AVOIDANCE IN INTERNATIONAL DISPUTE SETTLEMENT

This book offers a bold new perspective on how international adjudication operates.

While international courts claim to decide all disputes over which they have jurisdiction, this book argues that sometimes they strategically choose not to. Through detailed case studies and a close analysis of international procedural law, it reveals that courts decide most disputes most of the time – but not all.

By unpacking how courts use doctrines of jurisdiction and admissibility to avoid or narrow down certain issues, the book exposes the covert techniques of judicial avoidance. It shows how the flexibility of international procedural law allows judges to manage politically sensitive disputes without openly acknowledging that they are relying on avoidance doctrines.

This book offers a nuanced and realistic account of international adjudication, one that recognises how legal principle is often weighed against political and practical realities.

Volume 107 in the series Studies in International Law

Studies in International Law

RECENT TITLES IN THIS SERIES

The Effectiveness of the Inter-American Court of Human Rights: The Case of Indigenous Territorial Rights
Gabriela CB Navarro

Individuals in International Humanitarian Law: A Historical Analysis
Sarina Landefeld

The Pathology of Plenty: Natural Resources in International Law
Lys Kulamadayil

The United Nations Security Council and the Authorisation of Force: Form, Character and Nature
Marko Svicevic

Protecting the Right to Leave in an Era of Externalised Migration Control
Emilie McDonnell

Pluralising Actors and Norms in Human Rights Treaties: Beyond Monolithic States
Hinako Takata

Systemic Economic Offences as International Crimes: Theorising a New Paradigm of Mass Criminality
Nicole Citeroni

A Central Asian Perspective on International Law
Sergey Sayapin

Responsibility for the Crime of Aggression under International Law
Nikola Hajdin

Judicial Discretion in the Interpretation of International Crimes: Revisiting the Legality Principle
Ligeia Quackelbeen

Solidarity in International Disaster Response Law
Thomas Mulder

Avoidance in International Dispute Settlement: Jurisdiction, Admissibility, and Justiciability
Manuel Casas Martinez

For a complete list of titles in this series see www.bloomsbury.com/uk/series/studies-in-international-law/

Avoidance in International Dispute Settlement

Jurisdiction, Admissibility, and Justiciability

Manuel Casas Martínez

•HART•
OXFORD • LONDON • NEW YORK • NEW DELHI • SYDNEY

HART PUBLISHING
Bloomsbury Publishing Plc
Kemp House, Chawley Park, Cumnor Hill, Oxford, OX2 9PH, UK
1385 Broadway, New York, NY 10018, USA
Bloomsbury Publishing Ireland Limited, 29 Earlsfort Terrace, Dublin 2, D02 AY28, Ireland

HART PUBLISHING, the Hart/Stag logo, BLOOMSBURY and the Diana logo are trademarks of Bloomsbury Publishing Plc

First published in Great Britain 2026

1

A catalogue record for this book is available from the British Library.

A catalogue record for this book is available from the Library of Congress.

ISBN: HB: 978-1-50999-355-0
ePDF: 978-1-50999-353-6
ePub: 978-1-50999-352-9

Typeset by Amnet

For product safety related questions contact productsafety@bloomsbury.com

To find out more about our authors and books visit www.hartpublishing.co.uk. Here you will find extracts, author information, details of forthcoming events and the option to sign up for our newsletters.

To my abuelas, *Nieves María Margarita y María de la Chiquinquira.*

One baked me cake; the other told me to do my homework.

Both rock.

Tell all the truth but tell it slant —
Success in Circuit lies
Too bright for our infirm Delight
The Truth's superb surprise
As Lightning to the Children eased
With explanation kind
The Truth must dazzle gradually
Or every man be blind —

Emily Dickinson

Preface

READER (IF THERE ARE any): this is a book in good faith. I have mainly tried to achieve two things. The first is intellectual honesty. The second is clarity. So, I've done my best to say what I truly think and to say it in a way that is straightforward and easy to understand. So hopefully of all the criticisms that could – fairly or unfairly – be made about this book, those are not amongst them. Given that my main argument is that judgments are not always candid and sometimes require reading between the lines, the irony is not lost on me.

This book is a revised and condensed version of my doctoral dissertation, at the Yale Law School. I was lucky enough that the dissertation received Yale's *Ambrose Gherini* prize for international law.[1] Time, thoughtful comments and further reflection have, I hope, helped to improve the final product.

At its simplest, the question I set out to answer was what happens when an international court would prefer not to have to decide a certain case. One option is that they dutifully decide all cases before them, with an 'eat your vegetables' style of stoicism. But another option is that sometimes international courts find other ways of getting rid of a case, like five-year-olds get rid of their broccoli by discreetly giving it to the dog under the table.

Some context may help to explain why I found this question interesting. It starts with my experience in Venezuela. In the aughts and early tens I was a law student and also worked as a legal intern. Those were hard times. They involved a relentless erosion of the rule of law. One of my main tasks as a legal intern was to spend (countless) hours sitting in different courts' archives reviewing court files to see if something had happened.[2] One of the most important cases I had to keep track of was a highly salient, politically sensitive dispute before the Supreme Court.[3] For years, nothing happened. Newer cases worked their way through the system, but this one seemed to be forever stuck in some early-stage procedural limbo. When I asked one of my bosses why nothing ever happened, he laughed and said that the case was a political hot potato that had been '*drawered*' and was going to stay drawered to '*sleep the deep sleep of the just*'. Then it clicked: non-decisions were a thing.

My interest in this topic increased during my time as a judicial fellow at the International Court of Justice. Saying I had a first-row seat to the workings of one of the most relevant international courts would be misleading. The

[1] Apparently social proof is important.

[2] The way you found out if something had happened was if there was a new document at the back of the case file.

[3] SPA-07-411. I am not the only person to have that file number memorised.

nature of the international judicial function means that it is only the judges who are both actors and first-row spectators. But at least I was in the theatre. And during that season the *Marshall Islands* cases and the *Nicaragua v Colombia* cases were playing. Being able to follow them so closely was a privilege. Now, in my experience, international judges are particularly circumspect. No one ever mentioned that the Court had relied on jurisdictional or admissibility doctrines to avoid deciding those disputes. Nor, in fairness, did I ever have the audacity to ask if that was the case. Nevertheless, I was left with a strong gut feeling that international courts may have some techniques up their sleeves to avoid deciding certain cases or issues. I started to think that perhaps in international adjudication sometimes things were left unsaid and underlying motivations were not always fully articulated.

And so, I went down this rabbit hole of decisions not to decide. On the way down I found that international procedural law was very exciting. It is jagged, flexible and constantly evolving. It is apparently technical, but that very technicality can sometimes act as a subterfuge for policy considerations. This meant I had a lot of fun writing this book[4] – and I hope others will find it at least half as fun to read.[5]

I should also briefly explain the origin of my approach to legal theory. That, as Holmes said, has not been based on logic, but on experience. For some reason, the Venezuelan legal academy has a mild obsession with Kelsen's *Pure Theory of Law*. Great book that it is, I nevertheless had some fundamental problems with it. As an engineering school drop-out, the attempt to apply a 'scientific' approach to the law struck me as misguided. Moreover, I thought, the laws were *made* by people (politicians) and they were *applied* by people (government officials and judges).[6] There was not much that was pure there. Plus, there was a chasm between the Venezuelan law in the books and what was actually happening in reality.[7] Venezuelan law guarantees due process, the right to property and freedom of expression. Yet dissidents were being jailed, businesses were being confiscated and critical TV and radio stations were being shuttered. Looking at just the black letter law would not be enough. Yet the mere exercise of power was not – and could not be – an adequate explanation either. It is in that context that I found the New Haven school's balancing of normative commitments with the acknowledgment of the important role of policy, of legitimacy and effectiveness, so attractive.

[4] I have personally written every single word in this book. I liked dashes before LLMs overused them. I have used them throughout, and I intend to continue doing so.

[5] Otherwise, this would confirm a longstanding fear: that I like boring things.

[6] Perhaps I should say: government officials/judges.

[7] I hesitate to call this the *law in action, because a good deal of it wasn't legal.*

Acknowledgments

THIS BOOK IS BASED on a doctoral dissertation, so I should start by thanking my doctoral advisor, Michael Reisman, whose guidance, kindness and patience have been unfailing throughout the years. Although what he has taught me is too long to list, perhaps the most important one is that it is okay to have an opinion. I likewise need to thank the two members of my doctoral committee, Harold Koh and Leah Brilmayer, for their continued support and encouragement. One particular characteristic of this troika is that they all have excellent (albeit very different) senses of humour. Through it they have shown me (and many others) that scholarship can be fun.

Institutionally, thanks are due to the graduate programme at the Yale Law School, as well as to the brilliant staff at the Lilian Goldman Law Library, who indulged my multiple requests for scanned copies. Critically, thanks are due to the unknown individuals at the financial aid office who decided my studies were worth funding.

The circumstances in which I did my doctorate were peculiar. I was planning to ensconce myself in a library in New Haven for a couple of years. But, to paraphrase Lennon, life, adulting and migration regimes are what happens when you're busy making other plans. Fortunately, those years found me in The Hague and London, two places that managed to supply both companionship and intellectual stimulation in abundance. I have learned a ton from, and am very grateful for, my past and current friends, colleagues and teachers at UCAB, D'Empaire, Yale Law School, the International Court of Justice, WilmerHale, and Twenty Essex. Meeting people who make you raise your standards and push you to be better is one of life's privileges. I have been lucky to have come across many of them in all those institutions.

I am also grateful to the editorial staff at Hart. In particular, to Sinead Moloney, Verity Stuart and Paula Devine for their trust and support. Likewise, I am grateful to the anonymous reviewers for their thoughtful comments.

Last, but very much not least, infinite gratitude is due to Tefy and *los salvajes*. For their unconditional love and support and, importantly, for bearing with me.

Gracias, totales.

Contents

Table of Cases

France

Germany

Interamerican Court of Human Rights

International Centre for Settlement of Investment Disputes

International Court of Justice

Permanent Court of International Justice

United States

United States—Venezuela Mixed Claims Commission

World Trade Organization

1

Introduction

'In theory there is no difference between theory and practice. In practice there is'

Yogi Berra

I. SETTING THE SCENE

THIS IS A BOOK about avoidance. Avoidance is the broad term for the techniques that courts, both domestic and international, use to abstain from deciding certain cases or issues.[1] Basically ducking or dodging a case or issue, punting a decision or kicking it into touch. This book only focuses on one type of avoidance – what I call *jurisdictional* avoidance – as exercised by international courts and tribunals.[2]

The main question that motivates this book is: do *all* international courts exercise *all* the jurisdiction they have been granted *all* of the time?[3] Or would it be more accurate to say that *almost all* international courts exercise *almost all* of the jurisdiction they have been granted *almost all* of the time. I argue that the latter is the right answer. And avoidance techniques explain why the answer is *almost all* rather than *all*.

In short, jurisdictional avoidance refers to the techniques that international courts use to abstain from deciding a case or issue by relying on doctrines of jurisdiction, admissibility or justiciability.[4] Jurisdictional avoidance happens when two conditions are met. The first is that an international court declines jurisdiction over a dispute (or a specific issue within a dispute); when a dispute or claim is held to be inadmissible; or, more rarely, when a dispute or issue is declared to be non-justiciable. The second is that those decisions are mainly motivated by the international court's preference to refrain from deciding that case or issue. There are many grounds that could lead an international court to prefer abstention: the disputes' subject matter, the political sensitivities around it, the potential for backlash, the threats to a court's institutional legitimacy or

[1] EF Delaney, *'Analyzing Avoidance: Judicial Strategy in Comparative Perspective'* (2016) 66 *Duke Law Journal* 1, 3.

[2] For simplicity, I will refer throughout this book just to 'international courts', taking that expression to include both courts *and* tribunals.

[3] This is, of course, a play on Lou Henkin's statement about compliance with international law, see L Henkin, *How Nations Behave* (Columbia University Press, 1979).

[4] Other types of avoidance are dealt with in detail in chapters 2 and 3.

authority, or the possibility of rendering a completely ineffective judgment,[5] are just some examples. Some would say these are contextual, extra-legal factors and, as such, that they should not form part of legal analysis. Nevertheless, I argue that a close reading of some judgments suggests that that may not always be the case: that these contextual factors *may* play a role in international courts' approach to issues of jurisdiction and admissibility.

The second condition is important because not all decisions of an international court declining jurisdiction or declaring a claim to be inadmissible are an instance of jurisdictional avoidance. Some may be based on an entirely formal, strictly black-letter application of the law. For instance, art 25(2) of the ICSID Convention bars nationals from one State from pursuing claims against their State of nationality.[6] So, if a UK citizen tries to bring a claim against the UK and the tribunal dismisses that claim on grounds of lack of personal jurisdiction, there is likely no avoidance there. Jurisdictional avoidance should be rare. It should, one hopes, be something that seldom happens – that only comes up in marginal cases. It is the exception rather than the rule. To use a culinary metaphor, avoidance is like salt: you can't eat a dishful of it, but adding a pinch here and there is necessary for your food to taste better. Or, in automotive terms, avoidance is like an emergency brake: you can't rely on it for your daily driving but, once in a while, it can save you from an accident.

After all, jurisdiction is power. An international court's exercise of jurisdiction involves an exercise of power: the power to adjudicate a dispute involving a State or States, in theory with binding effects for the parties involved.[7] Jurisdictional avoidance implies abstaining from exercising that power. These types of decisions are, to use Alexander Bickel's eloquent expression,[8] an exercise of the *passive virtues*. They imply *not* deciding. The techniques and mechanisms that international courts and tribunals use to exercise those passive virtues are a fascinating – if somewhat underexplored – part of international procedural law.[9]

[5] These issues are addressed in detail in chapter 2, section II(C).

[6] In relevant part this provision states: 'National of another Contracting State' means: (a) any natural person who had the nationality of a Contracting State other than the State party to the dispute'.

[7] Yet States can ultimately exit and refrain from complying with those judgments, see eg C McLachlan, 'The Assault on International Adjudication and the Limits of Withdrawal' (2019) 68 *International and Comparative Law Quarterly* 499, 503–10; J Pauwelyn and RJ Hamilton, 'Exit from International Tribunals' (2018) 9 *Journal of International Dispute Settlement* 679, 683.

[8] AM Bickel, 'Foreword: The Passive Virtues' (1961) 75 *Harvard Law Review* 40.

[9] Although as of late there has been more work done on these issues, see eg WJ Davey, 'Has the WTO Dispute Settlement System Exceeded Its Authority? A Consideration of Deference Shown by the System to Member Government Decisions and its Use of Issue-Avoidance Techniques' (2001) 4 *Journal of International Economic Law* 79, 96; J Odermatt 'Patterns of Avoidance: Political Questions before International Courts' (2018) 14 *International Journal of Law in Context* 221; A John, 'Inarticulate and Unconscious: Non-Justiciability before the International Court of Justice' (2021) 20 *The Law & Practice of International Courts and Tribunals* 77; M Jackson, 'Judicial Avoidance at the European Court of Human Rights: Institutional Authority, the Procedural Turn, and Docket Control' (2022) 20 *International Journal of Constitutional Law* 112, 114; F Fouchard, *The Standard of Review before the International Court of Justice: Between Principle and Pragmatism* (Hart, 2024). And by myself at M Casas, 'Functional Justiciability and the Existence of a Dispute: A Means of Jurisdictional Avoidance?' (2019) 10 *Journal of International Dispute Settlement* 599.

The basic ideas I explore here are *whether* and *how* international adjudicators exercise those passive virtues through avoidance techniques. These can be used either as a case-selection mechanism (i.e., as techniques that allow international courts, to a certain degree, to determine which disputes they wish to decide) or as issue-selection mechanisms (i.e., as techniques that allow international courts to narrow or carve-out certain aspects of a dispute, for instance, by excising the most politically sensitive parts).[10] These are issues not only of international procedural law relating to jurisdiction and admissibility, but they also go to a core underlying issue: the role – and limits – of international adjudication.[11]

Yet a superficial analysis of this would quickly lead a naïve observer to the conclusion that there is no such thing as avoidance, as international courts *don't* apply doctrines of jurisdiction and admissibility in these ways. Rather, international courts diligently and straightforwardly exercise the jurisdiction they have been given and dutifully decide all cases and issues that properly come before them, without giving any (supposedly) improper consideration to extra-legal factors. A naïve observer could point out that, other than the ICJ's judgment in *Northern Cameroons*[12] – a judgment that has been extensively criticised *because* it expressly applied a non-justiciability doctrine,[13] judicial propriety – international courts simply do not apply these doctrines.

Our naïve observer could also point to the recent judgment in *Alleged Violations of the 1955 Treaty of Amity, Economic Relations, and Consular Rights*.[14] The dispute arose from the United States' decision to withdraw from the Joint Comprehensive Plan for Action (i.e., the Iran Nuclear Deal) and (re) impose sanctions on Iran. The latter initiated proceedings against the United States before the ICJ, arguing that the sanctions were imposed in breach of the 1955 Treaty of Amity.[15] The United States challenged the Court's jurisdiction. Among other things, the United States argued that the Court lacked jurisdiction because the subject-matter of the dispute was its decision to withdraw from the JCPOA, which it defined as a 'multilateral political arrangement', that was not

[10] This framework is developed cogently in Y Shany, *Questions of Jurisdiction and Admissibility before International Courts* (CUP, 2015).

[11] See eg GI Hernández, *The International Court of Justice and the Judicial Function* (OUP, 2014); L Gross, 'Limitations on the Judicial Function' (1964) 58 *American Journal of International Law* 415; WM Reisman, *Nullity and Revision: The Review and Enforcement of International Judgments and Awards* (Yale University Press, 1971).

[12] *Northern Cameroons (Cameroon v United Kingdom)*, ICJ, Judgment (Preliminary Objections) of 2 December 1963.

[13] See eg DHN Johnson, 'The Case concerning the Northern Cameroons' (1964) 13 *International and Comparative Law Quarterly* 1143; JR Stevenson, 'Case Concerning the Northern Cameroons (Cameroon v United Kingdom), Preliminary Objections' (1964) 58 *American Journal of International Law* 488; 'The Northern Cameroons Case' (1964) *Duke Law Journal* 550; G White, 'International Court of Justice: Judgment in Case concerning the Northern Cameroons. The Judicial Function' (1965) 23 *Cambridge Law Journal* 9.

[14] *Alleged Violations of the 1955 Treaty of Amity, Economic Relations, and Consular Rights (Islamic Republic of Iran v United States of America)*, ICJ, Judgment of 3 February 2021, 9.

[15] ibid paras 42–43.

capable of creating legal obligations.[16] In essence, the United States was arguing that this was a political dispute that was not suitable for international adjudication. The Court acknowledged this. It held that:

> It is true that this dispute arose in a particular political context, that of the United States' decision to withdraw from the JCPOA. However, as the Court has had occasion to observe: 'legal disputes between sovereign States by their very nature are likely to occur in political contexts and often form only one element in a wider and long-standing political dispute between the States concerned. Yet never has the view been put forward before that, because a legal dispute submitted to the Court is only one aspect of a political dispute, the Court should decline to resolve for the parties the legal questions at issue between them.[17]

And the Court *unanimously* rejected this preliminary objection.[18] In fact, our naïve observer could argue that in an even more recent and highly salient judgment – *South Africa v Israel* – there was only one judge on the Court that considered, in a criticised dissent, that the Court should refrain from adjudicating that dispute because of its subject matter.[19]

Our naïve observer could contend that this extends beyond the ICJ. They could refer to the WTO's Appellate Body's approach in *Mexico – Soft Drinks*, a dispute between the United States and Mexico, involving soda sweeteners.[20] Mexico invited the Panel to decline jurisdiction arguing, among other things, that the proper forum to hear the dispute was a NAFTA arbitral tribunal. The Panel rejected that argument. It held that 'it had no discretion to decide whether or not to exercise its jurisdiction in a case properly before it'.[21] On appeal, Mexico contended that, although it accepted that the Appellate Body (and the Panel) had jurisdiction to decide the dispute, the Appellate Body had discretion

[16] ibid para 46.

[17] ibid para 55, citing: *United States Diplomatic and Consular Staff in Tehran (United States of America v Iran)*, ICJ, Judgment of 24 May 1980 37.

[18] ibid para 114(1). The other of the United States' objections to jurisdiction were either also rejected unanimously, or rejected 15:1, with the U.S.' judge ad hoc, Charles Brower, being the sole vote in favour.

[19] *Application of the Convention on the Prevention and Punishment of the Crime of Genocide in the Gaza Strip (South Africa v Israel)*, ICJ, Order of 26 January 2024, Dissenting Opinion of Judge Sebutinde, stating at para 35: 'I reiterate that in my respectful opinion the dispute between the State of Israel and the people of Palestine is essentially and historically a political one, calling for a diplomatic or negotiated settlement.'

[20] WTO Appellate Body Report, *Mexico – Tax Measures on Soft Drinks and Other Beverages* WT/DS308/AB/R (adopted 24 March 2006) ('*Soft Drinks*'); WTO Panel Report, *Mexico – Tax Measures on Soft Drinks and Other Beverages* WT/DS308/R (adopted 24 March 2006). For commentary see WJ Davey and A Sapir, 'The Soft Drinks Case: The WTO and Regional Agreements' (2009) 8 *World Trade Review* 5; C Henckels, 'Overcoming Jurisdictional Isolationism at the WTO–FTA Nexus: A Potential Approach for the WTO' (2008) 19 *European Journal of International Law* 571; A Alvarez-Jiménez, 'The WTO AB Report on Mexico – Soft Drinks, and the Limits of the WTO Dispute Settlement System' (2006) 33 *Legal Issues of Economic Integration*.

[21] *Soft Drinks* (Panel Report) (n 20) para 7.1.

to decide *not* to exercise that jurisdiction on the basis of 'implied powers' to abstain from exercising such jurisdiction.[22]

The Appellate Body rejected that argument. Whilst it acknowledged that WTO panels have 'certain powers that are inherent in their adjudicative function', including the power to 'determine whether they have jurisdiction in a given case, as well as to determine the scope of their jurisdiction',[23] it considered that the mandatory wording of the WTO's constitutive dispute resolution treaty – the Dispute Settlement Understanding – meant that 'once jurisdiction has been validly established', WTO panels did not 'have the authority to decline to rule on the entirety of the claims that are before them in a dispute'.[24]

What more evidence is needed, our naïve observer may ask, to conclude that international courts – even courts such as the ICJ, which lack compulsory jurisdiction and strong enforcement mechanisms – do not *select* which disputes or which issues they adjudicate? What more evidence is needed to show that international adjudicators *always* dutifully exercise the jurisdiction they have been given and that they do not take into account extra-legal considerations to determine *whether* they exercise that jurisdiction? We should, after all, take the judgments and pronouncements of international courts at face value – and they are expressly saying, and saying very clearly, that they are not applying avoidance techniques.

And yet. A closer look at some decisions on jurisdiction and admissibility would cast significant doubt on that conclusion. For example, did the ICJ *really* decline jurisdiction in the *Marshall Islands* cases because of (very) technical reasons regarding the procedural requirements for the existence of a dispute?[25] Or did the fact that the case ultimately involved the legality of nuclear weapons influence the outcome? Staying with nuclear weapons, did the dispute between Australia and New Zealand AGAINST France on grounds of nuclear testing *really* become moot following a declaration of the French president?[26] Did the European Court of Human Rights *really* decide that the European Convention did not apply extraterritorially in Yugoslavia in *Bankovic* because, although NATO forces carried out air strikes in that territory, they had no ground forces there, thus the doctrinal conditions for the extraterritorial application of the

[22] *Soft Drinks* (Appellate Body Report) para 44.

[23] ibid 45.

[24] ibid 46 and ff.

[25] *Obligations concerning Negotiations relating to Cessation of the Nuclear Arms Race and to Nuclear Disarmament (Marshall Islands v United Kingdom),* ICJ, Judgment (Preliminary Objections) of 5 October 2016; *Obligations concerning Negotiations relating to Cessation of the Nuclear Arms Race and to Nuclear Disarmament (Marshall Islands v India),* ICJ, Judgment (Preliminary Objections) of 5 October 2016; *Obligations concerning Negotiations relating to Cessation of the Nuclear Arms Race and to Nuclear Disarmament (Marshall Islands v Pakistan),* ICJ, Judgment (Preliminary Objections) of 5 October 2016.

[26] *Nuclear Tests (Australia v France),* ICJ, Judgment (Questions of Jurisdiction and Admissibility) of 20 December 1974; *Nuclear Tests (New Zealand v France),* ICJ, Judgment (Questions of Jurisdiction and Admissibility) of 20 December 1974.

Convention were not satisfied?[27] Or was the European Court reluctant to declare unlawful the conduct of sixteen Convention States (with considerable clout), in relation to humanitarian intervention in the face of potential ethnic cleansing?

A more clear-eyed analysis of those decisions suggests that international courts may sometimes rely on different procedural doctrines of jurisdiction and admissibility to avoid adjudicating certain disputes or issues. Those often involve politically sensitive issues, the risk of a backlash which may jeopardise an international court's authority or legitimacy or present particularly high enforcement and compliance risks. The key point is that international courts do not expressly articulate that they are relying on avoidance techniques. International courts are not openly saying: 'this case involves sensitive political issues and we therefore abstain from deciding it on the merits'. However, for all practical purposes, the ultimate result is the same: the court manages to decline jurisdiction and avoids dealing with the merits of the dispute. Avoidance techniques, I argue, are mainly applied impliedly or covertly: there is no candour as to their application.[28] So my starting hypothesis is that, *in theory,* our naïve observer may be right; but, in *practice,* they are not. This starting intuition is bolstered by Yogi Berra's (perhaps apocryphal) epigram: in theory there is no difference between theory and practice. In practice, there is.

II. THE ARGUMENT IN SHORT

Because some people only read the introduction of books,[29] I will now try to distil the core ideas of this book here. The goal is that someone who just reads this, will at least walk away with the gist of what I'm trying to say.

First, international courts operate in a particular institutional context – one that is quite different from domestic courts. Although each international court is different, with differences in structure and institutional design and powers, there are some overarching characteristics that apply across most of them. Two of those characteristics are particularly important here. The first is that international courts are not courts of general personal jurisdiction; rather, their jurisdiction is limited and is mainly based on State consent.[30] The second is that

[27] *Banković and Others v Belgium and Others* App no 52207/99 (ECtHR (GC), Decision, 12 December 2001). On the same issue, see *Behrami and Behrami v France* App no 71412/01 and *Saramati v France, Germany and Norway* App no 78166/01 (ECtHR (GC), Decision, 2 May 2007), all concerning NATO air strikes in Serbia; and also *Hanan v Germany* App no 4871/16 (ECtHR (GC), 16 February 2021). This line of cases is analysed in detail in chapter 5.

[28] The issue of the implied use of avoidance techniques and its relation to judicial candour is examined in detail in chapter 3.

[29] Sometimes understandably. But this book is different and is worth reading from cover to cover (but I would say that, wouldn't I?).

[30] See chapter 2, section III(B).

international courts lack coercive enforcement mechanisms; the effectiveness and enforceability of their judgments are therefore not a given.[31]

Second, avoidance – jurisdictional or otherwise – is happening in international adjudication. Although international courts claim, sometimes loudly,[32] that they do not take into account extra-legal factors (i.e., factors that would motivate avoidance), there are grounds to doubt that assertion. There is by now relatively wide acceptance that avoidance happens in domestic courts, particularly in apex courts.[33] If avoidance is happening in domestic courts, which have both a stronger institutional footing and more effective coercive mechanisms available, why would it not be happening in international courts, with generally their consent-based jurisdiction and their lack of coercive enforcement regimes?[34]

Third, avoidance doctrines may be applied expressly or impliedly. Express avoidance doctrines are those where the international court is openly acknowledging that it will abstain from deciding an issue, mainly because of its subject matter. The paradigmatic example of an express avoidance doctrine is a finding of non-justiciability.[35] But express avoidance doctrines are rarely used by international courts. With notorious exceptions, like *Northern Cameroons,* where the ICJ relied on 'judicial propriety' to abstain from deciding the case, there are very few instances where international courts have relied on express avoidance doctrines.

In contrast, implied avoidance techniques operate as sub-text or *sotto voce* – Straussianly.[36] The international court is not expressly holding that it is declining to adjudicate a case because it is, say, concerned with the potential backlash. Rather, the international court is relying on the technical intricacies of the law on jurisdiction and admissibility to refrain from deciding the case or dispute. So I argue that when the ICJ is relying on a somewhat contorted reading of the requirements for the existence of a dispute to decline jurisdiction over the *Marshall Islands* cases on nuclear disarmament,[37] or when the European Court of Human Rights is going back and forth on the extraterritorial application of the European Convention in cases of the use of force abroad,[38] that supposedly technical or doctrinal nuance is covering for what in reality – practically and functionally – is an implied avoidance technique.

[31] ibid section III(C).

[32] Perhaps a bit *too* loudly.

[33] See eg Delaney, *Analyzing Avoidance* (n 1); T Roux, *The Politics of Principle: The First South African Constitutional Court, 1995–2005* (CUP, 2013); C Alves das Chagas, *Judicial Avoidance: Balancing Competences in Constitutional Adjudication* (Hart, 2023).

[34] In fact, there is now quite some acceptance that avoidance takes place before international courts, see (n 9).

[35] This is addressed in detail in chapter 2, section 1(C)–(D). See also I Brownlie, 'The Justiciability of Disputes and Issues in International Relations' (1967) 42 *British Yearbook of International Law* 123; JA King, 'Institutional Approaches to Judicial Restraint' (2008) 28 *Oxford Journal of Legal Studies* 421.

[36] This issue is dealt with extensively in chapter 3, section IV(A). Mainly, see L Strauss, *Persecution and the Art of Writing* (University of Chicago Press, 1988).

[37] See chapter 5, section II(A).

[38] ibid section II(C).

Fourth, the inherent characteristics of international procedural law allow international courts to rely on the law on jurisdiction and admissibility when deploying implied avoidance techniques. International courts have wide, almost free-ranging discretion to ascertain the scope and limits of their own jurisdiction under the competence-competence principle.[39] And critically, international procedural law is relatively indeterminate. Many of its provisions are vague. Most of them are created by judges through case law. They are standards or evaluation rules; not narrow, bivalent verification rules.[40] In consequence, many rules of international procedural law allow multiple plausibly correct answers. The ductility of these provisions affords international courts some discretion in their application. My view is that international courts sometimes rely on that flexibility to use jurisdiction and admissibility rulings as avoidance techniques to abstain from deciding a case or issue.

Fifth, the use of implied avoidance techniques may be normatively justified, but only contingently. That normative justification will depend on the circumstances of the case; it is entirely casuistic. The normative justification of avoidance is easier to understand when viewed through the lens of the New Haven school of international law, for three reasons. First, because it views law as a process rather than as a fixed set of rules. Second, because it considers that two of the key requisites for a decision to be lawful are that it be legitimate (authoritative) and effective (that is has 'control intention'). Third, because it has strong normative commitments, which cover minimum order, the rule of law and human rights/human dignity. I argue that there are some circumstances in which the decision to abstain – to refrain from deciding a case – may be the path that most contributes to minimum order. This is for multiple reasons, including that sometimes a dispute may be best addressed through diplomatic or political channels,[41] because an eventual judgment has no or very low probabilities of being enforced or because abstention will help preserve the authority (and sometimes the very existence) of an international court.

Sixth, there are limits to the international judicial function.[42] The last decades have seen an increased (perhaps excessive) judicialisation of international affairs.

[39] See chapter 3, section III.

[40] See eg TAO Endicott, *Vagueness in Law* (OUP, 2000).

[41] Commenting on how international lawyers don't 'own' international relations, see D Bethlehem, 'The Secret Life of International Law' (2012) 1 *Cambridge Journal of International and Comparative Law* 23, 26.

[42] For eloquent articulation of these views from the international bench, see: *Legality of the Threat or Use of Nuclear Weapons,* ICJ, Advisory Opinion dated 8 July 1996, Dissenting Opinion of Judge Oda, para 54; see also Judge Eicke's lone separate opinion in *Verein Klimaseniorinnen Schweiz v Switzerland*, para 15: 'It seems to me that, even more so in the light of the political complexities arising in the context of identifying and implementing the necessary measures to counter climate change effectively and swiftly, there must be significant doubt that proceeding before this Court can make a meaningful contribution. In fact there must be a real risk that . . . proceedings before this Court are much more likely to distract the Contracting Parties and slow down the necessary processes and, even if a judgment is obtained, any delay and/or failure in the implementation of any judgment is only likely to undermine the need for urgent action and, potentially, the rule of law.'

Politically salient and sensitive issues are making their way more regularly to the dockets of international courts.[43] That is not necessarily a good thing. Backlash against international courts is rife, even from States that have strong commitments to the international rule of law. The legitimacy of international courts to resolve some types of highly politicised disputes is questionable. And when they do attempt to decide those issues, the effectiveness of their judgments may be debatable. Yet there are 'incurable judicial romantics' that believe that international courts are the silver bullet that will solve some of the most intractable problems the international community faces. Avoidance, in turn, is, if not a complete cure, at least a way of mitigating the symptoms of that pathology.

Seventh, through a close reading of three case studies of doctrines of jurisdiction and admissibility – the existence of a dispute, the indispensable third party or *Monetary Gold* principle, and the extraterritorial application of the European Convention on Human Rights – I argue that there is credible evidence to suggest that international courts are using the inherent flexibility of those doctrines as avoidance techniques.

I suspect some – perhaps many – will take issue with these arguments. Some may find the very notion of avoidance objectionable or distasteful, even repugnant. They may view avoidance as a threat to law's normativity – as a way of ditching principle in the name of expediency.[44] Aesthetically, some may consider avoidance cowardly or even pusillanimous: an international court's failure to step up to the challenges that parties put before them. And although I hesitate to engage in armchair psychoanalysis, both scholars and practitioners tend to over-index on the importance of international adjudication. The idea that the judgment of an international court will, *ipse dixit,* operate to solve some intractable problem is widespread. Perhaps that is because if that is the case, then the status of international lawyers rises. This is linked with social-desirability bias, which may also be at play. On that ground, the increased judicialisation of international affairs and the expansion of the jurisdiction of international courts is considered desirable.[45]

Accepting avoidance, in turn, implies acknowledging the limits of the international judicial function. Avoidance is based on prudence and humility – traits usually considered virtuous. Avoidance allows international courts to consider some contextual factors that may otherwise fall outside of the scope of traditional, formalist legal analysis. It is a tool that allows international courts to navigate the increasingly challenging scenarios in which they operate, subject to the vagaries of State consent and the ever-increasing risk of backlash. Avoidance allows international courts to attempt to preserve their institutional legitimacy

[43] See eg R Hirschl, *Towards Juristocracy* (Harvard University Press, 2004).

[44] The paradigmatic example is G Gunther, 'The Subtle Vices of the "Passive Virtues"—A Comment on Principle and Expediency in Judicial Review' (1964) 64 *Columbia Law Review* 1, stating that the application of Bickel's approach results in the application of 100% of principle, 20% of the time.

[45] On judicialisation, see chapter 2, section II(A).

and authority, avoiding adjudicating on issues on which a judgment is likely to remain an ineffective exercise in futility. Avoidance is thus a way of inserting some contextual and policy considerations into the exercise of an important – if somewhat frail – power: the jurisdiction of an international court.

III. METHODOLOGICAL APPROACH

Declaring outright the methodology adopted in this book runs the risk of being overly restrictive. Tribal, dogmatic attachment to a specific school of thought can lead to a jurisprudential bed of Procrustes. But as this is a book written in good faith and I am striving for as much intellectual honesty as possible, it makes sense to clarify some of the main mental models, conceptual influences, and theoretical frameworks applied. The main influence is the historic and contemporary New Haven school of international law (also recently called the 'Yale School' of international law).[46] This means a combination of policy-oriented jurisprudence (or the 'original) New Haven School with the 'New' New Haven School). Nonetheless, I do not unreflexively adopt all its tenets. For instance, there is basically no reliance on the neologisms articulated by the oldest version of the New Haven school. Unsurprisingly, legal realism and pragmatism also play roles as secondary influences.

Both legal realism and the New Haven school have sometimes been misrepresented and even caricaturised. Despite its profound insights into the legal process, American legal realism has been ridiculed as boiling down to what the judge had for breakfast and labelled as nightmarish by HLA Hart.[47] Similarly, despite the New Haven school's emphasis on connecting values to policy and its balancing of idealism and realism, it has been derided by some critics as an apology for the United States' position during the Cold War. That is unfair.[48]

The main advantage of the New Haven approach to international law is actually its moderation and even-keeledness. Some may find that claim surprising, even provocative. But I mean it. Consider these three factors. First, the New Haven approach has strong normative commitments, including to the rule of

[46] See generally HH Koh, 'The Yale School of International Law' (2024) 9/22 *The Yale Journal of International Law Online 1*.

[47] HLA Hart, *The Concept of Law*, 3rd edn (OUP, 2012), ch 7.

[48] See eg O Schacter, 'Remarks at the 79th Annual Meeting of the American Society of International Law' (1985) 79 *Proceedings of the American Society of International Law, McDougal's Jurisprudence: Utility, Influence, Controversy* 272. For an appraisal that is also somewhat ambiguous, see M Koskenniemi, *The Gentle Civilizer of Nations, the Rise and Fall of International Law 1870–1960* (CUP, 2001), in particular ch 5. A good friend just says that it is mere 'fortune-cookieism'. In any event, claims of the New Haven school being a mere apologia for US foreign policy should have been quelled by the criticisms that leading figures in the New Haven school made of the United States' position during the US' invasion of Iraq, see eg WM Reisman, 'The Manley O. Hudson Lecture: Why Regime Change is (Almost Always) A Bad Idea' (2004) 98 *American Journal of International Law*, 515.

law (and to international law *as law*) whilst at the same time being cognisant of the realities of State power. Most other theories that are openly concerned about State power are, in reality, sovereigntist.[49] Second, the view of law as process gives due weight to legal rules but does not consider that rules themselves exhaust the totality of legal analysis. Third, although there are some anti-formalist elements, including some rule scepticism, these are considerably milder than the absolute or radical views of indeterminacy espoused by the critical legal studies movements or other contemporary legal realisms (e.g., the Genovese realists).[50] If I could offer my own distillation of what the New Haven approach entails, I'd say that it is a very soft form of legal realism that – unlike most other realistic theories about law – has some normative commitments. Ultimately, by balancing those normative commitments with at least an acknowledgement of power dynamics the New Haven approach proposes a pragmatic jurisprudence of common sense.

A. Basic Notions

This is a short summary of the basic notions of the New Haven approach,[51] particularly those that are relevant for this book.

First, and most importantly, the New Haven school assumes a particular definition of *law*. Law is not a mere set of *rules* (as the formalists or positivists would say); rather, law is a 'process of decision that is both authoritative

[49] Koh, *The Yale School* (n 46) 10–12.

[50] See eg M Koskenniemi, *From Apology to Utopia: The Structure of International Legal Argument* (CUP, 2005) 590–1. For the Genovese realist perspective, see P Chiassoni, 'Legal Interpretation without Truth' (2016) 29 *Revus – Journal for Constitutional Theory and Philosophy of Law* 93, 117; P Comanducci, 'Principios jurídicos e indeterminación del derecho' (1998) 21(II) *Doxa: Cuadernos de Filosofía del Derecho* 89, 103.

[51] See eg WM Reisman, *The Quest for World Order and Human Dignity in the Twenty First Century* (Brill, 2013); W Michael Reisman, 'The View from the New Haven School of International Law' (1992) 86 *Proceedings of the Annual Meeting (American Society of International Law)* 118; WM Reisman, S Wiessner and AR Willard, 'The New Haven School: A Brief Introduction' (2007) 32 *Yale Journal of International Law* 575; MS McDougal, HD Lasswell and WM Reisman, 'Theories about International Law: Prologue to a Configurative Jurisprudence' (1967–1968) 8 *Virginia Journal of International Law* 188; HH Koh, 'Is There a New New Haven School of International Law? Commentary' (2007) 32 *Yale Journal of International Law* 559; S Wiessner, 'The New Haven School of Jurisprudence: A Universal Toolkit for Understanding and Shaping the Law' (2010) 18 *Asia Pacific Law Review* 45; E Suzuki, 'The New Haven School of International Law: An Invitation to Policy-Oriented Jurisprudence' (1970) 1 *Yale Journal of World Public Order*. For an intellectual history, see R Derrig, *The New Haven School: American International Law* (OUP, 2025). Derrig's work is both thoughtful and thorough. Although perhaps it somewhat underestimates the post-McDougal and Lasswell developments of the New Haven school. The contrast of opinions about the school is perhaps illustrated by the fact that the series editor's preface considers that the texts of the New Haven school 'almost completely unread' whilst at the same time Martti Koskenniemi, one of the commenters that provide advance praise of the book considers, stated four pages before that the school is 'far from marginal or eccentric' and that it has 'been strikingly effective in articulating an approach to international law and policy that dominates scholarship and practice in the United States'.

and controlling'.[52] Law is viewed as a *process,* not the 'neutral application of rules'.[53] Put simply, the New Haven school does not reduce law to mere words on text. It does not 'examine only words in documents'.[54] Its concept of law is *contextual* rather than merely *textual.* A contextual approach is fundamental, as it allows analysing legal issues with 'comprehensiveness and realism'.[55] However, despite viewing law as *process*, the New Haven school is not nihilistic about the importance of *rules.*[56] Its approach to rule scepticism is moderate. And while it considers that 'international law rules are intended to be sensitive to international policy arguments',[57] at the same time it considers that the view of international relations realism, with its emphasis on naked power, 'underestimates the role of rules, and of legal processes in general'.[58]

This is the focal lens through which the New Haven school approaches legal problems. It aims to have a comprehensive view 'regarding the various factors that influence decision'.[59] Put another way, it considers that to 'remain "legal" is not to ignore everything that is not "rules"'.[60] Taking into account the broader legal process requires taking into account factors that traditional legal scholarship considers extraneous to legal analysis (or deems extra-legal), but that the New Haven school considers an inherent part of the legal process.[61] This approach is thus concerned with the 'normativity of process' and is also 'sensitive to practice'.[62] At its most basic, this means that when analysing a case, the New Haven school, following the views of the different realistic theories of law, suggests looking very carefully at facts and context. This includes factual and contextual information that is not necessarily expressed in the pages of a

[52] Reisman and others, *The New Haven School: A Brief Introduction* (n 51) 576.

[53] R Higgins, *Problems & Process: International Law and How We Use It* (OUP, 1994) 267. See also A Chayes, T Ehrlich and AF Lowenfeld, *International Legal Process* (Little Brown, 1968); HH Koh, 'Transnational Legal Process and the "New" New Haven School of International Law' in JL Dunoff and MA Pollack (eds), *International Legal Theory: Foundations and Frontiers* (2022) 101, 104–05. Some challenge this notion: *Prosecutor v Dražen Erdemović* (ICTY Appeals Chamber, Judgment, 7 October 1997) (Dissenting Opinion of Judge Cassese) para 11(ii), contending that the ICTY 'is called upon to apply international law, in particular our Statute and rules of international humanitarian law . . . Our International Tribunal is a court of law; it is bound only by international law. It should therefore refrain from engaging in meta-legal analyses', as those 'policy considerations . . . [were] extraneous to the task of our tribunal'. See also RA Falk, 'Casting the Spell: The New Haven School of International Law' (1995) 104 *Yale Law Journal* 1991.

[54] Reisman, *The View from New Haven* (n 51) 121.

[55] McDougal and others, *Theories About International Law* (n 51) 196.

[56] Unlike, say, the critical legal studies movement.

[57] Harold Hongju Koh, 'The 1994 Roscoe Pound Lecture: Transnational Legal Process' (1996) 75 *Nebraska Law Review.*

[58] Myres S McDougal, 'International Law, Power and Policy: A Contemporary Conception' (1953) 82 *Recueil des Cours de l'Académie de Droit International* 137, 157.

[59] Reisman, *The View from New Haven* (n 51) 121.

[60] Higgins, *Problems & Process* (n 53) 9.

[61] Rosalyn Higgins, 'Policy Considerations and the International Judicial Process' (1968) 17 *International and Comparative Law Quarterly* 58, 62.

[62] Koh, 'Transnational Legal Process' (n 57) 107.

judgment or award. This factually detailed analysis contrasts with the approach taken by some doctrinalists, which limit their analysis to a few isolated lines or pages of text.

Second, the New Haven school is goal-oriented or consequentialist. There is an explicit normative element. The objective of the New Haven school is to 'map the decision processes', asses them and, perhaps most importantly, 'improve the performance of decision processes . . . and hence their capacity to achieve outcomes more consonant with human dignity'.[63] In essence, the New Haven approach considers that the appraisal of a decision (widely understood) requires looking at 'their degree of contribution to the achievement of a public order of human dignity'.[64] The New Haven approach thus has a strong normative commitment to both the rule of law and human rights.[65] Because of this, outcomes are assessed based on their aggregate consequences for minimum and optimum world order and the respect of human rights. Additionally, influenced by Transnational Legal Process, the New Haven school is also interested in transnational legal substance, understood as global standards that, although initially developed in international law, have made their way into domestic law.[66] These global standards tend to also contribute to the achievement of minimum and optimum world order.

Third, the New Haven school is a theory 'about making social choices'. This view – essentially, that of the decision-maker – contrasts with the traditional view associated with positivism – that of the rule-taker or the political inferior.[67] Viewing law as process through which 'human beings try to influence the way social choices are made',[68] means that policy-oriented jurisprudence openly assumes a 'social interventionist' stance, concentrated on the appraisal of alternatives and recommendations (and their consequences).[69]

Fourth, the New Haven school balances normativity with effectiveness. For a particular decision to be considered lawful it must simultaneously be legitimate (i.e., authoritative) and effective in the real world (i.e., controlling). This excludes 'exercises in irrelevance', understood as decisions that lack either authority or control – or both[70] – as well as the exercise of 'naked power' (i.e., raw power without any legitimate basis).[71] Basically this framework requires distinguishing

[63] Reisman and others, *The New Haven School: A Brief Introduction* (n 51) 577.

[64] WM Reisman, 'Theory about Law: Jurisprudence for a Free Society' (1999) 108 *Yale Law Journal* 935, 939.

[65] Koh, *The Yale School* (n 46) 5.

[66] Koh, *Transnational Legal Process* (n 57) 114.

[67] Reisman, *The View from New Haven* (n 51) 119–20.

[68] ibid.

[69] S Wiessner and AR Willard, 'Policy-Oriented Jurisprudence Focus Section: International Theory' (2001) 44 *German Yearbook of International Law* 96.

[70] Note, however, that 'in certain contexts a decision that is not immediately realizable can still evoke consequences favourable to public order', see *Nullity and Revision* (n 10) 243.

[71] WM Reisman, 'Sovereignty and Human Rights in Contemporary International Law' (1990) 84 *American Journal of International Law* 866, 872.

between 'authority formally provided' and what actually happens in reality. A related distinction is that between international law's myth system (the law in the books) and the operational code (the law in action).[72]

Viewing international adjudication as part of a process of legitimate and effective decisions requires identifying what, exactly, must be looked at: the *parts* of that process. Again, some particularly important issues that are considered here are broader than those in traditional positivist legal analysis.

First, the participants. There are several important participants to international adjudication. Focusing *only* on the international adjudicators themselves is a mistake.[73] The *parties* to the proceedings, be they States or individuals, are also relevant. Moreover, there is also a broader notion of transnational actors and compliance constituencies, which include State officials, domestic courts, non-governmental organizations and individuals, who play an important part in the different stages of the international legal process.[74]

Second, the perspectives. There are three *key* perspectives that are relevant in international adjudication. That of the parties, that of the adjudicators, and those of interested third parties (understood broadly).[75] One of the main differences between these perspectives is whether they take a short or long-term view as to the authority of an international court. Whereas parties, logically, will be inclined to focus on the specific outcome of their cases, international adjudicators, particularly those in *permanent* adjudicative bodies, may be more concerned with the potential long-term effects of their decisions.[76]

Third, the situations in which the relevant decisions are taken. In international adjudication, one must assume that the decisions are made *within* international courts, often in the deliberation room or other scenarios where the adjudicators deliberate on the outcome of a dispute.[77] There may be distinctive properties in each one, depending on their institutional design and sometimes on the distinctive culture of each international court. Additionally, the parties also frame decisions, particularly when determining whether to resort to

[72] WM Reisman, 'Myth System and Operational Code' (1976–1977) 3 *Yale Studies in World Public Order* 229.

[73] International adjudication still mostly depends on State consent, as explained in detail in chapter 2. Because States may ultimately withdraw their consent (or carry out similar processes of backlash or dejudicialisation), their reaction to the work of international courts and tribunals is of particular relevance.

[74] See eg K Alter, *The New Terrain of International Law* (Princeton University Press 2014); Koh, *Transnational Legal Process* (n 57) 114.

[75] Again, it is important to consider the perspectives not only of the parties to a specific dispute but also that of the broader transnational actors and compliance constituencies.

[76] This will be covered in detail in chapter 2. See generally M Shapiro and A Stone Sweet, *On Law, Politics, and Judicialization* (OUP, 2002).

See eg K Alter, E Hafner-Burton and L Helfer, 'Theorizing the Judicialization of International Relations' (2019) 63 *International Studies Quarterly* 449. See also C Neal Tate and Torbjorn Vallinder (eds), *The Global Expansion of Judicial Power* (New York University Press, 1995).

[77] See eg Article 54 of the ICJ's Statute; Article 6 of the International Criminal Court's Code of Judicial Ethics.

international adjudication, which types of disputes to pursue, and how those claims are framed.[78]

Fourth, the bases of power. International courts are not all created equal. They have different institutional designs and operate in sometimes vastly differing political contexts.[79] Accordingly, they have differing bases of power. Nevertheless, even taking all those differences into account, international adjudicators tend to have relatively restricted power bases. This is best illustrated by the lack of coercive enforcement mechanisms (or, in the few instances where there are mechanisms that are coercive or close to being so, the reluctance to rely on them).[80]

Fifth, strategies. The inherent nature of international adjudication has effects on the available strategies. After all, the formal strictures of the judicial or arbitral process mean that there are severe limits on the strategies that may lawfully be manipulated to achieve objectives.[81] However, as I will explain below, within those limits there are strategies available to international courts, namely, the explicit or the implied application of avoidance techniques. Most of these relate to the application of the law.[82] One critical aspect is the relative indeterminacy of the rules of international procedural law applied by international adjudicators.[83] That indeterminacy means that, quite often, they enjoy a degree of flexibility when applying those rules. This is achieved by a series of doctrinal techniques, including how precedent is interpreted (i.e., broadly or narrowly), how it is applied or not (i.e., distinguished), and how facts are treated (i.e., characterised). These tools are available because in international adjudication 'the formal elements of decision are highly ambiguous, allowing decision makers wide discretionary latitude for appreciation of context or milieu'.[84] Despite this strategic tool-kit being somewhat limited, particularly when compared to the strategies available in more informal or less structured areas of international law, in many (albeit not all) cases it is enough to advance particular policy goals.

Sixth, the outcomes. Analysing the outcome of international judgments and awards must go beyond appraising them in their own terms.[85] This would limit

[78] The general history of the types of disputes that are susceptible of being submitted to international adjudication is dealt with in detail in chapter 2. The key work is still H Lauterpacht, *The Function of Law in the International Community* (OUP, 2011).

[79] See eg RO Keohane, A Moravcsik and AM Slaughter, 'Legalized Dispute Resolution: Interstate and Transnational' (2000) 54 *International Organization* 457–488; Shapiro and Stone Sweet, *On Law, Politics, and Judicialization* (n 76) 71.

[80] This is explored in detail in chapter 2, including differing views on the meaning of enforcement and effectiveness.

[81] Reisman, *Nullity and Revision* (n 10) at 230.

[82] See eg H Dagan, 'The Realist Conception of Law' (2007) 57 *University of Toronto Law Journal* 607; K Llewellyn, *The Bramble Bush* (OUP, 2008); B Leiter, *Naturalizing Jurisprudence: Essays on American Legal Realism and Naturalism in Legal Philosophy* (OUP, 2007).

[83] These issues are addressed in detail in chapters 3–5.

[84] Reisman, *Nullity and Revision* (n 10) 235.

[85] AP Llamzon, 'Jurisdiction and Compliance in Recent Decisions of the International Court of Justice' (2007) 18 *European Journal of International Law* 815; TM Franck, *The Power of Legitimacy among Nations* (OUP, 1990); HH Koh, 'Why Do Nations Obey International Law' (1996–1997) 106 *Yale Law Journal* 2599.

the appraisal to issues such as internal consistency, reasoning, conformity with previous authorities, and style.[86] A broader appraisal of the outcome is required, one that considers a judgment's or award's aggregate effects for minimum and optimum world order and for human rights. One factor in the latter appraisal is whether a judgment or award contributes to the preservation of the authority of international adjudication and the availability of that specific court or tribunal as a viable institution for the settlement of international disputes.[87]

B. An Epistemic Note

I should clarify one point: a central thread that I have tried to pursue throughout this book is epistemic humility. I am aware – and openly acknowledge – that some of the claims I make are inherently speculative. The New Haven approach is both theoretical and practical. I thus focus on a combination of a close reading of legal texts (the textual mode of analysis) with broader policy-contextual considerations, focusing on a case's facts and the broader policy-context that could be at play.[88] Despite the 'empirical turn in international legal scholarship',[89] given the issues I am focusing on, namely the *implied* application of avoidance techniques, there are considerable limits to some types of empirical analysis. How do you accurately reflect that point in a data-driven analysis? Further, this is not even something that can be teased out through qualitative interviews with experienced international adjudicators. Most codes of judicial ethics would forbid sitting or even former judges from revealing what was said in deliberations.[90] In any event, this is a legal book centred on legal analysis. It does not purport to be a political science book (much less a *manqué* version of that).

Because of that, I am comfortable adopting a probabilistic approach. My view is not that international courts are in some cases *certainly* relying on the flexibility of international procedural law to avoid cases or issues. My claim is more modest: I am only saying that in some cases they *may* be doing that. And I further claim that, based on a close reading of those judgments, together with a broader look at the context in which they were issued, it is more likely than not that what we are seeing is not doctrinal flip-flopping or technical/doctrinal incompetence in the application of clear-cut rules of jurisdiction and admissibility, but rather the application of implied avoidance techniques. But that is as high as I am willing to put it and, ultimately, I recognise this is a finely balanced

[86] Reisman, *Nullity and Revision* (n 10) 221.

[87] ibid.

[88] Reisman, *The Quest for World Order* (n 51) 168–90.

[89] G Shaffer and T Ginsburg, 'The Empirical Turn in International Legal Scholarship' (2012) 106 *American Journal of International Law* 1.

[90] Article 54(3) of the ICJ's statute, for instance, provides that the 'deliberations of the Court shall take place in private and remain secret.' Similarly, Article 6 of the ICC's Code of Judicial Ethics requires judges to 'respect the confidentiality . . . and secrecy of deliberations'.

issue. In consequence, I proceed by way of a probabilistic estimate and illustration rather than by suggesting an absolute, hard-and-fast rule. Indeed, given that the covert application of avoidance techniques is essentially a *prudential* exercise, it is hard – or perhaps even conceptually impossible – to develop these kinds of rules. Given these limitations, like a lawyer dealing with a difficult and opaque fraud case, I am left to rely on indicia – and a dash of speculation. With these caveats, I am happy to do so.

The probabilistic or even slightly speculative nature of these claims, however, should not be an issue. Law, after all, often deals with situations where it is hard or sometimes impossible to achieve certainty. In those circumstances the law is generally comfortable with relying on circumstantial evidence to draw inferences.[91] That is the approach I take below and why my arguments are at best probabilistic[92] and inferential.[93] Part of my claim is based on Bayesian or conditional probability.[94] The relevant prior is that avoidance happens. There is cogent evidence showing that domestic courts – including apex courts – engage in avoidance.[95] With that as a prior, then the question that follows is how likely is it that international courts are also engaged in avoidance. I invite the reader to look at the case studies mentioned in chapter 5 and then ask themselves whether they have updated their subjective probabilities. I certainly have.

IV. SUMMARY

This book has five chapters. Below is a summary of the remaining four.

Chapter 2 addresses two key points. The first defines several of the foundational doctrinal concepts that are relevant, mainly jurisdiction, admissibility, justiciability, and avoidance. The second places international adjudication in its proper institutional and political context. This covers some of the current trends which international adjudication faces, including the expansion of the judicialisation of international law, the proliferation of international adjudication, and different forms of backlash (including dejudicialisation and what I call non-judicialisation) as well as some of the core characteristics of international adjudication, which are the lack of compulsory jurisdiction (and the resulting

[91] *JSC BM Bank v Kekhman* [2018] EWHC 791 (Comm) [78] (Bryan J). See also *R v Kilbourne* [1973] AC 729, 758 where Lord Simon stated that 'circumstantial evidence is evidence of facts from which, taken with all the other evidence, a reasonable inference is a fact directly in issue. It works by cumulatively, in geometrical progression, eliminating other possibilities'.

[92] A good, straightforward introduction is available at D Levy, *Maxims for Thinking Analytically: The Wisdom of Legendary Harvard Professor Richard Zeckhauser* (Dan Levy, 2021) at 66–70.

[93] See eg 'Bayes Theorem – a primer'. Available at: wwwreflect.ucl.ac.uk/ad-veturi/2021/03/09/bayes-theorem-a-primer/.

[94] Some judicial decisions have been critical to applying Bayes Theorem, at least in the context of a jury trial: *R v Adams* [1996] 2 Cr App R 467.

[95] Delaney, *Analyzing Avoidance* (n 1).

importance of State consent) and the lack of coercive enforcement mechanisms, and how that may affect the exercise of the international judicial function.

Chapter 3 offers a deep dive into jurisdictional avoidance. It deals with three issues. First, it provides a historical background and a definition of different types of avoidance techniques. Second, it develops the distinction between express and implied avoidance techniques and considers why international courts generally do not rely on express avoidance techniques. Third, it sets out a theoretical and normative framework for avoidance.

Chapter 4 explores the legal theory of international procedural law – a topic that is generally overlooked. The chapter focuses on three inherent characteristics of international procedural law. It mainly focuses on the relative indeterminacy of international procedural law and argues that the inherent vagueness of many rules of international procedural law provide international courts with some flexibility in their application. The chapter also considers some other particular characteristics of international adjudication which also contribute to the relative indeterminacy of the rules of international procedural law, namely the broad discretion that international courts enjoy when establishing their own jurisdiction (the competence–competence principle) and the lack, or reduced scope of, appellate or review mechanisms in international adjudication.

Chapter 5 analyses how implied or covert avoidance doctrines operate in practice. It does so by a series of case studies from different international courts. The chapter starts by considering some historical examples that illustrate that avoidance has potentially always been part of international adjudication. It then goes on to focus on how three specific doctrines may have been used as jurisdictional avoidance techniques: the existence of a dispute, the indispensable third party or *Monetary Gold* principle, and the extrajudicial application of treaties. This chapter then provides a New Haven influenced analysis of those judgments with the objective of determining whether international courts were using them as avoidance techniques to abstain from deciding a specific case or issue.

2

International Dispute Settlement in Context

'The future ain't what it used to be'

Yogi Berra

THIS CHAPTER ADDRESSES TWO issues. First, it covers foundational concepts of international procedural law, focusing on jurisdiction, admissibility and justiciability (with a particular emphasis on the latter). Second, it provides an overview of the broader context in which international court operate, namely without compulsory jurisdiction and without coercive enforcement mechanisms, and considers how that may impact the exercise of the international judicial function. Think about it as setting the scene for more detailed discussions later.

I. SOME ESSENTIAL CONCEPTS OF INTERNATIONAL PROCEDURAL LAW

One complicating factor about international procedural law is that it lacks a uniform lexicon. There is no standard usage of concepts such as jurisdiction or admissibility across international courts. So, for instance, the European Court of Human Rights tends to use the term 'admissibility' to cover issues that other international tribunals would consider to be either of 'admissibility' (narrowly understood) or jurisdiction.[1] There is thus a risk of imprecision caused by terminological drift. Although it is rare for legal concepts to be complete homonyms, there is often some nuance in what different legal systems mean when they refer to specific terms.[2] Therefore, it is important to set out precise definitions of some of the key concepts that will be used throughout this book.

[1] See eg European Court of Human Rights, Registry, *Practical Guide on Admissibility Criteria*, Section II 'Grounds for inadmissibility relating to the Court's jurisdiction', 64, last updated 28 February 2025. Available at: echr.coe.int/documents/d/echr/admissibility_guide_eng.

[2] For a perspective from comparative law, see J Ellis, 'General Principles and Comparative Law' (2011) 22 *European Journal of International Law* 949; M Cohn, 'Form, Formula and Constitutional Ethos: The Political Question/Justiciability Doctrine in Three Common Law Systems' (2011) 59 *American Journal of Comparative Law* 675. For a specific look at the issue of translation, see CJW Baaij, 'EU Translation and the Burden of Legal Knowledge' in S Šarčević (ed), *Language and Culture in EU Law* (Routledge, 2015).

A. Jurisdiction[3]

'Jurisdiction' is a complicated concept. Some say it is one 'of the most difficult words in the legal lexicon to delineate'.[4] In the words of one domestic court, *jurisdiction* is 'a word of many, too many, meanings'.[5] For international law, jurisdiction is about sovereignty. This means that jurisdiction is about power:[6] about '*entitlements* to act'.[7] It is thus a concept 'at the heart of an international legal order'.[8] Understanding *jurisdiction* as *power* is intuitive.[9] The Latin etymology of the word, after all, is to 'speak the law' (*ius dicere*). Despite its importance, *jurisdiction* is often considered a dry, technical area of law.[10] It is anything but.

As a preliminary issue, it is important to clarify the different meanings that the term *jurisdiction* has in international law. Generally, jurisdiction is divided into three categories: prescriptive (or legislative) jurisdiction,[11] enforcement jurisdiction,[12] and adjudicative jurisdiction.[13] This book is mainly concerned with the third type, and particularly with the narrower issue of *international* adjudicative jurisdiction.[14] This means an international court's authority to adjudicate a dispute and to subject the parties to that dispute to judicial proceedings. In the words of Shabtai Rosenne, this type of jurisdiction 'relates to the capacity of

[3] See eg: C Ryngaert, *Jurisdiction in International Law*, 2nd edn (OUP, 2015); see also: M Akehurst, 'Jurisdiction in International Law' (1972 -73) 46 *British Yearbook of International Law* 145; DW Bowett, 'Jurisdiction: Changing Patterns of Authority over Activities and Resources' (1983) 53 *British Yearbook of International Law* 1; A Mills, 'Rethinking Jurisdiction in International Law' (2014) 84 *British Yearbook of International Law*; FA Mann, *The Doctrine of International Jurisdiction Revisited After Twenty Years*, The Hague Academy Collected Courses 186 (Brill, 1984); FA Mann, *The Doctrine of International Jurisdiction*, The Hague Academy Collected Courses 111 (Brill, 1964).

[4] BJ George, 'Extraterritorial Application of Penal Legislation' (1966) 64 *Michigan Law Review* 609, 621.

[5] *United States v Vanness,* 85 F3d 661, 663, n 2 (DC Cir 1996).

[6] See Bowett (n 3); AJ Colangelo, 'Spatial Legality' (2012–13) 107 *Northwestern University Law Review* 69, 106; M Shaw, *International Law,* 8th edn (CUP, 2017) 572, defining jurisdiction as 'the power of the state to affect people, property and circumstance'.

[7] R Higgins, *Problems & Process: International Law and How We Use It* (OUP, 1995) 146.

[8] Mills, 'Rethinking Jurisdiction' (n 3) 188.

[9] S Allen, D Costelloe, M Fitzmaurice, P Gragl and E Guntrip, 'Introduction' in S Allen, D Costelloe, M Fitzmaurice, P Gragl and E Guntrip (eds), *The Oxford Handbook of Jurisdiction in International Law* (OUP 2019) 4.

[10] B Simma and AT Müller, 'Exercise and Limits of Jurisdiction', in J Crawford and M Koskenniemi (eds) *The Cambridge Companion to International Law* (CUP 2012) 134.

[11] See eg Ryngaert (n 3) 6, stating that it 'ensures that States, especially powerful States, do not assert jurisdiction over affairs which are the domain of other States, it is closely related to the customary international law principles of non-intervention and sovereign equality of States'. There is also a helpful definition in: Restatement (Third) of US Foreign Relations Law §401(a).

[12] B Oxman, 'Jurisdiction of States' in *Max Planck Encyclopedia of Public International Law* (2007); see also Restatement (Third) of US Foreign Relations Law §401(c).

[13] Bowett (n 3); Mills (n 3) 194–195. See also A T von Mehren, 'Adjudicatory Jurisdiction: General Theories Compared and Evaluated' (1983–84) 6 *Tel Aviv University Studies in Law* 50.

[14] The different types or meanings of jurisdiction in international law are addressed in Ryngaert (n 3) 6–11.

the Court to decide a concrete case with a binding force'.[15] This is thus similar to the concept of jurisdiction as it is used under many domestic legal systems. Procedurally, international adjudicative jurisdiction is often sub-divided, covering issues of temporal,[16] personal,[17] subject-matter and, in some cases, territorial[18] jurisdiction, which will be explored in detail throughout this book.

B. Admissibility

Jurisdiction and admissibility are closely related concepts. They are sometimes hard to distinguish. In fact, some even question the usefulness of the distinction.[19] Yet the distinction is important[20] and one which often arises in relation to the exercise of jurisdictional avoidance techniques, as explained below.

Understanding the distinction between jurisdiction and admissibility requires a precise understanding of what admissibility relates to. According to Heiskanen, admissibility 'is about whether the claim, as presented, can or should be resolved by an international tribunal, which otherwise has found jurisdiction'.[21] Gerald Fitzmaurice explains that the distinction between jurisdiction and admissibility lies in the fact that admissibility relates to a decision to 'rule a claim to be inadmissible on some ground other than its ultimate merits', whilst jurisdiction relates to a decision that 'the tribunal itself is incompetent to give any ruling at all whether as to the merits or as to the admissibility of the

[15] S Rosenne, The Law and Practice of the International Court, 1920–2005 (Brill, 2006) 301–02. There is some debate as to whether the English term jurisdiction is conceptually different from the French term competence. This debate first arose from Albania's Judge *ad hoc* Daxner, in Corfu Channel, who stated that 'In my opinion, the word "jurisdiction" has two fundamental meanings in international law. This word is used: (1) to recognize the Court as an organ instituted for the purpose jus dicere and in order to acquire the ability to appear before it; (2) to determine the competence of the Court, ie to invest the Court with the right to solve concrete cases', Corfu Channel (UK v Albania), ICJ, Preliminary Objections Judgment, 25 March 1948 (Daxner J dissenting). See also G Fitzmaurice, 'The Law and Procedure of the International Court of Justice, 1951–4: Questions of Jurisdiction, Competence and Procedure' (1958) 34 British Yearbook of International Law 1; V Heiskanen, 'Ménage à trois? Jurisdiction, Admissibility and Competence in Investment Treaty Arbitration' (2013) 29(1) ICSID Review – Foreign Investment Law Journal pp 231 and ff.

[16] N Gallus, *The Temporal Jurisdiction of International Tribunals* (OUP, 2017).

[17] See eg *Serafín García Armas and Karina García Gruber v Venezuela*, PCA Case No 2013-3, Decision on Jurisdiction (15 December 2014) paras 176 and following.

[18] See eg *Al-Skeini and Others v United Kingdom* App No 55721/07 (ECtHR [GC], 7 July 2011) and the case studies set out in chapter 5.

[19] H Thirlway, *The Law and Procedure of the International Court of Justice: Fifty Years of Jurisprudence* (OUP, 2013) 74.

[20] In general, see: F Fontanelli, *Jurisdiction and Admissibility in Investment Arbitration: The Practice and the Theory* (Brill, 2018). See also F Fontanelli and A Tanzi, 'Jurisdiction and Admissibility in Investment Arbitration: A View from the Bridge at the Practice' (2017) 16(1) *Law and Practice of International Courts and Tribunals* 3–20.

[21] Heiskanen, *Menage a Trois?* (n 15). See also: Y Shany, 'Jurisdiction and Admissibility' in CP Romano, KJ Alter and C Avgerou (eds), *The Oxford Handbook of International Adjudication* (OUP, 2013), 779.

claim'.[22] Or, as Highet put it: 'lack of jurisdiction refers to the jurisdiction of the Tribunal and inadmissibility refers to the admissibility of the case'.[23]

James Crawford explains the distinction between jurisdiction and admissibility as follows. On the one hand, objections that go to the court's jurisdiction 'relate to conditions affecting the parties' consent to have the tribunal decide the case at all'.[24] They are fatal to an international court's attempts to adjudicate a dispute as they 'deprive the tribunal of the authority to give rulings' on the claim.[25] On the other hand, objections that go to admissibility, rather than questioning the court or tribunal's authority to decide that claim 'invite the tribunal to dismiss (or perhaps postpone) the claim on a ground which, while it does not exclude its authority in principle, affects the possibility or propriety of its deciding the particular case at the particular time'.[26]

Similarly, Yuval Shany considers that whilst jurisdictional challenges 'reflect legal power – that is, the power to adjudicate a dispute', issues of admissibility, in contrast, relate to the 'terms permitting an international court to decline to exercise its legal powers'.[27] Thus, Shany considers that admissibility criteria imply some discretion and that international courts use admissibility doctrines as an avoidance technique, as a way of abstaining from deciding disputes that may jeopardise the court's judicial function. He concludes that the 'link between rules of admissibility and judicial propriety and expediency (or legitimacy and effectiveness) is quite straightforward'.[28]

Basically, the key distinction between the two is that whereas jurisdiction relates to the *existence* of the court's power to adjudicate a dispute, admissibility relates to the *exercise* of that power, at that particular moment, over that particular claim. International courts have considered this issue. The ICJ articulated the relevant principles in its 2008 judgment in *Croatian Genocide*. The Court observed that an objection based on admissibility: 'consists in the contention that there exists a legal reason, even when there is jurisdiction, why the Court should decline to hear a case, or more usually, a specific claim therein'.[29]

The distinction between the two concepts is not always universally accepted, however. For example, the Tribunal in *Pan American Energy LLC and BP Argentina Exploration Company v Argentine Republic* brushed away the distinction between the two. It held that: '[T]here is no need to go into the possible – and

[22] Fitzmaurice, 'The Law and Procedure' (n 15).

[23] *Waste Management Inc v United Mexican States*, ICSID Case No ARB(AF)/98/2, Decision on Jurisdiction (2 June 2000), Dissenting Opinion of Keith Highet, para 57.

[24] J Crawford, *Brownlie's Principles of Public International Law*, 8th edn (OUP, 2012) 667.

[25] ibid.

[26] ibid.

[27] Y Shany, *Questions of Jurisdiction and Admissibility before International Courts* (CUP, 2015) at 47.

[28] ibid 52.

[29] *Application of the Convention on the Prevention and Punishment of the Crime of Genocide* (*Croatia v Serbia*), ICJ, Judgment (Preliminary Objections) of 14 November 2008, para 120.

somewhat controversial – distinction between jurisdiction and admissibility', thus disregarding the '*labelling*' of the objections.'[30]

In my view, the distinction between the two concepts is important and should be affirmed. As Fitzmaurice explained, there is a clear jurisprudential distinction between an objection to the jurisdiction of a tribunal, and an objection to the substantive admissibility of the claim'. That conceptual distinction, he argued, meant that there was a 'considerable differences in treatment and procedure' when dealing with the two different types of objections.[31] Moreover, for the purpose of avoidance techniques, this is a distinction without a difference: both admissibility and jurisdictional doctrines may be used as avoidance techniques to reach the same result: abstaining from deciding a particular case or issue.

C. Justiciability: Domestic Law

The third key concept – and perhaps the most complex – is justiciability. Justiciability is a chameleonic concept.[32] It is also an important one: some suggest that it is 'one of the moral principles that determine the ideal content of the rule of law'.[33] Non-justiciability doctrines are particularly relevant for a study on avoidance, as declaring an issue as non-justiciable is a way of preventing disputes involving said issue to be decided by international courts. Non-justiciability is, by definition, the principal express avoidance technique. This warrants looking at justiciability from both a domestic and an international perspective.

Like admissibility, this is another concept that must be distinguished from jurisdiction. In some domestic contexts, jurisdiction and justiciability (and admissibility) are sometimes used interchangeably.[34] The better view, however, is that they are separate concepts. The US Supreme Court has explained that the key distinction is that issues of justiciability relate to the *subject matter* of a dispute and the 'inappropriateness of the subject matter for judicial consideration'.[35]

[30] *Pan American Energy LLC v Argentina*, ICSID Case No ARB/03/13, Decision on Preliminary Objections (27 July 2006) para 54. Other tribunals have followed a similar approach; see eg *Bayindir Insaat Turizm Ticaret ve Sanayi AS v Pakistan*, ICSID Case No ARB/03/29, Decision on Jurisdiction (14 November 2005) para 87 stating that: 'without distinguishing between objections to the jurisdiction of the Tribunal and objections to the admissibility of the claims'.

[31] Fitzmaurice (n 15) 11–12.

[32] D McGoldrick, 'The Boundaries of Justiciability' (2010) 59 *International and Comparative Law Quarterly* 981.

[33] TAO Endicott, *Vagueness in Law* (OUP, 2000) 97.

[34] McGoldrick (n 32) 983. See also R Fallon, 'The Linkage between Justiciability and Remedies: And Their Connections to Substantive Rights' (2006) 92 *Virginia Law Review* 633, stating that 'First, the court determines justiciability – involving whether the plaintiff has standing, the suit is ripe, and so forth'.

[35] *Baker v Carr* 369 US 186, 198 (1962).

Geoffrey Marshall writes about the prescriptive aspect of justiciability: the 'aptness of a question for judicial solution'.[36] Lou Henkin, when considering the political question doctrine – an important non-justiciability doctrine – said: '[t]hat there are political questions – issues to be resolved and decisions to be made by the political branches of government and not by the courts – is axiomatic in a system of constitutional government built on the separation of powers'.[37]

A British judge, Lord Scarman, put it pithily: an issue will be justiciable when it is 'a matter upon which the court can adjudicate'.[38] Timothy Endicott considers that Lord Scarman's phrase needs a qualifier, so that it reads: a matter which the court 'can *properly* adjudicate'.[39] Endicott further contends that justiciability does involve considering whether judges have the required expertise to address a certain type of dispute, or whether certain types of decisions should be taken by judges that are insulated from political control mechanism (i.e., who could be deposed at the ballot box). Justiciability, he argues, also 'involves understanding what the judicial process is good for . . . an issue is not justiciable if the way in which courts make decisions is not a good way to resolve that issue'.[40]

There are several classifications of justiciability doctrines. One division is between normative (or rule-based) justiciability and institutional justiciability.[41] Normative justiciability[42] is based on the absence of applicable legal rules or principles to decide a dispute. Perhaps it would be best to characterise this type of justiciability as rules-based justiciability (or legal lacunae justiciability).[43] The second category is institutional justiciability. This is based on separation of powers and the allocation of authority between different branches of government.[44] Accordingly, a dispute will be non-justiciable on this basis when there is a:

[36] G Marshall, 'Justiciability' in AG Guest (ed), *Oxford Essays in Jurisprudence* (OUP, 1961), 267–68. For a thorough discussion of these issues, see JA King, 'Institutional Approaches to Judicial Restraint' (2008) 28 *Oxford Journal of Legal Studies* 409, 420 and following.

[37] L Henkin, 'Is There a 'Political Question' Doctrine?' (1976) 85 *Yale Law Journal* 597.

[38] *Council of Civil Service Unions v Minister for the Civil Service* [1985] AC 374.

[39] See eg TAO Endicott, 'The Reason of the Law' (2003) 48 *American Journal of Jurisprudence* 83.

[40] McGoldrick (n 32) 98 takes a similar view, opining that a dispute will be justiciable 'in a particular forum if it is capable of being decided in that legal forum and it is considered appropriate to do so'.

[41] A Barak, *The Judge in a Democracy* (Princeton University Press, 2008) 178–86. There is a cogent definition of both types of justiciability in *Baker v Carr* (n 35), 369 US 186, 217 (1962). This, of course, is one of the seminal US decisions on the political question doctrine.

[42] This is perhaps a misnomer, as it is not based on *normative,* ie based on evaluative or value, judgments.

[43] Justice Brennan, considering a narrow ground of non-justiciability (the political question doctrine, as understood in US law), stated that there were cases where there was 'a lack of judicially discoverable and manageable standards for resolving it' 369 US 186, 217 (1962). Some heavily criticise this approach. See eg Barak (n 41) 179: 'In my opinion, every dispute is normatively justiciable. Every legal problem has criteria for its resolution. There is no "legal vacuum." According to my outlook, law fills the whole world. There is no sphere containing no law and no legal criteria.'

[44] See eg L Sossin, *Boundaries of Judicial Review: The Law of Justiciability in Canada* (Carswell, 1999); King (n 36).

> [T]extually demonstrable constitutional commitment of the issue to a coordinate political department... or the impossibility of a court's undertaking independent resolution without expressing lack of the respect due coordinate branches of government.[45]

In the UK, Lord Hoffmann has also articulated this principle. In a case regarding the legality of a decision to deport a suspect of terrorism, he observed that courts should be deferential to the executive branch in matters of national security, as there was a:

> [N]eed for the judicial arm of government to respect the decisions of ministers . . . It is not only that the executive has access to special information and expertise in these matters. It is also that such decisions . . . require a legitimacy which can be conferred only be entrusting them to persons responsible to the community through the democratic process.[46]

This type of non-justiciability doctrine is seldom applied in international law[47] – at least expressly, as will be explored in detail in chapter 3.

Another classification distinguishes between primary and secondary justiciability.[48] This distinction has been advanced in the context of English public law, in relation to whether certain acts by public authorities are subject to judicial review. Harris considers that primary justiciability refers to broad, generic categories that refer to 'a particular class of executive decision-making' and whether they are 'amenab[le] at all to judicial review'.[49] If this first hurdle is satisfied, then issues of secondary justiciability arise. Those are more specific. They involve determining whether 'particular decision-making can be reviewed upon particular grounds'.[50] This categorisation has so far not been applied to international law – and there are no obvious reasons why it should be otherwise.

Although non-justiciability doctrines are not entirely absent from civil law jurisdictions,[51] they are less developed and generally have less relevance than in some common law systems,[52] and therefore are not addressed in detail.

[45] *Baker v Carr* (n 35) 217. The Israeli Supreme Court has taken a similar approach, observing in *Ressler v Minister of Def* HC 910/68 that: 'Institutional justiciability therefore deals with the question whether the law and the court are the proper frameworks for deciding the dispute. The question is not whether it is possible to decide the dispute according to the law and in a court . . . The question is whether it is desirable to decide the dispute—which is normatively justiciable—according to legal criteria in court', 488–489.

[46] *Secretary of State for the Home Department v Rehman* [2001] 3 WLR 877, 897.

[47] The only obvious example being *Northern Cameroons*.

[48] BV Harris, 'Judicial Review, Justiciability and the Prerogative of Mercy' (2003) 62 *CLJ* 631, 644. But see TRS Allan, *Law Liberty and Justice* (Clarendon Press, 1994) 212–13.

[49] Harris (n 48) 644.

[50] ibid. At this point, the analysis is context dependent. Criticising a 'spatial approach' to justiciability, see: M Hunt, 'Sovereignty's Blight: Why Contemporary Public Law Needs the Concept of "Due Deference"' in N Bamforth and P Leyland (eds), *Public Law in a Multi-Layered Constitution* (Hart Publishing, 2003) 346–48.

[51] See eg the doctrine of *actes de gouvernement* under French law.

[52] See eg German Constitutional Court Judgment of 19 May 2020, 1 BvR 2835/17 (regarding restrictions to foreign surveillance on non-German nationals); see also: E Garcia de Enterria, *Democracia, jueces y control de la administración,* 5th edn (Navarra, Civitas, 2000) 171.

D. Justiciability: International Law

Justiciability has received much attention in international law, both in State practice and scholarship. I will only address the issue in summary. Like in domestic law, justiciability in international law refers to certain *categories* of disputes, or certain *issues* or *subject matters,* that are considered as inherently not susceptible to be decided by international courts.

Most recent discussions on justiciability in international law start with Lauterpacht;[53] but they should start before, with Vattel. Vattel considered arbitration to be a very reasonable method to solve disputes – and one that is very much in accordance with natural law – provided that it *only* apply to disputes that do not affect the 'health of the nation'.[54] Some rely on that comment to argue that Vattel was the first to introduce the notion of nonjusticiable disputes to international law, albeit without expressly using what would later become the technical term.[55] Although Vattel does not specify what types of disputes may affect the 'health of the nation', he does make two separate distinctions between types of rights, with the second distinction being that between important rights and less important rights.[56] In the case of important rights, Vattel considered that States should not even consider having those solved through conciliatory means, but rather that States should deploy all efforts to protect them, including, somewhat ominously, to shed all the blood that may be necessary for doing so.[57]

Writing in the nineteenth century, John Westlake articulated an elegant argument on justiciability. He developed the dichotomy between legal and political disputes advanced by Vattel, further substantiating that distinction.[58] Westlake's distinction is based on what he considers the political actions of States; those instances where States act *politically,* which, in his view, means beyond law.[59] Westlake then goes on to elaborate his dichotomy between legal and political disputes, stating that the political disputes are those that touch 'the national honour of the state, or its superior or vital interests and its imprescriptible assets . . . and it is pointed out that on such questions depend in a large part the security and prosperity of the state, and that only the sovereign

[53] J Odermatt 'Patterns of Avoidance: Political Questions before International Courts' (2018) 14(2) *International Journal of Law in Context,* 221, 224.

[54] E De Vattel, Albert De Lapradelle and Charles Ghequiere Fenwick, *Le Droit Des Gens Ou Principes de La Loi Naturelle Appliqués à La Conduite et Aux Affaires Des Nations et Des Souverains* (Washington, Carnegie Institution, 1916) 329 (the original term is 'salut de la nation', my translation).

[55] H Lauterpacht, *The Function of Law in the International Community* (OUP, 2011) 7.

[56] Vattel and others (n 54) 332.

[57] ibid 331.

[58] J Westlake, *International Law* (CUP, 1910) 300. Westlake's dichotomy between political and legal disputes influenced the Russian proposal in the First Hague Conference, see RY Hedges, 'Justiciable Disputes' (1928) 22 *American Journal of International Law* 560.

[59] Westlake (n 58) 302.

power can be the judge of them'.[60] In short, he was referring to politically sensitive issues.

Lauterpacht, however, is the scholar that has addressed the issue of justiciability in most depth. He is also, perhaps, its greatest critic.[61] Lauterpacht considers that justiciability doctrines were 'an obstacle in the way of legal progress'[62] and so vague that they could 'mean so much that it does not mean anything'.[63] He divides justiciability doctrines in four main categories.[64] The most important is the second one: the distinction between legal and political disputes. Lauterpacht considered that the distinction was spurious. According to him, *all* disputes involving States are, in some way, political as the 'State is a political institution, and all questions which affect it as a whole, in particular in its relations with other States, are therefore political'.[65] Despite that, Lauterpacht concludes that ultimately all of those disputes are legal.[66] Indeed, he considered that the distinction between political and legal disputes was based exclusively on subjective considerations – not on the subject matter of the dispute itself. Lauterpacht contended that what makes the dispute political was 'the refusal of the State to submit the dispute to judicial settlement, and not the intrinsic nature of the controversy, which makes it political'.[67] So State consent to adjudication – rather than the subject matter of the dispute – was the key criteria.

Lauterpacht considers that the only legally sound – and normatively coherent – position is the recognition of compulsory jurisdiction in international law,[68] asserting that the 'reign of law, represented by the incorporation of obligatory arbitration as a rule of positive international law, is not the only means for securing and preserving peace among nations. Nevertheless it is an essential

[60] ibid 302–303.

[61] It is one of the main objects of study of his classic *The Function of Law in the International Community*. And see also H Lauterpacht, 'The Absence of an International Legislature and the Compulsory Jurisdiction of International Tribunals' (1930) 11 *British Yearbook of International Law* 134; H Lauterpacht, 'The Doctrine of Non-Justiciable Disputes in International Law' (1928) *Economica* 277.

[62] ibid 443.

[63] ibid.

[64] Each of these broad categories is then analysed in detail the different parts of *The Function of Law*. As to the first category, Lauterpacht considered that the combination of the completeness of the international legal system and the prohibition on *non liquet* would suffice, see Lauterpacht *The Function of Law* (n 55) 142; for the third category, the absence of an international legislature, he considered that it was even more important to allow international adjudicators to gradually develop the law, 352–53; as for the fourth category, Lauterpacht argues that it is ultimately a distinction without a difference, as what really matters is States' willingness to submit an issue to international adjudication, 377.

[65] Lauterpacht, *The Function of Law* (n 55) 161.

[66] ibid 166.

[67] ibid 172.

[68] ibid 444 '[I]t is a duty incumbent upon the lawyer to adopt a critical attitude in regard to that doctrine in the interest not only of the dignity of the science of international law, but also of an effective peaceful organization of the international community which it is the legitimate business of international lawyers to promote.'

condition of peace'.[69] Lauterpacht's arguments are formidable. Given the reluctance of international adjudicators to expressly invoke justiciability doctrines,[70] it could be said that Lauterpacht's views prevailed. Yet 90 years have passed since the publication of *The Function of Law in the International Community* and the history of international adjudication has not confirmed Lauterpacht's views. As explained in more detail below, States have been reluctant to embrace his rather idealistic views on international adjudication.

In the first half of the twentieth century, other scholars were not as critical of justiciability doctrines as Lauterpacht. Morgenthau,[71] for instance, accepted the distinction between legal and political (i.e., non-justiciable) disputes, considering that what was needed was 'objective criteria' to distinguish between disputes that were legal and those that were not.[72] Count Leonidas Kamarowsky, the author of one of the first monographs on international courts,[73] and one of the earliest proponents of a permanent international court, considered nevertheless that such court's jurisdiction would need to be subject to important restrictions. Carlos Calvo, a jurist well known for his scepticism towards international adjudication,[74] unsurprisingly also had reservations regarding the subject-matter jurisdiction of international courts. While Calvo *considered* that mediation was a suitable means of resolution for 'all kinds of international questions', he opined that international adjudication 'will not address those [international disputes] that directly affect a state's honour or national independence . . . each nation is the sole judge of its dignity and of the rights that ensure it'.[75] Thomas Balch,[76]

[69] ibid 445.

[70] As explained in detail in chapters 3–5.

[71] Before becoming one of the chief exponents of international relations realism, Hans Morgenthau was a legal scholar, see H Morgenthau, K Thompson and D Clinton, *Politics Among Nations* 7th edn (McGraw-Hill Education, 2005).

[72] H Morgenthau, *La Notion du Politique et la Théorie des differends internationaux* (Paris, Recueil Sirey, 1933). There is an English translation: Hans Morgenthau, *The Concept of the Political* (Maeva Vidal trans., 2012 ed.). Citations, however, are from the French version. See also O Jütersonke, *Morgenthau, Law and Realism* (CUP, 2010), particularly ch 2; L Gross, 'On the Justiciability of International Disputes' in *Essays on International Law and Organization* (Transnational Publishers 1984).

[73] L Kamarowsky, S De Westman and J Lacointa, *Le Tribunal International* (Paris, G Pedone-Lauriel, 1887); and a newer edition, L Kamarowsky, S De Westman and J Lacointa, *Le Tribunal International* (Gale, 2013); for a brief appreciation of Kamarowsky, see 'In Memoriam: Mr Auguste Beernaert' (1913) 7 *American Journal of International Law* 371, 373–74.

[74] His main contribution to international law is the 'Calvo Clause', which was very influential across Latin America. See eg P Juillard, 'Calvo Doctrine/Calvo Clause' (2007) *Max Planck Encyclopedia of Public International Law*; AV Freeman, 'Recent Aspects of the Calvo Doctrine and the Challenge of International Law' (1946) 40 *American Journal of International Law* 121; AH Feller, 'Some Observations on the Calvo Clause' (1933) 27 *American Journal of International Law* 461; LM Summers, 'The Calvo Clause' (1932) 19 *Virginia Law Review* 459.

[75] C Calvo, *Le Droit international théorique et pratique: précédé d'un exposé historique des progrès de La science du droit des gens,* Vol. 3 (HardPress, 2010) 472.

[76] Who is credited with suggesting the submission of the *Alabama* claim to arbitration (making him perhaps the most underrated contributor to the development of international dispute settlement). For an account of Balch's role in the *Alabama* Arbitration see eg VV Veeder, 'The Historical Keystone to International Arbitration: The Party-Appointed Arbitrator – From Miami to Geneva' (2013) 107 *Proceedings of the ASIL Annual Meeting* 387, 391.

also considered that arbitration was not suitable for certain important disputes. He thought that it was hopeless to expect that disputes 'involving the "place in the sun" of nations' would be submitted to international tribunals.[77] Balch then provides some examples of the types of disputes that could not be settled 'on the basis of jural rules' (i.e., non-justiciable disputes), and mentions the Franco-Prussian War, the Russo-Japanese War, and World War I.[78] Jackson Ralston, a man with ample practical experience of international adjudication, was more bullish about expanding the scope of subject matter jurisdiction. Ralston considered that the notion of obligatory arbitration had developed significantly in the first decades of the twentieth century, and noted that, gradually, the types of disputes submitted to arbitration had increased, and now included disputes that were both political *and* domestic, such as boundary disputes.[79] Finally, John Fischer-Williams thought that there were disputes that were not justiciable, including those in which a State was seeking 'something different from what the law will give it'[80] and also considered that self-judging reservations regarding disputes involving national honour and vital interests, although problematic, could 'not be dismissed as a mere piece of human frailty or obstinacy'.[81]

The *Institut de Droit International* also did important work on the topic. Between the late nineteenth and the early twentieth century the *Institut* attempted to define and elaborate on the distinction between justiciable and non-justiciable disputes and also to list the types of dispute that were justiciable (something that was a common theme in the first few decades of the twentieth century, as explained below). The first effort came as early as 1873.[82] The *Institut* then made a second attempt in 1922, in which it tried – and failed – to establish a list

[77] TW Balch, *Legal and Political Questions between Nations* (Allen, Lane and Scott, 1924) 18.

[78] ibid 19–20.

[79] JH Ralston, *International Arbitration from Athens to Locarno* (Lawbook Exchange, 2004) 44–45.

[80] JF Williams, 'Model Treaties for the Pacific Settlement of Disputes – Mutual Assistance and Non-Aggression' (1929) 7 *International Affairs* 407; JF Williams, 'Justiciable and Other Disputes' (1932) 26 *American Journal of International Law* 31; JF Williams, 'Treaty Revision and the Future of the League of Nations' (1931) 10 *International Affairs* 326.

[81] JF Williams, 'The Place of Law in International Affairs: Paper Read on February 28th, 1928' (1928) 7 *Journal of the Royal Institute of International Affairs* 94, 100.

[82] Draft Regulations for International Arbitral Procedure. See Institut de Droit International, '*Project de réglement pour la procedure arbitrale internationale*', Session de La Haye – 1875, *Annuaire* (1877). The Draft itself, however, does not expressly address the issue of justiciability. Nevertheless, Goldschmidt's preliminary remarks to the draft do, however, address the issue. Two points are particularly interesting. The first is Goldschmidt's views on the limits of international adjudication. His view was that the main objective of judicial settlement was nothing other than restraining the use of force. Goldschmidt understood that there were some intrinsic limits to international adjudication, noting that 'it is hard to imagine that sovereign States, and particularly Great Powers, will ever consent in advance to submit *all* possible disputes to the decision of an arbitral tribunal', 423. He illustrates the point with a colourful example, mentioning that that neither Louis XIV nor Napoleon would have ever agreed to 'submit to arbitrators their pretensions of world domination'. Nor, we could add, would their modern-day equivalents. The second point is Goldschmidt's position on the distinction between legal and political disputes, which he supported. He considered that some disputes, particularly those of a 'complex political nature' are 'by their very nature, more a question of power than of law', 425.

classifying which disputes were justiciable, concluding that it was not a useful approach as ultimately it was a matter best left for States.[83]

The distinction between justiciable and non-justiciable disputes has also received extensive treatment in State practice, particularly before the creation of the United Nations. Indeed, for a long time it was generally acknowledged that some international disputes were political or non-justiciable. The 1899 and 1907 Hague Peace Conferences,[84] although wildly optimistic about the benefits of compulsory arbitration,[85] still recognised that some disputes were not justiciable. In the 1899 Conference, the limits of compulsory arbitration were eloquently captured by the note the Russian delegation circulated prior to the Conference.[86] In short, the Russian note contended that international disputes fell into two categories: those concerning a 'material indemnity for damages and losses caused to it or to its nationals',[87] so essentially claims for monetary damages and those concerning the exercise of sovereign power.[88] The note

[83] Institut de Droit International, '*La Classification des conflits comportant un reglement judiciare, rapport par MM Ph Marshall-Brown et N. Politis*', *Annuaire* (1922) 23 and ss. The Rapporteurs considered (correctly) that even the paradigmatic case of a justiciable dispute – a dispute regarding the interpretation of a treaty – stops being justiciable the second it touches upon a State's political interests, at p 28, and further recognised that it was incorrect to equate political disputes with non-justiciable disputes, observing that it was almost impossible to properly define what constitutes 'political disputes', at p 31. The Report further developed – in a nuanced way – the distinction between legal and justiciable disputes (note that the rapporteurs chose to use justiciable, rather than *political*), at pp 26–27. There was a third report, published in 1927, see: Institut de Droit International Institut, '*L'extension de l'arbitrage obligatoire et la competence obligatoire de la Cour Permanente de Justice Internationale*', *Annuaire* (1927), at 679 and ff. Although this report did not expressly consider justiciability, including on grounds that the issue had been covered in the 1922 Report, the *travaux preparatoires* includes an interesting contribution from Max Huber, who by that time had spent some years as the President of the PCIJ. He observed that it was pointless to try to define justiciable disputes based on an 'abstract criteria of delimitation', as that was not in line with the 'political requirements of Powers in matters of arbitration', observing that from the point of view of diplomats charged with concluding arbitration convention, a system that distinguishes between justiciable and non-justiciable disputes is, 'despite its deficiencies, completely natural', as States would be able to decide themselves whether a dispute fell within the scope of the vital interests reservation, at pp. 763–65 (my translations).

[84] I am referring to the Hague Convention for the Pacific Settlement of International Disputes, Convention for the Pacific Settlement of International Disputes, 29 July 29, not the other conventions regarding the laws of war, the Convention respecting the Laws and Customs of War on Land and the Convention for the Adaptation to Maritime Warfare of the Principles of the Geneva Convention, Convention (IV) respecting the Laws and Customs of War on Land and its annex, The Hague, 29 July 29, 1899. See also MO Hudson, 'Present Status of the Hague Conventions of 1899 and 1907' (1931) 25 *American Journal of International Law* 114.

[85] See eg DD Caron, 'War and International Adjudication: Reflections on the 1899 Peace Conference' (2000) 94 American Journal of International Law 4; TR White, 'Limitations Upon the Initiation of War' (1925) 19 *Proceedings of the American Society of International Law at Its Annual Meeting* 102, 106; PC Jessup, 'A Record of the Arbitration Treaties' (1928) 138 *The Annals of the American Academy of Political and Social Science* 120.

[86] J Brown Scott, *Reports to the Hague Conferences of 1899 and 1907* (Clarendon Press, 1917), 98. The Russian note was considered to have been quite influential, because Russia had convened the conference, see: M Hudson, *The Permanent Court of International Justice: 1920–1942* (The Macmillan Company, 1943) 457.

[87] ibid 98.

[88] ibid. This is one of the first articulations of the distinction between political and legal disputes that would eventually be the basis of the League of Nations' dispute settlement system.

considered that the second category should not be subject to adjudication,[89] as those disputes involve 'questions of which none but the sovereign Power can be the judge'.[90] The Report to the Convention also developed this idea.[91] In turn, the 1907 Hague Conference also accepted the distinction between legal and political disputes[92] and tried – and failed – to classify which types of disputes were justiciable.[93]

[89] ibid 399.

[90] ibid. The Note further stated that 'In introducing international arbitration into the international life of States we must proceed with extreme care in order not to extend unreasonably its sphere of application, so as to shake the confidence which may be inspired therein, or discredit arbitration in the eyes of Governments and peoples.'

[91] ibid 56. Given the implausibility of general compulsory arbitration, the Russian delegation proposed that the States represented at the Conference agree to compulsory arbitration of a limited list of issues. These included disputes over pecuniary damage to aliens and the interpretation of treaties (two of the issues that States had until then most often submitted to arbitration). Although there was some support for the idea of having a list of justiciable disputes, the delegations could not agree on the *contents* of that list (the traditional problem of the enumeration approach). Indeed, the delegates were not even able to agree to compulsory arbitration for issues as trivial as wages and estates of deceased seamen or weights and measures, see eg W Hull, *The Two Hague Conferences and their Contribution to International Law* (Boston, Ginn & Company, 1908) 329–30. One of the main hurdles was German opposition to any form of compulsory arbitration. Four of the Great Powers that participated in the Conference – the United States, the United Kingdom, France, and Russia – were in general terms favourable to international adjudication. The United States in particular was reluctant to accept compulsory arbitration over certain types of disputes, including the navigation of rivers and the international monetary system and the United States were concerned with the possibility of arbitration undermining the Monroe doctrine. Germany, however, was not favourable to international arbitration and that opposition almost derailed the effort, see Caron (n 85) 16 and AD White, *Autobiography of Andrew Dickson White* (Washington, Library of Congress, 2016) 265.

[92] This is most evident in the work regarding the establishment of a permanent international court. On first impression, the 1907 Draft Convention appears not to establish any limitation regarding the types of disputes that could be submitted to it. Article 17 of the 1907 Draft Convention provides that: 'The Court of Arbitral Justice is competent to deal with all cases submitted to it.' That provision, however, should not be interpreted as implying that there are no limits on the types of disputes that would be susceptible of international adjudication. The Report to the Conference clarifies that the authors of the Draft Convention recognised the distinction between legal and political disputes, stating that 'it is evident that questions of a judicial nature were deemed peculiarly susceptible to arbitration'. The drafting commission was aware of, and accepted, the dichotomy between legal and political disputes. This was eloquently articulated by the president of the drafting commission, the French delegate, Léon Bourgeois (once characterised as 'the Pope of radicalism'). Bourgeois, operating under a different conception of arbitration than that used today (ie which considers that arbitrators may decide cases not necessarily on legal points; although some could say there is no distinction with contemporary practice), tried to temper concerns about the role of the proposed court. He emphasised that it would only have jurisdiction to decide legal disputes, see J Brown Scott, *The Project Relative to a Court of Arbitral Justice* (Washington, The Endowment,1920) 2.

[93] HM Cory, *Compulsory Arbitration of International Disputes* (Columbia University Press, 1932) 69. See also: Caron (n 85) 21; Hull (n 91) 332 for the full list. The list includes matters as varied as aid to sick indigents, wages and estates of deceased sailors, pecuniary claims resulting from civil war, customs duties, rules on epizooty, phylloxera and other pests, the acquisition of wealth by foreigners, postal and telegraph systems, and copyrights, patents and trademarks, see MO Hudson, 'Legal and Political Questions' (1924) 18 *Proceedings of the American Society of International Law at Its Annual Meeting* 126. The Conference nevertheless did issue a (merely symbolic) declaration in support of compulsory arbitration, particularly regarding disputes about the interpretation and application of treaties. Some delegations were unhappy. The United States was so dissatisfied with the Conference's failure to include a draft treaty on compulsory arbitration in the final conventions that it abstained from voting in favour of the declaration.

The end of the First World War galvanised the supporters of international adjudication.[94] One consequence was the creation of the League of Nations.[95] The Covenant adopted a dual approach to the solution of international disputes. It established both legal *and* political mechanisms to address them, which sometimes were intertwined in operation. The Covenant did include two articles that address legal disputes. Article 13 of the Covenant addressed issues of justiciability,[96] which recognises the dichotomy between justiciable and non-justiciable disputes,[97] as it provides that States could pursue the legal settlement of disputes 'which they recognise to be suitable for submission to arbitration or judicial settlement'.[98] In fact, Article 15 of the Covenant further reaffirms that distinction, by referring to non-justiciable 'political' disputes,[99] which would be submitted either to the Council or to the League's Assembly. But the Statute of

[94] See eg MD Dubin, 'Elihu Root and the Advocacy of a League of Nations, 1914–1917' (1966) 19 *Western Political Quarterly* 439, 442; WH Taft, 'A World League to Enforce Peace' (1915) 2 *The New York Times Current History of the European War* 667; P Kruger, 'From the Paris Peace Treaties to the End of the Second World War' in B Fassbender and A Peters (eds), *Oxford Handbook on the History of International Law* (OUP, 2012) 685; Treaty of Versailles, arts 227–30.

[95] As a starting point, the Covenant itself did not establish an international judicial organ. Rather, Article 14 of the Covenant required the League's Council to 'formulate and submit . . . plans for the establishment of a permanent Court of International Justice' which would be 'competent to hear and determine any dispute of an international character'. There are no records as to what the Covenant's drafters meant by those words. Some early drafts indicate that the objective was to postpone discussion of the nature and authority of the court to be established. The Council, in turn, tasked a Committee of Jurists to formulate said plan, see E Beneš, 'The League of Nations: Successes and Failures' (1932–33) 11 *Foreign Affairs* 66.

[96] For a view of one of the original drafts, agreed by Robert Cecil and Wilson in 1919, see D Miller, *Drafting of the Covenant* (P Putnam's Sons, 1928), vol II, 585. In that draft Article 13 of the Covenant provides that disputes should be solved *either* through arbitration *or* through inquiry by the Executive Council."

[97] One of the leading proposals for the league of nations, the Smuts Plan, authored by Marshall Jan Smuts. Article 20 of Smuts' proposal is close to the final text of Article 13 of the Covenant. Smuts' proposal recognises that some disputes may not be justiciable: 'It may, however, be that the circumstances of the dispute are not of a justiciable nature . . . The issues are generally vague and intangible . . . they involve large questions of policy, of so-called vital interests, and of national honour. It is round these issues and questions that national and international passions gather like storm-clouds, until the thunder of war alone can clear the air again. They cannot be disposed of on judicial lines, and require entirely different treatment . . . Unlike arbitration on definite issues of fact or law, the object in these cases is not to arrive at a definite decision, but to mediate between the parties with a view to an amicable or peaceful settlement.' Miller (n 96) 57.

[98] The article also provides that there are certain categories of disputes that are 'generally suitable for submission to arbitration or judicial settlement' and those types of disputes relate to the interpretation of a treaty, any question of international law, as to the existence of a fact which if established would constitute a breach of any international obligation, and as to the extent and nature of the reparation to be made for any such breach. See also DH Miller, *My Diary at the Conference of Paris* (Appeal Printing, 1924) 312, 468; Hudson (n 84) 106. Nevertheless, some distinguished jurists, including Loder, consider, without a solid basis in the wording of the Covenant, that the court, by its 'very nature' had to have compulsory jurisdiction, see: BCJ Loder, 'The Permanent Court of International Justice and Compulsory Jurisdiction' (1921–22) 2 *British Yearbook of International Law* 6, 12.

[99] For an overview of the League's record in solving political disputes, see L Lloyd, '"A Springboard for the Future": A Historical Examination of Britain's Role in Shaping the Optional Clause of the Permanent Court of International Justice' (1985) 79 *American Journal of International Law* 28.

the Permanent Court of International Justice brought a change of approach. The Statute rejected compulsory jurisdiction.[100] This is reflected in Article 36, which provides that 'The jurisdiction of the Court comprises all cases which the parties refer to it' (the inclusion of the plural – *parties* – was critical, as it made clear that *both* parties, rather than only one, had to consent).[101] That Article, however, also addresses justiciability and mentions that the Permanent Court has jurisdiction over *all* cases that the parties submit to it. On first impression, the use of the expression 'all cases' suggests an expansive notion of justiciable disputes, with the main constraint being State consent rather than the subject matter of a dispute, i.e., an approach like that proposed by Lauterpacht. Although Article 36 then immediately qualifies that by referencing '*classes of legal dispute*',[102] and by setting out the same four categories mentioned in Article 13 of the Covenant,[103] arguably the distinction between justiciable and non-justiciable disputes was blurred.

Other international dispute settlement agreements entered into during the inter-war period also recognised the distinction between justiciable and non-justiciable disputes, but that distinction had been gradually losing force. Just to name a few examples, the Locarno Treaties;[104] the 1928 General Act of Arbitration (Pacific Settlement of International Disputes),[105] better known as the

[100] See eg N Kebbon, 'The World Court's Compulsory Jurisdiction under the Optional Clause – Past, Present and Future' (1989) 58 Nordic Journal of International Law 257 and ff.

[101] But Article 36 of the Statute further provides for the possibility of States unilaterally accepting the Court's compulsory jurisdiction. This Article was contentious. According to Hudson, it was 'the result of the greatest contest waged in the creation of the Court'. Hudson (n 84) 193. It is also worth noting that, in late 1925, the Council of the League of Nations commissioned a survey of all the arbitration treaties that had been entered into and deposited with the League – League of Nations, *Arbitration and Security* (1927), 5. The distinction between justiciable and non-justiciable disputes was not always articulated on those terms, as sometimes it distinguished legal and non-legal or political disputes, or between disputes regarding rights and those regarding interest, as well as disputes regarding a State's independence, honour or vital interests. The Survey was a conscientious compilation of State practice on the matter and it shows that, at least until that point, the distinction between justiciable and non-justiciable disputes was widespread and widely accepted. In fact, the Survey's introductory comments recognised – quite matter-of-factly – the distinction between justiciable and non-justiciable disputes.

[102] Lauterpacht, The Function of Law (n 55) 36–7, explaining that the adjective legal in the Statute is not meant to be a qualifier but is, rather, meant as being solely descriptive.

[103] Article 36 must be evaluated in its historical context. According to Hudson, between the end of the nineteenth century and 1920, three types of disputes were 'widely recognised as suitable for compulsory arbitration agreements'. Those are, not coincidentally, the first three of the four types of disputes mentioned in Article 13 of the Covenant and Article 36 of the Statute of the PCIJ (ie disputes regarding the interpretation of treaties; questions of international law; and the existence of facts which, if established, would result in a breach of an international obligation). Hudson (n 84) 457–58.

[104] PO Cohrs, 'The First "Real" Peace Settlements after the First World War: Britain, the United States and the Accords of London and Locarno, 1923–1925' (2003) 12 *Contemporary European History* 1. See also J Jacobson, 'The Conduct of Locarno Diplomacy' (1972) 34 *Review of Politics* 67; G Glasgow, *From Dawes to Locarno – Being a Critical Record of an Important Achievement of European Diplomacy 1924–1925* (Harper & Brothers 1926). In particular, Article 3 of the Treaty of Mutual Guarantee, known as the Security Pact, recognised this distinction.

[105] The Kellogg-Briand Pact is laconic; it was supplemented by the General Act of Arbitration.

Kellogg-Briand Pact, as supplemented by the General Act of Arbitration 1928;[106] and the Inter-American Treaties,[107] all still hinted at a separation between justiciable and non-justiciable disputes. But the lines were getting ever more blurred.

And the line had almost disappeared by the time the ICJ Statute was negotiated. By then, the distinction between justiciable and non-justiciable disputes had almost completely been cast aside. The distinction was 'abandoned', Kolb writes, because 'there is no dispute, however sensitive it may be, which cannot be technically reduced to legal terms and thus decided by a tribunal'.[108] Similarly, Tomuschat, observes that '[r]ightly, legal doctrine has ceased focusing on the issue [the distinction between legal and political disputes]', further noting that the 'position has undergone dramatic changes since the coming into force of the Statute of the PCIJ'.[109] Tomuschat categorically affirms that 'it would be fatal for the ICJ to deny its jurisdiction solely on the ground that inevitably its decision will contribute to shaping the political circumstances from which it arose'.[110] This is the generally accepted position.

So, although Article 36(2) of the ICJ Statute provides that States may accept the Court's compulsory jurisdiction to decide 'all legal disputes', and then listing the four broad types of legal disputes also set out in Article 36 of the PCIJ's Statute, the qualifier legal is not understood as implying a recognition of the distinction between legal and political disputes. The Court addressed the issue in *Tehran Hostages*, noting that it 'never' considered that it should decline to address a legal question 'because a legal dispute submitted to the Court is only one aspect of a political dispute'.[111] The Court has also somewhat defiantly held that it 'has never

[106] League of Nations Treaty Series vol 93 343, see also JL Brierly, 'The General Act of Geneva, 1928' (1930) 11 *British Yearbook of International Law* 119. The General Act recognised that justiciable disputes would be solved by judicial settlement (Chapter II), whereas political disputes would be solved through conciliation (Chapter III). Note that Brierly considered that the General Act's main problem was that it assumed that every dispute was intrinsically capable of being settled, although, I would argue that that was tempered by the Act's acceptance of very broad reservations.

[107] According to Hudson, the Inter-American Conference tasked with preparing the General Treaty of Inter-American Arbitration was buoyed by the contemporaneous European developments, namely the Kellogg-Briand Pact and the General Act, see see MO Hudson, 'The Inter-American Treaties of Pacific Settlement' (1936–37) 15 *Foreign Affairs* 165. For a history of the development of the Inter-American Conferences, see JO Murdock and HJ Gobbi, 'The Inter-American Juridical Committee' (1960) 9 *American Journal of Comparative Law* 596; J Kunz, 'International Arbitration in Pan American Developments' (1948–1949) 27 *Texas Law Review* 182, 183. OAS Treaty Series No 16. The other three treaties are: (1) the Treaty to Avoid or Prevent Conflicts between the American States of 1923 (generally called the 'Gondra Treaty'); (2) the General Convention of Inter-American Conciliation of 1929; and (3) the Anti-War Treaty of 1933 (generally called the 'Saavedra Lamas Treaty'). The main distinction between justiciable and non-justiciable disputes was based on the recognition that judicial settlement would be for 'claim of right' that were 'juridical in their nature', see: General Treaty, Article 1.

[108] R Kolb, *The International Court of Justice* (Hart, 2013) 335.

[109] C Tomuschat, 'Article 36' in A Zimmermann, C Tams, K Oellers-Frahm and C Tomuschat (eds), *The Statute of the International Court of Justice: A Commentary* (OUP, 2019) 724.

[110] ibid 725.

[111] *United States Diplomatic and Consular Staff in Tehran (United States of America v Iran)*, ICJ, Judgment of 24 May 1980 para 37; *Military and Paramilitary Activities in and Against Nicaragua (Nicaragua v United States of America)*, ICJ, Judgment of 27 June 1986, para 33; *Border and Transborder Armed Actions (Nicaragua v Honduras)*, ICJ, Judgment of 20 December 1988, paras 52–54.

shied away from a case brought before it merely because it had political implications or because it involved serious elements of the use of force'.[112]

Indeed, even in its advisory function, where the Court's Statute uses the conditional *may,* the Court has refused to expressly exercise that discretion. Rather, as the Court explained in the *Wall* advisory opinion, its 'long-standing jurisprudence' was that the '"political" character of the question posed' was not a factor that could lead it to decline jurisdiction.[113]

Yet the Court's reluctance to *expressly* recognise a distinction between legal and political (or justiciable and non-justiciable) disputes, does not mean that that is the position in reality. As I will explain throughout this book, the political or policy issues arising in some disputes may influence an international court's decision to avoid them, albeit never by expressly admitting that the political or policy-sensitive issues are the motivating factor for that decision. Perhaps Ian Brownlie, always an acute observer, was right when he said in one of the last articles he published that 'there are certain limitations upon the justiciability of disputes which are dictated by rule of law considerations' observing that there was still a 'distinction between legal and political disputes'.[114] One of the central points of my argument is that this distinction, which as Brownlie suggests still exists, has been relegated to subtext.

E. Avoidance

The central concept of this book is avoidance. The topic is addressed fully in the next chapter; I only provide this as a very short introduction. Avoidance refers to the techniques that courts rely on to abstain or refrain from deciding contentious cases or issues within those cases.[115] It is what is informally called *ducking* or *dodging* a case (or issue).

There are many types of avoidance. One of the main ways of classifying avoidance techniques is based on the moment in the proceedings in which they are applied. Delaney thus talks about *ex ante* avoidance, which prevents the court from having to decide the case at all; *in medio* avoidance, which allows some flexibility in the approach to the merits of an issue; and *ex post* avoidance, which is focused on how remedies are structured.[116] Similarly, Alves das

[112] *Military and Paramilitary* (n 111) para 96. This, I argue, is not entirely true.

[113] *Legal Consequences of the Construction of a Wall in the Occupied Palestinian Territory*, ICJ, Advisory Opinion dated 9 July 2004 para 41.

[114] I Brownlie, 'The Peaceful Settlement of International Disputes' (2009) 8 *Chinese Journal of International Law* 267, 267–68.

[115] E Delaney, 'Analyzing Avoidance: Judicial Strategy in Comparative Perspective' (2016) 66 *Duke Law Journal*, 1, 3.

[116] ibid 5.

Chagas groups avoidance techniques in two, splitting them between admissibility control and merits avoidance.[117]

My focus is on the first type of avoidance: the doctrines that allow a court to avoid even having to decide the merits of a case. This includes the different doctrines that international courts may rely on to dismiss a case on admissibility or jurisdictional grounds. For simplicity, I will refer to this type of avoidance as *jurisdictional avoidance*, but the term *jurisdictional* is used broadly and is meant to include instances where international courts dismiss a case on admissibility grounds. Accordingly, this book will not put too much emphasis on avoidance techniques deployed at the post-jurisdictional stage of proceedings, whether in dealing with merits or remedial issues.[118] Nor will it focus on avoidance techniques that do not imply issuing a judgment such as practices of timing and docket control.[119]

Another important distinction is whether avoidance doctrines are applied expressly or implied. Some avoidance doctrines expressly include non-justiciability. But I argue that avoidance techniques are, almost inherently and, by definition, applied implicitly. Jurisdictional avoidance implies that concepts of international procedural law are applied in a way that results in a case being dismissed on jurisdictional grounds, without the international court expressly stating that they are doing so because they want to avoid deciding that dispute. This issue is addressed in chapters 3 and 4.

II. INTERNATIONAL ADJUDICATION IN CONTEXT

Context is that which is scarce.[120] Understanding how international courts approach the exercise of their jurisdiction requires understanding the context in which those international courts operate. This section addresses that context, with a particular emphasis on some recent institutional developments – trends – which may affect international adjudication more broadly. It covers the following topics: judicialisation, the proliferation of international courts, contestation and backlash, dejudicialisation, and non-judicialisation.

[117] C Alves das Chagas, *Judicial Avoidance: Balancing Competences in Constitutional Adjudication* (Hart, 2023), particularly chs 7 and 8.

[118] For an excellent approach to avoidance on the merits, and how the use of differential standards of review is useful for that objective, see: F Fouchard, *The Standard of Review before the International Court of Justice: Between Principle and Pragmatism* (Hart, 2024).

[119] See M Jackson 'Judicial Avoidance at the European Court of Human Rights: Institutional Authority, the Procedural Turn, and Docket Control' (2022) 20 *International Journal of Constitutional Law* 112.

[120] Tyler Cowen, 'Context is That Which is Scarce' (*Marginal Revolution,* 10 Feb 2022). Available at: www.marginalrevolution.com/marginalrevolution/2022/02/context-is-that-which-is-scarce-2.html.

A. Judicialisation

Judicialisation is the acceptance that a certain dispute or issue may be submitted for judicial decision, i.e., the notion that a particular type of dispute can be resolved by a court. Alec Stone-Sweet, one of the early proponents of the concept, defines it as 'the construction of judicial power', noting that judicialisation involves a process in which adjudication 'appears, stabilizes, and develops authority over the normative structure governing exchange in a given community'.[121] Other scholars have defined it as the 'process by which courts and judges increasingly dominate politics and policy-making'[122] or as the 'expansion of judicial involvement in the formation and regulation of international governance'.[123]

There has been an increase in the judicialisation of international law. The number of international courts grew dramatically following the end of the Cold War. There are now 24 international courts in operation.[124] The number of cases brought before them has, logically, also increased.[125] These developments show that there has been an increase in the judicialisation of international affairs – to an extent. Until about a decade ago, scholars and practitioners of international law confidently predicted that the trend towards the increasing *judicialisation* of international disputes could only continue.[126] International courts would continue to proliferate and the scope of their subject matter jurisdiction would increase, expanding the types (and number) of disputes they would adjudicate. Indeed, they considered that it would only be a matter of time before international courts would match the institutional solidity of their domestic counterparts (which had also experienced increased judicialisation). The expansion of international jurisdiction was a one-way ratchet; it could only ever go in one direction.[127] This optimism fails to consider that judicialisation

[121] M Shapiro and A Stone Sweet, *On Law, Politics, and Judicialization* (OUP, 2002) 71. In general, for a more casual approach to the issue, see also P Sands, 'Reflections on International Judicialization' (2016) 27 *European Journal of International Law* 885.

[122] K Alter, E Hafner-Burton and L Helfer, 'Theorizing the Judicialization of International Relations' (2019) 63 *International Studies Quarterly* 449. See also C Neal Tate and Torbjorn Vallinder (eds), *The Global Expansion of Judicial Power* (New York University Press, 1995). For a discussion of the issue in broader terms R Hirschl, *Towards Juristocracy* (Harvard University Press, 2004).

[123] D Abebe and T Ginsburg 'The Dejudicialization of International Politics?' (2019) 63 *International Studies Quarterly* 521, 522.

[124] Alter, Hafner-Burton and Helfer 'Theorizing the Judicialization of International Relations' (n 122) 451.

[125] See CPR Romano, 'The Proliferation of International Judicial Bodies: The Pieces of the Puzzle' (1999) 31 *NYU Journal of International Law and Politics* 709, 752. See also K Alter, *The New Terrain of International Law* (Princeton University Press 2014).

[126] See n 122.

[127] There are several theories regarding what motivates or leads to judicialisation. Functionalist theories are based on the complexity and intertwined nature of international governance; institutionalist theories are based on democratic governance and the delegation of decisions from States to international bodies; court-centred theories suggest that international judges have been slowly expanding their powers; and rights-centred theories suggest that there is a growing awareness of

is a dynamic – and generally *slow* – process. It may involve contestation. Some advances may trigger a backlash. It is not, as some would have it, a story of linear, continual progression, as current developments show.

There are many reasons why States agree to submit certain types of dispute to international courts.[128] Judicialisation is complex and multi-causal. They often depend on the political context and the specific issue.[129] The amount and degree of judicialisation varies, both geographically and across different areas of international law.[130] Two examples, based on the subject matter of the disputes, illustrate this.

First, in the case of boundary disputes, often the decision to submit those disputes to international adjudication aims to give 'political cover' to the politicians that made that decision, thus allowing them to 'counter domestic political opposition to a controversial settlement agreement'.[131] Simply put: submitting the dispute to international adjudication allows domestic politicians to shift the blame for any negative outcome, as well as avoiding the political flak of making concessions in a negotiation process.[132]

---

the importance of rights that has led to an increase in the scope of international adjudication. For a good overview, see Abebe and Ginsburg 'Dejudicialization of International Politics?' (n 123) 522–24 (2019). See also M Byers (ed), *The Role of Law in International Politics* (OUP, 2000); A Stone Sweet and TL Brunell, 'The European Court of Justice, State Noncompliance, and the Politics of Override' (2012) 106 *American Political Science Review* 204; Alter (n 27); Alter, *The New Terrain* (n 125); Romano 'The Proliferation of International Judicial Bodies' (n 125).

[128] See Hirschl *Towards Juristocracy* (n 122), focusing on the domestic context.

[129] See, eg KW Abbott and others, 'The Concept of Legalization' (2000) 54 *International Organization* 401.

[130] K Alter, C Romano and Y Shany, 'Mapping International Courts and Tribunals, the Issues and Players' in K Alter, C Romano and Y Shany (eds), *The Oxford Handbook of International Adjudication* (OUP, 2014); Alter (n 125); B Kingsbury, 'International Courts: Uneven Judicialization in Global Order', in J Crawford and M Koskenniemi (eds), *The Cambridge Companion to International Law* (CUP, 2012).

[131] TL Allee and PK Huth, 'Legitimizing Dispute Settlement: International Legal Rulings as Domestic Political Cover' (2006) 100 *American Political Science Review* 219, 219. The authors also include a table of decisions regarding territorial disputes between 1919–1995, at 221. Although, for a more pessimistic view, see SR Ratner, 'Land Feuds and their Solutions: Finding International Law Beyond the Tribunal Chamber' (2006) 100 *American Journal of International Law* 808, stating at 828 that: 'The last century has revealed that states will not send most of [territorial] disputes to courts and that when they do, the disputes often persist. This experience has also not proved . . . that courts are institutionally the best actors for solving territorial disputes. In those cases they have decided it is difficult to know if some other border would have better resolved the legal and political claims of the parties. And as for those cases they have not decided, it is hard to imagine how they could settle some of them—one wonders whether the ICJ would really wish to determine Israel's borders, or the final status of Kashmir, Kosovo, or Western Sahara.'

[132] Ratner 'Land Feuds and their Solutions' (n 131) 223: 'international disputes typically are not arbitrated or adjudicated because state leaders expect to 'win' based on the legal merits of the case . . . Rather, legal procedures are pursued when the parties may be willing to offer some concessions as part of a settlement agreement, but they are reluctant to do so in direct bilateral negotiations'. See also TL Allee and K Huth, 'The Pursuit of Legal Settlements to Territorial Disputes' (2006) 23 *Conflict Management and Peace Science* 285, stating at 301 that: 'In particular, we found that executives attempting to resolve a territorial dispute were more likely to seek the cover of an international legal ruling when: 1) they faced strong domestic and political opposition, 2) they faced a high degree of accountability due to the presence of democratic

Second, in the case of trade disputes, the reason for pursuing international adjudication is often also domestic. For example, to show domestic constituencies that the government is pursuing the State's economic interests,[133] as well as to pursue international cooperation,[134] and, perhaps crucially, to attempt to shape the interpretation of treaty provisions through test cases in a way that will ultimately favour a State's self-interest.[135]

But not all circumstances lead to the judicialisation of a certain type of international dispute. A specific set of circumstances is required. Alter, Hafner-Burton and Helfer consider that there are two pre-conditions to judicialisation. The first is delegation: the transfer of authority from domestic actors (i.e., domestic elites, a State's executive, legislative, and judiciary) to international actors or institutions.[136] The institutional design choices made when setting up international courts affect their performance.[137] The second is that the mechanisms of international adjudication are actually used, which they deem 'rights-claiming' as this leads to the 'authoritative [ ] naming [of] legal violations'.[138]

Those authors propose four criteria to determine whether an international court can foster judicialisation (and even judicialise part of international politics). They are:

1. Formal authority to decide concrete legal dispute between contesting parties.
2. Independent decision-makers that apply pre-existing rules and procedures to review facts, evidence, and legal claims.
3. Decisions that result in authoritative determinations of violations of law (binding or nonbinding).
4. Orders or suggested actions to remedy legal violations and prevent their recurrence.[139]

---

political institutions, and 3) the dispute was highly salient to domestic groups due to the presence of ethnic co-nationals located in the disputed territory'; B Simmons, 'See you in "Court"? The Appeal to Quasi-Judicial Legal Processes in the Settlement of Territorial Disputes', in PF Diehl (ed), *A Road Map to War: Territorial Dimensions of International Conflict* (Vanderbilt University Press, 1999) 205.

[133] CL Davis and S Blodgett Bermeo, 'Who Files? Developing Country Participation in GATT/WTO Adjudication' (2009) 71 *Journal of Politics* 1033, observing at 1035 that, based on an empirical analysis, 'when countries with a low income choose to initiate a dispute, it is *more* likely to be against a wealth trade partner'. One of the authors has treated the issue in book length, see C Davis, *Why Adjudicate?* (Princeton, Princeton University Press, 2012).

[134] Davis, *Why Adjudicate?* (n 133) 2

[135] KJ Pelc, 'The Politics of Precedent in International Law: A Social Network Application' (2014) 108 *American Political Science Review* 547, particularly at 557–61.

[136] `Alter, Hafner-Burton and Helfer (n 122) 450.

[137] RO Keohane, A Moravcsik and AM Slaughter, 'Legalized Dispute Resolution: Interstate and Transnational' (2000) 54 *International Organization* 457.

[138] ibid.

[139] Alter, Hafner-Burton, Helfer (n 122) 451.

Yet the narrative of the development and advance of judicialisation should not be overstated. Yes, there are more international courts (although there are fewer than some years ago). And yes, there are more international disputes being solved through international adjudication. But some of those new international courts have a narrow geographical jurisdictional scope – and often an even narrower subject-matter jurisdiction.[140] Additionally, there are some areas where there is substantial reluctance to submit disputes to international adjudication, most notably the use of force.[141]

One issue that should be kept in mind is that, as described by Benedict Kingsbury, judicialisation in international law has been *uneven*. Although population size is not a perfect proxy for political clout, Kingsbury observed that the 'world's most populous states tend not to accept in advance the jurisdiction of the ICJ, the ICC, human rights courts, or the UN Human Rights Committee'.[142] A brief survey of the relevant armed conflicts of the twenty-first century also shows that, despite some advances in international criminal law, prosecuting those engaged in hostilities is still far from certain – and legal actions regarding current conflicts, either in Ukraine,[143] Gaza[144] or Sudan[145] seem to have been ineffective in practice.

Furthermore, the judicialisation of international disputes is not necessarily a positive development. There is a tendency for international lawyers to engage in incurable judicial romanticism. But some are critical. In a recent speech, Dame Rosalyn Higgins said – quite unambiguously – that 'simply not every major issue is suitable for litigation [before international courts]'.[146] Similarly, when asked whether the ICJ would benefit from having compulsory jurisdiction, Alain Pellet emphatically answered 'No!' He explained that:

[140] G Hernández, 'The Judicialization of International Law: Reflections on the Empirical Turn' (2014) 25 *European Journal of International Law* 919, stating at 925–26 that: 'Most of Alter's "new style" international courts are smaller, regional institutions with very limited subject-matter competence . . . most of these smaller actors operate only within limited geographical spaces and within three limited issue areas'; see also N Krisch, 'The Path of Judicialization: A Comment on Karen Alter's The New Terrain of International Law' *EJIL:Talk!* (23 April 2014). Available at: www.ejiltalk.org/the-path-of-judicialization-a-comment-on-karen-alters-the-new-terrain-of-international-law/. Krisch mentions that these 'new style' courts constitute 'islands' of judicialisation.

[141] This issue is discussed in detail in chapter 5.

[142] Kingsbury 'International Courts' (n 130) 212.

[143] See eg Allegations of Genocide under the Convention on the Prevention and Punishment of the Crime of Genocide (Ukraine v Russian Federation), ICJ, Order of 16 March 2022 (Provisional Measures); as well as the European Court of Human Rights' Decision in Ukraine, in Ukraine and the Netherlands v Russia Apps nos 8019/16, 43800/14, 28525/20 and 11055/22 (ECtHR, 25 January 2023).

[144] *Application of the Convention on the Prevention and Punishment of the Crime of Genocide in the Gaza Strip (South Africa v Israel)*, ICJ, Order of 26 January 2024 (Provisional Measures).

[145] *Application of the Convention on the Prevention and Punishment of the Crime of Genocide in Sudan (Sudan v United Arab Emirates)*, ICJ, Order of 5 May 2025 (Provisional Measures). The Court struck out based on a manifest lack of jurisdiction.

[146] Rosalyn Higgins, remarks at the London Conference on International Law, Plenary 4: Taking Stock, 11 October 2022.

> Salvation does not lie in the compulsory jurisdiction of the Court but in the patient learning by States of the virtues of settling disputes by judicial means. It is not major and politically sensitive disputes that should be submitted to the Court, but the 'lambda' disputes that poison bilateral relations without threatening international peace and security.[147]

The expansion of the *types* of disputes submitted to international adjudication may have accelerated this trend. And it may have also accelerated the backlash against international adjudication. Moreover, the issue has become more salient because international adjudication now covers some 'mega political' issues. This notion was initially developed in the domestic context by Ran Hirschl, who defined 'mega politics' as:

> [M]atters of outright and utmost political significant that often define and divide whole polities. These range from electoral outcomes and corroboration of regime change to matters of war and peace, foundational collective identity questions, and nation-building processes pertaining to the very nature and definition of the body politic.[148]

Hirschl says that due to the increased adjudication of these types of matters 'courts today are significantly more involved in dealing with core political predicaments than they were, say, a generation ago', as the number of 'policy-making areas that are insulated from judicial intervention is distinctly smaller . . . than it was 25 years ago'.[149] Bearing in mind the risks involved by the submission of mega political issues to international adjudication, Alter and Madsen comment that, when international adjudicators are 'called upon to adjudicate hotly-contested and socially or politically divisive issues', they are acutely aware of the potential consequences and that 'no matter how they rule, powerful actors and segments of society are likely to be frustrated or disappointed'.[150] Logically, they then observe that international adjudicators 'are also well aware that resistance, contestation, and forms of actual or symbolic backlash . . . might follow from such involvement'.[151]

[147] British Institute of International and Comparative Law, *Reimagining the International Court of Justice* (8 December 2020). Available at: www.biicl.org/reimagining/41/reimagining-the-international-court-of-justice-8-december?cookiesset=1&ts=1646740217.

[148] Hirschl (n 122) 94.

[149] ibid 113.

[150] K Alter and MR Madsen, 'Beyond Backlash: The Consequences of Adjudicating Mega-Politics' (2022) 84 *Law and Contemporary Problems* 219.

[151] ibid at 16. Those authors propose three categories of mega-political disputes. The first category is 'inter-State driven', where there are conflicting claims between States (and where the issue is also salient for the domestic populations), eg territorial disputes. The second is 'social cleavage driven', that is, disputes involving mainly domestic issues that are socially divisive, eg issues involving religious rights and secularism. The third category is 'sovereignty driven', meaning disputes involving what essentially are domestic issues but that are often seen as tightly linked to State sovereignty, eg amnesty laws or some disputes with foreign investors related to a State's right to regulate.

In fact, as I will explain in more detail in the next chapter, one potential normative justification for the use of avoidance techniques is tempering the extent of judicialisation, particularly in relation to politically sensitive or mega political issues. That is, international courts may deploy jurisdictional avoidance techniques when they are faced with a dispute that they consider should not have been submitted to international adjudication.

B. Proliferation

The number of international courts has increased drastically, particularly since the end of the Cold War.[152] According to one scholar, 'the enormous expansion and transformation of the international judiciary' is probably 'the single most important development of the post-Cold War age', at least for international lawyers.[153] The expansion of international adjudication coincided, of course, with the heyday of globalisation. As one experienced international judge put it, this increase was the 'largely a response to recent transformations in international society: the growing role of law in globalized liberal economies and national societies'.[154]

James Crawford also provides a pithy explanation for the increase in numbers of international courts and tribunals:

> Two broad reasons for this proliferation may be identified. In the first place, the traditional reluctance of States to submit bilateral disputes to third party adjudication has decreased. In the second, globalization and increasing interdependence has resulted in complex problems of interaction, and the corresponding production of detailed norms of international law.[155]

During this time of continued expansion, the main concern was not whether these international courts would be effective in solving international disputes

[152] Alter (n 122) Chapter 4.

[153] Romano (n 125) 709.

[154] G Guillaume, 'Advantages and Risks of Proliferation: A Blueprint for Action' (2004) 2 *Journal of International Criminal Justice* 300, 301. Judge Guillaume also raised this issue when, as President of the ICJ, he addressed the General Assembly of the United Nations (30 October 2001). Available at: www.icj-cij.org/files/press-releases/5/2995.pdf.

[155] J Crawford, *Chance, Order, Change: The Course of International Law* (Brill, 2014) 292. See also C Brown, 'Review Essay: The Proliferation of International Courts and Tribunals: Finding Your Way Through the Maze' (2002) 3(2) *Melbourne Journal of International Law*. Brown considers that there are more reasons, but they all point in the same general direction. He proposes five: 'First, there is an "increased density of international norms", which require correspondingly sophisticated dispute settlement institutions. Second, there is a greater commitment to the rule of law in international relations. Third, the end of the Cold War has seen an 'easing of international tensions' which had hampered the growth of international adjudicative procedures. Fourth, the "positive experience with some international courts and tribunals" has inspired the creation of more such bodies. Finally, the realization that the ICDJ was unsuitable for the resolution of all types of disputes, be they regional, trade or investment-related, or focused on the protection of human rights, has encouraged the establishment of more adjudicative bodies'.

or whether they would maintain their legitimacy despite increasingly deciding more disputes that touched on politically sensitive topics. Instead, and perhaps in what, in retrospect, could be seen as an excess of confidence, the focus was on whether the continual expansion of international adjudication would lead to jurisdictional conflicts between different international courts[156] or contribute to the fragmentation of international law.[157] The latter concern led the International Law Commission to study the issue of fragmentation, ultimately concluding that there really wasn't that much to worry about.[158]

Some predictions made during the early phases of the expansion of international adjudication have not turned out to be particularly accurate. For instance, Thomas Buergenthal, himself an experienced international judge, predicted that 'the proliferation of international judicial institutions has a socializing effect on states that leads to the ever greater accepted by them of the jurisdiction and role of international tribunals'.[159] In retrospect, that was too optimistic an assessment. Investment arbitration has also been held out as an example of the problems with the proliferation of international adjudication. This is because, given its decentralised nature, it has allowed arbitral tribunals to issue apparently contradictory decisions, sometimes interpreting similarly worded treaty-provisions or (although in admittedly exceptional circumstances) deciding what is for all practical purposes the same claim in opposite ways.[160] This, in the words of one scholar, leads to the 'drama of arbitral decision-makers uttering conflicting and diverging opinions about central legal issues', a practice that may 'cast

[156] See eg Y Shany, *The Competing Jurisdiction of International Courts and Tribunals* (OUP, 2003).

[157] Writing at the turn of the century, Roger Alford observed that 'The past two decades have seen an explosion of new international courts and tribunals. Depending on one's count, more than fifty international courts and tribunals are now in existence, with more than thirty of these established in the past twenty years. The rate of growth has been so furious that government leaders now express concern over "tribunal fatigue"', at RP Alford, 'The Proliferation of International Courts and Tribunals: International Adjudication in Ascendance' (2000) 94 *Proceedings of the ASIL Annual Meeting* 160. Similarly, Benedict Kingsbury, thinking about potential jurisdictional conflicts, questioned whether this proliferation of international courts would cause problems, particularly given the fact that 'there are very few formal links between different courts and tribunals, let alone hierarchies of appeal or review'. B Kingsbury, 'Foreword: Is the Proliferation of International Courts and Tribunals a Systemic Problem?' (1999) 31 *NYU Journal of International Law and Politics* 679, 680–81.

[158] See, eg International Law Commission, *Fragmentation of International Law: Difficulties Arising from the Diversification and Expansion of International Law* (Report of the Study Group of the International Law Commission, 2006). For example, the Report mentions that: 'What once appeared to be governed by "general international law" has become the field of operation for such specialist systems as "trade law", "human rights law", "environmental law", "law of the sea", "European law", and even such exotic and highly specialized knowledges as "investment law" or "international refugee law" etc. – each possessing their own principles and institutions', at 11.

[159] T Buergenthal, 'Proliferation of International Courts and Tribunals: Is It Good or Bad?' (2001) 14 *Leiden Journal of International Law* 267, 275.

[160] *CME Czech Republic BV v Czech Republic* (Final Award) (UNCITRAL, 14 March 2003); and *Ronald S Lauder v Czech Republic* (Final Award) (UNCITRAL, 3 September 2001). See also: C Dupont, T Schultz, J Yackee, 'Investment Arbitration and Political Systems Theory' in T Schultz and F Ortino (eds), *Oxford Handbook of International Arbitration* (OUP, 2019).

doubt on the reliability and predictability of the entire system'.[161] This is one reason why proposals to centralise investment arbitration through a permanent investment court have gained traction.[162]

Overall, both the fears and hopes of the proliferation of international courts and tribunals may have been overstated. On the one hand, save for a few exceptions,[163] there have not been many instances of jurisdictional conflicts between international courts and tribunals; nor has their proliferation led to the fragmentation of international law. In fact, the stance adopted by some prominent international courts is a 'spirit of systemic harmonization'.[164] On the other hand, while there have been some advances in States' acceptance of international adjudication, the process has been dynamic, fluid, and subject to contestation, push back, backlash, and dejudicialisation.

C. Contestation and Backlash

One intrinsic feature of all litigation is that, traditionally, in most cases, one side loses. No one likes to lose a case. And politically powerful actors – including governments – are no exception. So, often when politically powerful actors find themselves on the losing end, particularly when the judgment relates to a politically sensitive or salient topic (e.g., the use of force or a contentious boundary), they may attempt to 'punch back' at the international court that rendered the offending judgment. Sometimes those punches land. Traditional formalist views that equate law with fixed legal rules may have difficulty appreciating the impact that contestation and backlash may have on the development of international adjudication. Of course, this is different under a policy-oriented approach. This difficulty subsides if law is viewed as a dialectical process, where the 'prevailing allocation of power as well as the calculus of fairness or justice' will constantly

[161] A Reinisch, 'The Proliferation of International Dispute Settlement Mechanisms: The Threat of Fragmentation vs. the Promise of a More Effective System? Some Reflections from the Perspective of Investment Arbitration', in I Buffard, J Crawford, A Pellet and S Wittich (eds), *International Law Between Universalism and Fragmentation, Festschrift in Honour of Gerhard Hafner* (Brill, 2008) 125.

[162] See eg European Commission, 'Public Consultation on a Multilateral Reform of Investment Dispute Resolution' (December 2016). Available at: https://ec.europa.eu/eusurvey/runner/mutlilateralinvestmentcourt; B Beaumont, F Brodlija, R Ashdown and A Terrien, *The Future of Investor-State Dispute Settlement: Reforming Law, Practice and Perspectives for a Fast-Changing World* (Wolters Kluwer, 2024); O Ama (ed), *International Investment Law Reform: Contemporary Issues and Solutions* (Routledge, 2025); European Yearbook of International Economic Law, Special Issue: Permanent Investment Courts: The European Experiment.

[163] See the *CME* example (n 160).

[164] This was the term used by the Grand Chamber of the European Court of Human Rights in Al-Dulimi and Montana Management Inc v Switzerland App no 5809/08 (ECtHR, 21 June 2016) para 140. For a more general view on the issue, see A Peters, 'The Refinement of International Law: From Fragmentation to Regime Interaction and Politicization' (2017) 15 *International Journal of Constitutional Law* 671.

be subject to demands for its 'adjustment, amendment or replacement'.[165] Contestation and backlash are thus relevant issues for the dynamic operation of international courts – and they should not be ignored.

There are several key concepts to bear in mind when discussing contestation and backlash.

(i) Backlash: Broadly Understood

This is my simple definition of backlash: political actions aimed at either punishing or reducing the power of international courts that are considered to have issued decisions that are contrary to the interests of politically influential actors. Others have provided nuanced definitions. At the domestic level, discussions about backlash tend to focus on the role of apex courts. For instance, Alter and Zürn define backlash as 'a particular form of political contestation with a retrograde objective as well as extraordinary goals and tactics, which has reached the threshold level of entering public discourse'.[166] They further note that the deployment of backlash is often accompanied by 'emotional appeals, nostalgia, taboo breaking practices, and institutional reshaping'.[167]

Post and Siegel consider that, from a domestic judicial perspective, backlash refers to a 'threat to the maintenance of legal authority and control',[168] which may result in an 'impediment to judicial efforts to endow . . . ideals with legal form'.[169] A constant concern among scholars of backlash is that a particular decision (and it's political fallout) may 'undermine [ ] both the Court and its holdings'.[170] That is why some scholars observe that courts 'deciding an issue that leads to any meaningful disagreement or political backlash can be dangerous'.[171]

At the international level, Hillebrecht recently defined backlash against international courts as:

> [A] sustained attack on the tribunals that fundamentally challenges their structural, adjudicative, and moral authority . . . backlash [means] the politics of states and individual political leaders' seeking to undermine and subvert the tribunals by working

[165] WM Reisman, The Quest for World Order and Human Dignity in the Twenty First Century (Brill, 2013) 90.

[166] KJ Alter and Michael Zürn, 'Conceptualising Backlash Politics: Introduction to a Special Issue on Backlash Politics in Comparison' (2020) 22 *British Journal of Politics and International Relations* 563, 576–77.

[167] ibid 577.

[168] R Post and R Siegel, '*Roe* Rage: Democratic Constitutionalism and Backlash' (2007) 42 *Harvard Civil Rights-Civil Liberties Law Review* 373, 379.

[169] ibid 390.

[170] L Krugman Ray, 'Justice Ginsburg and the Middle Way' (2003) 68 *Brooklyn Law Review* 629, 636.

[171] D Fontana, 'Docket Control and the Success of Constitutional Courts', in T Ginsburg and R Dixon (eds), *Comparative Constitutional Law* (Edward Elgar, 2011) 624, 629.

> within the judicialized and legalized landscape of international human rights and criminal law.[172]

Similarly, Madsen, Cebulak and Wiebusch draw some useful distinctions to differentiate pushback and backlash.[173] They consider pushback to be narrower: it is a form of resistance that only affects the development of the law.[174] Backlash, in contrast, is broader: it seeks to 'overturn the system', at an *institutional* level, including by 'exiting' it.[175] These authors also consider that it is important to distinguish the *mechanisms* by which States resist international courts from the *outcomes* of that resistance. Sometimes, as they point out, very vocal resistance leads to little change in practice.[176] Interestingly, the authors suggest that international adjudicators rely on legal reasoning as a way of eluding backlash. As they point out: 'to prevent critique, the most obvious tool available to international judges is legal reasoning'. And 'what most likely is important . . . is not the way an IC reaches its conclusions, but the conclusions it reaches and the implications these might have for its constituencies'.[177] In other words, they suggest that the fear of backlash – an extra-legal factor – may be influencing how international courts apply the law, one of the central topics explored in this book.

Since the mid-aughts the backlash against international courts has increased. As one scholar put it, 'international courts seem to be living in hard times',[178] as 'more intrusive international authority will generally provoke a higher degree of resistance at the domestic level'.[179] This has led some to consider that the current moment is 'dangerous' for international adjudication, as the 'violations of international law are rising and compliance supporters of ICs and the international liberal order are under siege'.[180]

So, what causes backlash? There are several explanations. One of the most persuasive is populism,[181] which itself has been (non)defined as a 'largely amorphous phenomenon'.[182] Broadly, populists rely on local mobilisation of the

[172] C Hillebrecht, *Saving the International Justice Regime* (CUP, 2021) 5.

[173] MR Madsen, P Cebulak and M Wiebusch, 'Backlash Against International Courts: Explaining the Forms and Patterns of Resistance to International Courts' (2018) 14 *International Journal of Law in Context* 197, 206.

[174] For another related study, see L Zimmermann, N Deitelhoff, M Lesch, A Arcudi and A Peez, *International Norm Disputes: The Link Between Contestation and Norm Robustness* (OUP, 2023).

[175] Madsen, Cebulak and Wiebusch 'Backlash Against International Courts' (n 173).

[176] ibid 207.

[177] ibid 212.

[178] N Krisch, 'The Backlash against International Courts' *Verfassungsblog* (16 December 2014).

[179] ibid.

[180] K Alter, 'Critical Junctures and the Future International Courts in a Post-Liberal World Order' (2018) 140 *iCourts Working Paper Series* 30.

[181] See eg E Voeten, 'Populism and Backlashes Against International Courts' (2020) 18 *Perspectives on Politics* 407.

[182] D Landau, 'Populist Constitutions' (2018) 85 *University of Chicago Law Review* 521, 523 (stating that populism 'is a fiercely contested concept'); AZ Huq, 'The People Against the Constitution' (2018) 116 *Michigan Law Review* 1123, 1124; S Issacharoff, 'Democracy's Deficits' (2018) 85 *University of Chicago Law Review* 485, 486; A Schäfer, 'Cultural Backlash? How (Not) to Explain the Rise of Authoritarian Populism' (2022) 52 *British Journal of Political Science* 1977; JL Broz,

'pure people' against the 'corrupt elites' (in the case of international courts, even worse, *international* elites).[183] International courts are an easy target for populism, as they can operate as a constraint on majoritarian politics.[184] Another one is based on public opinion more broadly. Eric Posner, not exactly an enthusiast of international adjudication, considers that backlash is motivated by public opinion: many ordinary people, left behind by globalization, have united in their opposition to further international legalization. 'They have lost faith in international institutions . . . and in national leaders who supported them'.[185]

Yet another explanation is a perception among certain States that international courts treat them unfairly. For example, some African States have had issues with the International Criminal Court, particularly after its decision to prosecute Omar al-Bashir.[186] Similarly, some Latin American states have issues regarding investment arbitration, as some studies have suggested that the outcomes 'have been significantly less favourable to states than they have been in other regions'.[187]

(ii) Backlash: In Practice

A common thread in these different definitions of backlash is rejection and contestation of international adjudication. How does this backlash manifest? There is ample State practice on the matter. Some of the most conspicuous examples of States' conduct are:

- Withdrawing their consent to the jurisdiction of international courts. This includes, for instance, withdrawing an optional clause declaration before the International Court of Justice (e.g., the United States' withdrawal in 1985 following the ICJ's decision on jurisdiction in the *Nicaragua* case).[188]
- Amending declarations recognising an international court's jurisdiction to withdraw consent over certain subject-matters (e.g., Japan removed the ICJ's

J Frieden and S Weymouth, 'Populism in Place: The Economic Geography of the Globalization Backlash' (2021) 75 *International Organization* 464.

[183] Voeten 'Populism and Backlashes' (n 181) 407.

[184] ibid. C Sunstein, 'If People Would be Outraged by Their Rulings, Should Judges Care?' (2010) 60, *Stanford Law Review* 155.

[185] EA Posner, 'Liberal Internationalism and the Populist Backlash' (2017) 49 *Arizona State Law Journal* 795, 813.

[186] See eg T Murithi, 'The African Union and the International Criminal Court: An Embattled Relationship?' (Institute for Justice and Reconciliation Policy Brief No 8, March 2013). Available at: www.ijr.org.za/home/wp-content/uploads/2017/05/IJR-Policy-Brief-No-8-Tim-Miruthi.pdf; JM Mbaku, 'International Justice: The International Criminal Court and Africa' (Brookings Institution Foresight Africa, 20 December 2013). Available at: www.brookings.edu/wp-content/uploads/2016/07/03-foresight-international-criminal-court-africa-mbaku-1.pdf; CB Murungu, 'Towards a Criminal Chamber in the African Court of Justice and Human Rights' (2011) 9 *Journal of International Criminal Justice* 1067.

[187] KL Remmer, ''Investment Treaty Arbitration in Latin America' (2019) 54 *Latin American Research Review* 795, 797.

[188] See eg K Highet, 'Litigation Implications of the US Withdrawal from the Nicaragua Case' (1985) 79 *American Journal of International Law* 992.

jurisdiction over disputes involving 'living resources of the sea' following an adverse judgment on whaling).[189]

- Terminating a treaty that provides for international adjudication (e.g., Venezuela's withdrawal from the American Convention on Human Rights;[190] or the 26 EU Member States who terminated approximately 130 BITs (and their sunset clauses) following the CJEU's decision in *Achmea*).[191]
- Abolishing an international court altogether (e.g., as Zimbabwe managed to achieve in relation to the Southern African Development Community tribunal).[192]
- Proposing structural reforms to international courts to restrict or limit their powers, including modifying the applicable substantive law and the types of cases they are able to adjudicate (e.g., the European Union's proposal for a multilateral investment court).[193]
- Refusing to appoint members to an international court, thus depriving it of quorum (e.g., the US' blocking of appointments to the WTO's appellate body).[194]
- Creating alternative adjudicative (or quasi-adjudicative) institutions to compete with already established international courts (e.g., Venezuela's proposal to create, through UNASUR, an alternative to the Inter-American Human Rights

[189] MA Becker, 'Japan's New Optional Clause Declaration at the ICJ: A Pre-Emptive Strike?' (*EJIL:Talk!* 20 October 2015). Available at: www.ejiltalk.org/japans-new-optional-clause-declaration-at-the-icj-a-pre-emptive-strike.

[190] D Mejia-Lemos, 'Venezuela's Denunciation of the American Convention on Human Rights' (2013) 17(1) *ASIL Insights*. On this issue more generally, see X Soley and S Steininger, 'Parting Ways or Lashing Back? Withdrawals, Backlash and the Inter-American Court of Human Rights' (2018) 14 *International Journal of Law in Context* 237; J Contesse, 'Resisting the Inter-American Human Rights System' (2019) 44 *Yale Journal of International Law* 179.

[191] Agreement for the Termination of Bilateral Investment Treaties between the Member States of the European Union [2020] OJ L169/1. Available at: https//eur-lex.europa.eu/legal-content/EN/TXT/?uri=CELEX%3A22020A0529%2801%29. For a thorough analysis, see J Tropper and August Reinisch, 'The 2020 Termination Agreement of Intra-EU BITs and Its Effect on Investment Arbitration in the EU – A Public International Law Analysis of the Termination Agreement' (2022) 16 *Austrian Yearbook on International Arbitration* 301; G Nardell and L Rees-Evans, 'The Agreement Terminating Intra-EU BITs: Are Its Provisions on "New" and "Pending" Arbitration Proceedings Compatible with Investors' Fundamental Rights?' (2021) 37 *Arbitration International* 197. See also M Casas, 'The Enforcement of Intra-EU Arbitral Awards: Some Additional Policy Considerations' (2025) 42 *Journal of International Arbitration* 77.

[192] KJ Alter, JT Gathii and LR Helfer, 'Backlash against International Courts in West, East and Southern Africa: Causes and Consequences' (2016) 27 *European Journal of International Law* 293.

[193] See eg M Bungenberg and A Reinisch, *From Bilateral Arbitral Tribunals and Investment Courts to a Multilateral Investment Court: Options Regarding the Institutionalization of Investor-State Dispute Settlement* (Springer, 2020); JM Alvarez Zarate, 'Legitimacy Concerns of the Proposed Multilateral Investment Court: Is Democracy Possible?' (2018) 59 *Boston College Law Review* 2765; C Titi, 'The European Union's Proposal for an International Investment Court: Significance, Innovations and Challenges Ahead' (2017) 1 *Transnational Dispute Management*.

[194] P Van den Bossche, 'The Demise of the WTO Appellate Body: Lessons for Governance of International Adjudication?' (2021), *World Trade Institute Working Paper No 02/2021*; J Miranda and M Sanchez Miranda, 'Chronicle of a Crisis Foretold: How the WTO Appellate Body Drove Itself into a Corner' (2023) 26 *Journal of International Economic Law* 435.

System; the African Union's attempts to implement the Malabo Protocol to grant the African Court of Justice and Human Rights with jurisdiction over certain international crimes, overlapping with the ICC's jurisdiction).[195]

- Reducing the operative budget for international adjudication (e.g., as happened to the Inter-American Human Rights System throughout a good part of 2010–2020, where member States systematically reduced their budgetary contributions).[196]

Having set out this list of examples of how backlash operates, it is useful to set out two particularly important trends that are often-overlooked: dejudicialisation and non-judicialisation.

(iii) Dejudicialisation

The first trend is dejudicialisation. This implies that an issue that, at one point, was subject to international adjudication, is no longer so. In other words, a certain issue has been removed from the purview of international adjudication; it is the narrowing of an international court's subject matter jurisdiction. This concept was originally articulated by Abebe and Ginsburg, who considered it one of the more extreme types of backlash. They define dejudicialisation as the 'complete removal from judicial cognizance of a policy issue that had previously been subject to judicialization'.[197]

The concept of dejudicialisation is related to the idea that, in international law, it is generally the subjective views of States (i.e., their consent) that often determine whether a particular dispute should be resolved through international adjudication.[198] Although it is acknowledged that dejudicialisation may be 'politically costly', and that it will only happen 'under limited circumstances', dejudicialisation will nevertheless happen when 'the losses from the court's decisions exceed the costs of dejudicialization'.[199] The end result of this process is that power shifts back to the domestic level.[200]

[195] See eg D Flemes, D Nolte and L Wehner, 'Una comunidad de seguridad regional en formación: la unasur y su Consejo de Defensa/A regional security community in the making: unasur and its South American Defence Council (2011) 44 *Estudios Internacionales* 105.

[196] ibid; R Cetra and J Nascimento, 'Counting Coins: Funding the Inter-American Human Rights System', in Due Process of Law Foundation (ed), *The Inter-American Human Rights System: Changing Times, Ongoing Challenges* (2016) 53.

[197] Abebe and Ginsburg (n 123) 521.

[198] It could be said that there is a *subjective* or *voluntarist* notion of justiciability, based on the will of States.

[199] Abebe and Ginsburg (n 123) 527. The authors also set out a table with the different mechanisms of backlash that may be implemented by the different actors, including states, domestic courts, the public, and litigants. In the case of states, the more severe mechanism identified is to 'cooperate with other states to *dejudicialize* the regime entirely'.

[200] ibid 529.

Abebe and Ginsburg's theory is based on feedback politics. They discuss how states react to adverse rulings from international courts – and the mechanisms they could deploy when reacting:

> If the draw of costs and benefits reveal payoffs that are dramatically lower than those anticipated at the moment of institutional design, states may attempt to limit the activity of the court through some form of backlash. . . . Backlash might take the form of cooperating with other states to change the jurisdiction of the court, or perhaps engaging with other states to change the jurisdiction of the court. Communicating dissatisfaction or seeking to undermine the court is also a form of backlash. If the payoffs for a state are extremely low, it might decide to exit the regime entirely. An unhappy state can unilaterally effectuate any of these reactions . . . In the most extreme cases, however, a state might seek to destroy the court, or remove the relevant issue area from judicial purview.[201]

In Abebe and Ginsburg's view, the main causes for dejudicialisation, and for backlash more generally, are either when anticipated benefits fail to materialise or when, mainly due to changes in governmental preferences, the cost–benefit analysis of accepting an international court's jurisdiction changes.[202] Ginsburg and Abebe explain that, whilst judicialization transfers power 'from states to international actors', dejudicialisation, conversely, 'marks the decisive return of power to national executives and legislatures'.[203]

There has been some substantial dejudicialisation in the context of international investment law, for example. Consider the following three instances. First, the removal of international adjudication for investment disputes between the United States and Canada in USMCA.[204] International adjudication had been available under USMCA's predecessor, the NAFTA. Second, the complete elimination of Intra-EU Bilateral Investment Treaties (and the accompanying elimination of investment arbitration for disputes between EU investors and EU States). This was mainly the result of two decisions from the Court of Justice of the European Union: *Achmea*[205] and *Komstroy*.[206] Third, the increased use of internal exceptions in investment treaties. Recent internal exemptions include non-precluded measures provisions (i.e., provisions that expressly allow

[201] ibid 525.
[202] ibid 526.
[203] ibid 529.
[204] See eg A Lopez, 'ISDS Under the USMCA: The First Three Years at a Glance' (Kluwer Arbitration Blog, 25 November 2023). Available at: www.arbitrationblog.kluwerarbitration.com/2023/11/25/isds-under-the-usmca-the-first-three-years-at-a-glance [https://perma.cc/YYU2-25A5]; C Amirfar and others, 'From NAFTA to USMCA: Main Changes to the Investor-State Dispute Settlement System' (Debevoise & Plimpton, 7 May 2020). Available at: www.debevoise.com/insights/publications/2020/05/from-nafta-to-usmca-main-changes-to-the-investor [https://perma.cc/9XLC-3XMC]. See also M Casas, 'Dejudicialization and Non-Judicialization in International Law' (2025), *Yale Journal of International Law* 107.
[205] *Slowakische Republik v Achmea BV* Case C-284/16, ECLI:EU:C:2018:158 (6 March 2018).
[206] *République de Moldavie v Komstroy LLC* Case C-741/19, ECLI:EU:C:2021:655 (2 September 2021).

States to implement certain measures); essential security clauses; and general public health or environmental exceptions.[207] In some cases, these clauses are self-judging,[208] meaning that they allow states *themselves* to decide whether they will comply with their treaty obligations.[209]

Further, by including self-judging internal exception clauses in their treaties, States are, for all practical purposes, giving themselves the authority to remove the issues covered by the self-judging clauses from judicial scrutiny.[210] Essentially, self-judging clauses allow the respondent State in a dispute – rather than the adjudicator – to decide whether the subject matter of the dispute is suitable for adjudication. Without those clauses, the international adjudicator would determine whether those measures engaged the State's international responsibility. So, an issue that was at one point commonly submitted to international courts has been slowly but surely – albeit discreetly – either fully withdrawn from international adjudication or has had its scope narrowed down.

(iv) Non-Judicialisation

The second trend is what I call non-judicialisation. While dejudicialisation refers to subject matters and issues that were at one point subject to international adjudication but are no longer so, non-judicialisation refers to the subject matters and issues which, from the start, are not subject to international adjudication – and are unlikely to be in the near future. Essentially, this refers to the constant, reiterated refusal of States to agree to submit certain disputes to international adjudication. This is different from non-justiciability because the claim is not that a specific issue or subject matter is conceptually or in principle unsuitable for international adjudication, but rather that, in practice, States are systematically refusing to consent to that issue or subject matter being adjudicated. The issue is State consent to adjudication, not some inherent characteristic of the dispute itself.

Abdulqawi Yusuf, then President of the ICJ, observed that most cases now brought before the Court were based on compromissory clauses included in multilateral and bilateral conventions and treaties. Nevertheless, he cautioned that 'now there is a growing trend not to include compromissory clauses on judicial settlement of disputes in multilateral conventions'.[211] Perhaps the most obvious example of this trend is the Paris Agreement. The Agreement does not

[207] F Paddeu and M Waibel, 'Necessity 20 Years On: The Limits of Article 25' (2022) 37 *ICSID Review – Foreign Investment Law Journal* 160.

[208] KP Sauvant, M Ong, K Lama and T Petersen, 'The Rise of Self-Judging Essential Security Interest Clauses in International Investment Agreements' (2016) *Columbia FDI Perspectives* 188.

[209] S Schill and R Briese, '"If the State Considers": Self-Judging Clauses in International Dispute Settlement' (2009) 13 *Max Planck Yearbook of United Nations Law* 61, 63.

[210] E Shirlow, *Judging at the Interface: Deference to State Decision-Making Authority in International Adjudication* 116 (CUP, 2021).

[211] A Yusuf, 'Remarks' (2021) 115 *Proceedings of the ASIL Annual Meeting* 215.

even have its own dispute resolution provision.[212] Instead, Article 24 of the Paris Agreement provides that the dispute settlement provisions set out in Article 14 of the United Nations Framework Convention on Climate Change 'shall apply *mutatis mutandi*'.[213] Yet Article 14 of the Framework Convention does not include a compromissory clause or otherwise make any form of binding requirement for international adjudication. Rather, the Framework Convention provides that, in case of disputes, 'the Parties concerned shall seek a settlement of the dispute through negotiation or any other peaceful means of their own choice'.[214] Additionally, it provides that, when parties are ratifying, approving, or acceding to the Framework Convention, they '*may declare*' that they consent for disputes to be submitted to the ICJ or to arbitration.[215]

In practice, as Amirfar and Lawry-White observe, 'only a handful of states have made declarations under Article 14 of the [Framework Convention] to submit disputes to the ICJ and/or arbitration'.[216] The only state that has so far consented to the compulsory jurisdiction of the ICJ, or of an arbitral tribunal, to solve disputes arising under the Paris Agreement is the Netherlands.[217]

For a treaty which François Hollande, the then French President, celebrated exclaiming 'history is here'[218] and which Barack Obama characterised as an 'historic agreement',[219] States' lack of enthusiasm for compulsory adjudication of any disputes arising from the Paris Agreement is surprising. This, in itself, is telling – and may potentially influence how the treaty is interpreted, given that, at least for now, there will be no authoritative, adjudicative interpretation of

[212] C Reichenbach, 'The Missing Dispute Resolution Mechanisms in International Climate Change Agreements' (2023) 3 *Global Energy Law and Sustainability* 129.

[213] Paris Agreement art 24, 4 November 2016, 3156 United Nations Treaty Series 79.

[214] United Nations Framework Convention on Climate Change art 14, para 1, 9 May 1992, 1771 United Nations Treaty Series 107.

[215] ibid art 14, 2. It is telling that one of the main commentaries to the Paris Agreement has only one short paragraph dealing with the Agreement's dispute resolution provision. See C Voigt, 'Institutional Arrangements and Final Clauses (Articles 16–29)', in D Klein, MP Carazo, M Doelle, J Bulmer and A Higham (eds), *The Paris Agreement on Climate Change: Analysis and Commentary* (OUP, 2017) 352, 369.

[216] C Amirfar and M Lawry White, 'The Paris Agreement's Conciliation Annex: If Not Now, Then When?' (2021), *ASIL Insights*, 25(17). Available at: www.asil.org/insights/volume/25/issue/17> [https://perma.cc/9YT9-RF9R].

[217] The text of the Netherlands' declaration reads: 'The Kingdom of the Netherlands, for the European part of the Netherlands, declares in accordance with Article 14, paragraph 2, of the United Nations Framework Convention on Climate Change in conjunction with Article 24 of the Paris Agreement, that it accepts both means of dispute settlement referred to in that paragraph as compulsory in relation to any Party accepting one or both means of dispute settlement'. Declaration of Netherlands (Kingdom of the) to Paris Agreement, 28 July 2017, *U.N. Treaty Collection*. Available at: http//treaties.un.org/Pages/ViewDetails.aspx?src=IND&mtdsg_no=XXVII-7-d&chapter=27&clang=_en [https://perma.cc/7HVP-9WY2.

[218] J Vidal, A Vaughan, S Goldenberg, L Taylor and D Boffey, 'World Leaders Hail Paris Climate Deal as "Major Leap for Mankind"' *The Guardian* (12 December 2015). Available at: www.theguardian.com/environment/2015/dec/13/world-leaders-hail-paris-climate-deal [https://perma.cc/YH9F-8PJB]. There is perhaps something ironic here.

[219] J Eilperin, 'Obama Hails Historic Ratification of Paris Climate Agreement' *The Washington Post* (5 October 2016). Available at: www.washingtonpost.com/news/energy-environment/wp/2016/10/05/obama-hails-historic-ratification-of-paris-climate-agreement [https://perma.cc/N3WU-42MZ].

it.[220] Nevertheless, this overwhelming lack of acceptance of international adjudication for disputes arising under the Paris Agreement is a strong indication that States consider climate change-related disputes as non-judicialised – at least for the time being. As an aside, the lack of enthusiasm for the Paris Agreement's compromissory clause can be contrasted – perhaps not without irony – with the contrasting effervescence regarding advisory proceedings on climate change.[221]

Another conspicuous example is the Regional Comprehensive Economic Partnership (RCEP), the largest trade bloc in history. It covers the largest economies in Asia, accounting for approximately 30 per cent of the world's population and approximately 30 per cent of global GDP.[222] During early negotiations, there was momentum towards including a dispute settlement mechanism in RCEP, but ultimately States decided to forego this.[223] Consequently, RCEP does not yet include any investor-State dispute settlement mechanisms.[224]

The decision to exclude investor-state dispute settlement was important, particularly given how widespread those dispute settlement mechanisms are in bilateral and regional trade agreements. Nonetheless, the State parties to RCEP ultimately decided that they did not wish to include any such mechanisms (although they left open the possibility of including them in the future).[225] Again, this is an important case where an entire *category* of disputes were deliberately excluded from international adjudication from the very start of the treaty's operation.

Two further observations. The first is that despite the advances in judicialisation and the expansion of formalised mechanisms of international adjudication, a substantial number of treaties still lack dispute resolution mechanisms.[226] The objective of those treaties is chiefly to set standards – to create rules and, potentially (hopefully), to influence States' conduct. Here, the notion of *lex simulata* or *lex imperfecta* is useful to analyse treaties or other international agreements that systematically refuse to include provisions for international dispute settlement (i.e., non-judicialisation) or other types of effective enforcement provisions. Those treaties may have an *expressive* function.[227] This may be positive. Although

[220] However, the current advisory opinions on climate change may be a way around this.

[221] *Climate Change and International Law*, ITLOS, Advisory Opinion of 21 May 2024; *Emergencia Climatica y derechos humanos,* IACtHR, Advisory Opinion No 32 of 29 May 2025; *Obligations of States in Respect of Climate Change,* ICJ, Advisory Opinion of 23 July 2025.

[222] See eg PL Hsieh, 'New Investment Rulemaking in Asia: Between Regionalism and Domestication' (2023) 22 *World Trade Review* 173, 174.

[223] A Lugg and others, 'Why is There No Investor-State Dispute Settlement in RCEP? Bargaining and Contestation in the Investment Regime' (2024) *Business and Policy (First View)* 1, 15–17.

[224] ibid.

[225] J Riley, 'A Multilateral Approach to Investor-State Dispute Settlement Issues in the Asia-Pacific Region' (2021) 14 *Journal of East Asia and International Law* 147.

[226] See eg I Johnstone and S Ratner (eds), *Talking International Law: Legal Argumentation Outside the Courtroom* (OUP, 2021); E Methymaki, 'Thinking Beyond International Adjudication: Inspections as Instruments of Order Production in the International System' (2022) 21 *Law and Practice of International Courts and Tribunals* 520, 522.

[227] See eg C Sunstein, 'On the Expressive Function of Law' (1996) 144 *University of Pennsylvania Law Review* 2022.

States may not be willing to provide those treaties with coercive enforcement mechanisms (i.e., with teeth), their existence may show (even if sometimes only an incipient) commitment to certain underlying values or goals.

But the objective of those treaties is to prevent States from submitting disputes to international adjudication.[228] Again, this must be viewed in proper context. Although international adjudication has gained more importance in the last decades, it is still not the main stage where these issues are sorted.[229] A clear-eyed view of the situation suggests that States are aware of the limits of international adjudication – and that, to an extent, they can influence and even determine those limits, which operate in the dynamic continuum of the political process rather than in the fixed rules of the legal process. The second observation is that the lack of institutional, adjudicatory dispute resolution mechanisms does not mean that dispute resolution is not happening in practice. Rather than taking place in the highly formalised context of international courts,[230] it is taking place in the more informal (and perhaps more effective) province of diplomatic negotiations.[231]

III. TWO INTRINSIC PROBLEMS OF INTERNATIONAL ADJUDICATION

A. Domestic and International Courts Are Not Equal

International and domestic courts are not created equal. They operate in a very different institutional context; they have differences in legitimacy, authority and effective power. However, there is a current trend in some scholarship to equate domestic and international courts, and the judicialisation of domestic disputes with the judicialisation of international ones.[232] Some have even observed that

[228] M Chiam, 'Public Invocation of International Law and Legacies of the Iraq War' (2021) 9 *London Review of International Law* L 271, 277; see also F Zarbiyev, 'On the Judge Centredness of the International Legal Self' (2021) 32 *European Journal of International Law* 1139.

[229] Some would even consider international courts and tribunals relatively marginal actors. See Reisman, *The Quest for World Order* (n 166) 19.

[230] S Murphy, 'The Concept of International Law' (2009) 165, *Proceedings American Society International Law Annual Meeting* 6.

[231] *Legality of the Threat or Use of Nuclear Weapons,* ICJ, Advisory Opinion dated 8 July 1996, Dissenting Opinion of Judge Oda.

[232] JK Staton and WH Moore, 'Judicial Power in Domestic and International Politics' (2011) 65 *International Organization* 553, 581, stating that there is an '(implicit) choice to view the separation of judicial power research in international relations and comparative politics as appropriate . . . that domestic politics are carried out under hierarchy, whereas international politics are carried out under anarchy', further stating that 'we do not have the data necessary to sustain an empirical rationale for dividing the international from the domestic'; see also Alter, Hafner-Burton and Helfer (n 122) 451: 'we embrace Jeffrey Staton and William Moore's suggestion that international relations scholars shed the classic assumption that domestic politics is hierarchical while international politics is anarchical, and with it the corollary presumption that legalized domestic politics must be fundamentally different from legalized international politics.'

'like international courts, national supreme and constitutional courts have no means to compel governments to follow their rulings'.[233]

The basis of this proposition is that, in reality, the lack of coercive enforcement mechanisms is not a defining feature of international law, as domestic constitutional law (and public law more generally) suffers from the same deficiency. This was Alexander Hamilton's point when he said that the judiciary wields neither the sword nor the purse.[234] Following that line of argument, Goldsmith and Levinson contend that domestic 'constitutional law, just as much as international law, lacks a coercive enforcement mechanism standing above the state to ensure that the government complies'.[235] They draw the analogy between domestic and international courts arguing that courts 'lacking the powers of the purse and sword that might be used to coerce the compliance of other government officials and their constitutions . . . constitutional law shares with international law the challenge of coercing the compliance of powerful political actors – or the inability to do so'.[236]

I disagree with this approach for four reasons.

First, there are different bases of jurisdiction in domestic and international law. As Judge Schwebel observed, 'jurisdiction is not consensual in national law'; but it is in international law.[237]

Second, this approach ignores the relevance of the rule of law domestically.[238] There is no advanced democracy that does not respect the rule of law. The latter

[233] Alter, Hafner-Burton, Helfer (n 122) 451. That these authors accept this is somewhat surprising, as one of them at least had previously accepted the distinction between domestic and international courts. In *Establishing the Supremacy of European Law: The Making of an International Rule of Law in Europe*, KJ Alter stated that: 'While national governments appeared to be willing to ignore ECJ jurisprudence, ignoring their own courts was a different matter entirely . . . But few governments want to claim a right to ignore their own courts, and few citizens want their governments to have such a right . . . The rule of law means that governments follow the law. In a rule-of-law society, governments follow their courts.'

[234] A Hamilton, 'No. 78', in C Rossiter (ed), *The Federalist Papers* (New American Library, 1961).

[235] J Goldsmith and D Levinson, 'Law for States: International Law, Constitutional Law, Public Law' (2009) 122 *Harvard Law Review* 1791, 1823.

[236] ibid 1831. Stephenson puts the claim even more provocatively, asking: 'Why would people with money and guns ever submit to people armed only with gavels?' Stephenson, like Goldsmith and Levinson, relies on the Federalist Papers, albeit in his case to Madison's reference to constitutional limits on power as 'parchment barriers'. Stephenson's empirical analysis, however, leads him to conclude that an independent judiciary (capable of controlling the actions of the executive and legislative branches) 'serves a valuable insurance function for competitors in a stable democracy', see M Stephenson, '"When the Devil Turns . . .": The Political Foundations of Independent Judicial Review' (2003) 32 *Journal of Legal Studies* 59, 60.

[237] *Certain Phosphate Lands in Nauru (Nauru v Australia)*, ICJ, Judgment (Preliminary Objections) dated 26 June 1992, dissenting opinion of Schwebel J, 329-330.

[238] For instance, German Federal Constitutional Court Justice Hans G Rupp observed that: 'The only marshal there is to enforce the Court's ruling is its moral authority, the conscience of the parties concerned, and in the last resort, the people's respect for law and good government.' HG Rupp, 'Some Remarks on Judicial Self-Restraint'(1960) 21 *Ohio State Law Journal* 507. There is a question as to whether the rule of law applies between States vis-à-vis each other. For a strong argument against this idea, see J Waldron, 'Are Sovereigns Entitled to the Benefit of the International Rule of Law?' (2011) 22 *European Journal of International Law*.

has become an inherent and intrinsic characteristic of the former. One of the core definitions of the rule of law is the 'requirement that people in positions of authority should exercise their power within a constraining framework of public norms'.[239] The rule of law is one of the pillars of the modern State.[240]

Third, Goldsmith and Levinson rely on the intrinsic vagueness and indeterminacy of US constitutional provisions to equate them with international law.[241] This is wrong for two reasons. The first is that, although constitutional law is often framed at a higher level of generality than regular laws, it is not always ambiguous or uncertain.[242] That is a particular issue of *US* constitutional law, but it cannot be extrapolated to *all* constitutions.[243] Likewise, whereas some international legal provisions are broad and abstract,[244] others are narrow rules.[245] The second is that legal systems have developed sophisticated ways of addressing or tempering the uncertainty that arises from the higher level of abstraction used in constitutional law. In some legal systems, the tempering mechanisms may operate 'by precedent, by reason, by institutional structure and context';[246] whereas in others, it may be through techniques such as proportionality analysis.[247]

[239] J Waldron, 'The Concept and the Rule of Law' (2008) 43 *Georgia Law Review* 55, 56. As MacCormick notes, when the rule of law applies, 'the government of a state . . . is carried on within framework laid down by law', see N MacCormick, *Rhetoric and The Rule of Law* (OUP, 2005), 12.

[240] As such, it exercises a normative pull. Waldron explains, the 'Rule of Law is one of the most important political ideals of our time', considering it, together with human rights and democracy, as 'one of the cluster of ideals constitutive of modern political morality': see Waldron (n 239) 3. A von Bogdandy and I Venzke, *In Whose Name? A Public Law Theory of International Adjudication* (OUP, 2014), approaching the issue from a (civilian) public law context, observe that: 'In developed and well-functioning legal systems, if a decision of a domestic court is not adhered to, a coercive apparatus will enforce it almost automatically', and this applies to judgments against the State. And not only is the rule of law important as an issue of political philosophy, but, additionally, it has been a central feature of economic development, thus highlighting its importance for States. The leading work on this is D Acemoglu, S Johnson and J Robinson, 'Institutions as the Fundamental Cause of Long-Run Growth' in P Aghion and SN Durlauf (eds), *Handbook of Economic Growth* (Elsevier, 2005), where they identify 'institutions of private property' as a cluster of 'economic institutions, including the rule of law and the enforcement of property rights', as being a key issue in economic development. See also R Barro, 'Democracy and the Rule of Law' in BB de Mesquita and H Root (eds), *Governing for Prosperity* (Yale University Press, 2000).

[241] Goldsmith and Levinson (n 235) 1802–03.

[242] In the civil law constitutional law context, see eg S Muñoz Machado, *Tratado de derecho administrative y derecho público general* (Madrid, BOE, 2015), particularly Vol 5, La constitución como norma, 106.

[243] Grimm compares *prescriptive* and *descriptive* types of constitutions: D Grimm, 'Types of Constitutions' in M Rosenfeld and A Sajó (eds), *The Oxford Handbook of Comparative Constitutional Law* (OUP, 2012).

[244] The indeterminacy of some rules of international procedural law is addressed in chapter 4.

[245] See eg WM Reisman, 'Canute Confronts the Tide: States versus Tribunals and the Evolution of the Minimum Standard in Customary International Law' (2015) 30 *ICSID Review* 616, 616–18.

[246] S Sherry, 'Putting the Law Back in Constitutional Law: Symposium – Is American Constitutional Law in Crisis: Association of American Law Schools Section on Constitutional Law (January 2009)' (2008) 25 *Constitutional Commentary* 461.

[247] See R Alexy, 'Constitutional Rights and Proportionality' (2014) 22 *Revus: Journal for Constitutional Theory and Philosophy of Law* 51 and ff; A Stone Sweet and J Mathews, *Proportionality Balancing and Constitutional Governance: A Comparative and Global Approach* (OUP, 2019).

Fourth, Goldsmith and Levinson's approach, at a basic level, assumes that only those State entities that *directly* wield coercive enforcement mechanisms are able to enforce their decisions. Taken to its logical consequence this means only law enforcement agencies and the military, which is obviously not the case. The question is who actually wields the sword? Judges may only make judgments (i.e., pieces of paper), but what, in reality, are other branches of the State armed with? In that regard, legislators are also only armed with pieces of paper too (laws). In principle, it is only the executive that may command actual kinetic forces.

Perhaps the most cogent argument to support the distinction between international courts and domestic ones is that even outright autocracies have not completely dispensed with their domestic judiciaries. Those judiciaries may well be ineffective (and perhaps completely so) when it comes to controlling the exercise of State power. It may even be that courts can often be useful to dictators, insofar as they give a veneer of legitimacy to some decisions, even if they were determined entirely politically rather than legally. They nevertheless exist and, at least in theory, public officials are subject to their jurisdiction. Put bluntly: even dictators pay lip service to having courts.

According to the World Justice Project's Rule of Law Index, the five States with worst rule of law indicators are: Cameroon, Egypt, the Democratic Republic of Congo, Cambodia and Venezuela.[248] But all those States have domestic judiciaries and those have compulsory jurisdiction over public authorities. None of those States have taken the step to get rid of their judiciaries. That those judiciaries – despite their flagrant ineffectiveness, the corruption of their judges or their general toothlessness – still exist, indicates that even autocratic States consider that they cannot go as far as dispensing with them entirely. The point may be summarised as: domestically, a judiciary is a must have; internationally, it is a nice to have – that still depends on State consent.

The distinction between domestic and international courts becomes even more apparent when two of the defining institutional features of international courts are analysed in detail: the lack of compulsory jurisdiction and the absence of coercive enforcement mechanisms.

B. The First Issue: Lack of Compulsory Jurisdiction

International adjudication still depends on State consent.[249] This is a well-established (i.e., old) principle. The PCIJ explained it in the *Eastern Carelia* advisory opinion in 1923, when it stated that: '[i]t is well established in international

---

See also Be Schlink, 'Proportionality (1)' in M Rosenfeld and A Sajó (eds), *The Oxford Handbook of Comparative Constitutional Law* (OUP, 2012); A Barak, 'Proportionality (2)' in M Rosenfeld and A Sajó (eds), *The Oxford Handbook of Comparative Constitutional Law* (OUP, 2012).

[248] World Justice Project, *Rule of Law Index 2022*. Available at: https://worldjusticeproject.org/rule-of-law-index/global.

[249] Fouchard, *The Standard of Review* (n 118).

law that no State can, without its consent, be compelled to submit its disputes with other States . . . to arbitration, or to any other kind of pacific settlement'.[250] More recently, in *Certain Questions of Mutual Assistance in Criminal Matters* the ICJ reaffirmed this principle, stating that: 'the jurisdiction of the Court is based on the consent of States, under the conditions expressed therein'.[251]

As Reisman observed: 'International tribunals are bodies of limited competence, empowered to adjudicate only those matters which have been submitted to them by the parties and only in the manner prescribed by their constitutive documents.'[252] This lack of compulsory jurisdiction has, reasonably, made international courts careful in exercising their jurisdictional powers. Similarly, Fontanelli observes that 'if anything, the Court has been a rigorous guardian of the State's consent, rigour being both a virtue and a survival strategy'.[253] In international adjudication, then, consent cannot be overlooked. As Voeten recognised: 'it is not clear that high levels of trust in an international court mean that the court can withstand a firestorm of critique if it takes an unpopular decision'.[254] It is not clear at all. Even less so with low levels of trust.

Some scholars consider that most current international courts *do* have compulsory jurisdiction. For example, Alter remarks that 'eighty percent of operational

[250] *Status of Eastern Carelia*, PCIJ, Advisory Opinion of 23 July 1923, 27. See generally CPR Romano, 'The Shift from the Consensual to the Compulsory Paradigm in International Adjudication: Elements for a Theory of Consent' (2006–2007) 39 *NYU Journal of International Law and Politics* 791. In the words of Judge Mosler: 'the Court, like all other international courts and tribunals, still derives its jurisdiction in contentious cases from the voluntary submission of potential parties. Its competence is based on a jurisdictional link between the parties, which may be established by various types of technical devices, but always involves the feature that the State concerned have incurred an obligation to subject themselves to the Court': H Mosler, 'The Area of Justiciability: Some Cases of Agreed Delimitation in the Submission of Disputes to the International Court of Justice', in J Makarczyk (ed) *Essays in International Law in Honour of Manfred Lachs* (Brill, 1984) 409.

[251] *Certain Questions of Mutual Assistance in Criminal Matters (Djibouti v France)*, ICJ, Judgment of 4 June 2008, para 4.

[252] WM Reisman, 'Has the International Court Exceeded its Jurisdiction?' (1986) 80 *American Journal of International Law* 128, 128.

[253] F Fontanelli, 'Once Burned, Twice Shy: The Use of Compromissory Clauses before the International Court of Justice and Their Declining Popularity in New Treaties' (2021) 104 *Rivista di Diritto Internazionale* 7. Gleider Hernández raises a similar point. He explains that: 'The Court's restraint is a logical corollary flowing from its consensual jurisdiction', as that requires the Court to operate with 'a natural "judicial caution" . . . to avoid strained or difficult constructions as a ground for seeking to impose its jurisdiction upon unwilling States'. GI Hernández, *The International Court of Justice and the Judicial Function* (OUP, 2014) 50.

[254] E Voeten, 'Public Opinion and the Legitimacy of International Courts' (2013) 14 *Theoretical Inquiries in Law* 411. In her dissenting opinion in an international investment dispute, *Garanti Koza LLP v Turkmenistan*, Laurence Boisson de Chazournes raised similar concerns. She observed cogently that: 'The trust and confidence in third-party adjudication is dependent on the respect by international courts and tribunals to the limits to the jurisdiction conferred upon them. Tribunals should not create a *de facto* system of compulsory jurisdiction, which in the present stage of positive international law remains the exception. The international legal order still rests largely on a system of facultative jurisdiction, and because of that essential characteristic, a tribunal should never attempt to impose its jurisdiction and adjudicate the merits of a dispute when the parties have not consented to its jurisdiction.' *Garanti Koza LLP v Turkmenistan*, ICSID Case No ARB/11/20, Award (3 July 2013) para 6 (Dissenting Opinion of Laurence Boisson de Chazournes).

[international courts] have a broad compulsory jurisdiction'.[255] In fact, Alter suggests that there is a distinction between 'old style' international courts, which lack compulsory jurisdiction; and 'new style' international courts, which have compulsory jurisdiction. In these 'new style' courts, 'cases will proceed despite the reluctance of the defendant state'.[256]

On one level, this observation is correct. Newer international courts – particularly those that are part of regional and supranational integration mechanisms – tend to have compulsory jurisdiction, insofar as often acceptance of the international court's compulsory jurisdiction is a requirement for membership in said regional or supranational organisations. For example, membership of, say, the World Trade Organisation, the European Union, or the Andean Community, requires States to accept the compulsory jurisdiction of the WTO's dispute settlement mechanism,[257] the Court of Justice of the European Union[258] or the Andean Tribunal of Justice, respectively.[259]

Yet at another level that claim is debatable. First, some consider that *supranational* courts – such as the Court of Justice of the European Union – should not be classified as properly *international* courts. Their argument is based on the different institutional background in which courts like the CJEU operate as compared to other international courts. So, whereas the CJEU 'is legally and institutionally bound into the framework of the European Union' and it operates effectively as a third branch, interacting with the European Parliament and the European Commission, other international courts simply do not have such a 'centralized political framework'.[260] Second, in all of these cases States *voluntarily* decide whether they want to join or be part of these international organisations. And they can leave. The shift is in the *moment* and the *place* where such consent to jurisdiction is given – but States are still giving their consent. This change has been described as a shift in international courts' centre of gravity, which has moved from case-specific consent (e.g., a *compromis* before the ICJ or an arbitral tribunal) to a court's (or international regime's) constitutive

[255] Alter (n 122) 4. Alter argues that 'the extension of compulsory jurisdiction is arguably the most prevalent and important IC design change since the end of the Cold War. Granting an IC a broad compulsory jurisdiction, and associating this jurisdiction with community membership, means that the only way to "opt out" is to withdraw entirely from the multilateral institution'.

[256] ibid.

[257] For a comprehensive view of this process grounded on the 'exit' and 'voice' theory, see J Pauwelyn, 'The Transformation of World Trade' (2005) 104 *Michigan Law Review* 1, 2–7.

[258] The development of a European judiciary has received much attention. For an insightful view of the issue, see J Weiler, 'The Transformation of Europe' (1991) 100 *Yale Law Journal* 2403. See also A Stone Sweet, *The Judicial Construction of Europe* (OUP, 2004), particularly ch 2; Alter, *Establishing the Supremacy* (n 234).

[259] Romano, *The Shift from the Consensual* (n 251) 809 mentions that: 'the ECJ has fundamentally broken with the hitherto prevailing consensual paradigm . . . the Court was granted wide and, most importantly, compulsory jurisdiction to ensure observation of the law in the interpretation and application of the Treaties establishing the European Communities'.

[260] See eg Von Bogdandy and Venzke *In Whose Name?* (n 240) 25.

or foundational documents (e.g., the WTO's dispute settlement system or the CJEU).[261] The price of exit may be higher, but the option is still there.

Being subject to the jurisdiction of the Court of Justice of the European Union was one of the reasons relied on by those that campaigned for Brexit.[262] Similarly, Venezuela left the Andean Community, among other things, because it did not want to be subject to the Andean Tribunal of Justice.[263] So, despite some of these 'new style' international courts having something that comes closer to compulsory jurisdiction, that quasi compulsory jurisdiction – like the jurisdiction of (almost) all international courts – initially arose from State consent.

Indeed, as explained above, exit – understood as termination of a treaty or a State's withdrawal from a treaty regime – is one of the harshest forms of backlash. Its impact is broader than the mere withdrawal of consent to international adjudication as it may involve withdrawal from a wider treaty regime. For instance, the decision to terminate NAFTA not only affected the jurisdiction of arbitral tribunals to decide disputes under the treaty's investment chapter but also affected the considerably more important trade regime between the three member States. In light of this, international courts, explicitly (or at least implicitly), may sometimes be concerned about whether their decisions will ultimately lead States to withdraw from treaties as, in the context in which they operate, withdrawal is a real possibility.[264]

Pauwelyn and Hamilton recently identified four key exit drivers. Two are court-centred: judicial activism and bias; and two are State-centred: sovereignty costs and political change.[265] These authors also identified five different ways in which State discontent with an international court may turn out. This includes nothing happening, reform, exit, the asphyxiation of the tribunal or the creation of an alternative mechanism.[266] They also identify some issues that influence the likelihood that a State may withdraw from an international court. The main issue is whether the court is self-standing. As they explain, withdrawal is easier if a State 'can leave the tribunal without necessarily leaving the substantive regime or organization that tribunal is linked to'.[267]

In short, international courts are *not* like the Hotel California: States can, and sometimes do, checkout – and ultimately leave. Consent to jurisdiction is

[261] Y Shany, *Assessing the Effectiveness of International Courts* (OUP, 2014) 71.

[262] See eg C Baudenbacher 'The ECJ Used to Be a Neutral Court for the UK – It No Longer Is' *LSE Brexit Blog* (9 March 2021). Available at: https://blogs.lse.ac.uk/brexit/2021/03/09/the-ecj-didnt-used-to-be-a-foreign-court-it-is-one-now/, stating: 'The Brexiteers had promised to end the EU Court's jurisdiction.'

[263] JC Sainz Borgo, 'La salida de Venezuela de la Comunidad Andina' (2007) 38 *Politeia* 136. The main reason was the introduction of treaty instruments that the Venezuelan government considered to be akin to free trade agreements.

[264] For a relatively recent survey, see C McLachlan, 'The Assault on International Adjudication and the Limits of Withdrawal' (2019) 68 *International and Comparative Law Quarterly* 499, 503–10.

[265] J Pauwelyn and R J Hamilton, 'Exit from International Tribunals' (2018) 9 *Journal of International Dispute Settlement* 679, 683.

[266] ibid 686–88.

[267] ibid.

withdrawn; treaties providing for international adjudication are terminated; integration mechanisms are abandoned. The threat of exit looms over the heads of (almost) all international courts – in a way that it does not, at least not to the same degree, for domestic courts.

There is potentially one exception to this principle: some international criminal courts established by the UN Security Council. For instance, the International Criminal Tribunal for the Former Yugoslavia, the International Criminal Tribunal for Rwanda, the International Residual Mechanism for Criminal Tribunals and, arguably, the Special Tribunal for Lebanon. Instead of being created by State consent, these international courts were created by the Security Council acting under Chapter VII of the UN Charter, which refers to the Council's powers to address threats to the peace, breaches of the peace, and acts of aggression.[268] Of course, the jurisdiction of the main standing international criminal court – the International Criminal Court – does mainly depend on State consent.[269]

Some have been asking for an end to the voluntarist paradigm.[270] This is not new. In fact, this trend started towards the end of the nineteenth century, when several 'peace movements' sprung up in both Europe and the Americas. One of the key objectives of these movements was the establishment of compulsory arbitration of international disputes. This, they thought, would avoid any further instance of war.[271] As David Caron explains, at the time there existed

[268] See eg WA Schabas, 'International Criminal Courts' in CPR Romano, K J Alter and Y Shany (eds), *The Oxford Handbook of International Adjudication* (OUP, 2013); Romano, *The Shift from the Consensual* (n 251) 813; P Webb and M Bergsmo, 'International Criminal Courts and Tribunals, Complementarity and Jurisdiction' *Max Planck Encyclopedia of Public International Law* (2010) para 4, noting that: 'The ad hoc tribunals are able to request national courts to defer to their jurisdiction because they were created by resolutions of the United Nations Security Council. Consequently, their jurisdiction is based on the Security Council enforcement measures rather than State consent under a treaty.'

[269] Perhaps with the exception of jurisdiction over the crime of aggression.

[270] Some consider the requirement of State consent to be a major stumbling block for the development of international law: see N Politis, *The New Aspects of International Law* (Carnegie Endowment for International Peace, 1928); G Clark and LB Sohn, *World Peace Through World Law: Two Alternative Plans,* 3rd edn (Harvard University Press, 1966); N Singh, *The Role and Record of the International Court of Justice* (Martinus Nijhoff, 1989); F Przetacznik, 'The Compulsory Jurisdiction of the International Court of Justice as a Prerequisite for Peace' (1990) 68 *Revue de Droit International de Sciences Diplomatiques et Politiques*; H Steiger, 'Plaidoyer pour une juridiction internationale obligatoire' in J Makarczyk (ed), *Theory of International Law at the Threshold of the 21st Century: Essays in Honour of Krzysztof Skubiszewski* (Kluwer Law International, 1996); AA Cançado Trindade, *International Law for Humankind: Towards a New Jus Gentium* (Martinus Nijhoff, 2010) 567 and ff.

[271] The peace movements have been studied in detail. See eg ACF Beales, *The History of Peace: A Short Account of the Organized Movements for International Peace* (G Bell & Sons, 1931); see also J Chambers II (ed), *The Eagle and the Dove: The American Peace Movement and United States Foreign Policy 1900–1922* (Syracuse University Press, 1991); C Chatfield, *The American Peace Movement: Ideals and Activism* (Twayne, 1992); ME Curti, *The American Peace Crusade 1815–1860* (Duke University Press, 1929); CR Marchand, *The American Peace Movement and Social Reform 1898–1918* (Princeton University Press, 1972); C Phelps, *The Anglo-American Peace Movements in the Mid-Nineteenth Century* (Columbia University Press, 1930); MR Vesnic, *Deux Précurseurs Français du Pacifisme* (A Pedone, 1911). A basic reference is RS Meyer, *Peace Organizations Past and Present: A Survey and Directory* (McFarland, 1988).

'a popular belief . . . that the establishment of a permanent international court would be an important step toward a world free of war'.[272]

These scholars and activists have been asking for compulsory jurisdiction for international courts for more than 100 years. They have not been very persuasive. Almost all international adjudication is still dependent on State consent. And, in any event, even if compulsory jurisdiction was widely accepted throughout, that only sorts half the problem. International law is a process that must be both legitimate *and* effective. Compulsory jurisdiction goes to the legitimacy part of the equation. But that does not solve the effectiveness part, which requires that the judgments of international courts have practical effects. They must be complied with. They must be able to affect the reality that they address. That is precisely the second inherent issue with international adjudication.

C. The Second Issue: General Lack of Coercive Enforcement Mechanisms[273]

In Arthur Leff's memorable phrase, a key feature of United States courts is that, at least theoretically, every judgment issued by a US court has the 101st Airborne division of the US army backing it up.[274] Strictly speaking, this is not true. But the point remains: when push comes to shove, domestic courts often rely on the State's coercive apparatus to enforce their decisions. International courts lack anything resembling that.[275] Even if we accept Henkin's claim that 'Almost all nations observe almost all principles of international law and almost all of their obligations almost all of the time'[276] and even if we accept that rulings from international courts exert a 'normative pull'[277] that leads towards compliance (at least when they are accepted as legitimate),[278] it is not less true that,

[272] DD Caron, 'War and International Adjudication: Reflections on the 1899 Peace Conference' (2000) 94 *American Journal of International Law* 4, 4. More recently, one prominent international judge asserted that a 'current reassessment of international adjudication can thus be appropriately undertaken . . . in the context of the growth of international jurisdiction, bearing in mind the recurring need and quest for compulsory jurisdiction': see Cançado Trindade, *International Law for Humankind* (n 271) 567, 568.

[273] 'There's th' international coort, ye say, but I say where ar-re th' polis? A coort's all r-right enough, but no coort's anny good onless it is backed up by a continted constabulary', *Mr Dooley, An International Police Force* (1899).

[274] AA Leff, 'Law and' (1978) 87 *Yale Law Journal* 989, 997.

[275] In that sense, a detractor of legalism in international law, Robert H Bork, claimed that: 'there can be no authentic rule of law among nations until nations have a common political morality or are under a common sovereignty'. RH Bork, 'The Limits of "International Law"' (1989) 3 *The National Interest* 10.

[276] L Henkin, *How Nations Behave* (Columbia University Press, 1979) 47. Eric Posner has harshly criticised Henkin's view, claiming that: 'The empirical work on international law is in its infancy but some of it – particularly the work on human rights treaties – has blasted holes in the Henkin view.' See E Posner, 'Evaluating the Effects of International Law: Next Steps' (2010) 1(3) *Global Policy* 334, 334–35.

[277] T M Franck, *The Power of Legitimacy Among Nations* (OUP, 1990) 24-25.

[278] HH Koh, 'Why Do Nations Obey International Law' (1996–1997) 106 *Yale Law Journal* 2599, 2659.

despite the existence of some compliance mechanisms,[279] these are not *coercive*. International courts most definitely *do not* have the 101st Airborne backing up their decisions.[280] Indeed, some consider that this lack of coercive enforcement mechanisms means that, unlike domestic courts, international courts are not actually exercising public authority.[281]

One unfortunate, relatively recent example illustrates this. Russia invaded Ukraine on 24 February 2022. Two days later Ukraine initiated proceedings against Russia before the ICJ under the Convention on the Prevention and Punishment of the Crime of Genocide.[282] Ukraine requested interim measures. Among other things, Ukraine claimed that the Russian Federation 'shall immediately suspend the military operations commenced on 24 February 2022', and that Russian troops 'take no steps in furtherance of the military operations'.[283] The Court moved quickly. It issued an order less than a month afterwards. The Court granted Ukraine's request for provisional measures, ordering the Russian Federation to 'suspend the military operations'.[284]

Unsurprisingly, for almost four years Russia, which had not even appeared in the proceedings, has not complied with the order.[285] Although Ukraine's President Zelensky characterised the Court's decision as a 'complete victory' for Ukraine,[286] the Ukrainian government was, in reality, not expecting Russia to heed the Court's order. Commenting on the judgment, Emine Dzhaparova, Ukraine's then First Deputy Minister of Foreign Affairs, acknowledged that 'the aggressor will not significantly change this position, of course'.[287] Dzhaparova's statement, instead, illustrates the decentralised mechanisms of enforcement of international law.[288] The Court's judgment was legitimate – but unfortunately it was not effective – and, critically, there was no coercive mechanism at its disposal to make it effective. In fact, during the extensive diplomatic discussions

[279] See eg LF Damrosch, *Enforcing International Law through Non-Forcible Measures* (Martinus Nijhoff 1998).

[280] In theory, the International Court of Justice counts on the Security Council to ensure compliance with the Court's decisions. In practice, however, the political working of the council makes it highly unlikely that 101st Airborne-like enforcement mechanisms will be available.

[281] Von Bogdandy and Venzke (n 240) 111.

[282] *Allegations of Genocide under the Convention on the Prevention and Punishment of the Crime of Genocide (Ukraine v Russia)*, ICJ, Provisional Measures Order of 16 March 2022 at para 1.

[283] *Allegations of Genocide under the Convention on the Prevention and Punishment of the Crime of Genocide (Ukraine v Russia)*, ICJ, Request for the Indication of Provisional Measures Submitted by Ukraine on 2 February 2022, at para 20(a–b).

[284] *Allegations of Genocide under the Convention* (n 283) para 81.

[285] ibid para 12: 'By a letter dated 5 March 2022, the Ambassador of the Russian Federation to the Kingdom of the Netherlands indicated that his government had decided not to participate in the oral proceedings.'

[286] 'The ICJ Ordered Russia to Halt Military Operations in Ukraine. What Comes Next?' *Washington Post* (25 March 2022).

[287] 'Decision of International Court of Justice Another Argument for World Community to Increase Pressure on Russia' *Interfax Ukraine* (19 March 2022).

[288] ibid.

regarding the conflict in Ukraine, the Court's interim measures have, as far as I can tell, not been invoked or mentioned at all.

Traditionally, the lack of enforcement mechanisms has been one of the main grounds relied on by legal positivism to challenge the status of international law as law[289] (or at least as not having all the elements required for an advanced legal system).[290] Those arguments, however, have been refuted.[291] Another traditional response is that, unlike municipal law, the existence of international law is unrelated to its enforcement.[292] Nevertheless, compliance with international court's judgment is important.[293] An international court whose judgments are routinely ignored may quickly lose its authority. It is thus critical that its decision be both legitimate and effective. The importance of compliance is not really in question. Some contend that it 'is one of the central questions of international law', as [w]ithout a theory of compliance, we cannot examine the role of treaties, customary international law, or other agreements. Nor can we consider how to improve the functioning of the

[289] J Austin, *The Province of Jurisprudence Determined* (CUP, 1995) 123, stating: '[T]he law obtaining between nations is not positive law: for every positive law is set by a given sovereign to a person or persons in a state of subjugation to its author . . . [T]he law obtaining between nations is law (improperly so called) set by general opinion. The duties which it imposes are enforced by moral sanctions: by fear on the part of nations, or by fear on the part of sovereigns, of provoking general hostility . . . in case they shall violate maxims generally received and objected.'

[290] HLA Hart, *The Concept of Law*, 3rd edn (OUP, 2012) ch X, see particularly 214: 'the absence of an international legislature, courts with compulsory jurisdiction, and centrally organized sanctions have inspired misgivings . . . The absence of these institutions means that the rules for states resemble that simple form of social structure, consisting only of primary rules of obligation . . . It is indeed arguable, as we shall show, that international law not only lacks the secondary rules of change and adjudication which provide for legislature and courts, but also a unifying rule of recognition specifying "sources" of law and providing general criteria for the identification of its rules'. See also A D'Amato, 'Is International Law Really "Law"?' (1985) 79 *Northwestern University Law Review* 1293, 1293.

[291] See eg I Brownlie, 'The Reality and Efficacy of International Law' (1982) 52 *British Yearbook of International Law* 1. Where Brownlie observed that domestic law often also lacks centralised and coercive methods of enforcement, such as during periods of civil unrest. Thus, he observed wryly that: 'Of especial importance is the fact that the operation of the secondary rules may break down without affecting the operation of the primary rules to any great extent, or at all. Civil strife may place the secondary rules in jeopardy . . . yet during the time when the political foundations are being remade there is generally no legal vacuum . . . [T]he stability of international relations compares quite well with international law, given the grand total of municipal systems ruptured by civil strife since 1945. And whilst it may be said that international law lacks secondary rules, this matters less if one accepts the view that secondary rules do not play such a decisive role in maintaining the more basic forms of legality in municipal systems.'

[292] D Kritsiotis, 'International Law and the Relativities of Enforcement' in J Crawford and M Koskenniemi (eds), *The Cambridge Companion to International Law* (CUP 2012). See also O Hathaway and SJ Shapiro, 'Outcasting: Enforcement in Domestic and International Law' (2011) 121 *Yale Law Journal* 252, 256.

[293] Shany, for instance, admits that there are structural and procedural issues that may limit an international court's effectiveness. He observes that some courts, like the ICJ or the ICC, are 'constrained . . . by the fact that important states have not accepted their compulsory jurisdiction (structure) and by apparent weakness in the application of their enforcement machinery (process)': Shany, *Assessing the Effectiveness of International Courts* (n 261) 308.

international legal system'.[294] This premise is reflected in important international agreements.[295]

Although current thinking tends to distinguish compliance from the broader notion of effectiveness, compliance is still nevertheless *the* best indicator to assess whether an international court's judgment is effective.[296] In fact, in the case of compliance with *court orders or judgments* (as opposed to compliance with international obligations more broadly), it is not too difficult to draw a causal relation between the judgment and the State's conduct.[297] Some current scholarship,[298] however, takes a broader view of compliance,[299] focusing instead on the broader concept of *effectiveness*.[300] This is one area where the international legal process perspective has made important contributions, as it looks

[294] AT Guzman, 'A Compliance-Based Theory of International Law' (2002) 90 *California Law Review* 1823, 1826; A Llamzon, 'Jurisdiction and Compliance in Recent Decisions of the International Court of Justice' (2007) 18 *European Journal of International Law* 815.

[295] Consider, for instance, art 21(1) of the WTO's Dispute Settlement Understanding, which reads: '[p]rompt compliance with recommendations or rulings of the DSB is essential in order to ensure effective resolution of disputes to the benefits of all Members': Understanding on Rules and Procedures Governing the Settlement of Disputes, Annex 2 of the WTO Agreement. Reisman also observes that: 'Enforcement refers to the transformation, by community means, of authoritative pronouncement into controlling reality. Organized communities enforce their authority in two ways: By *direct enforcement* they supervise the physical transfer of what was decreed in authoritative decision. By *indirect enforcement* they impose sanctions on the miscreant in order to persuade him to comply with community norms': WM Reisman and others, 'The Enforcement of International Judgments' (1968) 62 *Proceedings of the American Society of International Law* 13.

[296] D Hawkins and W Jacoby, 'Partial Compliance: A Comparison of the European and Inter-American Courts of Human Rights' (2010) 6 *Journal of International Law and International Relations* 35, 40. Based on empirical research in the international human rights context, they state that: '[w]hen a country persists in behavior long enough for an international court to rule against that country's practices, and the country subsequently changes its practices, we assume that the court's ruling helped trigger the change in behavior' and conclude that 'any resulting behavioral changes after an adverse court ruling can suggest court effectiveness'.

[297] This point is advanced by Huneeus, in the human rights context: see eg A Huneeus, 'Courts Resisting Courts: Lessons from the Inter-American Court's Struggle to Enforce Human Rights' (2011) 44 *Cornell International Law Journal* 493, 505.

[298] See eg K Raustiala, 'Compliance and Effectiveness in International Regulatory Cooperation' (2000) 32 *Case Western Reserve Journal of International Law* 387, 391. Raustiala suggests that compliance and effectiveness are, in reality, different concepts. Compliance, on the one hand, implies conformity between a State's conduct and a rule of international law. Effectiveness, on the other hand, refers to 'observable, desired changes in behavior' that are themselves caused by a rule of international law. His specific phrasing is: 'Compliance generally refers to a state of conformity or identity between an actor's behaviour and a specified rule. In the international context, compliance is often specified as an "actor's behavior that conforms to a treaty's explicit rules".' The main insight from this distinction is that compliance may be high – regardless of a rule, eg when a treaty is drafted to reflect a State's current practice – and, conversely, that a rule may not be complied with – but may nevertheless be effective, eg when an international rule provides a high standard of conduct which, albeit not complied with, in fact alters State conduct.

[299] Although the concept of compliance, itself, is contested. See eg B Kingsbury, 'The Concept of Compliance as a Function of Competing Conceptions of International Law' (1998) 19 *Michigan Journal of International Law* 345.

[300] As to the debate regarding the concept of effectiveness, Shany observes that 'a significant portion of this empirical literature possesses an "Achilles heel", found in the crude and/or intuitive definitions of "effectiveness" it employs, which often equates judicial effectiveness with judgment-compliance, usage rate, and impact on state conduct': Shany (n 261) 4.

at the potential effects of a decision beyond the confines of compliance with an international court's judgment strictly understood. Transnational legal process[301] suggests that international law is made effective by a combination of transnational actors[302] – both domestic and international, public and private (these have also been called compliance constituencies)[303] – and the interaction between them. Harold Koh defined this as the theory of how all of these actors 'interact in a variety of public and private, domestic and international fora to make, interpret, enforce, and ultimately, internalize rules of transnational law'.[304] Those internalised (domesticated?) rules then 'create default patterns of international law-observant behavior for all participants in the process',[305] which are based, not on coercion, but rather on 'patters of obedience'.[306]

One prominent example of how this operates in practice is the internalisation, in US domestic law, of the prohibition against torture initially set out at the international level.[307] The reason for this change is that 'compliance cannot tell us the full extent of the law's impact because it excludes other important effects that law may have'.[308] This change of paradigm allows focusing more on

[301] *Transnational* law refers to a hybrid legal system first articulated by Philip Jessup that simultaneously combines both domestic and international, as well as public and private law. P Jessup, *Transnational Law* (New Haven, Yale University Press, 1956) 2; see also A Lowenfeld, 'Public Law in the International Arena: Conflict of Laws, International Law, and Some Suggestions for Their Interaction' (1979) 163 *Recueil des Cours* 311, 321. Lowenfeld contends that 'public international law has been too rigid, too rule-oriented, and therefore too abstract, in part because it has been insulated from the more flexible, approach-oriented developments of private international law'. In Koh's view, this hybrid legal system generates '*interactions* that lead to *interpretations* of international law that become *internalized* into, and thereby binding under, domestic law': HH Koh, 'The 1994 Roscoe Pound Lecture: Transnational Legal Process' (1994) 75, *Nebraska Law Review* 105, 184. This idea is further developed in HH Koh (n 279) 2626–27; HH Koh, *The Trump Administration and International Law* (OUP, 2018); HH Koh, 'Is There a New New Haven School of International Law Commentary' (2007) 32 *Yale Journal of International Law* 559; and HH Koh, 'Transnational Legal Process and the "New" New Haven School of International Law' in J Dunoff and M Pollack (eds), *International Legal Theory: Foundations and Frontiers* (CUP, 2022).

[302] HH Koh, 'The 1998 Frankel Lecture: Bringing International Law Home' (1998) 35 *Houston Law Review* 624, 647–48.

[303] Alter, *The New Terrain* (n 125). For an interesting review, see JE Alvarez, 'Global Judicialization Revisited' (2015) 109 *American Journal of International Law* 677 (reviewing KJ Alter, *The New Terrain of International Law: Courts, Politics, Rights*). While overall positive, Alvarez does criticise Alter's reading of judgments, observing that: 'with some exceptions, Alter's case studies tend to rely on the secondary literature and not close analysis of the decisions themselves . . . At that granular level, lawyers may wince at some of Alter's more dubious asides, particularly her speculative conclusions concerning the connections between judges and politics' at 685. For a more critical appraisal, see Krisch, *The Path of Judicialization* (n 140).

[304] Koh, *Is There a New New Haven?* (n 301) 568.

[305] Koh, *The Trump Administration?* (n 301) 7.

[306] ibid 8. Also, for a further elaboration of the theory of norm internalization, see T Tyler, *Why People Obey the Law* (Yale University Press, 1990).

[307] Koh, *Is There a New New Haven?* (n 302) 568.

[308] A Huneeus, 'Compliance with Judgments and Decisions' in CPR Romano, KJ Alter and Y Shany (eds), *The Oxford Handbook of International Adjudication* (OUP 2013) 439. Helfer and Slaughter were early proponents of this view. They defined an international judgment's effectiveness based on its 'ability to compel compliance with its judgments by convincing domestic government institutions, directly and through pressure from private litigants, to use their power on its behalf': see

'the manner in which international law creates effects in the world . . . [to] what happens to legal rules when they are out in the world'.[309] This broader, functional approach to compliance is welcome. Ultimately, what matters is the *actual* conduct of States, regardless of the specific formal labels applied.[310] However, the shift from compliance to effectiveness is viewed cynically by some. One critic suggests that attempts to re-define compliance in a way that circumvents the uncomfortable reality that States often do not comply with their treaty commitments is an attempt to 'resuscitate' Henkin's 'complacent' view about almost all States complying with their international obligations almost all of the time.[311]

LR Helfer and AM Slaughter, 'Toward a Theory of Effective Supranational Adjudication' (1997) 107 *Yale Law Journal* 273, 290. More broadly, Abraham and Antonia Chayes, for instance, observed that there will be compliance when 'nations alter their behavior, their relationships, and their expectations of one another over time', in accordance with their international obligations: A Chayes and AH Chayes, 'On Compliance' (1993) 47 *International Organization* 175, 176. Raustiala then suggested that compliance and effectiveness are, in reality, different concepts. Compliance, on the one hand, implies conformity between a State's conduct and a rule of international law. Effectiveness, on the other hand, refers to 'observable, desired changes in behavior' that are themselves caused by a rule of international law. The main insight from this distinction is that compliance may be high – regardless of a rule, eg when a treaty is drafted to reflect a State's current practice – and, conversely, that a rule may not be complied with – but may nevertheless be effective, eg when an international rule provides a high standard of conduct which, albeit not complied with, in fact alters State conduct.

[309] R Howse and R Teitel, 'Beyond Compliance: Rethinking Why International Law Really Matters' (2010) 1(12) *Global Policy* 127.

[310] Somewhat relatedly, Helfer provides a useful classification of different types of effectiveness: case-specific, *erga omnes*, embedded, and norm-effectiveness: see LR Helfer, 'The Effectiveness of International Adjudicators' in CPR Romano, K J Alter and Y Shany (eds), *The Oxford Handbook of International Adjudication* (OUP, 2013) 464. See also L Martin, 'Against Compliance' in J Dunoff and M Pollack (eds), *Interdisciplinary Perspectives on International Law and International Relations: The State of the Art* (CUP, 2012); EM Hafner-Burton, DG Victor and Y Lupu, 'Political Science Research on International Law: The State of the Field' (2012) 106 *American Journal of International Law* 47; LR Helfer, 'The Benefits and Burdens of Brighton' (2012) 1(1) *ESIL Reflections*; LR Helfer, 'Overlegalizing Human Rights: International Relations Theory and the Commonwealth Caribbean Backlash Against Human Rights Regimes' (2002) 102 *Columbia Law Review* 1832; D Cassel, 'Does International Human Rights Law Make a Difference?' (2001) 2 *Chicago Journal of International Law* 121, 128–34. See also R Graebner, 'Dialogue and Divergence: The Vienna Convention on Consular Relations in German, American, and International Courts' (2011) 42 *Georgetown Journal of International Law* 605, 607–11; S Besson, 'The Erga Omnes Effect of Judgments of the European Court of Human Rights – What's In A Name?' in Samantha Besson (ed), *The European Court of Human Rights After Protocol 14* (Schulthess 2011) 125, 141; J Kanargelidis, 'New Anti-Dumping Rules Applied by Canada: The Zeroing Debate' *Mondaq Business Briefing* (7 September 2005); C Binder, 'The Prohibition of Amnesties by the Inter-American Court of Human Rights' (2011) 12 *German Law Journal* 1203, 1222–23. See also J Cavallaro and SE Brewer, 'Reevaluating Regional Human Rights Litigation in the Twenty-First Century: The Case of the Inter-American Court' (2008) 102 *American Journal of International Law* 768, 816–22; GF Mancini, 'The Making of a Constitution for Europe' (1989) 26 *Common Market Law Review* 595; K Alter, *The European Court's Political Power: Selected Essays* (OUP, 2009), particularly chs 4 and 5; W Burke-White, 'Proactive Complementarity: The International Criminal Court and National Courts in the Rome System of International Justice' (2008) 49 *Harvard International Law Journal* 53; AO Enabulele, 'Sailing against the Tide: Exhaustion of Domestic Remedies and the ECOWAS Community Court of Justice' (2012) 56 *Journal of African Law* 268.

[311] E Posner 'Evaluating the Effects of International Law' (n 277) stating that: 'The empirical work on international law is in its infancy but some of it – particularly the work on human rights treaties – has blasted holes in the Henkin view. To resuscitate this view, scholars now argue that even if states

Regardless of the approach taken to understand or define compliance, the critical issue is still that international courts lack coercive enforcement mechanisms. They lack the institutional wherewithal to ensure that their decisions are complied with. There are two ways of approaching this. One is for international courts to simply ignore any potential compliance difficulties down the line and focus on issuing the correct legal decision. We could call this *let justice be done though the heavens fall* approach. That is the mainstream view. Another alternative is for international courts – expressly or, more realistically, impliedly – to take potential compliance difficulties into account when determining whether to decide or avoid a case or issue. As I will explain in detail, ignoring potential compliance difficulties is fraught. International courts whose rulings are ignored[312] risk following the fate of the boy who cried wolf and of being reduced to paper tigers issuing devalued judgments which, at most, may elicit a 'so what' response from the parties they sought to bind.[313]

IV. CONCLUSION

This chapter has addressed some foundational concepts of admissibility, jurisdiction, justiciability and avoidance. It also showed that international adjudication does not operate in a vacuum. International courts operate in a specific institutional and political context. Their judgments – particularly those that involve sensitive issues – risk causing backlash and contestation, including dejudicialisation and non-judicialisation, which can, in some instances, result in the obliteration of the international court or in the withdrawal of that subject matter or issue from international adjudication. Finally, this chapter explored some of the inherent characteristics of international adjudication. It highlighted the distinction between domestic and international courts and considered two of the main differences between them: international courts' lack of compulsory jurisdiction and coercive enforcement mechanisms.

---

do not always comply with human rights treaties, those treaties may nonetheless advance the cause of human rights through a range of alternative pathways . . . It should be kept in mind that when treaties are created but not complied with, this may breed cynicism about international law and interfere with its development.'

[312] Tai-Heng Cheng states the issue clearly: 'judges should also be concerned about the effectiveness of their decisions because a decision that is ignored is useless'. See *When International Law Works* (OUP, 2012) 131.

[313] This assumes that a ruling from an international court or tribunal is an authoritative prescription that seeks to influence the behaviour of the receptor through a process of communication. See WM Reisman, 'International Lawmaking: A Process of Communication: The Harold D Lasswell Memorial Lecture' (1981) 75 *Proceedings of the American Society of International Law* 101, 105.

3

Jurisdictional Avoidance

'If the world were perfect, it wouldn't be'

Yogi Berra

THIS CHAPTER FOCUSES ON avoidance. It addresses three points. First, it explains what avoidance is. Second, it explains and analyses the distinction between express and implied avoidance techniques. Third, it sets out a theoretical and normative framework for avoidance.

I. AVOIDANCE: DEFINITION

The central concept of this book is avoidance. The idea is straightforward. Avoidance is the practice of courts – both domestic and international – of finding ways to abstain from deciding cases or issues within cases.[1] It is what is informally called *ducking* or *dodging* a case (or issue), of punting or kicking to touch, of shelving or 'drawering' a decision.

Avoidance is not new. It gives contingent effect to the old principle of non-justiciability. Arguably, the use of avoidance techniques has increased before both domestic and international courts. Although it is hard to fully determine the cause of this, the leading explanation is probably a combination of several factors. These include the increased judicialisation of international law, including the judicialisation of politically sensitive issues (what Hirschl calls 'mega political' issues);[2] the decline of non-justiciability doctrines also likely plays a

[1] EF Delaney, 'Analyzing Avoidance: Judicial Strategy in Comparative Perspective' (2016) 66 *Duke Law Journal* 1, 3. For instance, the ICJ relied on the flexible notion of what constitutes a 'dispute' to carve out controversial or politically sensitive aspects of disputes. In *Obligation to Prosecute or Extradite*, the Court excluded the issue of potential obligations arising under customary international law because they were not *explicitly* mentioned in diplomatic correspondence, at 445. And in *Alleged Violations*, the Court relied on statements made by Nicaraguan military officials and the timing of the filing of the application to consider that there was no dispute regarding Colombia's purported threats to use force against—easily the most controversial issue in that case, at 32–33.

[2] As explained in chapter 2. See K Alter, E Hafner-Burton and L Helfer, 'Theorizing the Judicialization of International Relations' (2019) 63 *International Studies Quarterly*. See also

role, as this has increased the types of issues – particularly politically sensitive issues – that end up before international courts.

In the context of international adjudication, Davey has described avoidance techniques as 'a variety of . . . techniques to dispose of cases or issues within cases where a decision seems unnecessary, inappropriate, or perhaps simply too controversial'.[3] Jackson considers that avoidance is a third way that allows international courts to 'avoid deciding the issue at all—an option that comes with the additional benefit of neither legitimating the underlying measure or conduct nor upsetting existing doctrinal structures'.[4] I would add, for further clarification that there is a second requirement: avoidance requires that the main or preponderant motivation for the application of an avoidance technique is the international court's preference for refraining from deciding the case or issue. This could be due to a series of considerations including, but not exclusively limited to, its subject matter, the potential for backlash, the risk to a court's authority or legitimacy or concerns with the eventual effectiveness of a judgment. This second requirement highlights that not all decisions that imply some judicial abstentions are an instance of avoidance.

As explained in the previous chapter, one of the main criteria used to classify avoidance relates to its timing: the precise moment in the proceedings in which an avoidance doctrine is applied. Delaney thus talks about *ex ante* avoidance, which prevents the court from having to decide the case at all; *in medio* avoidance, which allows some flexibility in the approach to the merits of an issue; and *ex post* avoidance, which is focused on how remedies are structured.[5] Similarly, Alves das Chagas groups avoidance techniques in two, splitting them between admissibility control and merits avoidance.[6]

This book focuses on the first type of avoidance: the doctrines that allow a court to avoid even having to decide the merits of a case. This includes the different doctrines that international courts may rely on to dismiss a case on admissibility or jurisdictional grounds. This type of avoidance has been called different things: for Delaney it is ex ante avoidance, for Alves das Chagas it is *admissibility* avoidance, and for Fouchard it is *merits* avoidance. For simplicity, I will refer to this type of avoidance as *jurisdictional avoidance*, but the term *jurisdictional* is used broadly and is meant to include instances where international courts

C Neal Tate and T Vallinder (eds), *The Global Expansion of Judicial Power* (New York University Press, 1995). For a general discussion of the issue, see R Hirschl, *Towards Juristocracy* (Harvard University Press, 2004).

[3] WJ Davey, 'Has the WTO Dispute Settlement System Exceeded Its Authority? A Consideration of Deference Shown by the System to Member Government Decisions and its Use of Issue-Avoidance Techniques' (2001) 4 *Journal of International Economic Law* 79, 96.

[4] M Jackson, 'Judicial Avoidance at the European Court of Human Rights: Institutional Authority, the Procedural Turn, and Docket Control' (2022) 20 *International Journal of Constitutional Law* 112, 114.

[5] Delaney, 'Analyzing Avoidance' (n 1) 5.

[6] C Alves das Chagas, *Judicial Avoidance: Balancing Competences in Constitutional Adjudication* (Hart, 2023), particularly chs 7 and 8.

dismiss a case on admissibility grounds.[7] Accordingly, this book will not put too much emphasis on avoidance techniques deployed at the post-jurisdictional stage of proceedings, whether in dealing with merits or remedial issues.[8]

Another important distinction is whether avoidance doctrines are applied expressly or impliedly. Some avoidance doctrines are express: consider doctrines of non-justiciability or the political question doctrine. But, as I explain, many instances of avoidance see these techniques applied impliedly, *sotto voce*, without any articulation that an avoidance technique is being applied. So jurisdictional avoidance implies that concepts of international procedural law are applied in a way that results in a case being dismissed on jurisdictional grounds,[9] without the international court expressly stating that they are doing so because they would prefer to avoid deciding that dispute or issue.

A. Origin

The doctrinal precursor of avoidance techniques, as used in this book, is the doctrine of constitutional avoidance, developed under US law. The principle was articulated by Justice Brandeis in his concurrent opinion in *Ashwander v Tennessee Valley Authority*,[10] where he stated that the US Supreme Court had 'for its own governance in the cases confessedly within its jurisdiction, a series of rules under which it has avoided passing upon a large part of all the constitutional questions pressed upon it for decision'.[11]

The prudential argument for constitutional avoidance was then refined by Alexander Bickel.[12] To summarise, Bickel considered that when the US Supreme Court abstained from deciding a politically sensitive case, the Court was

[7] Given the terminological divergence, the choice to add yet another label may be questioned. But it is, I think, justified. Admissibility avoidance is not the most fitting term for international courts, given that most instances of avoidance take the form of a court declining jurisdiction over a case or issue. Merits avoidance (i.e., when the court avoids entering into the merits of the dispute) places the emphasis on what is being avoided, rather than the techniques used to avoid it. Finally, ex ante avoidance focuses too much on the timing rather than on the procedural mechanism – and I would rather avoid a term in Latin. It involves cases where there is an express decision to refrain from deciding a case, so I do not address issues of docket control or even of outright striking of cases, e.g., *Application of the Convention on the Prevention and Punishment of the Crime of Genocide in Sudan (Sudan v United Arab Emirates)*, ICJ, Order of 5 May 2025.

[8] The use of different standards of review as an avoidance technique is addressed in detail in F Fouchard, *The Standard of Review before the International Court of Justice: Between Principle and Pragmatism* (Hart, 2024).

[9] Again, for simplicity, I will say 'jurisdictional' but consider that to include both jurisdiction (strictly speaking) and admissibility.

[10] *Ashwander v Tennessee Valley Authority* 297 US 288 (1936).

[11] *Ashwander* ibid 297; ibid 346 (Brandeis J concurring). Bobbitt considered this concurrence 'majestic'– see P Bobbitt, 'Constitutional Fate' (1980) 58(4) *Texas Law Review*, 719. Those ideas were further developed in book form: *Constitutional Fate: Theory of the Constitution* (OUP, 1984).

[12] Described by B Ackerman as 'the revered . . . spokesman-in-chief for a school of thought that emphasizes the importance of judicial restraint'. BA Ackerman, 'The Storrs Lectures: Discovering the Constitution' (1984) 93 *Yale Law Journal* 1013, 1014.

exercising the *passive virtues*. Bickel considered that the US Supreme Court had developed a series of techniques 'loosely referred to as jurisdictional' that allow it to abstain from deciding certain cases (or certain issues in those cases),[13] including doctrines on standing, cases and controversies, ripeness, and the political question doctrine.[14] In his view, the Supreme Court deployed those techniques as a way to exercise its power to 'decline the exercise of jurisdiction which is given'.[15] To avoid deciding, Bickel observed that:

> [T]he Court has, over the years, developed an almost inexhaustible arsenal of techniques and devices . . . 'The most important thing we do,' said Brandeis, 'is not doing.' He had in mind all the techniques . . . for staying the Court's hand . . . These are the techniques that allow leeway to expediency without abandoning principle. Therefore they make possible a principled government. There can be no understanding of the Court without an appreciation of the variety and significance of these techniques, most of which are lumped roughly and often disingenuously together under the rubric of jurisdiction.[16]

This position is in sharp contrast with what Bickel called the formalist approach, which held that the Supreme Court must inexorably exercise its jurisdiction over a case. This opposing view, represented by, among others, Herbert Wechsler, stated that: 'for anyone who finds the judicial power anchored in the Constitution, there is no such escape from the judicial obligation'.[17] Bickel criticised those views, considering that they were 'inevitably tied to the conviction – never lacking in comfort yet fraught with risk – that there is no escape from the exercise of jurisdiction which is given'.[18]

[13] International disputes are not monolithic and indivisible. They have different aspects, different parts. Some parts of that dispute could be amenable to judicial determination; others may not. Hermann Mosler considered this the 'area of justiciability'. He observed that there are 'disputes which possess, in the eyes of the parties, both a legal and political character', noting that the distinction between both, rather than being a matter of legal principle, was 'more a pragmatic than a logical one': see H Mosler, 'The Area of Justiciability: Some Cases of Agreed Delimitation in the Submission of Disputes to the International Court of Justice' in J Makarczyk (ed), *Essays in International Law in Honour of Judge Manfred Lachs* (Martinus Nijhoff, 1984) 415. Note that, extolling the virtues of special agreements to jurisdiction, Mosler observed that: 'In their special agreement the parties have an opportunity to define which part of the controversy they consider as justiciable between them . . . Splitting a dispute into a major justiciable part to be decided definitely by the Court, and a smaller part reserved for settlement by other means, is, of course, easier to arrange in the terms of a special agreement . . . In order to promote the Court's effectiveness as a means of peaceful settlement of disputes on the basis of international law, this method of recourse to it should be welcomed in principle'.

[14] A Bickel, 'The Supreme Court 1960 Term, Foreword: The Passive Virtues' (1961) 75 *Harvard Law Review* 40, 42.

[15] ibid 47; see also A Bickel, *The Least Dangerous Branch: The Supreme Court at the Bar of Politics* 2nd edn (Yale University Press, 1986) 127.

[16] Bickel ibid 70–1.

[17] See H Wechsler, 'Toward Neutral Principles of Constitutional Law' (1959) 73 *Harvard Law Review* 1, 5.

[18] Bickel, *Forward: The Passive Virtues* (n 14) 48.

Bickel recognised the 'Lincolnian tension' between principle and expediency.[19] It is in that context that he considered the Supreme Court's institutional needs, namely, the need to survive and to be able to operate efficiently and conserve its legitimacy.[20] Further, Bickel argued that by avoiding making a decision on some sensitive issues the Court manages to *stay out* of politics;[21] yet it is in this process of opting to avoid certain issues where the 'Court is most a political animal'.[22] As Bobbitt explains, prudential arguments allow the 'introduction of political realities' into a court's 'decisional process'.[23] There are interesting parallels with how and why international courts rely on avoidance techniques, including the preservation of their legitimacy and authority, as well as avoiding backlash and contestation.

Critically, Bickel *normatively* defends the Supreme Court's decision to avoid certain cases or issues.[24] This justification arises from several factors, chief among them Bickel's view that judicial review was a 'counter-majoritarian force in our system'[25] and, in consequence, a 'deviant institution in American democracy'[26] that 'may, in a larger sense, have a tendency over time seriously to weaken the democratic process'.[27] Because of that, Bickel contended that the Supreme Court's reliance on avoidance techniques did not mean that it was operating in an unprincipled way. In effect, it was:

> [N]ot to concede unchanneled, undirected, uncharted discretion. It is not to concede decision proceeding from impulse, hunch, sentiment, predilection, inarticulable and unreasoned. The antithesis of principle in an institution that represents decency and reason is not whim or even expedience, but prudence.[28]

Indeed, prudence was the central value in Bickel's jurisprudence. As Anthony Kronman explains:

> The most important element in Bickel's political philosophy . . . is his belief in the value of prudence as a political and judicial virtue . . . A prudent judgment . . . is, above all, one that takes into account the complexity of its human and institutional setting . . . A prudent person . . . has a high tolerance for accommodation and

[19] Bickel, *The Least Dangerous Branch* (n 15) 68.

[20] JG Deutsch, 'Neutrality, Legitimacy, and the Supreme Court: Some Intersections between Law and Political Science' (1967) 20 *Stanford Law Review* 169, 213. For an analytical framework which studies how courts may assess legitimacy, see T Roux, *The Politics of Principle: The First South African Constitutional Court, 1995–2005* (CUP, 2013) 72–111.

[21] Bickel (n 15) 132.

[22] ibid.

[23] Bobbitt (n 11) 719

[24] Specifically, Bickel worries about what he called the 'countermajoritarian difficulty' observing that 'judicial review may, in a larger sense, have a tendency over time seriously to weaken the democratic process,' *The Least Dangerous Branch* (n 15) 21.

[25] ibid 16.

[26] ibid 18.

[27] ibid 21.

[28] ibid 132–33.

> delay . . . It was Bickel's view that prudence is an indispensable condition for success in the activities of both the politician and judge; indeed, Bickel believed prudence to be the defining excellence of their respective crafts.[29]

Bickel, Philip Bobbitt opined, was the 'most eloquent and creative exponent of prudential argument'.[30] In his view, this type of argument (in the constitutional context) was characterised by taking into account the 'political and economic circumstances surrounding the decision'.[31]

Unsurprisingly, Bickel's views have been criticised.[32] Gunther, for instance, considered that Bickel engaged in a 'manipulative use of jurisdictional techniques,' that overlooked the fact that jurisdiction was based on the Constitution's text and was thus not something that was exclusively within the Supreme Court's discretion.[33] This criticism is best encapsulated by Gunther's comment that Bickel's approach required '100% insistence on principle, 20% of the time'.[34] Similarly, Hellman considers that Bickel's 'advocacy of the covert deployment of prudential values indefensible.'[35]

Despite those criticisms, Bickel's insights have found empirical support. Scholarship suggests that apex courts do – and, quite frequently, must – rely on avoidance techniques to abstain from deciding a case or issue. Determining whether to rely on those avoidance techniques involves making strategic, pragmatic considerations. The reason domestic courts do this are for arguably valid grounds, including avoiding stepping into overly political territory, maintaining their legitimacy or authority or encouraging dialogue between other branches of government.[36] That insight may be extrapolated to international adjudication.[37]

[29] A Kronman, 'Alexander Bickel's Philosophy of Prudence' (1985) 94 *Yale Law Journal* 1567, 1569.

[30] Bobbitt (n 11) 717.

[31] ibid.

[32] In fact, in 1969, Yale student activists burned Bickel in effigy, see *Washington Post*, A Search for Order, an Answer in the Law. For more academic criticism, see G Gunther, 'The Subtle Vices of the "Passive Virtues"—A Comment on Principle and Expediency in Judicial Review' (1964) 64 *Columbia Law Review* 1; M Tushnet, 'Law and Prudence in the Law of Justiciability: The Transformation and Disappearance of the Political Question Doctrine' (2002) 80 *North Carolina Law Review* 1203; W Haltom and M Silverstein, 'The Scholarly Tradition Revisited: Alexander Bickel, Herbert Wechsler, and the Legitimacy of Judicial Review' (1987) 4 *Constitutional Commentary* 127; JS Wright, 'Professor Bickel, the Scholarly Tradition, and the Supreme Court' (1971) 84 *Harvard Law Review* 797.

[33] Gunther 'The Subtle Vices of the "Passive Virtues"' (n 32) 16.

[34] ibid 1.

[35] D Hellman, 'The Importance of Appearing Principled' (1995) 37 *Arizona Law Review* 1107, 1123.

[36] Delaney 'Analyzing Avoidance' (n 1) 8; see also V Blasi, 'The Role of Strategic Reasoning in Constitutional Interpretation: In Defense of the Pathological Perspective' (1986) *Duke Law Journal* 696; Roux *The Politics of Principle* (n 20).

[37] See eg Jackson 'Judicial Avoidance' (n 4); Fouchard *The Standard of Review before the International Court of Justice* (n 8); J Odermatt 'Patterns of Avoidance: Political Questions Before International Courts' (2018) 14 *International Journal of Law in Context* 221; A John, 'Inarticulate and Unconscious: Non-Justiciability before the International Court of Justice' (2021) 20 *The Law & Practice of International Courts and Tribunals* 77.

B. Jurisdiction and Policy Considerations

The idea that international courts may take into account contextual, policy considerations – such as the potential backlash that deciding a case or issue will generate or the potential effectiveness of a particular judgment – when considering whether to exercise jurisdiction over a dispute or issue may appear radical to some. But it is not new. After all, an international court's decision to adjudicate a case implies, to some degree, a policy choice. International courts are not courts of either general or compulsory jurisdiction.[38] Their jurisdiction mainly depends on State consent – and claims of the end of that principle have so far been wrong. State consent has been described as the 'link between the general political organization of international society and the functioning of the Court'.[39] Because of this, challenges to an international court's jurisdiction often have a political element.[40] Indeed, Rosenne considers that 'when a respondent raises a matter of jurisdiction . . . it frequently indicates the absence of political agreement that the Court should entertain the case. These are not mere technical issues. This imposes an attitude of caution in everything relating to jurisdiction'.[41] For this reason, he observed that whether the ICJ upholds jurisdiction over a case 'is frequently of political importance no less than the decision on the merits, if not more'.[42]

More recently, Yuval Shany has also acknowledged that an international court's approach to jurisdictional issues – rather than merely a technical legal principle – is, in fact, a 'policy tool'. Shany notes that:

> [O]ne may view the establishment of international courts, the conferral of jurisdiction upon them and their actual activation in concrete cases as means to an end: a way to advance the goals, interests and values of international actors belonging to relevant political communities . . . In this context, rules on jurisdiction typically serve as the method by which the mandate providers and disputing parties control the space reserved for the court's judicial operations and, consequently, the extent of its functional utility.[43]

Similarly, Tai-Heng Cheng has suggested that there is a normative imperative for international courts to exercise prudence and caution when asserting their jurisdiction over a dispute.[44] Cheng observes that: 'Overreaching the legal authority of judges to decide disputes also overreaches their moral authority. It

[38] See eg V Lamm, *Compulsory Jurisdiction in International Law* (Edward Elgar, 2014).
[39] Malcolm Shaw (ed), *Rosenne's Law and Practice of the International Court* 5th edn (Brill/Nijhoff, 2016) vol II, 827.
[40] ibid.
[41] ibid.
[42] ibid 803.
[43] Y Shany, *Questions of Jurisdiction and Admissibility before International Courts* (CUP, 2015) 8.
[44] TH Cheng, *When International Law Works: Realistic Idealism After 9/11 and the Global Recession* (OUP, 2012) 173.

undermines the international constitutional structure that by design respects the autonomy of territorial communities organised as states.'[45]

Accordingly, an honest, realistic analysis of international courts' approach to jurisdictional issues should acknowledge that policy considerations *may* be a factor that those courts take into account. Sometimes they may operate as second-order consequentialist reasons, as Neil MacCormick called them.[46] Emphasis on the *may*. Jurisdictional decisions are often complex. The operation of international courts – and their reasoning – tends to be multi-causal. Saying that decisions on jurisdiction are always determined by policy considerations would be simplistic, risky and probably wrong. But that is different from saying that policy considerations may often *influence* jurisdictional decisions, particularly when, as I argue in chapter 4, the applicable rules of international procedural law are often sufficiently indeterminate to allow courts some flexibility as to their application.

To be clear, I am neither articulating nor supporting the view that jurisdictional rulings will *always* be motivated or determined purely based on policy considerations (much less purely *political* factors or expediency). Far from that. Nevertheless, while political or policy considerations may not be the *exclusive* determining factors of those decisions, they may often influence or play a role in them (either explicitly or implicitly). Critically, I also contend that the current structure of international adjudication and international procedural law permit this, as it provides international courts considerable (although not unfettered) discretion in the application of admissibility and jurisdictional doctrines. Accordingly, although it is impossible to make any categorical assertions, my argument is that, probabilistically and inferentially, it is more likely than not that policy considerations sometimes play a role in jurisdictional decisions. Say that, in some instances, there is at least a 60% probability of that being the case. To reiterate, I make this claim with some hesitation and, I hope, with sufficient epistemic humility.

The very structure of international procedural law – some of its core, inherent features – allows this. These are explained in more detail in chapter 4, but to summarise:

First, international procedural law is relatively indeterminate, both rationally and causally.[47] It is characterised by loose, relatively vague rules and principles, often developed by international courts or arbitral tribunals directly. As Palchetti observed in relation to the ICJ, the Court 'appears to enjoy a relatively wide freedom in procedural matters . . . [c]ommentators have long highlighted the freedom of action retained by the ICJ in procedural matters'.[48]

[45] ibid.

[46] N MacCormick, *Legal Reasoning and Legal Theory* (Clarendon Press, 1978) 101 ff.

[47] B Leiter, *Naturalizing Jurisprudence* (OUP, 2007).

[48] See eg P Palchetti, 'Making and Enforcing Procedural Law at the International Court of Justice' (2019) *Questions of International Law Questions de Droit International*; A Pellet and D Muller 'Article 38' in A Zimmermann, C Tams, K Oellers-Frahm and C Tomuschat (eds), *The Statute of the International Court of Justice: A Commentary* (OUP, 2019).

Second, the principle of *competence-competence*, which enables a court or tribunal to determine whether it has jurisdiction over a dispute. The ICJ has routinely observed that it is a matter for the Court itself – and not for the parties to a dispute – to determine whether it has jurisdiction and, importantly, the *extent* of that jurisdiction. This last issue is often overlooked. For instance, in *Fisheries Jurisdiction*, the Court held that: 'there is no burden of proof to be discharged in the matter of jurisdiction. Rather, it is for the Court to decide based on all the facts and arguments advanced by the Parties 'whether an intention on the part of the Parties exist to confer jurisdiction upon it'.[49]

Third, with some exceptions, mainly in the context of international criminal tribunals and in the World Trade Organization's dispute settlement mechanism, most international adjudication is structured as a single-instance proceeding. The result is that international courts' determination of their own jurisdiction often go unchallenged.

II. EXPRESS AVOIDANCE TECHNIQUES

This section analyses express avoidance doctrines. Illustrating the distinction between express and implied avoidance techniques is best done by first looking at how some express avoidance techniques operate under domestic law. After doing so, it considers how express avoidance doctrines have been applied by international courts – and explains why they may be inclined to rely on implied avoidance doctrines instead.

A. Express Avoidance Techniques Before Domestic Courts

Some avoidance techniques are applied expressly. This means that domestic courts apply them openly: the courts acknowledge that they are refraining from adjudicating a dispute, often because of its subject matter.[50] This is the case, for instance, with non-justiciability or the political question doctrine, where a court expressly says that it will refrain from deciding a dispute. These express avoidance techniques may be applied either before a decision on the merits is issued (i.e., by declining jurisdiction or considering a claim inadmissible) or when analysing the merits or the applicable remedies.[51] In the latter scenario, rather than declining jurisdiction over a dispute, the domestic court may simply acknowledge that there are issues that it will not adjudicate or to which it will

[49] *Fisheries Jurisdiction (Spain v Canada)*, ICJ, Judgment (Jurisdiction) of 4 December 1998 paras 37–38. This judgment summarises the Court's case law on the issue.

[50] For a comparative overview, see S Weill, *The Role of National Courts in Applying International Humanitarian Law* (OUP, 2014), particularly ch 2: 'The Avoiding Role of National Courts: Law as a Political Doctrine'.

[51] Delaney (n 1).

apply a deferential (sometimes *very* deferential) standard of review when so doing.[52]

That is not always the case. There are many instances where domestic courts *impliedly* or *covertly* apply avoidance techniques; that is, where they do not acknowledge that they are refusing to adjudicate a dispute for pragmatic or prudential reasons. In those cases, domestic courts tend to rely on other procedural and jurisdictional techniques, for example standing, mootness or ripeness.

Express avoidance techniques are more common before domestic courts than international ones. One potential explanation for this is that domestic courts have fewer institutional concerns regarding their legitimacy and may thus be more self-confident in applying express avoidance doctrines. Three examples, from the US, the UK and France show how *express* avoidance techniques operate.

First, the US Supreme Court's decision in *Goldwater v Carter*.[53] The Supreme Court relied on the political question doctrine to dismiss the claim.[54] The dispute was whether some members of Congress could issue legal proceedings on President Carter's decision to unilaterally terminate a joint defence treaty with Taiwan, a part of his policy of recognising the People's Republic of China. The claim was dismissed without oral argument. Writing for the plurality, Justice Rehnquist concluded that the question was non-justiciable, stating that:

> I am of the view that the basic question presented by the petitioners in this case is 'political,' and therefore nonjusticiable because it involves the authority of the President in the conduct of our country's foreign relations and the extent to which the Senate or the Congress is authorized to negate the action of the President . . .
>
> The controversy in the instant case is a nonjusticiable political question that should be left for resolution by the Executive and Legislative Branches of the Government.[55]

[52] Of course, some domestic courts, particularly apex courts, have some control over their docket, and that is a way of exercising ex ante avoidance by simply precluding a certain dispute from being adjudicated. Although this type of avoidance technique is implied insofar as those courts are not declaring that they are using docket control to avoid adjudicating that dispute, that is not the focus of the implied avoidance techniques discussed here, which concentrate on the somewhat flexible application of rules of international procedural law.

[53] *Goldwater v Carter* 444 US 996 (1979).

[54] For more detailed considerations of this decision, see CT Oliver, 'Goldwater v Carter: Crisis in American Constitutional Arrangements for the Conduct of International Relations Symposium: Goldwater v Carter' (1979–1980) 6 *Yale Studies in World Public Order* 11; E McGlynn Gaffney Jr, 'Goldwater v Carter: The Constitutional Allocation of Power in Treaty Termination Symposium: Goldwater v Carter' (1979–1980) 6 *Yale Studies in World Public Order* 81; H Konar, 'Termination of Treaties as a Political Question: The Role of Congress after Goldwater v Carter Comment' (1980–1981) 4 *Fordham International Law Journal* 81; KL Lawson, 'The Constitutional Twilight Zone of Treaty Termination: Goldwater v Carter Note' (1979–1980) 20 *Virginia Journal of International Law* 147; GM Miller, 'Treaty Termination under the United States Constitution: Reassessing the Legacy of Goldwater v Carter Notes' (1994–1995) 27 *New York University Journal of International Law and Politics* 859. More recently, Curtis Bradley and Eric Posner argue that, although the US Supreme Court is relatively reluctant to apply the political question doctrine, the doctrine is frequently applied by lower appellate courts: 'The Real Political Question Doctrine' (2023) 75 *Stanford Law Review* 1031.

[55] *Goldwater* (n 53) 1002–03 (Chief Justice Burger, Justices Stewart and Stevens concurring).

This passage shows how the Court was expressly relying on the subject matter of the dispute – the decision to terminate the joint defence treaty – as the basis for abstaining from deciding the case on the merits.

Second, the UK Supreme Court's decision in *'Maduro Board' of the Central Bank of Venezuela v 'Guaidó Board' of the Central Bank of Venezuela*.[56] This claim involved determining which of two rival boards of the Central Bank of Venezuela were entitled to control monetary gold stored in the Bank of England's vaults. For all practical purposes, the Maduro Government was the de facto government of Venezuela, as it exercised effective control over the territory. The UK and others considered the 2018 Venezuelan election in which Maduro claimed to have been re-elected president of Venezuela to be 'deeply flawed'.[57] Making an exception from its policy of recognising States (not governments) the UK recognised Mr Guaidó as interim president of Venezuela.[58] The question then was whether it was entitled to recognise and give effect to Mr Guaidó's executive acts, including the appointment of the Central Bank's board. The answer was: yes. The acts of a foreign executive were an issue which English courts would not address. Lord Lloyd-Jones held that there was a rule that 'courts in this jurisdiction will not adjudicate or sit in judgment on the lawfulness or validity under its own law of an executive act of a foreign state, performed within the territory of that state'.[59] The Court thus expressly stated that it would not adjudicate the dispute based on its subject matter.

Third, in the civil law context, the decision of the French *Conseil d'État* in Cases Nos 455744, 455745, and 455746.[60] The dispute involved the (chaotic) fall of Afghanistan to Taliban control and the evacuation at Kabul airport. Some Afghan nationals who had obtained international protection and were based in France requested the French administrative courts to order that their family members in Kabul be included in the repatriation flights being operated by the French military.[61]

The Conseil d'État refused to adjudicate the merits of that dispute. It considered that it was not possible to separate 'evacuation operations in a foreign

[56] *Maduro Board of the Central Bank of Venezuela v Guaidó Board of the Central Bank of Venezuela* [2021] UKSC 57.

[57] ibid paras 11–14.

[58] ibid para 18.

[59] ibid para 135. Note that at para 169 Lord Lloyd-Jones observed that the act of state doctrine 'can have no application, however, where courts in this jurisdiction merely give effect to a judicial decision whereby the courts of the foreign state concerned, acting within their proper constitutional sphere, have previously declared the executive acts to be unlawful and nullities.' The Court also observed that: 'The rule also has a sound basis in principle. It is founded on the respect due to the sovereignty and independence of foreign states and is intended to promote comity in inter-state relations.'

[60] Conseil d'État, Ord, 25 August 2021, 455744-455745-455746. See also A Jully, 'Propos orthodoxes sur l'acte de gouvernement' (2019) 43 *Civitas Europa* 165; G Durand, 'L'acte de gouvernement, l'exemple afghan' (2022) *Actualité juridique Collectivités territoriales* 111.

[61] Conseil d'État ibid paras 1–2.

territory from France's international relations'[62] and therefore concluded that French administrative courts lacked jurisdiction to adjudicate those issues.[63] This was based on the doctrine of *acte de gouvernement,* which provides that courts will not adjudicate on matters which concern some aspects of the conduction of foreign affairs. As the Conseil reiterated in that case: 'the evacuation of Afghan nationals from the Kabul airport . . . relates to the conduct of France's international affairs and thus falls outside the scope of the administrative judge's jurisdiction'.[64] Here, too, the Conseil d'État expressly claims that it is the subject matter of the dispute that keeps it from deciding it.

These courts all relied on *express* avoidance techniques: the political question doctrine, the act of state doctrine and the *actes de gouvernement* doctrine. In all three examples the courts referred to the subject matter of the dispute when declining to decide it, as they considered that they were not suitable for adjudication.

The theoretical underpinnings of those techniques vary. In the case of the political question doctrine, the theoretical basis is the separation of powers.[65] In the case of the act of state doctrine, it is either abstention, or an 'attitude of judicial reluctance to adjudicate issues involving foreign States'.[66] In the case of the *actes de gouvernement* doctrine, it is the notion of absolute jurisdictional immunity of some government conduct.[67] In all three cases the end result is the same: avoidance – an apex court abstaining from rendering a judgment on a sensitive issue.

B. Express Avoidance Techniques Before International Courts

There are fewer (recent) examples of international courts expressly relying on avoidance techniques to refrain from adjudicating the merits of a dispute.[68]

[62] ibid para 6 (my translation).

[63] ibid.

[64] ibid para 9 (my translation).

[65] See eg RE Barkow, 'More Supreme than Court? The Fall of the Political Question Doctrine and the Rise of Judicial Supremacy' (2002) 102 *Columbia Law Review* 237, 240, explaining that, historically: 'to the extent that a constitutional question raises questions . . . reasons to defer to the judgment of Congress and the Executive'.

[66] MV Newbury, 'Foreign Act of State – A Practical Guide' *Amicus Curiae* Series 2, No 1(1) 7. See also A Dickinson, 'Acts of State and the Frontiers of International Law' (2018) 14 *Journal of Private International Law* 1; Z Akhtar, 'Act of State, State Immunity and Judicial Review in Public International Law' (2016) 7(3) *Transnational Legal Theory* 354–82; M Alderton, 'The Act of State Doctrine: Questions of Validity and Abstention from Underhill to Habib' (2011) 12 *Melbourne Journal of International Law* 1.

[67] B Plessix, *Droit administratif général* 2nd edn (LexisNexis, 2018) para 301. See also S Roussel and C Nicolas, 'De l'injusticiabilité des actes de gouvernement' (2018) *Actualité Juridique Droit Administratif* 491.

[68] See eg Odermatt 'Patterns of Avoidance' (n 27) 234, observing that: 'International and regional courts employ a range of techniques to avoid politically sensitive questions. ICs are rarely upfront about this, and are reluctant to refrain from adjudicating because the dispute involves political, rather than legal, questions. Rather, ICs tend to avoid disputes in a more subtle fashion, relying

Writing about the ICJ, Rosenne observed that, when determining whether it had jurisdiction over a dispute, the Court 'has little freedom to decide whether to deal with a case' and that only 'essential deficiencies or overriding requirements of judicial propriety can lead it to refrain from determining a case'.[69] Based on the Court's track record, on first impression he would be right: there is only *one* judgment where, arguably, the Court refused to adjudicate a dispute based on what could be characterised as prudential reasons: *Northern Cameroons*.[70] Although the Court expressly admitted that it was abstaining from deciding the issue because of the subject matter of the dispute, it relied on the rather woollier principle of 'judicial propriety' to do so, rather than on other more categorical non-justiciability doctrines or other express avoidance doctrines.[71]

The *Northern Cameroons* case was controversial.[72] Sir Gerald Fitzmaurice, who was on the bench when it was decided, considered that it is 'almost unique in the annals of international litigation'.[73] The background of the case is well-known. To summarise, the claim arose under the Trusteeship Agreement for the Territory of the Cameroons under British Administration.[74] The territories were divided in two and placed under the League of Nations' mandate system. They were then transformed to trust territories after the creation of the UN and were administered by the UK and France, respectively.[75] In 1960, the French-administered territory became independent (the Republic of Cameroon).[76]

The British-administered territory was itself divided in two: the Northern and the Southern Cameroons.[77] The Northern Cameroons were administered from Nigeria.[78] In 1961 the UN organised two plebiscites. The Southern

---

on procedural rules to exclude a case . . . or resolving the dispute in a way that avoids the most politically sensitive questions and controversies.' One notorious exception is the issue of decisions taken under the EU's Common Foreign and Security Policy, some of which are expressly excluded from review by the Court of Justice of the European Union. See L Lonardo, 'How the Court Tries to Deliver Justice in Common and Foreign Security Policy, Where the Need for Judicial Protection Clashes with Principles of Conferral and Institutional Balance' (2024) 9 *European Forum* 830.

[69] S Rosenne, *The Law and Practice of the International Court, 1920–2005* (Brill, 2006) 804.

[70] See generally *Military and Paramilitary Activities in and Against Nicaragua (Nicaragua v United States of America)*, ICJ, Judgment of 27 June 1986, dissenting opinion of Judge Oda.

[71] Only one of the judges, Wellington Koo, expressly mentioned justiciability: *Northern Cameroons (Cameroon v United Kingdom)*, ICJ, Judgment (Preliminary Objections) of 2 December 1963, separate opinion of Judge Wellington Koo, stating at para 46 that: 'The interest which the Republic of Cameroon now claims to have cannot be of a legal character; it is only a political interest of its own.'

[72] *Northern Cameroons* (n 71). See also DHN Johnson, 'The Case concerning the Northern Cameroons' (1964) 13 *International and Comparative Law Quarterly* 1143; John R Stevenson, 'Case Concerning the Northern Cameroons (Cameroon v United Kingdom), Preliminary Objections' (1964) 58 *American Journal of International Law* 488; 'The Northern Cameroons Case' (1964) *Duke Law Journal* 550; G White, 'International Court of Justice: Judgment in Case concerning the Northern Cameroons. The Judicial Function' (1965) 23 *Cambridge Law Journal* 9.

[73] *Northern Cameroons* (n 71), separate opinion of Judge Fitzmaurice 98.

[74] Stevenson, Case Concerning the Northern Cameroons' (n 72) 489.

[75] *Northern Cameroons* (n 71) 22-24.

[76] ibid 23.

[77] ibid 22.

[78] ibid.

Cameroons voted to join the Republic of Cameroon; the Northern Cameroons voted to join Nigeria.[79] Two years before the plebiscite, the General Assembly had recommended that the UK should administer the Northern Cameroons independently (i.e., separately from Nigeria).[80] The UK did not do that. The Republic of Cameroon argued that, had the UK complied with the GA's recommendation, the plebiscite would have had a different result.[81]

Cameroon invited the UK to enter into a special agreement to submit the dispute to the Court.[82] The UK rejected that offer. So, Cameroon relied on the jurisdictional provision in the Trusteeship Agreement to initiate proceedings against the UK. Yet the Court, despite finding that it had been properly seised by Cameroon (i.e., that it had jurisdiction), essentially refused to exercise its jurisdiction on grounds of judicial propriety.[83] The Court held that:

> It is the act of the Applicant which seises the Court but even if the Court, when seised, finds that it has jurisdiction, the Court is not compelled in every case to exercise that jurisdiction. There are inherent limitations on the exercise of the judicial function which the Court, as a Court of justice, can never ignore . . . The Court itself, and not the parties, must be the guardian of the Court's judicial integrity.[84]

The main criticism of the Court's approach was the 'somewhat obscure' source of that principle, as Hugh Thirlway put it.[85] Indeed, there is no language in the Court's Statute – nor in the Court's rules – that expressly grants the Court discretion to decide whether to exercise its jurisdiction (or not).[86] Some, however, consider that international courts have an 'inherent jurisdiction' which allows them to 'exercise [ ] powers not expressly conferred on them'.[87] Judge Oda, for instance, considered that 'judicial propriety' gave the Court a 'prudential ground' to decline to adjudicate a case by declaring it non-admissible. I consider that view to be based on authority and correct.

Interestingly, most academic criticism of the Court's judgment tends to omit any reference to the *political context* of the Court's judgment.[88] A decision

[79] ibid 23.

[80] UNGA Res 1473 (XIV) (12 December 1959).

[81] ibid.

[82] L Gross, 'Limitations on the Judicial Function' (1964) 58 *American Journal of International Law* 415, 417.

[83] G Abi-Saab, *Les exceptions préliminaires dans la procédure de la Cour internationale* (1967); I Brownlie, 'The Justiciability of Disputes and Issues in International Relations' (1967) 42 *British Yearbook of International Law* 123.

[84] Northern Cameroons (n 71) 29.

[85] H Thirlway, 'The Law and Procedure of the International Court of Justice 1960–1989: Part Nine' (1998) 69 *British Yearbook of International Law* 1, 150.

[86] ibid.

[87] C Brown, *A Common Law of International Adjudication* (OUP, 2007) citing as examples the *competence-competence* principle and the possibility of addressing jurisdictional and admissibility objections separately from the merits.

[88] But see WM Reisman, *Nullity and Revision: The Review and Enforcement of International Judgments and Awards* (Yale University Press, 1971) 782: 'A declaratory judgment would indeed have been effective in the conventional sense of the term. In a more comprehensive sense, it would

on the merits from the Court would have concerned territory and population between two recently independent, post-colonial States, at a time of relative political instability involving the amalgamation of separate territories and populations. Further, the allocation of territory and population between both States had been achieved under the UN's auspices.

As the UK noted during oral argument, the Court, in reality, had before it a case 'affecting territories and people who have been incorporated in accordance with a decision of the General Assembly of the United Nations', as well as referenda, further asserting that those territories and peoples 'now form part of, and an integral and indivisible and indistinguishable part of, the Federation of Nigeria and the Federal Republic of Cameroon'.[89] Put simply, the UK highlighted that, because the Northern Cameroons had already voted for – and in fact had already been incorporated into Nigeria – it was no longer possible to judicially unscramble the egg.

The Court, unsurprisingly, did not place too much emphasis on this point in its judgment. But at the same time, it is hard to imagine that this issue did not at least partly influence the case's outcome. Although *Northern Cameroons* is an unpopular precedent, I consider it to be correct – or at least a deployment of an express avoidance technique. Justifying the Court's decision is easier once the dispute's political context is considered. From the point of view of promoting stability and minimum order in the region, the decision's consequences were positive. Test the point this way: would potentially questioning the results of a contentious plebiscite (or at least giving the disappointed party authoritative grounds to do so), in the context of two newly independent States, contribute to the stability of those two nascent States? Moreover, would the decision have been effective? Would it have been enforced (and, if so, how)? Would it had contributed to minimum order? The more likely answer to all those questions is: no.

Yet it is only in that very particular context that the Court felt it was able to expressly rely on an avoidance technique. In the 60 years since its judgment in *Northern Cameroons* it has not declined to adjudicate any other dispute on grounds of judicial propriety. In fact, I have not been able to identify *any* other decision from an international court that has declined jurisdiction on judicial propriety grounds.

C. International Courts' Reluctance to Apply Express Avoidance Techniques

Why has the Court repeatedly refused to rely on express avoidance techniques to abstain from deciding certain disputes? Why are there so surprisingly few examples of international adjudicators expressly invoking avoidance techniques?

have been highly ineffective, since it appeared likely to disrupt a local border regime with no probable gains for long-range world order.'

[89] *Northern Cameroons (Cameroon v United Kingdom)*, ICJ, Oral Proceedings, at 259 (argument of Sir John Hobson for the UK). This was, indeed, the UK's *main* argument in the proceedings.

In the case of the ICJ, the lack of more recent examples of the Court invoking express avoidance techniques is closely intertwined with its *declared* rejection (at least theoretically) of the relevance of policy or contextual considerations in the exercise of its jurisdiction. Many a respondent has raised the political or sensitive nature of the claim as a ground for the Court to refrain from adjudicating a dispute.[90] To name but a few: Turkey, in *Aegean Sea Continental Shelf*;[91] Iran, in *United States Diplomatic and Consular Staff in Tehran*;[92] the United States, in *Certain Iranian Assets*; [93] and Qatar, in *Appeal relating to the Jurisdiction of the ICAO Council*.[94] And all of them have failed. This is not a successful argument. The Court has expressly – and categorically – rejected that political aspects of disputes before it act as a bar to adjudication. Perhaps this is due to a (conceptually incorrect) tendency to equate express avoidance techniques with the US political question doctrine. In any event, in *Border and Transborder Armed Actions*,[95] the Court held that:

> [T]he Court is aware that political aspects may be present in any legal dispute brought before it. The Court, as a judicial organ, is however only concerned to establish, first, that the dispute brought before it is a legal dispute, in the sense of a dispute capable of being settled by the application of principles and rules of international law . . . The purpose of recourse to the Court is the peaceful settlement of such disputes; the Court's judgment is a legal pronouncement, and it cannot concern itself with the political motivation which may lead a State at a particular time or in particular circumstances, to choose judicial settlement.[96]

[90] Even in cases that deal with highly politicised issues – such as the Israel/Palestine conflict – the Court has been reluctant to invoke express avoidance doctrines.

[91] *Aegean Sea Continental Shelf (Greece v Turkey)*, ICJ, Judgment of 19 December 1978.

[92] *United States Diplomatic and Consular Staff in Tehran (United States of America v Iran)*, ICJ, Judgment of 24 May 1980.

[93] *Certain Iranian Assets (Iran v United States of America)*, ICJ, Judgment (Preliminary Objections) of 13 February 2019, para 36.

[94] Of course, perhaps the paradigmatic example would be the United States, in *Military and Paramilitary Activities* (n 70). But the symmetry of having Iran and the United States back-to-back on this list was too good to pass.

[95] *Border and Transborder Armed Actions (Nicaragua v Honduras)*, ICJ, Judgment of 20 December 1988. This has been considered as setting out the Court's 'final word' on the issue: C Tomuschat, 'Article 36' in A Zimmermann, C Tams, K Oellers-Frahm and C Tomuschat (eds), *The Statute of the International Court of Justice: A Commentary* (OUP, 2019) 645.

[96] *Border and Transborder Armed Actions* ibid para 52. This pronouncement has been cited in several other cases. See *Questions of Interpretation and Application of the 1971 Montreal Convention arising from the Aerial Incident at Lockerbie (Libyan Arab Jamahiriya v United Kingdom)*, ICJ, Judgment (Preliminary Objections) of 27 February 1998; *Questions of Interpretation and Application of the 1971 Montreal Convention arising from the Aerial Incident at Lockerbie (Libyan Arab Jamahiriya v United States of America)*, ICJ, Provisional Measures Order of 14 April 1992 para 123. In the preliminary objections phase of *Lockerbie*, the Court affirmed that the legal character of a dispute is sufficiently established when there is 'a disagreement on a point of law or fact, a conflict of legal views or of interests between two groups' in which 'the claim of one party is positively opposed by the other'. See also *Armed Activities in the Territory of the Congo (Congo v Uganda)*, ICJ, Judgment of 19 December 2005, para 26; *Application of the Interim Accord of 13 September 1995 (the former Yugoslav Republic of Macedonia v Greece)*, ICJ, Judgment of

Even Judge Xue – arguably one of the few judges to openly take a moderate or restrictive view of the scope of the Court's jurisdiction[97] – considered that the Court 'does not shy away from cases simply because they involve complicated political, military and other important aspects', further noting that those sensitive issues 'do not by themselves render a cases unjusticiable'.[98]

Throughout the Court's history, some judges (who are always in the minority; sometimes a minority of one) have expressly invoked, or at least referred, to the unsuitability of the subject matters of some disputes for adjudication. Consider, for instance, Judge Oda's dissenting opinion in *Military and Paramilitary Activities*. There, Judge Oda openly stated that the Court should have declined jurisdiction either on the basis of non-justiciability, as he did not consider the dispute to be a legal one, or on judicial propriety grounds.[99] Another example is Judge Gros in *Nuclear Tests* where, in his separate opinion, he said that the dispute before the Court was, in reality 'a conflict of political interests … clothed in the form of a legal dispute'[100] alluding to the classical distinction between political and legal disputes.[101] In their (much, and somewhat unfairly maligned) joint dissenting opinion in the *South West Africa* dispute, Judges Spender and Fitzmaurice also embraced the distinction between legal and political disputes, observing that the core of the dispute was one for which the 'proper forum' was 'unquestionably a technical or political one'.[102] More recently, also in a criticised dissent, Judge Sebutinde stated that she considered 'the dispute between the State of Israel and the people of Palestine is essentially and historically a political one, calling for a diplomatic or negotiated settlement'.[103]

---

5 December 2011, para 57; *Certain Iranian Assets* (n 93), para 36; *Appeal Relating to the Jurisdiction of the ICAO Council under Article 84 of the Convention on International Civil Aviation (Bahrain, Egypt, Saudi Arabia and United Arab Emirates v Qatar)*, ICJ, Judgment of 14 July 2020, para 48.

[97] *Obligations concerning Negotiations relating to Cessation of the Nuclear Arms Race and to Nuclear Disarmament (Marshall Islands v United Kingdom)*, ICJ, Judgment (Preliminary Objections) of 5 October 2016, see Declaration of Judge Xue. More recently, in *Application of the Convention on the Prevention and Punishment of the Crime of Genocide (The Gambia v Myanmar)*, ICJ, Judgment (Preliminary Objections) of 22 July 2022, Dissenting Opinion of Judge Xue, who considered that, although the Gambia's application had not been an abuse of process, the Court should have rejected the application on admissibility grounds including, possibly, on grounds of judicial propriety, para 9.

[98] Xue H, *Jurisdiction of the International Court of Justice* (Brill, 2017) 42. Interestingly, in a recent speech in London, Dame Rosalyn Higgins said – quite clearly – that 'simply not every major issue is suitable for litigation [before international courts]'. London Conference on International Law, Plenary 4: Taking Stock, 11 October 2022.

[99] *Military and Paramilitary Activities* (n 70), Dissenting Opinion of Judge Oda, paras 17–18.

[100] *Nuclear Tests (Australia v France)*, ICJ, Judgment (Preliminary Objections) of 20 December 1974, Separate Opinion of Judge Gros 296-97.

[101] As explored in detail in chapter 2.

[102] In this context, see also *South West Africa (Ethiopia v South Africa; Liberia v South Africa)*, ICJ, Judgment (Second Phase) of 18 July 1966, Dissenting Opinion of Judge Tanaka 250. *South West Africa (Ethiopia v South Africa; Liberia v South Africa)*, ICJ, Judgment (Preliminary Objections) of 21 December 1962, Dissenting Opinion of Judges Spender and Fitzmaurice, 466–67.

[103] See eg *Application of the Convention on the Prevention and Punishment of the Crime of Genocide in the Gaza Strip (South Africa v Israel)*, ICJ, Order of 26 January 2024, Dissenting Opinion of Judge Sebutinde, stating at para. 35: 'I reiterate that in my respectful opinion the dispute

Although there is some support in scholarship for the proposition that international courts have certain inherent powers, particularly when it comes to determining the admissibility of claims, to exercise some degree of case selection,[104] the Court has avoided taking a definitive view on this.[105] For instance, in *Alleged violations of the 1955 Treaty of Amity, Economic Relations, and Consular Rights,* in addition to disputing the Court's jurisdiction, the United States also raised arguments on admissibility.[106] It contended that, if it declared the case admissible, the Court would be compromising the integrity of its judicial function.[107] The United States alleged that the Court had the 'inherent power to decline to exercise its jurisdiction in order to protect the integrity of its judicial function'.[108] Yet the Court did not even bother to address that argument, focusing instead (and exclusively) on the abuse of process argument, which it ultimately rejected.[109]

In somewhat softer terms, the Court has taken a similar approach to its advisory jurisdiction. As explained previously, the wording used in the Court's Statute in relation to its jurisdiction to issue advisory opinions involves an element of discretion. While the Court *must* decide contentious cases, it '*may give*' an advisory opinion.[110] But even in that context, where the Statute undoubtedly grants the Court discretion to expressly abstain from issuing an advisory opinion, that option has not found favour. Not even at the start of the Court's life.

One early attempt to rely on that discretion was in the *Conditions of Admission of a State to Membership in the United Nations (Article 4 of the Charter)* advisory opinion.[111] In a joint dissenting opinion Judges Basdevant, Winiarski McNair, and Read (quite a formidable group) considered that, although entitled to give an advisory opinion, the Court should not have answered some of the questions posed to it (or it should not have answered them in the way it did). The joint dissenters were concerned that the majority's approach required the Court to delve into assessing political considerations – and that

between the State of Israel and the people of Palestine is essentially and historically a political one, calling for a diplomatic or negotiated settlement.'

[104] The most insightful one being Shany *Questions of Jurisdiction* (n 43), particularly chss 8 and 9.

[105] Some judges, however, have expressed their views on this in their separate or dissenting opinions. For example, in *Obligations concerning Negotiations relating to Cessation of the Nuclear Arms Race* (n 97) Judge Yusuf stated that the doctrine of non-justiciable disputes was a 'legal relic' that the UK had attempted to 'unearth', Dissenting Opinion of Judge Yusuf at para 11.

[106] *Alleged Violations of the 1955 Treaty of Amity, Economic Relations, and Consular Rights (Islamic Republic of Iran v United States of America),* ICJ, Judgment (Preliminary Objections) of 3 February 2021, para 85.

[107] ibid para 88.

[108] ibid.

[109] ibid paras 92–6.

[110] Article 65(1). The Court has highlighted this. See eg *Accordance with International Law of the Unilateral Declaration of Independence in Respect of Kosovo,* ICJ, Advisory Opinion of 22 July 2010, para 29 noting that the Court had discretion to give an advisory opinion 'so as to protect the integrity of the Court's judicial function and its nature as the principal judicial organ of the United Nations'.

[111] ICJ, Advisory Opinion of 28 May 1948 57.

such exercise was not compatible with the judicial function. They considered that the majority was attempting to provide 'a political consideration from a political point of view', something which, in their view, was an assessment that was 'not within the province of the Court'.[112] They further stated that asking 'the Court to assess the validity of any particular political consideration upon which a Member relies . . . is a political question and must not be answered'.[113] Yet the majority did not find those arguments persuasive.

Seventy-one years later, the Court is still as reluctant to invoke its discretion to refrain from issuing an advisory opinion. In *Legal Consequences of the Separation of the Chagos Archipelago from Mauritius in 1965*,[114] only one judge, Judge Donoghue, considered that the Court should have exercised its discretion to refrain from issuing an advisory opinion. In her dissenting opinion she criticised the majority for giving an advisory opinion in what, in her view (in my opinion, correctly), was essentially a bilateral dispute.[115] This approach, Judge Donoghue explained, 'signals that the advisory opinion procedure is available as a fallback mechanism to be used to overcome the absence of consent to jurisdiction in contentious cases'[116] and thus 'undermines the integrity of the Court's judicial function'.[117]

Other international courts have not taken a markedly different approach. For instance, in *Mexico – Soft Drinks*[118] the WTO's Appellate Body rejected the contention that, despite having jurisdiction over a dispute, it had an implied power to discretionarily refrain from exercising that jurisdiction.[119] Instead, the Appellate Body categorically stated that 'once jurisdiction has been validly established', WTO panels did not 'have the authority to decline to rule on the entirety of the claims that are before them in a dispute'.[120] No express avoidance techniques there.

[112] ibid. Dissenting Opinion of Judges Basdevant, Winiarski, McNair and Read, para 24.

[113] ibid.

[114] *Legal Consequences of the Separation of the Chagos Archipelago from Mauritius in 1965, Advisory Opinion*, ICJ, Advisory Opinion of 25 February 2019, Dissenting Opinion of Judge Donoghue 95.

[115] For cogent criticism of the (mis)use of advisory jurisdiction, see J Contesse, 'The Rule of Advice in International Human Rights Law' (2021) 115 *American Journal of International Law* 367; J Contesse, 'Judicial Interactions and Human Rights Contestations in Latin America' (2021) 12 *Journal of International Dispute Settlement* 271.

[116] *Legal Consequences of the Separation* (n 114), Dissenting Opinion of Judge Donoghue, para 23.

[117] ibid.

[118] *Mexico – Tax Measures on Soft Drinks and Other Beverages* (Appellate Body Report) WT/DS308/AB/R (6 March 2006) adopted 24 March 2006. See also W Davey & A Sapir, 'The Soft Drinks Case: The WTO and Regional Agreements' (2009) 8 *World Trade Review* 5; C Henckels, 'Overcoming Jurisdictional Isolationism at the WTO-FTA Nexus: A Potential Approach for the WTO' (2008) 19 *European Journal of International Law* 571; A Alvarez-Jimenez 'The WTO AB Report on Mexico – Soft Drinks, and the Limits of the WTO Dispute Settlement System' (2006) 33 *Legal Issues of Economic Integration*.

[119] Alvarez-Jimenez *Soft Drinks* (n 118) para 44.

[120] ibid para 46 and ss.

And investment tribunals have taken a similar approach.[121] To take just one example, consider *CMS Gas Transmission Company v Argentine Republic*, a case concerning economic measures Argentina took during a financial crisis. Argentina challenged the admissibility of the claims, arguing that the measures affecting the investor were not directed to it, but rather measures of 'general economic policy affecting the country as a whole'.[122] The Tribunal rejected that argument. Although it considered that issues of general economic policy were outside its jurisdiction, the Tribunal concluded that the measures fell within its jurisdiction if they violated specific treaty (or legislative) commitments given to the investor.[123]

Recently, there is one peculiar situation in the investment context where an ICSID annulment committee expressly invoked an avoidance technique. The annulment committee in *ConocoPhillips v Venezuela* was presented with the situation of which of the two competing governments of Venezuela had the authority to represent the State in the proceedings. The Committee refused to decide the point, on the basis that it was 'neither a political body nor the deliberative order of an International Organization' and, accordingly, it could not decide that issue.[124] Of course, the factual situation there was *particularly* unusual and so this approach should not be considered representative of a broader trend (which, as I have shown, goes in the opposite direction).

Finally, to mention a recent – and controversial – example, consider the International Criminal Court's Pre-Trial Chamber's decision on territorial jurisdiction in *Situation in the State of Palestine*.[125] To summarise, Palestine, shortly after acceding to the Rome Statute and accepting the ICC's jurisdiction, referred allegations of crimes committed in the West Bank and the Gaza Strip to the ICC. The Prosecutor then asked the Pre-Trial Chamber to determine the Court's territorial jurisdiction. This would require the Court to decide contested issues of sovereignty in the context of the Israel – Palestine conflict. Several participants in the proceedings (including *amici curiae* submissions by States) considered that the Pre-Trial Chamber should refrain from deciding that issue. For instance,

[121] A Reinisch, 'Necessity in Investment Arbitration' (2010) 41 *Netherlands Yearbook of International Law* 138, 141, noting that: 'Argentina has routinely raised the non-justiciability .... As a jurisdictional bar to ICSID cases. ICSID tribunals have not been willing to uphold such challenges.'

[122] *CMS Gas Transmission Company v Argentine Republic* (Decision on Jurisdiction) ICSID Case No ARB/01/8 (17 July 2003) para 23.

[123] ibid. Specifically, the Tribunal held at paras 26–27 that: '[Q]uestions of general economic policy not directly related to the investment, as opposed to measures specifically addressed to the operations of the business concerned, will normally fall outside the jurisdiction of the Centre. A direct relationship can, however, be established if those general measures are adopted in violation of specific commitments given to the investor in treaties, legislation or contracts. What is brought under the jurisdiction of the Centre is not the general measures in themselves but the extent to which they may violate those specific commitments.'

[124] *ConocoPhillips Petrozuata BV v Bolivarian Republic of Venezuela* (Annulment Proceeding) ICSID Case No ARB/07/30, Order on the Applicant's Representation (3 April 2020), para 29.

[125] *Situation in the State of Palestine* (Decision on the 'Prosecution request pursuant to article 19(3) for a ruling on the Court's territorial jurisdiction in Palestine') ICC-01/18-143 (5 February 2021).

Brazil stated that deciding the issue would involve a 'political use of the Rome Statute' and risked jeopardising the Court's 'own legitimacy and credibility',[126] concluding that the underlying dispute had to be 'addressed through political dialogue . . . and not through an international criminal process'.[127]

The Pre-Trial Chamber did not share that view. Rather, it brushed away the notion that the political context in which a dispute arose should influence the Chamber's exercise of its jurisdiction. The Chamber acknowledged that, given the nature of the crimes it had to address, cases before it 'arise from controversial contexts where political issues are sensitive and latent' but, the Chamber noted, it could not 'retreat when it is confronted with facts which might have arisen from political situations . . . but which also trigger legal and juridical issues'.[128]

As these cases show, it is most unusual for international courts and tribunals to expressly invoke avoidance techniques. Below I set out two potential explanations for this.

III. ARE EXPRESS AVOIDANCE TECHNIQUES STILL NECESSARY?

A superficial reading of the cases mentioned above would indicate that express avoidance techniques are no longer needed. It is easy to conclude that they are done, outdated, passé. A relic from before the Second World War. An anachronistic doctrine that we have evolved out of (although it is worth noting that some domestic courts have not even gone that far). This view suggests that international courts have completely eschewed express avoidance techniques and that, as a logical consequence, international courts consider that they are generally capable of adjudicating any dispute before them, regardless of context, political sensitivity, or subject matter. And it also implies that international courts have no discretion whatsoever, no flexibility, regarding the exercise of their jurisdiction. But in reality, that is not the case.

One possible explanation for the reduced relevance of express avoidance techniques is that the main underlying policy objective that those techniques were meant to ensure – namely, abstaining from deciding a particular dispute – is now satisfied by other means. The main one is the marked shift in how international courts approach the merits of the cases before them; the change in the standards of review they apply to determine the legality of State conduct. In other words, jurisdictional avoidance has given way to *in medio* or ex post avoidance, which focuses on how the merits of a dispute are addressed and what remedies, if any, are ordered. As Delaney explains, much avoidance takes place *during* proceedings (i.e., through deference in the substantive review of States'

[126] *Situation in the State of Palestine* (n 125), Brazil, 'Observations on ICC Territorial Jurisdiction in Palestine' para 10.

[127] ibid para 33.

[128] *Situation in the State of Palestine* (n 125), para 55.

conduct) or *after* proceedings, in terms of remedies.[129] Those *in medio* or ex post avoidance techniques are outside the scope of this book.

There have been some relatively recent changes as to how international courts assess the merits of disputes. To use investment arbitration as an example, consider the inherent flexibility of the Fair and Equitable Treatment standard. This evaluation rule is vague and indeterminate. It is perfectly plausible that different tribunals, analysing exactly the same facts, would reach diametrically opposed conclusions[130] and thus a tribunal that was minded to avoid deciding a case related to a sensitive policy issue could find it easier to find there has been no FET breach rather than declining jurisdiction.[131] Or consider how some international courts apply different standards of review depending on the subject matter of a dispute, applying more deferential standards in disputes that are considered to touch issues that are more politically sensitive.[132] Two developments illustrate this point. The first is the 'procedural turn' at the European Court of Human Rights. The second is the increased use of exception clauses in investment treaties. These examples are only meant to be illustrative.

Additionally, there are other reasons why the reduction of the use of non-justiciability doctrines is positive. As King explains 'the precedential force of a non-justiciability finding can be extremely strong and potentially sweeping'.[133] By excluding further disputes that fall within the subject matter held to be non-justiciable, there is a risk of creating legal blackholes or areas of unaccountability.[134] In contrast with avoidance techniques, that are applied essentially on a case-by-case basis, a declaration of non-justiciability has potentially much stronger forward-facing effects, as it may operate to exclude an entire category of cases.

A. The Procedural Turn at the European Court of Human Rights

The 2010s were not an easy decade for the ECtHR. The Strasbourg Court was under pressure.[135] Several States had openly said that they wished to see the

[129] Delaney, *Analyzing Avoidance* (n 1) 15–16. See also Fouchard (n 8), arguing that the ICJ adopts a flexible approach to the applicable standard of review in part as an *in medio* avoidance technique.

[130] See eg C McLachlan, L Shore and M Weiniger, *International Investment Arbitration: Substantive Principles* 2nd edn (OUP, 2017); WM Reisman, 'Canute Confronts the Tide: States versus Tribunals and the Evolution of the Minimum Standard in Customary International Law' (2015) 30 *ICSID Review* 616.

[131] Of course, an ephemeral arbitral tribunal's institutional concerns and incentives are markedly different from those of a standing court, which may also affect whether they consider they need to rely on avoidance techniques.

[132] Fouchard (n 8).

[133] JA King, 'Institutional Approaches to Judicial Restraint' (2008) 28 *Oxford Journal of Legal Studies* 421.

[134] ibid.

[135] So has the Inter-American Court of Human Rights. Consider, for instance, the joint statement from the governments of Argentina, Brazil, Chile, Colombia and Paraguay submitted to the Inter-American Commission on Human Rights on 23 April 2019.

ECtHR's role to be more limited.[136] In addition to a series of declarations regarding the Court,[137] member States agreed to, and adopted, Protocol 15[138] which included an amendment to the European Convention's preamble that added an express reference to the principle of subsidiarity and the margin of appreciation doctrine.[139] Even before Protocol 15 entered into force, then president Róbert Spanó had declared that the Court was entering into an 'age of subsidiarity'.[140] Put bluntly, this means that the Strasbourg Court will move to the backseat – whilst domestic courts were back in the driver's seat.[141] In short, the procedural turn involves the Strasbourg Court focusing more on 'domestic procedures when determining the merits of a case', which includes an assessment of the quality of the domestic decision-making processes that influences the Court's review of the merits of cases.[142] As Jackson explains, the procedural turn involves a 'form of deference to national authorities'.[143]

[136] Jackson (n 4) 113.

[137] Convention for the Protection of Human Rights and Fundamental Freedoms (European Convention on Human Rights) (4 November 1950) 213 UNTS 222 (ECHR); Interlaken Declaration of the High Level Conference on the Future of the European Court of Human Rights (19 February 2010). Available at: www.coe.int/t/dgi/brighton-conference/Documents/Interlaken-declaration_en.pdf; Brighton Declaration (20 April 2012); www.echr.coe.int/Documents/2012_Brighton_FinalDeclaration_ENG .pdf; Brussels Declaration (27 March 2015); www.echr.coe.int/Documents/Brussels_Declaration _ENG.pdf; Copenhagen Declaration (13 April 2018). Available at: www.echr.coe.int/Documents /Copenhagen_Declaration_ENG.pdf.

[138] Protocol No 15 amending the Convention for the Protection of Human Rights and Fundamental Freedoms, CETS No 213.

[139] On the principle of subsidiarity, see eg R Spano, 'Universality or Diversity of Human Rights – Strasbourg in the Age of Subsidiarity' (2014) 14 *Human Rights Law Review* 487; R Spano, 'The Future of the European Court of Human Rights: Subsidiarity, Process-Based Review and the Rule of Law' (2018) 18 *Human Rights Law Review* 473; MI Vila, 'Subsidiarity, Margin of Appreciation and International Adjudication within a Cooperative Conception of Human Rights' (2017) 15 *International Journal of Constitutional Law* 393. On the margin of appreciation doctrine, see eg G Letsas, 'Two Concepts of the Margin of Appreciation' (2006) 26 *Oxford Journal of Legal Studies* 705; HC Yourow, *The Margin of Appreciation Doctrine in the Dynamics of Human Rights Jurisprudence* (The Hague, Kluwer Press, 1996); Y Arai-Takahashi, *The Margin of Appreciation Doctrine and the Principle of Proportionality in the Jurisprudence of the European Court of Human Rights* (Intersentia, 2002); E Benvenisti, 'Margin of Appreciation, Consensus and Universal Standards' (1998–99) 31 *New York University Journal of International Law and Politics* 843. In the Inter-American context, see S Bertelsen, 'A Margin for the Margin of Appreciation: Deference in the Inter-American Court of Human Rights' (2021) 19 *International Journal of Constitutional Law* 887.

[140] Spano, *The Future of the European Court of Human Rights* (n 139). See also OM Arnardóttir, 'Organised Retreat? The Move from "Substantive" to "Procedural" Review in the ECtHR's Case Law on the Margin of Appreciation' (2015) 4 *European Society of International Law Conference Paper Series*; J Gerards and E Brems (eds), *Procedural Review in European Fundamental Rights Cases* (CUP, 2017); T Kleinlein, 'The Procedural Approach of the European Court of Human Rights: Between Subsidiarity and Dynamic Evolution' (2019) 68 *International and Comparative Law Quarterly* 91; P Popelier, 'Procedural Rationality Review after Animal Defenders International: A Constructively Critical Approach' (2019) 15 *European Constitutional Law Review* 272.

[141] Current debates regarding the open letter, dated 22 May 2025, that nine States, led by Denmark and Italy, sent the European Court of Human Rights in relation to migration issues are another example of potential backlash: 'Open letter to the European Court of Human Rights on migration' (22 May 2025).

[142] Kleinlein 'The Procedural Approach of the European Court of Human Rights' (n 140) 91.

[143] Jackson (n 4) 113.

Consider one case to illustrate how the procedural turn operates: *Belcacemi and Oussar v Belgium*. The case concerned Belgium's blanket ban on face coverings – a controversial, politically sensitive topic. The Strasbourg Court had previously upheld a similar ban in France.[144] It also decided to uphold the Belgian ban. When analysing the need for that restriction in a democratic society, the Court started by reiterating that its role was 'fundamentally subsidiary', as 'national authorities have direct democratic legitimacy regarding the protection of human rights'.[145] When considering whether to exercise control of conventionality, the Strasbourg Court focused on the '*decisional process*' through which the face-covering ban was enacted, noting that it was a process that had taken 'several years', had been characterised by a 'long debate' in parliament and had been reviewed by the Belgian constitutional court.[146]

Belcacemi shows two things. First, how the Strasbourg Court's reasoning focused on *procedural* aspects (i.e., the process through which the State decided to adopt the measure; the quality of the decision-making that led to its implementation) rather than on the substantive merits of the decision. Ultimately, the ECtHR deferred to domestic political institutions. Second, based on the (revised and laxer) standard of review that was applied, how was the ECtHR able to be deferential to the internal political processes of the respondent State. In short, the European Court's application of this more deferential standard of substantive review thus allows it some flexibility. That means that the Court can rely on those techniques to avoid rendering decisions that could threaten its institutional credibility, risk a backlash, or are likely to be ineffective or remain unenforced.

B. The Increased Use of Internal Exceptions in Investment Treaties

The ECtHR has not been the only international court to have recently faced some backlash. Investment arbitration has received its fair share, too.[147] One

[144] *SAS v France* App no 43835/11 (ECtHR (GC), 1 July 2014).

[145] *Belcacemi and Oussar v Belgium* App no 37798/13 (ECtHR, 11 July 2017) para 51 (my translation).

[146] ibid para 54 (my translation).

[147] There is abundant literature on this topic. See eg M Waibel and others (eds), *The Backlash Against Investment Arbitration: Perceptions and Reality* (Kluwer, 2010); D Ma, 'A BIT Unfair: An Illustration of the Backlash against International Arbitration in Latin America' (2012) *Journal of Dispute Resolution* 571; D Caron and E Shirlow, 'Dissecting Backlash: The Unarticulated Causes of Backlash and its Unintended Consequences' in Geir Ulfstein and Andreas Føllesdal (eds), *The Judicialization of International Law: A Mixed Blessing?* (2018); M Langford, D Behn and OK Fauchald, 'Backlash and State Strategies in International Investment Law' in T Gammeltoft-Hansen and T Aalberts (eds), *The Changing Practices of International Law: Sovereignty, Law and Politics in a Globalising World* (2018); M Langford and D Behn, 'Managing Backlash: The Evolving Investment Treaty Arbitrator?' (2018) 29 *European Journal of International Law* 551; G Dimitropoulos, 'The Conditions for Reform: A Typology of "Backlash" and Lessons for Reform in International Investment Law and Arbitration' (2020) 18 *The Law and Practice of International Courts and Tribunals* 416; TL Berge, 'Dispute by Design? Legalization, Backlash, and the Drafting of Investment Agreements' (2020) 64 *International Studies Quarterly* 919.

of the main criticisms levied against investment arbitration is that it curtails States' rights to regulate in the public interest – and that it lacks legitimacy to do so.[148] Neither general international law nor the text of the (relatively) traditional, (relatively) standard investment treaties afford States much flexibility in this regard. The difficulty in successfully invoking necessity to justify certain measures that may have impacted a foreign investor's rights is but one example of this.[149]

This has been one of the causes for an increase in the addition of internal exception provisions in international investment agreements.[150] In the investment context, the most common exceptions are: general exceptions (i.e., broad-based exceptions based on Article XX of the GATT), non-precluded measures provisions (i.e., provisions that expressly allow the State to implement certain measures); essential security clauses; and general public health exceptions.[151] In some cases, these clauses are self-judging,[152] meaning that they allow States *themselves* to decide whether they do not need to comply with their treaty obligations.[153]

Paddeu and Waibel have analysed recent investment agreements and conclude that, despite starting from a low base, 'States have increasingly included internal exceptions in their investment treaties in the decade 2010-20'.[154] By including self-judging clauses in their treaties, States are, for all practical purposes, giving themselves the authority to remove the issues covered by the self-judging clauses from judicial scrutiny – at their own discretion.[155] Essentially, self-judging clauses allow the respondent State in a dispute – rather

[148] M Sornarajah, 'Right to Regulate and Safeguards' in UNCTAD (ed), *The Development Dimension of Foreign Direct Investment: Policy and Rule-Making Perspectives* (2003) United Nations 205; C Titi, *The Right to Regulate in International Investment Law* (Nomos/Hart, 2014); A von Bogdandy and I Venzke, *In Whose Name? A Public Law Theory of International Adjudication* (OUP, 2014); C Henckels, 'Indirect Expropriation and the Right to Regulate: Revisiting Proportionality Analysis and the Standard of Review in Investor-State Arbitration' (2012) 15 *Journal of International Economic Law* 223; V Korzun, 'The Right to Regulate in Investor-State Arbitration: Slicing and Dicing Regulatory Carve-outs' (2017) 50 *Vanderbilt Journal of Transnational Law* 355; G Zarra, 'Right to Regulate, Margin of Appreciation and Proportionality: Current Status in Investment Arbitration in Light of *Philip Morris v Uruguay*' (2017) 14 *Brazilian Journal of International Law* 95.

[149] C Binder, 'Necessity Exceptions, the Argentine Crisis and Legitimacy Concerns: Or the Benefits of a Public International Law Approach to Investment Arbitration' in T Treves, F Seatzu and S Trevisanut, *Foreign Investment, International Law and Common Concerns* (Taylor & Francis, 2013).

[150] For a general overview of exceptions, see L Bartels and F Paddeu (eds), *Exceptions in International Law* (OUP, 2020).

[151] F Paddeu and M Waibel, 'Necessity 20 Years On: The Limits of Article 25' (2022) 37 *ICSID Review – Foreign Investment Law Journal* 160.

[152] KP Sauvant, M Ong, K Lama and T Petersen, 'The Rise of Self-Judging Essential Security Interest Clauses in International Investment Agreements' (2016) *Columbia FDI Perspectives* No 188.

[153] S Schill and R Briese, '"If the State Considers": Self-Judging Clauses in International Dispute Settlement' (2009) 13 *Max Planck Yearbook of United Nations Law* 61, 63.

[154] ibid.

[155] E Shirlow, *Judging at the Interface: Deference to State Decision-Making Authority in International Adjudication* 116 (CUP, 2021) 116.

than the adjudicator – to decide whether the subject matter of the dispute is suitable for adjudication. In my view, this represents a partial case of dejudicialisation, whereby States decide that they want to withdraw a certain issue from the purview of international courts.

In short, these examples show that international courts have been developing other avoidance techniques particularly aimed at how they assess the merits of a dispute. These techniques often involve withdrawing certain issues from international adjudication (partial dejudicialisation) or applying a standard of review that is more deferential to States. These techniques achieve a similar objective to avoidance techniques. Their development may also partly explain why international courts seldom apply express avoidance techniques.

IV. IMPLIED AVOIDANCE TECHNIQUES

Another possibility is that international courts are still functionally applying avoidance techniques – but that they are doing so covertly or impliedly. Put simply, the proposition is that although international courts do not normally *expressly admit* that they are applying avoidance techniques, for all practical purposes they are still doing so *impliedly*. The way they do this is through the flexible (some would say, manipulated or distorted)[156] application of admissibility and jurisdictional principles and doctrines in a way that allows them to decline jurisdiction over a case or issue or declare it inadmissible. This results in jurisdictional avoidance as it allows the international court to abstain from deciding a particular case or issue.[157]

Chapter 5 of this book explains in detail how international courts have, I argue, applied implied avoidance doctrines. This section addresses two issues. First, it sets out some theories that could explain the implied application of avoidance doctrines. Second, it sets out a contingent normative justification for the use of implied avoidance doctrines.

A. Theoretical Explanations

The main overarching theoretical explanation for why international courts could be applying avoidance doctrines impliedly is scepticism about the rational and causal impact of doctrine, as elaborated by the different realist theories. To grossly summarise: the main premise is that 'the rules and principles that

[156] For criticism, see Gunther, *The Subtle Vices* (n 32).

[157] I have initially set out some thoughts on this point in M Casas, 'Functional Justiciability and the Existence of a Dispute: A Means of Jurisdictional Avoidance?' (2019) 10 *Journal of International Dispute Settlement* 599. I would like to believe my thinking has become slightly more nuanced since then.

judges recite in their opinions do not reveal the real reasons and motives for their decisions or reveal them incompletely'.[158] There are two additional cognate theoretical frameworks that may be helpful. The first is the distinction between the myth system and the operational code in international law. The second is the lack of judicial candour.

First, accepting the possibility that avoidance techniques are applied impliedly is easier when the issue is analysed through the New Haven lens. Under this framework, a distinction between international law's 'myth system' and its 'operational code' is accepted, even assumed.[159] Although conceptually distinct, this dichotomy is reminiscent of Roscoe Pound's observation, made over 100 years ago, regarding the distinction between the law-in-the-books (i.e., what the law prescribes, as determined in statutes) and the law-in-action (i.e., how the law is actually applied in practice).[160]

In Reisman's view, the myth system and the operational code are 'two 'relevant' normative systems: one which is supposed to apply and which continues to enjoy lip service among elites and one which is actually applied'.[161] The existence of an operational code does not negate the existence of law. Reisman is careful to clarify that the application of an operational code does not mean that 'there is no law' or that those are areas where 'anything goes.' His framing is more nuanced. He explains that the 'myth system' is not necessarily a legal fiction:

> [T]he myth system is not widely appreciated as consciously false. It does not express values that are obsolete. On the contrary: it affirms values that continue to be important socially and personally. Although not applied in the 'jurisdiction' of the operational code, the myth system may yet influence decision-making.
>
> Precisely because discrepancies between myth system and operational code can erode the credibility of the myth system, maintenance of belief in the myth system is a dynamic process requiring ongoing contributions from many. By contrast, those who practise the operational code try to obscure it from the general public. But there is an almost symbiotic relationship between myth system and operational code, with the latter providing a degree of suppleness and practicality that the myth system could not achieve without changing much of its content and procedure of application.[162]

This observation, intended for the broader field of international law, is particularly apposite to international adjudication. The main premise of the myth system is that, in international law, things are not necessarily what they seem. '[M]uch formal law', Reisman argues, 'will not only <u>not</u> be effectively enforced,

[158] B Leiter, 'Legal Realisms, Old and New' (2013) 47 *Valparaiso University Law Review* 949, 954.

[159] This idea was initially developed in WM Reisman, 'Myth System and Operational Code' (1977) 3 *Yale Studies in World Public Order* 229.

[160] R Pound, 'Law in Books and Law in Action' (1910) 44 *American Law Review* 12, 12–13.

[161] Reisman, 'Myth System' (n 159) 230.

[162] ibid.

but its violation will be accepted by those charged with operating it'.[163] The myth system, for example, manifests itself in international courts' categorical and adamant rejection of express avoidance techniques. This rejection is best illustrated by the ICJ's statement in *Diplomatic and Consular Staff in Teheran* (and repeated in several other cases), where the Court brushed aside the contention that it should avoid deciding politically sensitive issues.[164] Another way the myth system manifests itself is in the rejection of any limits to the international judicial function, i.e., the view that international adjudication is capable of solving many intractable international problems. Reisman characterises this view as incurable judicial romanticism, stating that those who hold those views:

> [L]ook to courts as a type of deus ex machina, ready to descend, upon the mere utterance of some juridical incantations that summon forth mysterious powers inherent in the law, to bring order and justice to the most untidy, even violent political situations. Many judicial romantics subconsciously transpose some of the powerful emotive affects of the symbol 'courts' in municipal systems, where they have been significant struts of public order, to radically different environments. This transfer can be disappointing and even dangerous. A court, by itself, is only a college of people. Its power in any setting derive form a political process, of which it is a part, and which enfranchises it.[165]

This incurable judicial romanticism, often oblivious to the limitations on the international judicial function, expressed itself (quite forcefully) in some of the dissenting opinions in the *Marshall Islands* case.[166] Consider, for instance, Judge Robinson's strong condemnation of what he considered the Court's acceptance of its 'irrelevance . . . in the settlement of disputes that implicate highly sensitive issues such as nuclear disarmament'.[167] Given the importance of the role that nuclear weapons play in States' national security,[168] and the geopolitical

[163] ibid 232. The concept of the myth system is cognate to the notion of the expressive function of the law. This approach highlights the function of the law in 'making statements' (understood as conveying certain normative information), in contradistinction with the function of 'controlling behaviour directly', see C Sunstein, 'On the Expressive Function of Law' (2021) 144 *University of Pennsylvania Law Review* 2022, 2024.

[164] *United States Diplomatic and Consular Staff* (n 92) 20. Reiterated in *1955 Treaty of Amity* (n 106) para 55. The Court held that 'never has the view been put forward before that, because a legal dispute submitted to the Court is only one aspect of a political dispute, the Court should decline to resolve for the parties the legal questions at issue between them'. The Court made a similar statement in *Military and Paramilitary Activities* (n 70), where it held that it had 'never shied away from a case . . . merely because it had political implications', 439–40.

[165] WM Reisman, 'The Constitutional Crisis in the United Nations' (1993) 87 *American Journal of International Law* 83, 94.

[166] See eg *Obligations concerning Negotiations* (n 97), Dissenting Opinion of Judge Cançado Trindade; Dissenting Opinion of Judge Robinson.

[167] ibid Dissenting Opinion of Judge Robinson, para 70.

[168] See eg KN Waltz and SD Sagan, *The Spread of Nuclear Weapons: An Enduring Debate* 3rd edn (WW Norton & Company, 2012); SD Sagan, *The Limits of Safety: Organizations, Accidents, and Nuclear Strategy* 4th edn (Palgrave Macmillan, 2019); and T Schelling, *The Strategy of Conflict* (Yale University Press, 1966; reissued 2008). See also S Ranganathan, 'Nuclear Weapons and the Court' (2017) 111 *AJIL Unbound* 88.

complexity of the issue of nuclear disarmament, it is either disingenuous or, worse, presumptuous, to consider that the Court's *ipse dixit* would have sufficed to magically sort the issue.

The operational code, in contrast, acknowledges that there are some avoidance techniques being applied in international adjudication and, moreover, that those avoidance techniques are being applied impliedly rather than expressly. Put simply, acknowledging that there is an operational code – and that it operates in parallel to the strictly formal, textual reading of the rules on jurisdiction and admissibility – opens the possibility to considering that international courts may *sometimes* exercise *some* discretion when determining whether to uphold jurisdiction over *some* disputes (or *some* parts of it) and that they do so by relying on the inherent flexibility of some procedural doctrines. When determining whether to exercise those implied avoidance techniques, international courts may take into account contextual and policy factors – prudential factors, in the Bickelian sense – including: the political sensitivity of the dispute and its subject matter; the potential risk for the international court's legitimacy and authority, including the potential to generate backlash; the broader political and diplomatic context; and compliance risks/the risk of outright defiance or non-enforcement.[169] Unlike purely doctrinal approaches, which would consider these extra-legal issues that should be ignored, under the New Haven approach these are a valid – albeit far from exclusive – element of legal analysis.

Again, it is important to stress the moderate, probabilistic and inferential nature of this proposition. And again, it is also important to emphasise that the possibility that, in some instances, international courts may consider these policy-contextual factors does not mean that those are the *only* factors they consider or that they are outcome-determinative or entirely causal. The position adopted is moderately realistic, but without being entirely rule sceptical or nihilistic. As explained in more detail in chapter 4, the relative, inherent indeterminacy of international procedural law leads to *rational* and *causal* indeterminacy in some – but critically, not in *all* – cases. Conversely, that these policy factors are not always considered or, when considered, that they are not always determinative of the outcome does not mean that they may not in some circumstances do so.

The second theoretical basis for implied avoidance doctrines is the literature on judicial candour (and lack thereof): in short, the view that judicial opinions are not 100% candid. One of the strongest criticisms of Bickel's invitation for courts to deploy the passive virtues was the lack of candour such approach requires. Bickel's view of the passive virtues, one critic contends, 'actually requires the Justices to lie'.[170] '[F]idelity to law', David Shapiro said, could only be 'fairly measured only if [the judges] believe what they say in their opinions,'

[169] When analysing which issues influence the ICJ's application of different standards of review, Fouchard considers that four categories are relevant (n 8).

[170] Hellman 'The Importance of Appearing Principled' (n 35).

concluding therefore that the 'obligation to candor is absolute'.[171] Framed that way, the suggestion that some judgments may not be entirely candid may come across as shocking.

But is it? Are we to believe that courts – either domestic or international – are fully transparent in their reasoning, all the time? My intuitionistic view: of course not. One of the main ideas I aim to articulate in this book is that there are some *esoteric* or Straussian elements, some subtext, in some judicial decisions – including decisions on jurisdiction and admissibility. In those decisions a court's reasoning is neither entirely transparent nor candid. An international court's ruling may imply some underlying reasoning – including the consideration of supposedly extra-legal factors –that can only be deciphered by reading between the lines. To paraphrase Dickinson's poem: the reasons are there, only that they have been told slant, as they are 'too bright for our infirm Delight'.[172]

More broadly, this approach to interpretation is not novel (including because it is one of the core claims of legal realism).[173] John Dugard, for instance, briefly mentions this possibility in an excellent article on the Court's *Nuclear Tests* cases. There, he suggests that the majority was influenced by the view that the dispute at hand was 'political' and therefore . . . nonjusticiable' and that such notion was the 'silent inspiration for the decision'.[174] Yet he does not elaborate further on what he means by 'silent inspiration'. Similarly, Marko Milanovic, commenting on some ECtHR decisions, observes that 'the Court's policy-driven motivations behind it are entirely transparent' and that the Court was 'fearful of political backlash' that may arise from some decisions based on the use of force, to the point that it considered them an 'existential danger' and, in consequence, it wanted to 'avoid dealing with as much as it is possible to do so'.[175] In domestic law, particularly in the US, the idea that judgments may not be completely candid has been considered in detail. By 1881 Oliver

[171] DL Shapiro, 'In Defense of Judicial Candor' (1987) 100 *Harvard Law Review* 731, 750. For a similar view, SC Idleman, 'Prudential Theory of Judicial Candor' (1994–95) 73 *Texas Law Review* 1307; M Schwartzman, 'Judicial Sincerity' (2008) 94 *Virginia Law Review* 987, 102, stating: 'Because judges wield the power of the state, they must show that their decisions are justified according to the law.' For a good summary of the literary defending judicial candor, see S Zeppos, 'Judicial Candor and Statutory Interpretation' (1989) 78 *Georgetown Law Journal* 353. But Zeppos himself is not completely convinced that judicial candour is an absolute obligation.

[172] *The Poems of Emily Dickinson: Reading Edition* (The Belknap Press of Harvard University Press, 1998) 1263. For a recent expansive work on the broader issue of secrecy in international law, see J d'Aspremont, *The Epistemology of the Secret: International Law as Revelation* (CUP, 2025).

[173] Even when an international law scholar like Robert Howse addresses Strauss' esoterisms, he is focused on the philosophical aspect of the doctrine rather than how it potentially applies to international courts, see R Howse, 'Reading Between the Lines: Exotericism, Esotericism, and the Philosophical Rhetoric of Leo Strauss' (1999) 32 *Philosophy and Rhetoric* 60. See also R Howse, *Leo Strauss Man of Peace* (CUP, 2014) presenting a (I would say fair) re-evaluation of Strauss' views as aligned with peace and international law.

[174] J Dugard, 'The Nuclear Tests Cases and the South West Africa Cases: Some Realism About the International Judicial Decision' (1976) 16 *Virginia Journal of International Law* 463, 488.

[175] M Milanovic, 'Georgia v Russia No 2: The European Court's Resurrection of Bankovic in the Contexts of Chaos' (EJIL:Talk!, 25 January 2021).

Wendell Holmes had written about how the 'very considerations that judges most rarely mention', namely, expedience, were the 'secret room from which the law draws all the juices of life'.[176] And this idea was well developed by Bickel and afterwards. Before addressing that, it is best to briefly address the concept of esoteric writing more broadly.[177]

The contemporary thinker most closely associated with esotericism is Leo Strauss, who developed this concept in his essay *Persecution and the Art of Writing*.[178] Strauss considers that in a fair amount of philosophical writing 'the truth about all crucial things is presented exclusively between the lines'.[179] Strauss considers that there are two modalities of writing: *exoteric* and *esoteric*. The distinction between these two modalities, Klein explains, is that: 'with her text, an author offers certain ideas or meanings, the exoteric ones, that are explicit, obvious, or apparent, and between the lines offers additional or other meanings, the esoteric ones', thus Klein concludes that the 'distinction implies a multiplicity of interpretations, obvious and nonobvious'.[180]

To simplify, Strauss' core claim is that the true (hidden) meaning of some texts is only discoverable by very careful, close reading. According to Strauss, the hidden or esoteric meaning is only visible 'after very long, never easy, but always pleasant work'.[181] Strauss provides some guidance as to how to approach this 'always pleasant' exercise:[182]

> Reading between the lines is strictly prohibited in all cases where it would be less exact than not doing so. Only such reading between the lines as starts from an exact consideration of the explicit statements of the author is legitimate. The context in which a statement occurs . . . must be perfectly understood before an interpretation of the statement can reasonably claim to be adequate or even correct. One is not entitled to delete a passage, nor to emend its text, before one has fully considered all reasonable possibilities of understanding the passage as it stands.[183]

[176] OW Holmes Jr, *The Common Law* (Belknap Press, 2009), particularly Lecture I.

[177] See eg PJ Bagley, 'On the Practice of Esotericism' (1992) 53 *Journal of the History of Ideas* 231.

[178] The reference to Strauss is limited to his approach to the interpretation of texts – and nothing else. I invite the reader not to assume that the reference to Strauss' approach to textual interpretation implies approval of Strauss' views on other topics (or of his followers; some of which are a bit too fond of military intervention – and potentially misread Strauss, see Howse 'Reading Between the Lines' (n 173)). See also: Jane Psmith and John Psmith, 'Joint Review: Philosophy Between the Lines, by Arthur M. Melzer' (*Mr and Mrs Psmith's Bookshelf*, 26 Jan 2026). Available at: www.thepsmiths.com/p/joint-review-philosophy-between-the.

[179] L Strauss, *Persecution and the Art of Writing* (University of Chicago Press, 1988) 25.

[180] DB Klein, 'Foreword to republication of "a beginner's guide to esoteric reading"' (2015) 12 *Econ Journal Watch* 293. Another explanation, in the context of Leibniz's philosophy, is provided by: 'Roughly speaking an esoteric presentation is one that is fully rigorous while an exoteric or 'popular' presentation is less rigorous but easier to understand, which is more appropriate for a general audience', J Whipple, 'Leibniz's Exoteric Philosophy', in *Stanford Encyclopedia of Philosophy* (Fall 2022 edn).

[181] Strauss, *Persecution* (n 179) 37

[182] For further on this point, see Howse *Leo Strauss* (n 173) 64-6.

[183] Strauss (n 179) 30.

Strauss, of course, was not thinking about the judgments of international courts when discussing esoteric writing.[184] Even though Strauss elegantly articulated these ideas, they are, in fact, older.[185]

This type of opaque communication is also common in other contexts. Four examples illustrate the point.

First, diplomacy. The '*language* of diplomacy' Barbara Keys explains, is 'replete with euphemism and misleading or indirect formulations'.[186] Berridge and James also support this view, defining diplomatic language as being 'special' and characterised by being 'typically mild, euphemistic, and circumlocutory'.[187] Given the diplomatic background of a fair number of international adjudicators,[188] it would be unsurprising if some aspects of this form of communication have not seeped into their judicial writing.

Second, game theory. Thomas Schelling observed the importance of 'taking a hint' in the game-theoretical context – as a particular form of transmitting information. He noted that: '*taking a hint* is fundamentally different from deciphering a formal communication or solving a mathematical problem; it involves discovering a message that has been planted within a context by someone who

[184] Although there is a reference to Grotius' *De jure beli ac pacis* at 35. In a footnote Strauss mentions Book 3, Chapter 1, particularly the sections that address deceit in war – and the extent to which it is permissible. Grotius considers whether falsehoods spoken in the presence of enemies are permissible. He then quotes Eustratius, the Bishop of Nicea, who, commenting on Aristotle's *Nichomachean Ethics*, wrote that: 'He who gives good counsel does not necessarily speak the truth. It can in fact happen that he who plans aright makes falsehood itself a part of his plan, that he may lie intentionally, either to an enemy, in order to deceive him, or to a friend, to deliver the friend from evil; historical narratives are full of instances of this sort.' Book III, p. 618. In fact, there are specific passages in Grotius that could be taken as openly acknowledging esotericism. For example, when providing suggestions as to how to determine who has the 'sovereign power in every Nation', Grotius counsels that the first thing is to 'not be deceived by the Ambiguity of Words, or the Shew of outward things'. Book I, X.

The idea has been traced to ancient Greece. One of the chief exponents of esoteric writing is considered to be Maimonides, particularly in his *Guide of the Perplexed*. In fact, some suggest that in the 'Epistle Dedicatory' to that work, Maimonides openly admits that he is engaging in esoteric writing. Indeed, Strauss' *Persecution and the Art of Writing* is heavily focused on Maimonides.

[185] In *Philosophy between the Lines: The Lost History of Esoteric Writing* (University of Chicago Press, 2014), Arthur Melzer manages to distinguish the historical and analytical aspects of esoteric writing from Strauss' broader views and positions. For instance, in *De Cive*, when discussing classical philosophers, Thomas Hobbes mentions that 'rather than openly exposed to disputations', the ancients 'rather chose to have the science of justice wrapped up in fables'. Similarly, in *Valerius Terminus* (published around 1603), Francis Bacon observed that there was a need for 'discretion in the transmission of knowledge', requiring that certain ideas be articulated in ways that 'may not be to the taste or capacity of all', see: J Spedding, RL Ellis and D Heath (eds) *The Works of Francis Bacon* (CUP, 2013), in particular vol III, 236–37. See also Bagley 'On the Practice of Esotericism' (n 177) 237.

[186] B Keys, 'Diplomat's Two Minds: Deconstructing a Foreign Policy Myth' (2020) 44 *Diplomatic History* 1.

[187] GR Berridge and A James, 'Demarche' in GR Berridge and A James, *A Dictionary of Diplomacy* 2nd edn (Palgrave Macmillan, 2003) 64, 74.

[188] See eg A Bianchi 'Choice and (the Awareness of) its Consequences: The ICJ's "Structural Bias" Strikes Again in the *Marshall Islands* Case' (2017) 111 *AJIL Unbound* 81, 85. See also: M Waibel and Y Wu, 'Are Arbitrators Political? Evidence from International Investment Arbitration', working paper.

thinks he shares with the recipient certain impressions or associations'.[189] The core assumption is that the participants in the conversation share an underlying common understanding that will enable the recipient to decipher the message.

Third, sociology. The key concept is 'preference falsification'. This notion, developed by Timur Kuran, is essentially a 'specific form of lying'. The emphasis is on the *specific* part: preference falsification 'aims specifically at manipulating the perceptions others hold about one's motivations or dispositions'.[190] It is a more nuanced way of deception because it involves trying to game what *others* think about the underlying thought process of the preference falsifier. Indeed, one may wonder whether international courts' (sometimes loud) claims to be oblivious to the political sensitivities and context that surround the disputes they have before them involves a degree of preference falsification. As I argue later in this book, the 'revealed preference' here may be that there are some instances of the implied application of avoidance techniques.

Fourth, leaks are also a form of esoteric communication. Unsurprisingly, leaks do not always sincerely convey information. One commonly accepted purpose of leaks is for it to serve as a 'trial-balloon' 'to test the response of key constituencies'[191] or to 'test the consequences' of certain positions.[192] Indeed, those leaks can provide an 'observational window' that permits gauging 'how outside actors process new information and respond'.[193] In this context, the use of leaks and trial-balloons is considered justified; not something to normatively question, but rather as something 'programmatic, a mode of governance'.[194]

What these four examples of opacity in communication highlight is that the sort of *esoteric* writing Strauss had in mind is not a form of communication that is restricted to philosophical writing. Rather, as a phenomenon that has been observed in several other contexts – and that any acute observer will notice occurring throughout her daily life – it is widespread. My contention is that international adjudication is not completely immune from that and, in consequence, that there might be just a bit of esoteric communication and preference falsification in the field.

The justification both Strauss and Kuran had in mind for esoteric writing and preference falsification respectively was avoiding persecution. That same reasoning applies to international courts (with a difference of degree, of course). Given the context in which they operate, international adjudicators, particularly when they are dealing with politically sensitive or 'mega political' issues,

[189] Schelling *The Strategy of Conflict* (n 168) 163.

[190] T Kuran, *Private Truths, Public Lies: The Social Consequences of Preference Falsification* (Harvard University Press 1997) 4.

[191] D Pozen, 'The Leaky Leviathan: Why the Government Condemns and Condones Unlawful Disclosures of Information' (2013) 127 *Harvard Law Review* 512.

[192] WC Spracher, 'Mired in Gray: Juggling Legality, Lawfulness, and Ethics as an Intelligence Professional' (2016) 33 *American Intelligence Journal* 101.

[193] Pozen 'The Leaky Leviathan' (n 191) 612.

[194] ibid 562.

find themselves in a delicate situation: caught in the tension between expediency and principle as Bickel mentioned. They are exposed to criticism. They may jeopardise the legitimacy, authority or even the continued existence of their institutions. Or they can risk defiance or non-compliance with their judgments (and the ensuing threat to their authority). There are thus some situations where international courts will have strong incentives to obscure or, in some cases, even omit, the actual reasoning behind some of their decisions.

Reading between the lines to (try) to decipher the underlying reasons of a judgment is, of course, open to criticism. It is inherently speculative. And it can be dismissed as 'arbitrary guesswork'; or, in the words of one less-than-kind commentator, an exercise in 'perverse ingenuity'.[195] Or, as one ingenious magazine headline put it: 'The Art of Interpreting Nonexistent Inscriptions Written in Invisible Ink on a Blank Page.'[196] A Straussian reading of some judgments is not perfect. But, to borrow a line from Wallace Stevens, perhaps we need to make peace with the idea that 'the imperfect is our paradise'.[197] In any event, Strauss considered that an esoteric interpretation should only be considered when some stringent requirements were satisfied.[198] In the context of interpreting legal judgments the threshold should be even higher. However, once the threshold is met, I suggest that it should be at least *considered* as one potentially plausible explanation.[199] Again, taking a probabilistic approach, the odds that some esoteric or uncandid reasoning – that there is some of Dugard's *silent inspiration* – is well above zero.

To be absolutely clear: the proposition set out in this book is *not* that most, or even many, international judgments have esoteric interpretations. It's the opposite: only for *a few* judgments – judgments on the margin – will an esoteric reading be appropriate, including to ascertain whether implied avoidance techniques were applied. Again, although some will find this proposition objectionable, it is nonetheless intuitively plausible, especially when the other potential explanation for a particular judgment could be a level of doctrinal ineptitude by international courts that would perhaps be even more frightening and objectionable.[200] In short, it is worth asking why it is asserted with so much certainty that there is *complete* candour in the context of international adjudication.

Moreover, in the context of domestic courts there has been an increasing acceptance that Courts are not always transparent in their judgments.[201] After

[195] G Sabine, 'Review of Persecution and the Art of Writing' (1953) 63 *Ethics* 220.

[196] S Leys, 'The Art of Interpreting Nonexistent Inscriptions Written in Invisible Ink on a Blank Page' *The New York Review of Books* (11 October 1990).

[197] W Stevens, 'The Poems of our Climate' in *Wallace Stevens, Collected Poems* (Faber and Faber, 2006).

[198] See also Howse (n 173) 65.

[199] See eg, RJ Allen and MS Pardo, 'Relative Plausibility and Its Critics' (2019) 23 *International Journal of Evidence & Proof* 5.

[200] Casas 'Functional Justiciability' (n 157).

[201] Zeppos 'Judicial Candor'(n 171); R Fallon, 'A Theory of Judicial Candor' (2017) 117 *Columbia Law Review* 2265; Idleman 'Prudential Theory' (n 171); Schwartzman 'Judicial Sincerity' (n 171); ED Hageman, 'Judicial Candor and Extralegal Reasoning: Why Extralegal Reasons Require Legal Justifications (And No More)' (2015) 91 *Notre Dame Law Review* 405.

all, there is at least a kernel of truth in Jerome Frank's quip that legal opinions are but '*censored expositions*'. When analysing Oliver Wendell Holmes' opinions, Leflar noted that Holmes 'believed in real reasons but chose not to parade them'.[202] Making a similar comment about Benjamin Cardozo, Leflar observes that 'neither his times nor his colleagues left him free to bare in official opinions the nonlegalistic reasons that motivated both him and them . . . The tradition was that judicial decisions must be grounded on "legal" considerations altogether, and Cardozo could not completely escape from that tradition'.[203] Indeed, Leflar – who was both a legal academic *and* a judge – considered that:

> Candor is a virtue, in judicial opinions as elsewhere, and we need much more of it. But to 'tell all,' with complete and unmitigated candor, is not always a virtue in judicial opinions or elsewhere. Restraint may be a virtue too, for reasons sometimes of decency and sometimes of wise planning.[204]

The notion that judges may not always be completely candid in their reasoning has also been raised more recently. Commenting on one particular form of lack of candour, stealth overruling, Ronald Dworkin observed that the Roberts' Court was 'bent on remaking constitutional law by overruling, most often by stealth . . . central constitutional techniques'.[205] He then defines this modus operandi as overruling a case 'without conceding that they were overruling anything'.[206] He was not a fan of the concept, noting that the Court did not operate 'explicitly, but through a laughably cynical subterfuge'.[207]

Barry Friedman, also writing in the context of the US Supreme Court, mentions that decisions that engage in stealth overruling tend to speak to two audiences simultaneously. He observes that: 'The Justices can cloak what they are doing from the public at large while making their intentions perfectly plain to lower courts and to officials'.[208] The justification for this approach is to "duck" publicity, thus avoiding issues arising from 'how the public will perceive the decision.'[209] In other words, the argument goes that the Supreme Court prefers to *impliedly* or *stealthily* overrule certain precedents to avoid attracting 'broad,

[202] RA Leflar, *One life in the Law* (University of Arkansas Press, 1985) 124.
[203] ibid 123.
[204] RA Leflar, 'Some Observations concerning Judicial Opinions' (1961) 61 *Columbia Law Review* 810, 819.
[205] R Dworkin, 'The Supreme Court Phalanx' *The New York Review of Books* (27 September 2007).
[206] ibid.
[207] ibid.
[208] B Friedman, 'The Wages of Stealth Overruling (With Particular Attention to *Miranda v Arizona*)' (2010) 99 *Georgetown Law Journal* 1, 14. Although note that Friedman draws a distinction between stealth overruling and overruling *sub silentio* (despite admitting they are 'close cousins'). His distinction is based on intent: whilst stealth overruling is intentional ('the hallmark of stealth overruling is that the Justices are perfectly aware that they are overruling but hide the fact they are doing so'). In contrast, overruling *sub silentio* may be the result of 'an accidental or unknowing treatment of precedents' at 14.
[209] ibid 33.

negative attention' which, in turn, could 'encourage attacks and jeopardize the Court as an institution'.[210]

The supporters of judicial candour consider that its normative worth is 'self-evident', a 'truth of uncompromising importance'.[211] There are normative and pragmatic arguments in favour of candour. Normatively, the focus is on the pervasive, detrimental consequences of lying.[212] Pragmatically, the claim is that deception, particularly if constant, will undermine both the 'integrity of the judiciary'[213] and democratic accountability.[214] This view is tied to the notion that the court's public reason-giving allows transparency and predictability – two key characteristics of the rule of law.[215] But there is more to that debate. There is enough evidence that judicial writing is not absolutely or entirely candid – even in systems that are generally considered as upholding the rule of law – for the demand of absolute candour to be considered an indispensable condition of a functional legal system. So, if, leaving aside the normative debate, there is a general at least descriptive acceptance of this in the domestic context, there are no obvious reasons to doubt that something similar is happening at the international level.

B. Is There a Normative Justification for Implied Avoidance Techniques?

This section considers whether there is a normative justification for the exercise of avoidance techniques. This issue is not addressed by some recent scholarship on avoidance.[216] One exception is Alves das Chagas, who recently argued that, in some instances, avoidance is normatively justified, particularly when it respects the rule of law, access to justice and is based on a 'legal obligation established by norms of competence'.[217] As explained below I consider that, in some cases, avoidance may be normatively justified.[218]

Before that, two caveats. The first is that, as a threshold matter, my view is that there may be a normative justification for the use of avoidance techniques,

[210] ibid 39.

[211] Zeppos (n 171) 400.

[212] M Cohen, 'Sincerity and Reason-Giving: When May Legal Decisions Makers Lie' (2009) 59 *De Paul Law Review* 1091, 1110–11; see also M Cohen, 'When Judges Have Reasons Not to Give Reasons: A Comparative Law Approach' (2015) 72 *Washington and Lee Law Review* 483.

[213] Zeppos (n 171) 401.

[214] Fallon 'A Theory of Judicial Candor' (n 201) 2282.

[215] Schwartzman, 'Judicial Sincerity' (n 171) 1005–12; Delaney (n 1) 13.

[216] See eg Delaney (n 1); Jackson (n 4) 129; Odermatt (n 37). Of course, Bickel did set out a normative justification for avoidance, as set out above.

[217] Alves das Chagas *Judicial Avoidance* (n 6) 24.

[218] Insofar as I understand Alves das Chagas' argument, we reach the same conclusions, albeit by different routes: whereas she focuses on norms of competence, I base my argument on the inherent relative indeterminacy of the rules of international procedural law. In fairness, however, I suspect that I go further in normatively justifying the use of avoidance techniques, including in some cases where this would not be possible under Alves das Chagas' analysis.

but such justification is contingent. *Sometimes* reliance on avoidance doctrines will be normatively justified. The *sometimes* is critical. The normative justification of avoidance will be casuistic; it will depend on context, on the facts, on the law; and it will depend on the specific policy considerations at play. There is no blanket rule. My argument is not that all instances of avoidance are normatively justified. They may not be. There may be situations where jurisdictional avoidance will be mere abdication.

The second caveat is that jurisdictional avoidance techniques may not be doctrinally unsound. Normative justifications for avoidance imply that avoidance is not doctrinally defensible or that it implies some improper manipulation of the law which explains why it is often characterised as an exercise of pragmatism.[219] Yet, in the context of international adjudication, that may not necessarily be the case. Avoidance may have a doctrinal basis – or at least it may not be doctrinally unsound. As explained in detail in chapter 4, international procedural law is somewhat indeterminate and flexible. The open-ended nature of many of the relevant principles and doctrines, particularly on issues of jurisdiction and admissibility, may allow for some leeway in their application, hence claims of avoidance requiring the manipulation of doctrine are not necessarily right. With those two caveats out of the way, what are, then, the potential normative justifications for implied avoidance techniques:

First, avoidance may be pro-dialogic.[220] By abstaining from deciding a case, an international court may be allowing the issue to be resolved through other avenues, mainly those of politics and diplomacy. The idea is originally Bickel's. In short, he considered that by avoiding to decide an issue, the Supreme Court was promoting and, importantly, *framing* dialogue with the other branches of government.[221] Or, as David Shapiro put it, discretionally declining to exercise jurisdiction allows the 'easing of intergovernmental tensions in our complex system of government'.[222]Avoidance leads to delay. And delay often leads to further ventilation of issues at the political level. So, delay may be strategic. As Delaney explains:

> Strategic avoidance – postponing decision of contentious issues that might threaten a court's institutional viability – is a way of engaging various external actors to create and secure institutional support. Delaying a decision on substance might allow the

[219] Fouchard (n 8).

[220] Delaney (n 1) 10. Broadly speaking, there are outcome-orientated and structural conceptions of dialogue. For the latter, see eg K Roach, 'Dialogic Judicial Review and its Critics' (2004) 23 *Supreme Court Law Review* 249; B Friedman, 'Dialogue and Judicial Review' (1992–1993) *Michigan Law Review* 81 577. For the former, see R Dixon, 'Creating Dialogue About Socioeconomic Rights: Strong-Form Versus Weak-Form Judicial Review' (2007) 5 *International Journal of Constitutional Law* 391. At the international level, see: AF Perez, 'The Passive Virtues and the World Court: Pro-Dialogic Abstention by the International Court of Justice' (1997) 18 *Michigan Journal of International Law*, 399, 447.

[221] Bickel, *The Least Dangerous Branch* (n 15) 64. Discussing the *Birth Control* cases, Bickel saw the Supreme Court as engaging in a 'sort of colloquy with the political institutions' in a way that allowed it to 'fram[e] the conditions to invite a responsible legislative decision'.

[222] DL Shapiro, 'Jurisdiction and Discretion' (1985) 60 *New York University Law Review* 543, 545.

> time and space necessary for productive dialogue with (and within) the political branches to resolve the question outside of the courts. Delay may even allow for the evolution of popular consensus on the issue.[223]

Sunstein mentions that judicial minimalism – a cognate of avoidance – is about the 'constructive uses of silence'.[224] He observes that judges 'use silence for pragmatic or strategic reasons or to promote democratic goals'.[225] Here, the strategic use of silence leaves an issue open for deliberation through other, potentially more legitimate and more effective channels, including not only diplomatic or political channels, but other forms of international law-making, such as treaties and other international agreements or customary international law. In turn, this implies acknowledging the limits of the international judicial function – a sort of antidote to the incurable judicial romanticism discussed above.[226]

Explaining pro-dialogic avoidance in the human rights context, Jackson explains that, instead of having an international court 'pushing straight into confrontation', avoidance 'creates space for political dialogue and contestation in the domestic order', further noting that this would allow 'the Court as an institution with flexibility in evading potential confrontations harmful to its long-term authority'.[227] In fact, taking a transnational approach, the dialogic potentials of abstention increase, as the solutions may arise purely at the domestic level.[228] For these pro-dialogic effects to take place, international courts must arguably refrain from *expressly* revealing that they are engaging in pro-dialogic abstention. That would defeat the point. It may also have unsalutary effects on the intended dialogue itself: if one party is leaning towards recalcitrancy, the express knowledge that the relevant international court is reluctant to address the issue may incentivise them to move *away* from dialogue.

Second, there are institutional reasons for avoidance. As explained in chapter 2, international courts are not in an institutionally robust position. Broadly, they lack both compulsory jurisdiction and coercive enforcement mechanisms. They are also facing different forms of backlash, pushback, dejudicialisation and even non-judicialisation. In that context, an international court must preserve its

[223] Delaney (n 1) 4.
[224] C Sunstein, 'The Supreme Court 1995 Term Foreword: Leaving Things Undecided' (1996) 110 *Harvard Law Review* 7.
[225] ibid.
[226] Reisman, *The Constitutional Crisis* (n 165) 94.
[227] Jackson (n 4) 131.
[228] HH Koh, 'The 1994 Roscoe Pound Lecture: Transnational Legal Process' (1994) 75, *Nebraska Law Review* 105, 184; HH Koh, 'Why Do Nations Obey International Law' (1996-1997) 106 *Yale Law Journal* 2599, 2659. See also P Paiement, 'Urgent Agenda: How Climate Litigation Builds Transnational Narratives' (2020) 11 *Transnational Legal Theory*, 121–43; R Thiebaut, 'The Role of Transnational Legal Process in Advancing a Sustainable Agenda within the Brics' (2024) 12 *Journal of Law and Sustainable Developments*.

institutional legitimacy, its authority[229] and, in some cases, its very existence.[230] Assuming (as I do), that the continued existence and effective operation of international courts is a desirable outcome then, from a consequentialist stance, the application of avoidance doctrines to achieve that objective is normatively justifiable. This, of course, will vary between international courts given the different institutional contexts in which they operate.

Additionally, there are institutional reasons related to the judicial function – and its limits – that justify the use of avoidance techniques. There has been an increased judicialisation of international affairs, including to cover 'mega-political' issues as well as the increase in 'lawfare'.[231] International courts may not be the best avenue to solve all international disputes. As Vaughan Lowe famously said, there 'are many times when it is much better to call upon a politician, or a priest, or a doctor, or a plumber'.[232] Avoidance techniques allow international courts to temper the potential excesses of judicialisation by eliding potentially controversial issues. An analogy could be drawn with the normative justifications for the exercise of judicial restraint in the context of judicial review. For instance, Kavanagh argues that the normative justification for judicial restraint is 'rooted in the institutional limitations of the courts'.[233] She explains that courts will sometimes engage with second-order reasons regarding the limits of their institutional role and the propriety of intervening in a specific case.[234]

Yet, some would argue that there are strong countervailing institutional reasons that go against the exercise of avoidance techniques. Indeed, the application of avoidance techniques may, in itself, result in backlash. The fallout from

[229] K Alter, L Helfer and MR Madsen, 'International Court Authority in a Complex World' in K Alter, L Helfer and MR Madsen, *International Court Authority* (OUP, 2018). The authors distinguish legitimacy from authority, noting that: 'we separate the study of authority from the study of legitimacy. This bifurcation recognizes that a court can do everything normative theorists expect of a legitimate international judicial body and still not possess authority in fact'. See also Y Lupu, PH Verdier and M Versteeg 'The Strength of Weak Review: National Courts, Interpretative Canons, and Human Rights Treaties' (2019) 63 *International Studies Quarterly* 507.

[230] See eg KJ Alter, JT Gathii and LR Helfer, 'Backlash against International Courts in West, East and Southern Africa: Causes and Consequences' (2016) 27 *European Journal of International Law* 293.

[231] Hirschl *Towards Juristocracy* (n 2) 94. On the increase of lawfare, see CJ Dunlap Jr, 'Does Lawfare Need an Apologia?' (2010) 43 *Case Western Reserve Journal of International Law* 121 and ff. Dunlap Jr, a former military lawyer, defines lawfare as the 'strategy of using—or misusing—law as a substitute for traditional military means to achieve an operational objective', CJ Dunlap Jr, 'Lawfare Today: A Perspective' (2008) 3 *Yale Journal of International Affairs* 146.

[232] V Lowe, *International Law* (OUP, 2009) 290.

[233] E Kavanagh, 'Judicial Restraint in Pursuit of Justice' (2010) 60 *University of Toronto Law Journal* 23, 27. See also J Waldron, 'The Core of the Case Against Judicial Review' (2006) 115 *Yale Law Journal* 1346; R Ekins and G Gee, 'Putting Judicial Power in its Place' (2017) 36 *University of Queensland Law Journal* 375 and ff.

[234] Kavanagh 'Judicial Restraint' (n 231) 27. This is also a topic that has been developed by Jonathan Sumption in *Trials of the State* (Profile Books, 2020); see also N Barber, R Ekins and P Yowell (eds), *Lord Sumption and the Limits of the Law* (Hart, 2018).

the ICJ's *South West Africa* decision is but one example of this.[235] Further, some would argue that a decision to *avoid* adjudicating the merits of a dispute is, in itself, a decision on the merits – one that is in the Respondent's favour.[236] Lauterpacht's admonition that justice should be done though the heavens fall also militates strongly against the use of avoidance techniques. Or, at a more technical level, the claim that reasoned explanation is a way that courts build legitimacy and this could be jeopardised by the implied application of avoidance doctrines.[237]

But these objections are not persuasive. Avoiding deciding a case means that an international court is not taking a position on the issue; a decision declining jurisdiction is neither here nor there on the merits. This alternative may be preferable to an international court upholding jurisdiction and then, out of institutional, compliance or legitimacy concerns, refusing to rule that the defendant State's conduct is wrongful based on the application of a deferential standard of review. Moreover, it is by now evident that a plethora of domestic courts deploy avoidance techniques as part of their judicial toolkit and have done so without that jeopardising the integrity of their judicial role.

Third, from the New Haven perspective, the use of avoidance doctrines could assist in achieving minimum order. As explained previously, one of the main normative goals of international law is to secure minimum order, understood as 'freedom from expectations of severe deprivations by unauthorized coercion and violence'.[238] The use of avoidance doctrines is thus relevant on two fronts.

The first is that it allows the international court to evaluate whether a decision on the merits would further minimum order. A New Haven analysis is configurative and allows approaching legal analysis with a focus on both context and underlying policy objectives. This, as McDougal, Lasswell and Reisman explained, allows 'comprehensiveness and realism' in analysis.[239] So, international courts can evaluate whether deciding the merits of a dispute would assist in furthering minimum order. There are obviously situations where it will. But in other cases, where it is evident that a decision would be ineffective, would lead to aggressive backlash or may actually make matters worse (i.e., inflaming tensions by throwing judicial gasoline on what's already burning), abstaining from ruling on the issue may, in itself, be the best course of action. An international

[235] L Gross, 'Underutilization of the International Court of Justice' (1986) 27 *Harvard Journal of International Law* 571; M Pomerance, 'Case Analysis: The ICJ and South West Africa (Namibia): A Retrospective Legal/Political Assessment' (1999) 12 *Leiden Journal of International Law* 425. Although contrast that with the (mainly) academic criticism of the ICJ's decision in the *Marshall Islands* cases, discussed in detail in chapter 5.

[236] See eg Weill *The Role of National Courts* (n 50), ch 2.

[237] T Roux, 'Principle and Pragmatism on the Constitutional Court of South Africa' (2009) 7 *International Journal of Constitutional Law* 106; Roux (n 20). See also Shapiro (n 171).

[238] M McDougal & F Feliciano, *Law and Minimum World Public Order* (Yale University Press, 1961) 261.

[239] M McDougal, H Lasswell and WM Reisman, 'Theories About International Law: Prologue to a Configurative Jurisprudence' (1967–1968) 8 *Virginia Journal of International Law* 196.

judgment is not the only – nor necessarily the best – way of addressing international disputes.

The second ground is that the availability, continued existence – and, importantly, the effectiveness – of international courts is also relevant for furthering minimum order. Test the point this way: is a world without international adjudication a better alternative than one where that is a valid channel to address international disputes? As Reisman explains: 'It is of crucial importance that decision makers perceive that *all* their acts have a strategic potential that can either maximize or minimize the effectiveness and degree of realization of their goals', on that basis, he observes that the 'continued viability of organized authoritative decision processes is a basic component of minimum order.'[240]

So, in this context, and given the (overall) institutional fragility of a good percentage of international courts, there will be situations where the application of avoidance techniques – including implied ones – will be normatively justified as a mechanism to preserve the international adjudicators legitimacy and authority. Of course, this assessment, which has strong discretionary and prudential element, must be carried out with care and nuance; in Reisman's words: 'skilful navigation between the Scylla of ineffectiveness and the Charybdis of timorousness'.[241] It is worth noting that in the Odyssey, despite Ulysses' skilful navigation, he did end up losing several sailors to Scylla. That is a fitting analogy for the cases that are never decided on the merits because of the application of jurisdictional avoidance techniques.

V. CONCLUSION

In short, this chapter has covered the following issues. First, it defined avoidance, explaining that the focus of this book is on jurisdictional avoidance techniques (rather than other *in medio* and *ex post* avoidance techniques), and described the origin of current avoidance techniques. Second, it distinguished express and implied avoidance doctrines and argued why express avoidance doctrines are not widely applied in international adjudication. Third, it set out a theoretical framework for the operation of implied avoidance doctrines, including the distinction between the myth system and the operational code, and the lack of (absolute) judicial candour. And fourth, it set out a contingent normative justification for the application of implied avoidance doctrines, which will be case and context dependent.

[240] Reisman, *Nullity and Revision* (n 88) 242.
[241] ibid 243.

4

Legal Theory and International Procedural Law

'When you get to a fork in the road, take it'

Yogi Berra

I. INTRODUCTION

INTERNATIONAL PROCEDURAL LAW IS a curious thing. At one point, it was considered the 'Antarctica of international law'.[1] Cold, desolate, and too far out there for most international lawyers to care. The rudimentary nature of international procedural law has been long recognised; almost 100 years ago Philip Jessup commented that:

> There can be no doubt that . . . the settlement of controversies between states by judicial processes, is in continued course of rapid development. There is already a considerable body of substantive law which can be drawn from the decided cases. But in the procedural field the development has naturally been slower . . . Unlike the usual situation in private law, the development of international law preceded its application by regular judicial organs. Accordingly no judicial procedure arose synchronously with the substantive law, and in the absence or paucity of international legislation it has not been easy to achieve procedural definiteness.[2]

International procedural law is no longer so underdeveloped. The increase in international proceedings has led to the development of a series of principles that are applied across different international fora.[3] Although international procedural law has undoubtedly become more sophisticated in recent decades, it is still a relatively underdeveloped area of international law. Compare it to other more doctrinally 'thick' areas, such as the law of State responsibility, the law of

[1] AH Feller, *The Mexican Claims Commissions: 1923–34* (Macmillan, 1935) vii.

[2] PC Jessup, 'The Palmas Island Arbitration' (1928) 22 *American Journal of International Law* 735.

[3] For a good overview on the issue, see C Brown, *A Common Law of International Adjudication* (OUP, 2007); C Kotuby and L Sobota, *General Principles of Law and International Due Process: Principles and Norms Applicable in Transnational Disputes* (OUP, 2017).

treaties, or the law of the sea, and international procedural law, if no longer an infant, is at least still a teenager.

The relative underdevelopment of international procedural law is relevant for avoidance techniques. As explained previously, I argue that one of the main ways international courts abstain from deciding certain cases or issues is by relying on rules and principles on admissibility and jurisdiction as implied jurisdictional avoidance techniques. An important reason why that is possible is due to some of the inherent characteristics of international procedural law. I contend that some characteristics that are somewhat unique or idiosyncratic are of particular relevance. These are either absent in domestic procedural law, or they are much less salient or subject to greater strictures or controls. They are: (1) the relative indeterminacy of a (fair) number of rules of international procedural law; (2) the competence–competence principle; and (3) the (general) lack of appellate review. This chapter explains each of those characteristics and shows how they grant international courts considerable leeway in the application of those rules. In short, the ductility of international procedural law is one of the key aspects that permits the deployment of implied jurisdictional avoidance techniques.

II. INDETERMINACY AND INTERNATIONAL PROCEDURAL LAW

Below I set out why some parts of international procedural law are relatively indeterminate. To start, test the point this way: compare the degree of precision with which domestic procedural rules – in both common and civil law systems – are set out and contrast that with the much lower degree of specificity at which rules of international procedural law are formulated. Understanding the relative indeterminacy of international procedural law requires addressing some of its key theoretical aspects. Those characteristics play a relevant role in how international courts exercise their jurisdiction – and in consequence are relevant for how they may deploy avoidance techniques.

A. Types of Rules

As an overarching point, different legal provisions operate in different ways. Analysing this distinction between different types of provisions is one of the fundamental problems addressed by legal philosophy.[4] One of the main

[4] See eg I Ehrlich and RA Posner, 'An Economic Analysis of Legal Rulemaking' (1974) 3 *Journal of Legal Studies* 257; KC Davis, *Discretionary Justice: A Preliminary Inquiry* (Louisiana State University Press, 1969); A Ogus, 'Quantitative Rules and Judicial Decision Making' in P Burrows and CG Veljanovski (eds), *The Economic Approach to Law* (Butterworths, 1981) 210; PS Atiyah and

distinctions is that between bright line *rules* and more flexible *standards*.[5] The canonical example that illustrates the difference between the two is Holmes' and Cardozo's disagreement on the standard of care that a driver must apply when arriving at a railroad crossing.[6] Holmes thought a rule was applicable. A driver must stop at the crossing and look.[7] Cardozo, in contrast, thought that a standard was applicable. The driver, he considered, must act with *reasonable caution*.[8] Schlag explains the distinction in the following terms. Whereas rules 'draw a sharp line between forbidden and permissible conduct', standards describe the 'distinction between permissible and impermissible conduct in evaluative terms'.[9]

Although there has been some commentary on the nature of international legal provisions,[10] this has tended to focus on issues such as the hierarchy of

---

RS Summers, *Form and Substance in Anglo-American Law: A Comparative Study in Legal Reasoning, Legal Theory and Legal Institutions* (Clarendon Press, 1987); HLA Hart, *The Concept of Law*, 3rd edn (OUP, 2012); HM Hart and AM Sacks, *The Legal Process* (Foundation Press, 1994) 155–58; M Kelman, *A Guide to Critical Legal Studies* (Harvard University Press, 1987) 15–63; RA Posner, *The Problems of Jurisprudence* (Harvard University Press, 1990) 42–53; R Pound, *An Introduction to the Philosophy of Law* (Yale University Press, 1922) 115–23; F Schauer, *Playing by the Rules: A Philosophical Examination of Rule-Based Decisionmaking in Law and in Life* (Clarendon Press, 1991); RM Unger, *Knowledge and Politics* (Free Press, 1975) 88–100; RM Dworkin, 'The Model of Rules' (1967) 35 *University of Chicago Law Review* 14, 22–29; D Kennedy, 'Form and Substance in Private Law Adjudication' (1976) 89 *Harvard Law Review* 1685; R Pound, 'Hierarchy of Sources and Forms in Different Systems of Law' (1933) 7 *Tulane Law Review* 475, 482–87; L Alexander, 'What Are Principles, And Do They Exist?' (2013) 33 *Institute for Law and Philosophy*; C Sunstein, 'Problems with Rules' (1995) 83 *California Law Review* 953. The traditional caveat applies: it is beyond the scope of this book to examine the issue in detail.

[5] Although some consider that the dialectical distinction between rules and standards is insufficient, as there are further distinctions between types of rules. For example, Lawrence Solum suggests that there are five broad categories: rules, standards, principles, catalogs, and discretion, see LB Solum, 'Legal Theory Lexicon: Rules, Standards, Principles, Catalogs, and Discretion' (*Legal Theory Blog*, 8 August 2021). Cass Sunstein also offers a broader taxonomy: mentioning untrammelled discretion, rules, rules with excuses, presumptions, factors, standards, guidelines, principles and analogies, Sunstein, *Problem with Rules* (n 4). In civil law, the notion of 'indeterminate legal concepts' is also relevant and has some analogies with standards.

[6] See generally P Schlag, 'Rules and Standards' (1985) 33 *UCLA Law Review* 379.

[7] *Baltimore & Ohio RR v Goodman* 275 US 70 (1927).

[8] *Pokora v Wabash Ry* 292 US 98 (1934), 103–06.

[9] Schlag 'Rules and Standards' (n 6) 380. Following Austin, Michael Reisman proposes a dichotomy between *verification* rules and *evaluation* rules in international law. He defines the former as a type of rule that 'transfers to the ultimate rule-applier the most limited exercise of discretion'. The main characteristic of this type of rule is that it circumscribes the discretion of the applier of the rule to a mere verification of 'compliance with an explicit metric'. Verification rules are bivalent or binary — that is to say, they are *either–or*. Evaluation rules, in contrast, are neither bivalent nor binary: 'they establish a goal that is expressed at some level of generality'. In consequence, the application of an evaluation rule requires reliance on a different methodology, as they require 'potentially wide-ranging contextual as well as textual methodologies'. Essentially, because of their open texture, evaluation rules grant the rule-applier a greater degree of discretion to determine whether the rule applies in those particular circumstances, see 'Canute Confronts the Tide: States versus Tribunals and the Evolution of the Minimum Standard in Customary International Law' (2015) 30 *ICSID Review* 616.

[10] See eg K Raustiala, 'Form and Substance in International Agreements' (2005) 99 *American Journal of International Law* 581.

sources, relative normativity, the distinction between hard and soft law,[11] the status of peremptory norms,[12] and similar. The question of the nature of the types of *rules* that constitute international procedural law as such is almost entirely overlooked.

(i) International Procedural Law: Rules and Standards

Where do provisions of international procedural law, particularly on jurisdiction and admissibility, fall into this framework? The answer is straightforward: in both. Some provisions of international procedural law are rules. Consider, for example, the special agreement between the Gabonese Republic and the Republic of Equatorial Guinea. Article 4(1) of this *compromis* provides that it will enter into force 'the day after the date on which both Parties have notified each other in writing that the necessary formalities have been completed'.[13] This is, of course, a rule. It applies, as rules do, in an 'all or nothing' manner. It is algorithmic: once the requirement (i.e., notification by both parties) is met, the *compromis* will have entered into force.

Or consider a slightly more complex scenario relating to personal jurisdiction under the ICSID Convention. Article 25 of the Convention sets out a jurisdictional requirement providing that the claimant must be a 'national of another Contracting State.' Article 25(2)(a) of the Convention then provides a definition of that term, stating that it refers to 'any natural person who had the nationality of a Contracting State other than the State party to the dispute'. Despite the renvoi to domestic law, under which nationality is determined, this is also a rule. The parameters for its application – and thus for the satisfaction of the jurisdictional requirements – are precise.[14]

Yet a good part of international procedural law – including a significant part of the provisions that relate to jurisdiction and admissibility – are standards. They are open-ended. They require judgment. They allow for a plurality of potentially correct answers. Compare the *rules* of international procedural law with other, vaguer, jurisdictional provisions or doctrines. Some of these doctrines are analysed in more detail in chapter 5, in which I argue they are used

[11] G Shaffer and M A Pollack, 'Hard vs Soft Law: Alternatives, Complements, and Antagonists in International Governance' (2010) 94 *Minnesota Law Review* 706; AT Guzman, 'The Design of International Agreements' (2005) 16 *European Journal of International Law* 579; AT Guzman, *How International Law Works: A Rational Choice Theory* (OUP, 2008) particularly ch 5; KW Abbott and others, 'The Concept of Legalization' (2000) 54 *International Organization* 401.

[12] D Costelloe, *Legal Consequences of Peremptory Norms* (CUP, 2017); A Orakhelashvili, *Peremptory Norms in International Law* (OUP, 2008).

[13] Special Agreement between the Gabonese Republic and the Republic of Equatorial Guinea (5 March 2021).

[14] On this, see M Casas, 'Nationalities of Convenience, Personal Jurisdiction, and Access to Investor-State Dispute Settlement' (2016) 49 *NYU Journal of International Law and Politics*. Although, of course, the fact that there is a renvoi to domestic law already introduces some potential complications.

as implied avoidance techniques. Two of them illustrate this point. In fact, they also show the flexibility that international courts enjoy when determining the scope of their jurisdiction.

The first is the *indispensable third-party* principle (sometimes also called the *Monetary Gold* principle).[15] In short, this principle requires an international court to decline jurisdiction over a dispute when the legal rights or interests of a State that is not a party to the dispute would 'not only be affected by a decision, but would form the very subject-matter of the decision'.[16] The operative part of the rule seems to be whether an issue constitutes the 'very subject-matter of the decision'. Unlike the prior examples, this is not a rule. There is no algorithmic or all-or-nothing way of determining this. Rather, the international court addressing this issue will have some leeway and flexibility in determining its application. It is relatively easy to imagine reasonable judges or arbitrators disagreeing as to whether a particular issue constitutes the 'very subject matter' of a dispute, as both linguistically and substantively that concept is not ascertainable with surgical precision.

The second relates to how international adjudicators interpret the scope of their jurisdiction (i.e., how they determine which disputes they may actually adjudicate, including based on applicable law). The decisions below illustrate not only how those jurisdictional provisions are standards rather than bright-line rules, but also how the fact that they *are* standards may lead to diametrically opposed results.

Some tribunals have taken a cautious, restrictive approach in relation to the applicable law and what claims they can adjudicate. The *Eurotunnel*,[17] *Mox Plant*[18] and *Ospar*[19] tribunals are in this category. The *Eurotunnel* Tribunal had jurisdiction to decide claims under both a concession agreement and a treaty (insofar as it had been incorporated into the concession agreement). The Tribunal held that, when determining whether it had jurisdiction over a claim, 'it is necessary to ask whether the breaches pleaded . . . do or do not fall within the provisions of the Concession Agreement from which alone the Tribunal's jurisdiction derives'.[20]

The two arbitral tribunals dealing with the Mox Plant dispute also took this approach. In short, the dispute concerned the potential construction of a nuclear fuel processing plant in the United Kingdom, only 112 miles from the

[15] This is one of the case studies addressed in detail in chapter 5. See generally Z Mollengarden and N Zamir, 'The Monetary Gold Principle: Back to Basics' (2021) 115 *American Journal of International Law* 41; M Paparinskis, 'Long Live Monetary Gold *Terms and Conditions Apply' (2021) 115 *American Journal of International Law* 154; M Paparinskis, 'Revisiting the Indispensable Third Party Principle' (2020) 103 *Rivista di Diritto Internazionale* 49, 83–84.

[16] *Monetary Gold Removed from Rome in 1943 (Italy v France, United Kingdom and United States of America)*, ICJ, Judgment of 15 June 1954 17.

[17] *Eurotunnel Arbitration* Partial Award (30 January 2007).

[18] *Mox Plant (Ireland v United Kingdom)*.

[19] *OSPAR Arbitration (Ireland v United Kingdom)*.

[20] *Eurotunnel* (n 17) paras 135 and 153.

Irish coast. Ireland was unhappy with the construction of the plant – and filed legal claims against the UK. Tribunals were constituted under both UNCLOS and the Convention for the Protection of the Marine Environment of the North-East Atlantic (the OSPAR Convention).

The *Mox Plant* Tribunal (an UNCLOS Annex VII tribunal) analysed whether it also had jurisdiction to consider claims made under the 1992 OSPAR Convention.[21] The Tribunal held that, although the OSPAR Convention was 'relevant to some at least of the questions in issue', it was ultimately 'not persuaded that the OSPAR Convention substantially covers the field of the present dispute'.[22] The *Ospar* Tribunal struck a similar note. There, Ireland alleged that general international law was applicable and that the Tribunal would have jurisdiction to determine a breach of it. The Tribunal rejected that claim observing that the Convention lacked any language to the effect that those obligations had to be applied 'in accordance with international law'.[23]

Contrast those restrictive approaches with the markedly more expansive position adopted by the ITLOS.[24] This trend started with the Tribunal's first judgment in the *M/V Saiga*. The main claim involved Guinea's arrest of a vessel, but Saint Vincent and the Grenadines was also claiming that Guinea's use of force when arresting the vessel had been in breach of general international law and the UN Charter.[25] ITLOS – in my view, somewhat surprisingly – concluded that it also had jurisdiction to decide claims under general international law.[26]

ITLOS reiterated this approach more recently in *M/V 'Virginia G'*, where it considered that it had jurisdiction over a claim relating to the use of force under general international law.[27] ITLOS did not elaborate much on its jurisdictional basis to do so, limiting itself to citing its prior decision in *M/V Saiga*. The Annex VII tribunal in *Guyana v Suriname* took a similarly expansive

[21] *Mox Plant* (n 18), Order No 3 of 24 June 2003).

[22] ibid paras 18-19.

[23] *OSPAR Arbitration* (n 19) Final Award of 2 July 2003, para 85.

[24] The leading case on this issue was ITLOS's judgment in *M/V Saiga (No 2) (Saint Vincent and the Grenadines v Guinea)* ITLOS, Judgment of 1 July 1999.

[25] See P Tzeng, 'Jurisdiction and Applicable Law Under UNCLOS' (2016) 126 *Yale Law Journal* 242.

[26] The ITLOS stated that: 'In considering the force used by Guinea in the arrest of the Saiga, the Tribunal must take into account the circumstances of the arrest in the context of the applicable rules of international law. Although the Convention does not contain express provisions on the use of force in the arrest of ships, international law, which is applicable by virtue of article 293 of the Convention, requires that the use of force must be avoided as far as possible and, where force is unavoidable, it must not go beyond what is reasonable and necessary in the circumstances. Considerations of humanity must apply in the law of the sea, as they do in other areas of international law'. *M/V Saiga No 2* (n 24) para 155. The unarticulated proposition of law that appears to be set out above is that the invocation of humanity is sufficient to override the specific jurisdictional remit that an international treaty imposes on an international court or tribunal. As to the invocation of Art 293(1), it is an established principle of international procedural law that an applicable law provision does not expand an international court's jurisdiction, see: E De Brabandere, *Investment Treaty Arbitration as Public International Law* (CUP, 2014) 123; C Schreuer, 'Jurisdiction and Applicable Law in Investment Treaty Arbitration' (2014) 1 *McGill Journal of Dispute Resolution* 2.

[27] *M/V Virginia G (Panama v Guinea-Bissau)* ITLOS, Judgment of 14 April 2014 paras 359–62.

approach. There, in addition to maritime delimitation claims, Guyana was also claiming reparations based on Suriname's purportedly unlawful use of force. The claim was for breaches of UNCLOS, the UN Charter and general international law. Relying on the *M/V Saiga,* the tribunal considered that it had jurisdiction over those claims.[28] These examples show that different tribunals reached diametrically opposed conclusions when dealing with the seemingly technical issue of determining the applicable law and the extent of their jurisdiction over certain claims.

I argue that there are many provisions of international procedural law that, properly understood, should be characterised as standards rather than rules. To name but a few: the existence of a dispute, standing, mootness, *res judicata*, temporal, territorial, or subject-matter jurisdiction (i.e., the question of whether a specific dispute falls within the scope of a treaty). These all show the inherent characteristics of standards, insofar as they are open-ended, flexible and, to some degree, indeterminate. This, in turn, means that they can lead to diverging results – even when different international courts are essentially considering the same issue.

(ii) Indeterminacy: Relative and Radical

In Kress' simple (and useful) definition, legal indeterminacy means that at least some 'legal questions lack single right answers'.[29] I argue that some parts of international procedural law are indeterminate.[30] In fact, a significant part of international procedural law is composed of standards, which are, to differing degrees, relatively indeterminate. Again, and to be clear, the qualifiers are not idle. I do not argue that all of international procedural law is indeterminate – only a part of it – and that it is *rationally* and *causally* indeterminate. To properly understand how this may impact decisions, including how they can be used impliedly as avoidance techniques, it is important to look at legal indeterminacy at a general level. Indeterminacy is a complex subject and there are several different views, espousing different degrees of indeterminacy.

The American legal realists had substantial influence on the issue.[31] The claim that law is somewhat indeterminate is, indeed, a core claim of the

[28] *Guyana v Suriname*, Award (17 September 2007), paras 405–6. The tribunal held that: 'Suriname's contention that this Tribunal had "no jurisdiction to adjudicate alleged violations of the United Nations Charter and general international law" cannot be accepted.'

[29] K Kress, 'Legal Indeterminacy' (1989) 77 *California Law Review* 283.

[30] Also supporting a view that international law provisions 'are neither determinate nor indeterminate in absolute terms', see A Bianchi, 'Textual Interpretation and (international) law reading: the myth of (in)determinacy and the genealogy of meaning' in P Bekker, R Dolzer and M Waibel (eds) *Making Transnational Law Work in the Global Economy* (CUP, 2010) 54.

[31] It is important to distinguish the claims of the *legal* realists with those of the realist school of thought in international relations. And it is also important to distinguish the core realist claims from other marginal, fringe claims articulated by some American legal realists (e.g., Thurman Arnold).

American legal realists.[32] As Brian Leiter summarises, American legal realism argues that 'judges respond primarily to the stimulus of the facts' (i.e., to non-legal considerations).[33] This means judicial decisions are not exclusively or even preponderantly determined by legal rules which justify only one outcome. In consequence, the American legal realists argue that parts of the law are *causally* and *rationally* indeterminate.[34]

Importantly, and in contrast with the critical legal studies movement, realists never argued that *all* law was indeterminate, but made a rather narrower claim: that law tended to be indeterminate in those cases that were actually litigated, particularly those that reach the appellate stage – what Max Radin called 'marginal cases, in which prognosis is difficult and uncertain'.[35] There is an important difference in degree between *some* rule-scepticism and absolute rule-scepticism. As Schauer explains 'in looking for a legal justification for an outcome selected on other grounds, judges in complex, messy common-law systems will rarely (but not never) be disappointed'.[36] That conclusion may be extrapolated to international law, where it applies with even greater force.

Legal pragmatism also accepts that law is rationally indetermined.[37] Its chief exponent, Richard Posner, observes that '*law*' does not always 'generate acceptable answers to all the legal questions'.[38] Because of that, judges 'have occasional – indeed rather frequent – recourse to other sources of judgment, including their

[32] See B Leiter, *Naturalizing Jurisprudence* (OUP, 2007) 21–23. There are several works addressing legal realism, see eg MJ Horwitz, *The Transformation of American Law 1870-1960: The Crisis of Legal Orthodoxy* (OUP, 1992) 169–212; JW Singer, 'Legal Realism Now' (1988) 76 *California Law Review* 467, 475–95 (reviewing Laura Kalman, *Legal Realism at Yale: 1927-1960* (University of North Carolina Press 1986)); FB Cross, 'Political Science and the New Legal Realism: A Case of Unfortunate Interdisciplinary Ignorance' (1997) 92 *Northwestern University Law Review* 251; TJ Miles and CR Sunstein, 'The New Legal Realism' (2008) 75 *University of Chicago Law Review* 831; 'Symposium, Empirical Legal Realism: A New Social Scientific Assessment of Law and Human Behavior' (2003) 97 *Northwestern University Law Review* 1075; DA Farber, 'Toward a New Legal Realism' (2001) 68 *University of Chicago Law Review* 279 (book review); AF McEvoy, 'A New Realism for Legal Studies' (2005) *Wisconsin Law Review* 433; SE Merry, 'New Legal Realism and the Ethnography of Transnational Law' (2006) 31 *Law & Social Inquiry* 975; V Nourse and G Shaffer, 'Varieties of New Legal Realism: Can a New World Order Prompt a New Legal Theory?' (2009) 25 *Cornell Law Review* 61; E Patterson, *Jurisprudence: Men and Ideas of the Law* (Foundation Press, 1953) 537–56; A Altman, 'Legal Realism, Critical Legal Studies, and Dworkin' (1986) 15 *Philosophy & Public Affairs* 205; H Dagan, 'The Realist Conception of Law' (2007) 56 *University of Toronto Law Journal* 607; GE White, 'The Inevitability of Critical Legal Studies' (1984) 36 *Stanford Law Review* 649, 651; B Leiter, 'American Legal Realism' in M Golding and W Edmundson (eds), *The Blackwell Guide to the Philosophy of Law and Legal Theory* (Blackwell 2005) 52.

[33] Leiter, *Naturalising Jurisprudence* (n 32) 21.

[34] ibid 10.

[35] M Radin, 'In Defence of an Unsystematic Science of Law' (1942) 51 *Yale Law Journal* 1271. As Karl Llewelyn remarked: '[i]f rules were results there would be little need for lawyers', *The Bramble Bush* (OUP, 2008) 9.

[36] F Schauer, *Thinking Like a Lawyer* (Harvard University Press, 2009), 138.

[37] In addition to Posner, other leading legal pragmatists are Daniel Farber, Thomas Grey, and Margaret Radin.

[38] RA Posner, *How Judges Think* (Harvard University Press, 2010) 9. But see also D Farber, 'Legal Pragmatism and the Constitution' (1988) *Minnesota Law Review* 1343, 1343–44.

own political opinions or policy judgments, even idiosyncrasies'.[39] Posner's view of legal pragmatism is less far-reaching than his critics would have. As Posner explains, pragmatism is: 'widely misunderstood to be an "anything goes approach to judging".'[40] He clarifies that it is not, instead explaining that: 'The pragmatic judge is a constrained pragmatist' and she is 'boxed in, as other judges are, by norms that require of judges impartiality, awareness of the importance of the law's being predictable enough to guide the behaviour of those subject to it . . . and due regard for the integrity of the written word in contracts and statutes.'[41]

More recent studies on vagueness and the law also accept a degree of indeterminacy – and rejecting *bivalence,* the view that legal provisions require either/or answers. As Jules Coleman stated, there are strong grounds to argue that at least 'some sentences involving the application of vague predicates are neither true nor false'.[42] Timothy Endicott goes even further. He argues 'when the law is vague, judicial decision-making will in some cases be unconstrained by the law'.[43] For all practical purposes, Endicott considers that vagueness leads to the same conclusion reached by empirical rule scepticism.[44]

Focusing on international law more specifically, the New Haven School acknowledges that international law is subject to some degree of indeterminacy.[45] McDougal, who perhaps took the point too far, contended that: 'The function that "rules" perform is too often that of the squid that confuses its pursuers by squirting black ink. At the best the function of rules can only be to guide

[39] Posner, ibid 9.

[40] ibid 13.

[41] ibid.

[42] JL Coleman, 'Truth and Objectivity in Law' (1995) 1 *Legal Theory* 33, 49.

[43] TAO Endicott, *Vagueness in Law* (OUP, 2000) 4.

[44] There are theorists, most notably Kelsen and Dworkin, which some characterise as subscribing to the epistemic theory of vagueness. The adherents of this theory contend that law has 'special resources that eliminate such indeterminacy'. Kelsen recognises that legal norms will be subject to a certain degree of indeterminacy: 'every legal act applying a norm . . . is determined only in part by this norm and remains indeterminate for the rest', accepting that indeterminacy is caused by either the 'conditioning material fact as well as to the conditions consequence', H Kelsen, *Introduction to the Problems of Legal Theory* (Clarendon Press, 1997), 78–9. Dworkin, in turn, argues that, in the dispute context, indeterminacy does not cause any insurmountable issues because there will practically be a *single* right answer to the vast majority of legal disputes. Thus, Dworkin contends that even if the primary rule (i.e., the words of a statute or the contract) are vague, that does not necessarily lead to indeterminacy, as the relevant cannons of construction or interpretation 'determine what force a vague word must be taken to have in a particular occasion, or at least make its force depend upon further questions that in principle have a right answer. These tests may refer to matters of intention or other psychological fact', R Dworkin, 'On Gaps in the Law' in P Amselek and N MacCormick (eds), *Controversies about Law's Ontology* (Edinburgh University Press, 1991) 84; R Dworkin, *A Matter of Principle* (Harvard University Press, 1985), particularly the chapter *Is there Really No Right Answer in Hard Cases?*; see also R Dworkin, 'No Right Answer' (1978) 53 *NYU Law Review* 12.

[45] More recently, Tai-Heng Cheng explained that 'The New Haven School's solution to the indeterminacy of law was to embrace it and make policy recommendations to stabilize international relations to promote minimum order and human dignity', T-H Cheng, *When International Law Works* (OUP, 2012) 49.

decisionmakers to relevant features of a problem and its context and to appropriate policies.'[46] As Reisman observed, the applicable rules of international law are 'highly ambiguous, allowing decision makers wide discretionary latitude for appreciation of context or milieu'.[47] Because of this, Reisman explains that the policy-oriented approach to the interpretation of international rules goes beyond the 'exclusively textual examination of structures of decision'. Instead, policy-oriented jurisprudence suggests a 'functional approach,' based on a 'process model'.[48] The point was also made cogently by Rosalyn Higgins. She stated that: 'The problem exactly is that various, quite plausible, alternative prescriptions can be and have been argued for. The role of international law is to assist in choice between these various alternatives.'[49] In consequence, that indeterminacy provides the law-applier (here, the judge or arbitrator) with the possibility of making social choices to determine how to give specific content to that indeterminate provision. Higgins concludes that:

> Reference to 'the correct legal view' or 'rules' can never avoid the element of choice (thought it can seek to disguise it), nor can it provide guidance to the preferable decision. In making this choice on must inevitably have consideration for the humanitarian, moral, and social purposes of the law . . . Policy considerations, although they differ from 'rules', are an integral part of that decision making process which we call international law; the assessment of so-called extralegal considerations is part of the legal process, just as is reference to the accumulation of past decisions and current norms . . . I believe there is no avoiding the essential relationship between law and policy.[50]

It is precisely this reference to normative elements which distinguishes the policy-oriented approach from that of the American legal realists. More recently, Tai-Heng Cheng emphasised this normative aspect, explaining that: The New Haven School's solution to the indeterminacy of law was to embrace it and

[46] MS McDougal, 'Remarks at the 79th Annual Meeting of the American Society of International Law' (1985) 79 *Proceedings of the American Society of International Law, McDougal's Jurisprudence: Utility, Influence, Controversy*; Myres S McDougal, Harold D Lasswell and James C Miller, *The Interpretation of Agreements and World Public Order: Principles of Content and Procedure* (Yale University Press, 1967) 39–45.

[47] WM Reisman, *Nullity and Revision: The Review and Enforcement of International Judgments and Awards* (New Haven, Yale University Press, 1971) at 235. For a critical, if unfair, assessment, see Oscar Schacter, 'Remarks at the 79th Annual Meeting of the American Society of International Law' (1985) 272, stating that: 'Policy oriented writers stress the relative flexibility of international prescriptions. They come close to the legal realists' brand of rule-skepticism, in emphasizing that legal prescriptions leave a wide range of discretion to the law-applying organ. However, unlike the legal realists, McDougal and his followers take the strongly normative position that the indeterminacies in the legal process should be resolved by reference to basic purposes. Since competing major purposes still provide a choice of results in most cases, they increase the discretionary element in applying law.'

[48] Schacter ibid 278

[49] R Higgins, *Problems & Process: International Law and How We Use It* (OUP, 1994) 267.

[50] ibid 5.

'make policy recommendations to stabilize international relations to promote minimum order and human dignity.'[51]

In short, provisions of international procedural law are often framed as standards, rather than as rules. As such, they are subject to an inherent degree of indeterminacy; they are somewhat ambiguous. This degree of indeterminacy often provides international adjudicators with some leeway or flexibility, as the interpretation or application of those provisions do not require one (and only one) answer. This means there will often be a plurality of potentially legally correct ways of interpreting or applying that rule. The policy-oriented approach to the indeterminacy of rules of international law aims to take into account normative and policy considerations when deciding which of those potentially correct interpretations or applications to choose. Rather than being dismissed as 'extralegal factors', those policy considerations are relevant to inform that choice. One of the main policy considerations should be the principle of minimum order.[52]

The claims of indeterminacy addressed above – which express *some* degree of rule-scepticism and consider that at least some, but not all, legal provisions are subject to a degree of indeterminacy – are not absolute. They are claims to the *relative* indeterminacy of the legal system. They are not claims to maximalist or radical indeterminacy, which contend that *all* law is indeterminate, from which they must be distinguished. The latter position is adopted by the critical legal studies movement,[53] and in fact it is one of its key tenets.[54] Koskenniemi addressed the issue of indeterminacy cogently in the epilogue to *From Apology to Utopia*:

> [T]he main claim of indeterminacy here is not at all that international legal words are semantically equivalent. It is much stronger . . . and states that that even where there is no semantic ambivalence whatsoever, international law remains indeterminate

[51] Cheng *When International Law Works* (n 45) 49.

[52] As Reisman explained, this involves the 'continued viability of organized authoritative decision processes' and this, in turn, requires that there be some consideration to the decision's eventual effectiveness, as 'a decision incapable of mustering an adequate control base should be examined for the possible repercussions of its nonenforcement on the decision processes concerned', *Nullity and Revision* (n 47) 242.

[53] This goes much further than the claims advanced by other schools that acknowledge a relative degree of indeterminacy in the law. In fact, CLS' views of indeterminacy are so sweeping that they may be considered to make the (nuanced) American legal realists appear as formalists!

[54] It is, of course, also one of the main tenets of critical legal studies in the domestic context. Duncan Kennedy's *Form and Substance in Private Law Adjudication* (n 4) being one of the leading expositions of this approach. Two of the leading exponents of this approach are David Kennedy and Martti Koskenniemi. Kennedy's views on the issue were articulated, for example, in D Kennedy, *International Legal Structures* (Nomos, 1987) 293–94. Nevertheless, some, like Miles, have observed that 'a certain softening in Kennedy's views seems to have crept into his later work', noting that in *The Dark Sides of Virtue*, Kennedy 'assigns lawyers the role of managers within a system of rules with no intrinsic limits but which is at least present in the minds of senior political operatives' see C Miles, 'Indeterminacy' in J d'Aspremont and S Singh, *Concepts for International Law* (Edward Elgar, 2019).

> because it is based on contradictory premises . . . international law emerges from a political process whose participants have contradictory priorities and rarely know with clarity how such priorities should be turned into directives to deal with an uncertain future. Hence they agree to supplement rules with exceptions, have recourse to broadly defined standards and apply rules in the context of other rules and larger principles. Even where there is little or no semantic ambiguity about an expression in a rule . . . it is possible to defend any course of action – including deviation from a clear rule – by professionally impeccable legal arguments that look from rules to their underlying reasons, make choices between several rules as well as rules and exceptions, and interpret rules in the context of evaluative standards . . . The important point . . . is not that all of this should be thought of as a scandal or (even less) a structural 'deficiency' but that indeterminacy is an absolutely central aspect of international law's acceptability.[55]

More recently, the Genovese realists have, in the civil law context, put forward some adamant claims about the indeterminacy both of specific laws and of the legal system more generally. In very broad terms, this is based on the Genovese approach to legal interpretation. The position is summarised by Chiasoni, who claims that in sophisticated legal systems 'legal indeterminacy is not tantamount to linguistic indeterminacy . . . It is in fact a methodological and axiological indeterminacy, moving beyond the boundaries of linguistic indeterminacy'.[56] Similarly, Comanducci argues that one of the main characteristics of legal norms is vagueness, not only in their text, but also in their relation to other legal norms, hence why law is *ex ante* indetermined.[57]

These more expansive views on the indeterminacy of law are, in my view, overstated. The problem is mainly one of degree. The fact that there is *some* indeterminacy in law does not mean that *all* law is indeterminate. This overstatement is the main conceptual pitfall of the critical approach. Similarly, the fact that *some* extra-legal factors may influence the operation of international law does not mean that the totality of international law is determined by those extra-legal factors.

Indeterminacy, however, also has some (determined) critics.[58] One of them is James Crawford, who has articulated a robust critique of both linguistic and

[55] M Koskenniemi, *From Apology to Utopia: The Structure of International Legal Argument* (CUP, 2005) 590–1. But see I Scobbie, 'Towards the Elimination of International Law: Some Radical Scepticism about Sceptical Radicalism' (1990) 61 *British Yearbook of International Law* 339, 348.

[56] P Chiassoni, 'Legal Interpretation without Truth' (2016) 29 *Revus – Journal for Constitutional Theory and Philosophy of Law* 93, 117.

[57] P Comanducci, 'Principios jurídicos e indeterminación del derecho' (1998) 21(II) *Doxa: Cuadernos de Filosofía del Derecho* 89, 103.

[58] Of course, HLA Hart was one of the main critics of even moderate indeterminacy. He then contends that: 'in the vast majority of cases there is very little doubt. The head-note is usually correct enough', Hart, *The Concept of Law* (n 4) 131. Leiter has heavily criticised that statement, in my view, correctly, as it is naïve at best. In Leiter's view: 'every first-year litigation associate knows that this approach to precedent would be a recipe for disaster', Leiter, *American Legal Realism* (n 32) 64. That is right: any lawyer that has been seriously engaged in litigation knows that things are not

substantive indeterminacy. Starting with linguistic indeterminacy, Crawford admits that some particularly difficult issues of linguistic indeterminacy may arise in international law, particularly when one text has several authoritative versions in different languages (thus compounding the potential competing interpretations). Nonetheless, Crawford considers that international law – in particular, Article 31 of the Vienna Convention on the Laws of Treaties and the rules of interpretation set out therein – provide a 'powerful interpretive device capable of rendering sensible meaning to a text, whether or not that text was drafted with Article 31 in mind'.[59]

As to substantive indeterminacy Crawford, defending the concreteness of international law, draws a distinction between *arguing* and *justifying*. In his view, while an 'argument may be made for almost any legal position', that does not mean that the argument will be correct, as international law 'is not so open-ended or mutable as to justify just anything: there comes a point at which a particular argument or interpretation becomes untenable'.[60] I agree. Yet the example that Crawford chooses to illustrate this point is telling; he asks whether there is any correct legal answer to the question of 'how many judges are there on the bench of the International Court' other than 15. Albeit Crawford admits that the choice of example is somewhat facile,[61] it is notorious that he chose a provision that is *obviously* a rule – rather than one that was a standard. Answering how many judges are on the bench is easy; determining whether a dispute exists results in 14 separate or dissenting opinions.[62]

In summary, and to be clear, the theoretical proposition I set out in this book is that there are *some* provisions of international procedural law, mainly those articulated as standards and, as explained below, that are often created through judicial or arbitral decisions that are relatively indetermined. In some of those cases, the indeterminacy of those provisions may allow international courts some flexibility to determine whether to adjudicate a case or issue, that is, to take policy considerations into account when determining both the scope of their jurisdiction and whether to exercise it. This is a moderate, rational form of rule-scepticism.[63] It is in contrast with the maximalist, bolder assertion that *all* law is indeterminate.[64]

---

usually that simple. Were that the case, then one would expect almost no cases to be litigated. And the realists' claims were *mainly* focused on cases that *were* litigated – and not only that, but that were litigated at the appellate level.

[59] J Crawford, *Chance, Order, Change: The Course of International Law* (Brill, 2014) 156.

[60] ibid 172.

[61] ibid.

[62] *Obligations concerning Negotiations relating to Cessation of the Nuclear Arms Race and to Nuclear Disarmament (Marshall Islands v United Kingdom)*, ICJ, Judgment (Preliminary Objections) of 5 October 2016.

[63] Kress 'Legal Indeterminacy' (n 29) 296 and ss; Leiter, *Naturalizing Jurisprudence* (n 32); Schauer *Playing by the Rules* (n 4).

[64] Which is one of the central tenets of the critical legal studies movement and other deconstructionist approaches to interpretation. See eg (n 54) and the references to the critical legal studies movement set out therein; D Kairys, 'Law and Politics' (1984) 52 *George Washington Law Review*

(iii) How International Procedural Law is Created

The way that international law generally, and international procedural law specifically, are created also influences their degree of indeterminacy. The decentralised nature of the international legal system results, almost by definition, in international law having some degree of indeterminacy. For example, in the case of customary international law, there will always be, by definition, multiple interpreters.[65] This means that the content of customary international law is subject to at least a degree of fluidity that may lead to indeterminacy.[66] The situation is not necessarily different in the case of treaties and international agreements. As Cope and Versteeg observe, treaty negotiations usually involve clashing State interests; those opposing interests are ultimately 'reconciled and codified in terse, often vague or ambiguous treaty provisions that reflect a series of compromises.'[67] This, of course, leads to a result where there is no clear consensus about what specific treaty provisions actually mean.[68] Raustiala suggests that States 'use substantive ambiguity to address preference heterogeneity'.[69] This practice is sometimes referred to as 'constructive ambiguity'. Despite its hermeneutical shortcomings. This satisfies an important practical objective: it allows the States-parties to *agree* to certain treaty provision[70] – in a scenario where perhaps more concrete text would have made that impossible.[71] Moreover, the decentralised and mostly horizontal nature of the international system will often mean that there will be no

243, 244-47; D Kairys, 'Legal Reasoning', in D Kairys (ed), *The Politics of Law* 3rd edn (Basic Books, 1998) 11, 15; JW Singer, 'The Player and the Cards: Nihilism and Legal Theory' (1984) 94 *Yale Law Journal* 1; J Boyle, 'The Politics of Reason: Critical Legal Theory and Local Social Thought,' (1985) 133 *University of Pennsylvania Law Review* 685; G Peller, 'The Metaphysics of American Law' (1985) 73 *California Law Review* 1151.

[65] See generally G Novak, *Global Lawmaking and Social Change* (Hart, 2024) 175.

[66] M Byers, *Custom, Power and the Power of Rules: International Relations and Customary International Law* (CUP, 1999) 49; A Roberts, 'Traditional and Modern Approaches to Customary International Law: A Reconciliation' (2001) 95 *American Journal of International Law* 757, 784.

[67] KL Cope and M Versteeg, 'Review Essay: The Interpretation of International Law by Domestic Courts' (2017) 111 *American Journal of International Law* 538, 541.

[68] For an approach that focuses on discourse analysis, see E Friedman, 'Evasion Strategies in International Documents: When "Constructive Ambiguity" Leads to Oppositional Interpretation' (2017) 14(4) *Critical Discourse Studies* 385–401.

[69] Raustiala, *Form and Substance* (n 10) 594.

[70] See O Frishman and E Benvenisti, 'National Courts and Interpretative Approaches to International Law: The Case against Convergence' in HP Aust and G Nolte (eds), *The Interpretation of International Law by Domestic Courts: Uniformity, Diversity, Convergence* (OUP, 2016) 317, 326.

[71] Cope and Versteeg 'Review Essay' (n 67) 337. Nevertheless, some scholars consider that the use of more indeterminate treaty language can have a negative effect on the treaty's implementation and compliance with its provisions, see K Linos and T Pegram, 'The Language of Compromise in International Agreements' (2016) 70 *International Organization* 587. But see WM Reisman, 'Negotiating and Maintaining Investment Treaties: Mechanisms for Anticipating and Controlling Textual Drift' (2019) 9 *Journal of International and Comparative Law* 75, 78 stating that 'the price for securing total agreement may be the artful crafting of a "constructive ambiguity". Constructive ambiguities permit the parties to side-step a negotiating impasse, but these intentional creations are a ticking mandate for courts and tribunals down the line to engage, on a case-by-case basis, in potentially broad interpretation'.

hierarchically superior norm that will set the 'frame' in which an indeterminate provision must be interpreted or applied.

Similarly, while the principles of treaty interpretation are well developed and often provide useful guidance to address (some) issues of linguistic indeterminacy, it is often difficult to ascertain the political justification for entering into a treaty with a similar degree of certainty to that available in a domestic context. Also, arguably the VCLT expressly rejected that type of purpositivism. This may be possible in some instances of bilateral treaties with an easily ascertainable object and purpose, but consider the difficulty in determining this in the case of a multilateral treaty, where each State's internal political justifications for entering into the treaty may vary wildly.[72]

Another generally overlooked question is the *source* of international procedural law: how it is created. Most international courts are either expressly empowered to issue their own procedural rules or, even when they are not, they nevertheless tend to do so in practice. This takes two forms. One is by issuing their own procedural rules. Both standing international courts and arbitral tribunals do so. The other is by creating procedural rules and categories, including issues of jurisdiction and admissibility, at the moment a specific case is decided.

Pellet and Müller say that the ICJ 'commonly formulates new rules under the cover of interpretation', which they characterise as the exercise of a 'de facto legislative power'.[73] Those powers, of course, also apply to the creation of procedural rules. The origins of most relevant doctrines of international procedural law were developed by case law. There is no treaty on jurisdictional objections; the *Monetary Gold* principle was not set out in a convention; nor was the existence of dispute criteria developed by customary international law, for example. These are all mainly judge-created. Their contours, the exact scope of their application, has not been fully determined, either intentionally or not. Their development has been the product of casuistry.[74] In consequence and, as

[72] McDougal's views on purposive interpretation were not successful in the negotiations that led to the Vienna Convention on the Laws of Treaties. McDougal disapproved of an over-reliance on text, considering it 'the grossest, least defensible exercise of arbitrary formalism to arrogate to one particular set of signs – the text of a document – the role of serving as the exclusive index of the parties' shared expectations. We join with those who condemn textualism of this kind as a violation of the human dignity to choose freely' see J Mortensen, 'The Travaux of Travaux: Is the Vienna Convention Hostile to Drafting History?' (2013) 107 *American Journal of International Law* 780, 789. See also MS McDougal, Harold D Lasswell and James C Miller, *The Interpretation of Agreements and World Public Order: Principles of Content and Procedure* (Yale University Press, 1994). For Fitzmaurice's critique, see G Fitzmaurice, 'Vae Victis, or Woe to the Negotiators!: Your Treaty, or Our "Interpretation" of It?' (1971) 65 *American Journal of International Law* 358. For a discussion of the issue in the context of implied terms, see C Miles, 'Implied Terms in Treaties' (2025) 119 *American Journal of International Law* 57.

[73] A Pellet and D Muller 'Article 38' in A Zimmermann, C Tams, K Oellers-Frahm and C Tomuschat (eds), *The Statute of the International Court of Justice: A Commentary* (OUP, 2019) 956.

[74] This is fully articulated in C Sunstein, *One Case at a Time: Judicial Minimalism on the Supreme Court* (Harvard University Press, 2001).

I explain in detail in chapter 5, this has resulted in those doctrines having a particular ductility to them.

To conclude, this section argued that some provisions of international procedural law are relatively indeterminate and that such indeterminacy may allow some flexibility in their application, which in turn allow some policy considerations to play a role in an international court's approach to decisions on jurisdiction and admissibility.

III. COMPETENCE–COMPETENCE

The second particular characteristic of international procedural law is international courts' powers to determine their own jurisdiction. They have jurisdiction (i.e., power) to determine whether they have substantive jurisdiction (i.e., power) over a specific dispute or issue. Shihata provides a useful definition, explaining that competence-competence is: 'the power, or the jurisdiction, to decide whether that substantive jurisdiction exists'.[75] Boisson de Chazournes provides an even pithier definition: 'The Principle of compétence de la compétence refers to the power of an international court or tribunal to define the limits of its own jurisdiction.'[76] Because it is generally the international courts *themselves* who decide whether they have jurisdiction, this provides those courts with a substantial degree of autonomy in the way they decide to *exercise* that jurisdiction (or refrain from doing so). This is the *competence–competence* principle (often also called *Kompetenz-Kompetenz* or *compétence de la competence,* depending on linguistic preferences).

The principle is of old vintage. It was first developed in the mixed commissions that were created under the Jay Treaty of 1794 between the United States and the United Kingdom.[77] The case where the issue initially arose was the *Betsey*.[78] One often overlooked fact is that the competence–competence principle was articulated in a context where both the United States and British commissioners were trying to *derail* the proceedings and so prevent the commission from deciding certain issues. In short, the case involved two sets of proceedings, carried out in Philadelphia and in London. The commissioners in both sets of proceedings were up to mischief. With the objective of depriving the commission

[75] IFI Shihata, *The Power of the International Court to Determine its Own Jurisdiction: Compétence de la Compétence* (Martinus Nijhoff, 1965) 5.

[76] L Boisson de Chazournes, 'The Principle of Compétence de la Compétence in International Adjudication and its Role in an Era of Multiplication of Courts and Tribunals' in RD Sloane and others (eds), *Looking to the Future: Essays in Honor of W Michael Reisman* (Brill, 2010) 1028.

[77] G Schwarzenberger, 'Present-Day Relevance of the Jay Treaty Arbitrations' (1978) 53 *Notre Dame Law Review* 715.

[78] J Ralston and Permanent Court of International Justice, *The Law and Procedure of International Tribunals Being a Résumé of the Views of Arbitrators upon Questions Arising under the Law of Nations and of the Procedure and Practice of International Courts* (Byrne & Co, 1926).

of quorum, the United States commissioners withdrew from the Philadelphia proceedings and the British commissioners withdrew from those in London.[79]

The difference is that, unlike the British commissioners sitting in Philadelphia, the United States commissioners sitting in London filed opinions. The British commissioners had taken the position that if a dispute arose as to the commission's jurisdiction, it was not for the commission itself to decide the issue; rather, they said, the point had to be referred to the States party to the treaty. One of the United States' commissioners, Christopher Gore, disagreed. He observed that: 'A power to decide whether a Claim preferred to this board is within its Jurisdiction, appears to me inherent in its very Constitution, and indispensably necessary to the discharge of any of its duties.'[80] The other United States commissioner, William Pinkney, reached a similar conclusion. He wrote that: 'I think that we are, *of ourselves* and without consulting the high contracting parties, the proper judges . . . of the nature and extent of our powers.'[81]

Often, the *Alabama* tribunal's decision to decline jurisdiction over indirect claims is cited as laying the foundation of the competence–competence principle.[82] In my view, this is mistaken. The conceptual basis for the competence–competence principle has been laid out before, in the opinions of commissioners Gore and Pinkney. More importantly, the issue of the indirect claims in the Alabama arbitration is so particular – and the circumstances that led the tribunal to decline jurisdiction over the indirect claims so *peculiar* – that one should approach that precedent with caution.[83]

In any event, by the late nineteenth and early twentieth centuries the competence–competence principle had been codified in the two most important international treaties on international dispute resolution: the 1899 and 1907 Hague Conventions on the Pacific Settlement of International Disputes.[84] Some

[79] JB Moore, *History and Digest of the International Arbitrations to which the United States has Been a Party* (Government Printing Office, 1898) 2277.

[80] ibid 2278-9 and 2282. Further noting that: 'That a board . . . should have no power to decide whether the Subject matter of Complaint be submitted to it, is with me so palpable a contradiction, that the disrespect which, in my judgment, such a position reflects on the high contracting Parties . . . To say that power is given to decide on the justice of the Claim . . . and yet no Power to decide or examine if the Claim has any justice, any merit even sufficient to be the Subject of Consideration, is to offer in terms a substance, in truth a phantom.'

[81] ibid also stating that: 'it belongs to us and is our indispensable duty, in the first instance, to decide in every case referred to us . . . whether the claim is such a one as the treaty submits to our award . . . Without such a power it is extremely obvious that the authority expressly communicated by the treaty to decide the merits of a claim . . . is completely nominal and illusory.'

[82] G Berlia, *Jurisprudence des tribunaux internationaux en ce qui concerne leur compétence* (Recueil Sirey, 1955) 109.

[83] Shihata *The Power of the International Court* (n 75) 18–19 expressed some scepticism as to the relevance of the *Alabama* award on this issue: 'The *Alabama Arbitration* did not, therefore, create a clear-cut rule as to the *compétence de la compétence*. It emphasized, however, an important fact – the *compétence de la compétence* is a useful device which insures that adjudication will continue even when the parties disagree in the course of the proceedings . . . The assent of the parties was needed to allow the tribunal the power to determine the issue and was necessary to give its declaration a binding character.'

[84] At arts 48 and 73, respectively. The wording of both provisions is materially identical. Art 73 of

years before that, in 1877, the *Institut de Droit International* had also included the principle in its proposed rules for international arbitral procedure.[85] More importantly, international tribunals operating at the turn of the twentieth century were routinely applying the principle, which was not contested. A good example of this is the *Flutie* award, issued by the United States – Venezuelan Mixed Claims Commission. A jurisdictional issue arose regarding the claimant's nationality, as the Commission only had personal jurisdiction over claims brought by United States nationals. It held that, the Commission, as the sole judge of its jurisdiction, must in each case determine for itself the question of such citizenship upon the evidence submitted'.[86]

Yet despite the frequent application of the competence–competence principle by arbitral tribunals, the PCIJ's approach to the principle was ambivalent. At some points the Permanent Court seems to have wholeheartedly endorsed the principle. For instance, in the *Interpretation of the Greco-Turkish Agreement of December 1st, 1926* advisory opinion, the Permanent Court held that the mixed arbitral tribunal created under that treaty had competence–competence. After observing that the treaty was silent on the issue, the Permanent Court held that: 'as a general rule, any body possessing jurisdictional powers has the right in the first place itself to determine the extent of its jurisdiction'.[87] In other instances, however, it was more cautious. For example, in *Free Zones of Upper Savoy and the District of Gex,* the Permanent Court was more restrained, holding that jurisdictional clauses had to be interpreted somewhat strictly.[88]

---

the 1907 Convention provides that: 'The Tribunal is authorized to declare its competence in interpreting the 'Compromis', as well as the other Treaties which may be invoked, and in applying the principles of law.' The two Hague Conventions have been addressed in detail in Chapter 2.

[85] Institut de Droit International, '*Project de réglement pour la procedure arbitrale internationale'*, Session de La Haye – 1875, *Annuaire* (1877) 130. Article 14 provides that: 'In cases where the doubts regarding the tribunal's jurisdiction depends on the interpretation of a clause of a compromis, the parties are considered to have provided the arbitrators the power to determine that question, unless when a clause provides the contrary' (my translation).

[86] *Flutie Cases* 9 RIAA 152 (US-Ven Mixed Claims Comm 1903–1905). See also the *Walfish Bay Boundary* arbitration between Germany and Great Britain, where the tribunal held that: 'it is a constant doctrine of public international law that the arbitrator has powers to settle questions as to his own competence by interpreting the range of the agreement, submitting to his decision the question in dispute', 11 RIAA 263, 307 (1909).

[87] *Interpretation of the Greco-Turkish Agreement of 1 December 1926 (Final Protocol, art IV),* PCIJ, Advisory Opinion of 1 December 1926, 20–21.

[88] *Free Zones of Upper Savoy and the District of Gex (France v Switzerland),* PCIJ, Order of 19 August 1929, 13. Some scholars consider the PCIJ's approach too timid, characterising it as developing a *presumption of incompetence*, Boisson de Chazournes 'The Principle of Compétence de la Compétence (n 76) 50. See also J Basdevant, G Jeze and N Politis, 'Les principes juridiques sur la competence des jurisdictions internationales et, en particulier, des Tribunaux Arbitraux Mixtes organises par les Traites de paix de Versailles, de Saint-Germain, de Trianon (1927) 44 *Revue du Droit Public et de las science politique en France et a l'etranger* 45, 46–47, stating that: 'The jurisdiction of international tribunals is much narrower than that of national tribunals. Not only is it always exceptional, but further it derogates from a fundamental rule of general international law: that international disputes are not solved by tribunals' (my translation). The Permanent Court's approach in the *Peter Pázmány University* case (*Appeal from a Judgment of the Hungaro-Czechoslovak Mixed Arbitral Tribunal (The Peter Pázmány University v The State of Czechoslovakia) (Czechoslovakia v*

In modern times, the competence–competence principle has been adopted in the procedural rules of many international fora.[89] Three examples illustrate this:

1. Article 36(6) of the ICJ Statute provides that in 'the event of a dispute as to whether the Court has jurisdiction, the matter shall be settled by the decision of the Court'.
2. Article 288(4) of UNCLOS is worded in very similar terms: 'in the event as to whether a court or tribunal has jurisdiction, the matter shall be settled by decision of that court or tribunal'.
3. The ICSID Convention frames it differently (but achieves the same objective), stating at Article 41(1) that 'The Tribunal shall be the judge of his own competence.'

This acceptance of the competence–competence principle can be traced to the ICJ's early practice. Early on, the Court expressly discarded the *presumption of incompetence* approach mentioned above. Some consider that the first decisive step was Judge (*ad hoc*) Spiropoulo's individual opinion in the *Ambatielos* case in 1952.[90] The principle, however, was articulated in more detail the following year, in 1953, in the Court's preliminary objections judgment in the *Nottebohm* case.[91] Although the Court placed undue reliance on the *Alabama* precedent, it reiterated the importance of the competence-competence principle. The Court held that:

> Paragraph 6 of Article 36 [of the ICJ's Statute] is drafted in the broadest terms . . . [it] merely adopted, in respect of the Court, a rule consistently accepted by general international law in the matter of international arbitration. Since the Alabama case, it has been generally recognized, following the earlier precedents, that, in the absence of any agreement to the contrary, an international tribunal has the right to decide as to its own jurisdiction and has the power to interpret for this purpose the instruments which govern that jurisdiction . . . the Court has not hesitated to adjudicate on the question of its own jurisdiction.[92]

Hungary), PCIJ, Judgment of 15 December 1933, 220–21, where it considered whether it had jurisdiction (under the *competence–competence* principle), but without expressly admitting that it was relying on it, is cited as an example of this timidity.

[89] For example, at art 36(6) of the Statute of the International Court of Justice.

[90] *Ambatielos Case (Greece v United Kingdom)*, ICJ, Judgment (Preliminary Objection) of 1 July 1952, Individual Opinion of Judge Spiropoulos, 54: 'in questions of arbitration, it is at the present time well recognized that if one of the parties should, for any reason, consider that the arbitral tribunal lacks jurisdiction to deal with the dispute, the question whether it in fact has jurisdiction is one that cannot be decided, as an exercise of sovereignty, by the party raising the objection to the jurisdiction, but it must be decided by the arbitral tribunal itself. The tribunal which adjudicates on the case must also adjudicate on the objection. This is a point on which, at the present time, no one can have any doubt'.

[91] The substantive decision in that case on matters of nationality was, in my opinion, severely flawed. For my criticism, see Casas 'Nationalities of Convenience' (n 14) 75–80.

[92] *Nottebohm Case (Liechtenstein v Guatemala)*, ICJ, Judgment (Preliminary Objections) of 19 November 1953.

One year later, in 1954, the Court dispelled any lingering doubts regarding the importance of the competence–competence principle in the *Monetary Gold* judgment.[93] The Court further bolstered the application of the principle more recently: in *Croatian Genocide* it highlighted that the competence–competence principle applied *always* – even when there were purportedly severe deficiencies in the application to the Court. There, Serbia had contended that the *competence–competence* principle did not apply because the applicant, Croatia, lacked capacity to participate in the proceedings. In Serbia's view, that deficiency constituted a '*fundamental question*' that precluded any further jurisdictional examination and, in consequence, meant that the Court could not even apply the competence-competence principle to determine its own jurisdiction. The Court rejected that argument – roundly. It held that: 'the Court cannot endorse the radical interpretation advanced by Serbia, namely that whenever it is seised by a State which does not fulfil those conditions, the Court does not even have the competence de la competence, the competence to decide whether or not it has jurisdiction', concluding that the Court 'always possesses the *competence de la competence*'.[94]

Other international courts have also recognised the importance of competence–competence. This includes international criminal tribunals. One example is the Appeal Chamber of the International Criminal Tribunal for the Former Yugoslavia's judgment in *Tadić*. There, the Appellate Chamber considered, first, that competence–competence was part of an international court's inherent powers and, second, that those powers could be exercised even when they were *not* expressly included in the court's constitutive treaty or instrument. The Appellate Chamber held that competence–competence: 'is part, and indeed a major part, of the incidental or inherent jurisdiction of any judicial or arbitral tribunal, consisting of its "jurisdiction to determine its own jurisdiction".'[95]

Some scholars consider that there are two distinct approaches to the competence–competence principle: one expansive, one restrictive.[96] In short, the extensive approach applies when, other than the parties' consent to a court's jurisdiction, there are no other overarching or underlying jurisdictional requirements. In those cases, having established State consent, the court or tribunal will have a '*quasi-unlimited*' power to determine its own jurisdiction.[97] In contrast,

[93] *Monetary Gold* (n 16), 28.

[94] *Application of the Convention on the Prevention and Punishment of the Crime of Genocide* (*Croation v Serbia*), Judgment (Preliminary Objections) of 14 November 2008, para 86.

[95] *Prosecutor v Tadić* (Decision on the Defence Motion for Interlocutory Appeal on Jurisdiction) IT-94-1-AR72 (2 October 1995) para 18. The Appellate Chamber then held that: 'It is a necessary component in the exercise of the judicial function and does not need to be expressly provided for in the constitutive documents of those tribunals . . . This is not merely a power in the hands of the tribunal. In international law, where there is no integrated judicial system and where every judicial or arbitral organ needs a specific constitutive instrument defining its jurisdiction, the first obligati on of any [international court] is to ascertain its own competence.'

[96] Boisson de Chazournes (n 76) 1045–55.

[97] ibid 1045-48.

the restrictive approach applies when there are specific jurisdictional requirements that must be met – and that courts or tribunals *must* ensure are satisfied before exercising their jurisdiction and adjudicating a dispute.[98] This is the case of arbitrations under the ICSID Convention, which incorporates *objective requirements* (i.e., factors other than the parties' consent) that must be satisfied for an arbitral tribunal to have jurisdiction under the Convention.[99]

Both the expansive and the restrictive approaches to competence–competence give international courts broad powers to determine their own jurisdiction. As shown above, even when the competence–competence principle is not expressly provided for in an international court's constitutive treaty, courts have often found the principle to apply nonetheless, on grounds that it is considered part of its inherent jurisdiction. Similarly, it has also often been held that international courts may rely on competence-competence to consider, of their own volition, whether jurisdictional requirements are satisfied – even in relation to issues that have not been challenged by the parties.[100]

Put simply, international courts and tribunals enjoy a substantial, *almost* unchecked power to determine their own jurisdiction. Those powers are often exercised with a degree of flexibility that is greater than those enjoyed by domestic courts. This, in turn, is an important factor in allowing them to exercise jurisdictional avoidance, particularly when that power to determine their own jurisdiction is coupled with the relative indeterminacy of a good deal of international procedural law.

IV. THE (GENERAL) LACK OF APPELLATE OR SECOND LEVEL REVIEW

The third characteristic of international procedural law is the general absence of appellate or second level review mechanisms. Of course, there are a few international courts whose decisions are subject to *some* sort of review.[101] Decisions by ICSID tribunals may be challenged at the annulment phase, at least in theory.

[98] ibid 1050-53.

[99] See eg Art 25 of the ICSID Convention.

[100] See eg the ICJ's judgment in *Fisheries Jurisdiction (United Kingdom v Iceland)*, ICJ, Judgment of 2 February 1973, 52, where, although the respondent State, Iceland, did not appear, the Court nevertheless considered the potential objections to its jurisdiction. The Court held that: 'It is to be regretted that the Government of Iceland has failed to appear in order to plead the objections to the Court's jurisdiction which it is understood to entertain. Nevertheless the Court, in accordance with its Statute and its settled jurisprudence, must examine *proprio motu* the question of its own jurisdiction to consider the Application of the United Kingdom.' Invoking art 53 of the Statute, the Court further held that 'whenever one of the parties does not appear before the Court, or fails to defend its case, the Court, before finding upon the merits, must satisfy itself that it has jurisdiction . . . the Court, in examining its own jurisdiction, will consider those objections which might, in its view, be raised against its jurisdiction'.

[101] The 1899 and 1907 Hague Conventions (discussed in chapter 2) both included a right to request the revision of a judgment (although query whether that is in reality analogous to appellate review).

WTO panels may be reviewed by the Appellate Body. In international criminal law it is generally accepted[102] that defendants have the right to appeal their convictions.[103] And some regional tribunals, such as the ECtHR, have two-tiered mechanisms that provide for some review.[104] Yet international courts that are subject to some form of second-level review are the exception rather than the rule. Decisions from the ICJ, ITLOS, the IACtHR and inter-State arbitral tribunals are generally not subject to any type of review, as they are single-instance proceedings.

Even when international adjudication provides some form of second-level review, the *degree* of review is often narrower and more limited than that carried out by domestic courts.[105] Consider Article 52 of the ICSID Convention. That provision sets out the grounds on which an award may be annulled.[106] The grounds are narrow.[107] Essentially, they only allow the annulment of an award when egregious violations of due process have taken place. The result is that only 2.6% of awards are annulled.[108] So, in practice, the odds of an ICSID Award being annulled are minimal (which, in itself, raises questions as to the effectiveness of the annulment process as a control mechanism). This may explain why

[102] See eg D Djukic, *The Right to Appeal in International Criminal Law* (Brill, 2019).

[103] See 'Appeal and Revision' in BD Taylor III and others (eds), *International Criminal Law Practitioner Library: International Criminal Procedure* (CUP, 2011), vol III, 423, 426. In part this is a result of the inclusion of a right to appeal in criminal cases in several international human rights treaties and conventions, including the Universal Declaration of Human Rights, Protocol 7 to the European Convention on Human Rights, the International Covenant on Civil and Political Rights and the American Convention on Human Rights.

[104] European Convention on Human Rights, art 43. In any event, submission to the Grand Chamber is only permitted in 'exceptional cases'.

[105] Although there are some that argue that the annulment process is a de facto 'appeal on procedural grounds', see N Gal-Or, 'The Concept of Appeal in International Dispute Settlement' (2008) 19 *European Journal of International Law* 43, 53.

[106] In the words of Lucy Reed and her co-authors, the ICSID annulment mechanism is 'designed to safeguard the integrity, not the outcome, of ICSID arbitration proceedings', see L Reed and others, *Guide to ICSID Arbitration* 2nd edn (Kluwer Law International, 2011) 162.

[107] They are:

'(a) that the Tribunal was not properly constituted;
(b) that the Tribunal has manifestly exceeded its powers;
(c) that there was corruption on the part of a member of the Tribunal;
(d) that there has been a serious departure from a fundamental rule of procedure; or
(e) that the award has failed to state the reasons on which it is based.'

[108] ICSID, *Background Paper on Annulment* (2024) para 33. Despite that, some commentators criticise what they consider to be the expansive approach taken by some annulment committees. Bishop and Marchilli observe that those committees have 'effectively expand[ed] the scope of annulment to encompass the characteristics of a *de facto* appeal'. They further note that some committees, while 'emphasizing the different features that separate appellate courts from annulment committees, as well as the limited role of annulment committees under the ICSID Convention' have, nevertheless, 'effectively assumed the role of appellate courts' when deciding disputes. This, in their view represents a 'substantial departure from the ICSID system'. There is, of course, some irony in the fact that even in a system such as ICSID with a second-level review mechanism, there are still important discrepancies and uncertainties regarding the role and scope of the annulment process, see RD Bishop and SM Marchili, *Annulment Under the ICSID Convention* (OUP, 2012) paras 1.03–1.07.

there is so much divergence in the interpretation of legal – including procedural – concepts in investor-State arbitration.

Even the WTO's Appellate Body,[109] which has some wide-ranging powers at least as to treaty interpretation, still has more limited review powers than most domestic appellate courts.[110] The Appellate Body's jurisdiction is set out in Article 17.6 of the DSU. It is limited to 'issues of law covered in the panel report and legal interpretations developed by the panel'. This means that the Appellate Body 'cannot deal with any factual issue' although this prohibition is sometimes tempered by the fact that the distinction between fact and law is not always clear-cut.[111] The WTO Appellate Body has had success in providing some stability to international trade law. In international dispute settlement that may be a rare commodity.[112] According to one study, the application of Appellate Body precedents 'moderate the influence of political pressures' on WTO panels.[113] However, in the words of one prominent commentator, the Appellate Body's overall record is something of 'a mixed bag'.[114] More importantly, it is difficult to extrapolate too much from the WTO system. The WTO's dispute settlement mechanisms operate in a very particular, self-contained regime with an enforcement mechanism that is relatively robust.[115]

The situation is different in domestic courts. Their judgments are *generally* subject to appellate review. This includes first instance decisions on procedural and jurisdictional issues. Even in jurisdictions like England & Wales, where there is no automatic right to appeal, difficult decisions, including those on procedural and jurisdictional issues, tend to find their way to appellate courts. To name but one example, in *FS Cairo (Nile Plaza) LLC v Lady Brownlie*,[116] the Supreme Court considered issues of the English courts' jurisdiction to hear personal injury claims for injuries suffered abroad.

The above applies with even greater force in the case of legal systems that establish an automatic *right* to appeal (at least to first-level appellate courts). In

[109] M Matsushita, J Schoenbaum, P Mavroidis and M Hahn, *The World Trade Organization: Law, Practice, and Policy* 3rd edn (OUP, 2015) para 3.7.

[110] P Mavroidis, *The Process before the Appellate Body* (CUP, 2022) 216.

[111] M Matsushita, 'Some Thoughts on the Appellate Body' in PFJ Macrory, AE Appleton and MG Plummer (eds), *The World Trade Organization: Legal, Economic and Political Analysis* vol 1 (New York, Springer, 2005) 1389. See in the same book, V Donaldson, 'The Appellate Body: Institutional and Procedural Aspects') at 1277340. For an insightful discussion between several current and former members of the Appellate Body, see S Charnovitz 'WTO Appellate Body Roundtable' (2005) 99 *Proceedings of the Annual Meeting of the American Society of International Law.*

[112] M Matsushita, 'The Dispute Settlement Mechanism at the WTO: The Appellate Body—Assessment and Problems' in M Daunton, A Narlikar and RM Stern (eds), *The Oxford Handbook on the World Trade Organization* (OUP, 2012) 511.

[113] CD Creamer, 'Between the Letter of the Law and the Demands of Politics: The Judicial Balancing of Trade Authority within the WTO' (working paper, 2015).

[114] Mavroidis *The Process* (n 110) 217.

[115] AW Shoyer, EM Solovy and AW Koff, 'Implementation and Enforcement of Dispute Settlement Decisions' in PFJ Macrory, AE Appleton and MG Plummer (eds), *The World Trade Organization: Legal, Economic and Political Analysis* vol 1 (New York, Springer, 2005) 1341.

[116] *FS Cairo (Nile Plaza) LLC v Brownlie* [2021] UKSC 45.

those systems, decisions from first instance courts, at least when the issues they address are seriously debatable, also tend to find their way to appellate courts. And even in systems where appeals beyond the first-level appellate courts are not provided for as of right (e.g., the United States), decisions on complex procedural and jurisdictional issues are often reviewed by apex courts. For instance, the United States Supreme Court recently addressed federal court's jurisdiction to review arbitral awards in *Badgerow v Walters*.[117] The level of review of complex procedural and jurisdictional issues is even more intense in some civil law systems. Some, for instance, establish specific procedures and courts to address jurisdictional conflicts.[118] The questions are decided. Lower courts, at least in systems with *stare decisis*, are then bound by those decisions from their hierarchically superior courts; those that are not at least have the persuasive guidance of superior courts.

Therefore, the degree and extent of appellate or second-level review provides conceptual clarity on procedural issues – much more so than what is available at the international level. If there are mistakes at first instance on the application of procedural rules, it is usually possible for those mistakes to be corrected up the appellate chain. This is in stark contrast with the constant uncertainty found at the international level, as shown throughout this book. This lack of second-level review also plays a role in jurisdictional avoidance. Free from second-level review, most international courts have a high degree of flexibility to apply relatively indeterminate rules of procedural law, including as implied avoidance techniques.

V. THE RELATIVE INDETERMINACY OF INTERNATIONAL PROCEDURAL LAW IN PRACTICE

This section explores how the relative indeterminacy of international procedural law operates in practice. To do so, it focuses on three issues. Two are from the field of investment arbitration. Given the number of decisions and the varying composition of arbitral tribunals, investment arbitration is perhaps the ideal

[117] *Badgerow v Walters* 596 US ___, 9 (2022). With that decision, the Supreme Court clarified the role that federal courts would have at the challenge and enforcement stage of arbitrations governed by the Federal Arbitration Act (and determined that claims to confirm or vacate arbitral awards will now rarely be properly before federal courts), holding that: 'we can see why Congress chose to place fewer arbitration disputes in federal court ... The statutory plan, as suggested above, makes Section 9 and 10 applications conform to the normal – and sensible – judicial division of labor: The applications go to state, rather than federal, courts when they raise claims between non-diverse parties involving state law'.

[118] Consider the Spanish Organic Law of the Judicial Power, which regulates the Spanish judiciary. That Organic Law includes a specific section that addresses jurisdictional conflicts, including those between courts and the public administration, as well as jurisdictional conflicts between courts (as many civil law jurisdictions do, Spain has a judiciary that is divided between courts that cover specific subject matters), see Title III of the Organic Law of the Judicial Power (Organic Law 6/1985, dated 1 July), particularly arts 38 and 42.

sub-field of international adjudication to show the indeterminacy of international procedural law in action. The third example is from the International Court of Justice and relates to a fundamental concept of international procedural law: res judicata. These are just meant to be illustrative.

These examples illustrate the theoretical claim made earlier in this chapter: namely, that many provisions of international procedural law are standards; that, as such, they are somewhat indeterminate; that they are open to different interpretations and provide international courts with some flexibility in their application; and that such flexibility may allow policy considerations to come into play when international courts decide to adjudicate a case or issue.

A. First Example: The Requirement to Pursue Domestic Litigation

Some investment treaties require a party to pursue domestic remedies as a prerequisite to bringing a claim in arbitration. Given how often the issue comes up, and given the importance of the concepts involved, one would think this question would either be already settled (or at least close to being settled). Far from it.

Consider the Annulment Committee's decision in *Kiliç v Turkmenistan*.[119] Kiliç was a Turkish construction company carrying out construction projects in Turkmenistan. At one point, Kiliç was concerned with the performance of the contract and wrote to Turkmenistani institutions to seek to resolve those issues.[120] The Turkey-Turkmenistan BIT required that any party wishing to raise a claim in arbitration would first need to submit that dispute to domestic courts. Only if those courts had not rendered their judgment after one year would the investor be able to initiate arbitration.[121] Kiliç did not do so, as it considered it would have been 'obviously futile'.[122] So it initiated arbitration having skipped that step.

In *Kiliç*, the tribunal declined jurisdiction over the investor's claim because the investor had failed to pursue domestic remedies (i.e., the local litigation

[119] For general comments on this dispute, see MH Arsanjani and WM Reisman, 'Babel and BITs: Divergence Analysis and Authentication in the Unusual Decision of *Kiliç v Turkmenistan*' in D Caron, S Schill, A Cohen Smuty and E Triantafilou (eds), *Practising Virtue: Inside International Arbitration* (OUP, 2015) 407 and ff; B Demirkol, 'Interpretation of the Dispute Settlement Clause in Turkish Investment Treaties with Turkic States' (2016) 32 *Arbitration International* 29-43; R Sharma, 'Is There Any Role for Linguists Among Lawyers in Arbitration' (2016) 9 *Contemporary Asia Arbitration Journal* 249.

[120] *Kılıç İnşaat İthalat İhracat Sanayi ve Ticaret Anonim Şirketi v Turkmenistan* (Award) ICSID Case No ARB/10/1 (2 July 2013) paras 2.2.1–2.2.9.

[121] Article VII.2 of the Turkey-Turkmenistan BIT: 'if these disputes cannot be settled in this way within six month following the date of the written notification . . . the dispute can be submitted, as the investor may choose, to [ICSID, UNCITRAL, or ICC] provided that, if the investor concerned has brough the dispute before the courts of justice of the Party that is a party to the dispute and a final award has not been rendered within one year'.

[122] *Kiliç* (n 120) para 3.4.1.

requirement) for at least one year.[123] A majority of the tribunal considered that the requirement was jurisdictional rather than of admissibility, on the basis that it 'constitute[s] fundamental jurisdictional conditions to the Contracting Parties' offer to arbitrate . . . [and not] merely conditions for the implementation of a consent that has already been given'.[124]

The Annulment Committee upheld the Tribunal's award declining jurisdiction. Yet the Committee's position was surprising, even if only for its candour in admitting that, on some issues, there is no single right answer and, in consequence, that there will be some variation between the approaches different tribunals take:

> Irrespective of the merits of the reasoning of the Majority of the Tribunal, this is a matter that would be decided by another tribunal unbound by findings of the Tribunal . . . Faced with the same question, other tribunals have decided differently on questions of jurisdiction and admissibility; it is not for the Committee to favor one or the other of these positions.[125]

In fact, the Annulment Committee further acknowledged that the rule regarding the exhaustion of domestic remedies was a 'flexible rule' and so the tribunal had an 'implicit discretion' to set the threshold that was required to satisfy it.[126] The Annulment Committee expressly articulated that, when faced with exactly the same jurisdictional provision, different tribunals may validly reach diametrically opposing conclusions.[127] That is, indeed, the case. Many arbitral tribunals have reached the opposite conclusion, finding that an investor's failure to exhaust domestic remedies does not deprive an arbitral tribunal of jurisdiction. For example, the jurisdictional decision in *Ambiente Ufficio S.p.A. v. Argentine Republic*,[128] a claim concerning a mass claim by Italian holders of Argentinian sovereign bonds. The tribunal found that, despite the existence of a requirement to exhaust domestic remedies, the claimants' failure to do so did not cause any jurisdictional issues. The Argentinian Supreme Court had already held that bondholders could not sue before Argentinian courts to obtain payments for their bonds.[129] Because of that, the tribunal concluded that: 'having recourse to the Argentine domestic courts . . . would not have offered

[123] ibid para 11.1.

[124] ibid para 6.5.2. One of the arbitrators, William W Park, dissented. He considered that interpreting the requirement in Article VII.2 of the BIT as establishing a pre-condition to arbitrate would not contribute to a stable framework for investments; he considered that it should be characterised as a 'procedural requirement not reaching the level of jurisdictional precondition', Separate Opinion of William W Park paras 21–23.

[125] *Kılıç İnşaat İthalat İhracat Sanayi ve Ticaret Anonim Şirketi v Turkmenistan* (Decision on Annulment) ICSID Case No ARB/10/1 (14 July 2015) para 166.

[126] ibid paras 169–73.

[127] ibid para 166.

[128] *Ambiente Ufficio SpA and others v Argentine Republic* (Decision on Jurisdiction and Admissibility) ICSID Case No ARB/08/9 (8 February 2013).

[129] Corte Suprema de Justicia de la Nacion, *Galli Hugo G y otro/Poder Ejecutivo Nacional* s/ amparo, final, decision 5 Abril 2005 (Fallos: 328:690).

Claimants a reasonable possibility to obtain effective redress . . . and would have accordingly been futile'.[130] On that basis, it considered that they had not breached the BIT's jurisdictional pre-requisite for the exhaustion of domestic remedies.[131] From a doctrinal perspective, neither decision is obviously wrong. Both the exhaustion of domestic remedies rule – and the futility exception – are standards rather than rules.[132] Their open texture means that both options are defensible. This is far from single-right-answer territory.

B. Second Example: Most-Favoured Nation and Jurisdiction

The second example is whether it is possible for claimants to invoke most-favoured-nation (MFN) clauses in BITs to establish, modify, or expand the jurisdiction of arbitral tribunals.[133] MFN clauses allow one party to 'import' the substantive provisions of another treaty, which do not directly apply to it.[134] That is uncontroversial.[135] But the application of MFN clauses to jurisdiction provisions is not that straightforward. Essentially, this means using the MFN provision in one investment treaty (that covers the claimant) to 'import' more favourable jurisdictional provisions set out in *another* investment treaty (that does *not* cover the claimant). For example, this can be done to *attempt* to avoid the application of a jurisdictional requirement to exhaust domestic remedies or one that includes a more favourable choice of arbitral forum.[136] The issue is contentious – and has divided both tribunals and scholarship.

The first award that decided that it was possible to rely on an MFN provision to 'import' jurisdictional provisions from other treaties was *Maffezini v Spain*.[137] As Douglas explains, *Maffezini* 'was the first time that a party had been

[130] *Ambiente Ufficio* (n 128) para 620.

[131] ibid.

[132] Although arguably the exhaustion of domestic remedies is a standard that has become ruleified, see F Schauer, 'The Tyranny of Choice and the Rulification of Standards' (2005) 14 *Journal of Contemporary Legal Issues* 803.

[133] See eg Z Douglas, 'The MFN Clause in Investment Arbitration: Treaty Interpretation Off the Rails' (2011) 2 *Journal of International Dispute Settlement* 97; SW Schill, 'Allocating Adjudicatory Authority: Most-Favoured-Nation Clauses as a Basis of Jurisdiction—A Reply to Zachary Douglas' (2011) 2 *Journal of International Dispute Settlement* 353; E Gaillard, 'Establishing Jurisdiction Through a Most-Favoured-Nation Clause' (2005) 233 *New York Law Journal* 105.

[134] Originally, MFN provisions were designed to prevent a situation where, through a free trade agreement, a State granted preferential market access to specific trading partners. The MFN thus aims to equalise the playing field, preventing any nationality-based differential treatment. See UNCTAD, *Most-Favoured-Nation Treatment: A Sequel* (United Nations, 2010), particularly the Introduction.

[135] C McLachlan, L Shore and M Weiniger, *International Investment Arbitration: Substantive Principles* 2nd edn (OUP, 2017) para 7.161.

[136] The classic example of this is *Emilio Agustín Maffezini v Kingdom of Spain* (Decision on Objections to Jurisdiction) ICSID Case No ARB/97/7 (25 January 2000).

[137] *Emilio Agustín Maffezini v Kingdom of Spain* (Award) ICSID Case No ARB/97/7 (13 November 2000).

permitted to rely upon an MFN clause to modify the jurisdictional mandate of an arbitral tribunal'.[138] Other tribunals have followed suit, including those in *Gas Natural SDG v Argentina,*[139] *Suez v Argentina*,[140] and *National Grid v Argentina.*[141] The *Austrian Lines v Slovakia* award states that there was 'no conceptual reason why an MFN clause should be limited to substantive guarantees and rule out procedural protections, the latter being a means to enforce the former'.[142]

Other tribunals disagreed. Some expressed their reluctance in strong terms. The first to do so was the Tribunal in *Plama v Bulgaria*,[143] which concluded that:

> [T]he 'basket of treatment' and 'self-adaptation of the MFN provision' in relation to dispute settlement provisions (as alleged by the Claimant) has effect that the investor has the option to pick and choose provisions from the various BITs. If that were true, a host State which has not specifically agreed thereto can be confronted with a large number of permutations of dispute settlement provisions from the various BITs which it has concluded. Such a chaotic situation . . . cannot be presumed to be the intent of the contracting parties.[144]

The issue has not been definitely solved. In *Impregilo v Argentina*, the majority of the tribunal stated that 'It is true that, as stated above, the jurisprudence regarding the application of MFN clauses to dispute settlement provisions is not fully consistent.'[145] This is an understatement. Rather than an absence of full consistency, arbitral tribunals are interpreting materially identical provisions in opposite ways.

The difference in the precise text of the treaty provisions does not explain this divergence. Julie Maupin concluded that 'neither the type of MFN clause nor the type of MFN question nor the set of reasons considered determined the outcome of MFN-based jurisdiction decisions'.[146] Perhaps it is causal (as opposed to linguistic or semantic) indeterminacy which was ultimately guiding the different tribunals' approach. Douglas, somewhat indignantly, observes that it 'is notorious that this question has proved to be among the most divisive in

[138] Douglas 'The MFN Clause in Investment Arbitration' (n 133) 100–1.

[139] *Gas Natural SDG SA v Argentine Republic* (Decision on Preliminary Questions on Jurisdiction) ICSID Case No ARB/03/10 (17 June 2005).

[140] *Suez, Sociedad General de Aguas de Barcelona SA and InterAguas Servicios Integrales del Agua SA v Argentine Republic* (Decision on Jurisdiction) ICSID Case No ARB/03/17 (16 May 2006).

[141] *National Grid plc v Argentine Republic* (Decision on Jurisdiction) UNCITRAL (20 June 2006). The gist of the issue is captured in *Gas Natural* (n 139) para 49, where the Tribunal held that: '*Unless it appears clearly that the state parties to a BIT or the parties to a particular investment agreement settled on a different method for resolution of disputes that may arise, most-favoured-nation provisions in BITs should be understood to be applicable to dispute resolution.*'

[142] *Austrian Airlines v Slovak Republic* (Final Award) UNCITRAL (9 October 2009) para 124.

[143] *Plama Consortium Limited v Republic of Bulgaria* (Decision on Jurisdiction) ICSID Case No ARB/03/24 (8 February 2005) para 219.

[144] ibid.

[145] *Impregilo SpA v Argentine Republic* (Award) ICSID Case No ARB/07/17 (21 June 2011) para 108.

[146] JA Maupin, 'MFN-based Jurisdiction in Investor-State Arbitration: Is There Any Hope for a Consistent Approach?' (2011) 14(1) *Journal of International Economic Law* 157, 175.

the jurisprudence. This does not bode well for the future of precise questions in this field'.[147] In sum, despite many tribunals having addressed this question – a fundamental issue of international procedural law, which appears in a substantial number of international treaties and comes up in a non-negligible number of cases – there is no straight, unequivocal answer.

C. Third Example: res judicata

The third example is the ICJ's treatment of *res judicata* in its decision in *Question of the Delimitation of the Continental Shelf between Nicaragua and Colombia beyond 200 nautical miles from the Nicaraguan Coast*.[148] Colombia raised a series of preliminary objections, one of them being that the issue was *res judicata*.[149] This was not the first time the two States were disputing maritime delimitation issues before the Court. Less than four years before, the Court had decided *Territorial and Maritime Dispute*.[150] That dispute mainly concerned a maritime boundary in the Western Caribbean. Nicaragua had claimed for an extended continental shelf. In the 2012 judgment, the Court held that Nicaragua's claim for an extended continental shelf was admissible, but concluded that it could not 'uphold' that claim.[151] In *Question of Delimitation*, Colombia contended that Nicaragua was trying to re-submit to the Court an issue that had already been decided (against it), so Nicaragua was precluded from doing so due to *res judicata*.

[147] Douglas (n 133) 97. He also observed that none of the camps could 'claim a clear numerical supremacy of adherents'.

[148] *Question of the Delimitation of the Continental Shelf between Nicaragua and Colombia beyond 200 nautical miles from the Nicaraguan Coast (Nicaragua v Colombia)*, ICJ, Judgment (Preliminary Objections) of 17 March 2016.

[149] Generally, *res judicata* is accepted as a general principle of international law. For example, see H Lauterpacht, *Private Law Sources and Analogies of International Law: With Special Reference to International Arbitration* (Longmans, Green & Co, 1927) 206; B Cheng, *General Principles of Law: As Applied by International Courts and Tribunals* (CUP, 2006) 337; I Scobbie, 'Res Judicata, Precedent and the International Court: A Preliminary Sketch' (1999) 20 *Australian Yearbook of International Law* 299; Brown *Common Law* (n 3) 155–6; A Reinisch, 'The Use and Limits of Res Judicata and Lis Pendens as Procedural Tools to Avoid Conflicting Dispute Settlement Outcomes' (2004) 3 *Law and Practice of International Courts and Tribunals* 37, 44 (2004); M Ottolenghi and P Prows, 'Res Judicata in the ICJ's Genocide Case: Implications for Other Courts and Tribunals' (2009) 21 *Pace International Law Review* 37; E Sobenes Obregon, 'Res Judicata and the Test of Finality' (2018) 5 *Journal of Territorial and Maritime Studies*' 75; M Sarzo, '*Res Judicata*, Jurisdiction *ratione materiae* and Legal Reasoning in the Dispute Between Nicaragua and Colombia before the International Court of Justice' (2017) 16 *Law and Practice of International Courts and Tribunals* 224–44; N Riddi, 'Precarious Finality? Reflections on *Res Judicata* and the Question of the Delimitation of the Continental Shelf Case' (2018) 31 *Leiden Journal of International Law* 383; B Salas Kantor and ME Zavala Achurra, 'The Principle of *res judicata* before the International Court of Justice: in the Midst of Comradeship and Divorce between International Tribunals' (2019) 10 *Journal of International Dispute Settlement* 288–306.

[150] *Territorial and Maritime Dispute (Nicaragua v Colombia)*, ICJ, Judgment of 12 November 2012.

[151] ibid para 251.

The Court rejected that argument – but only barely. The decision was an 8–8 split, decided by President Abraham's casting vote. This, in itself, is remarkable: a sophisticated court evenly split over whether a judgment it issued less than five years ago was *res judicata*. And it is even more remarkable that most of the Judges sitting in the 2016 case had sat on the 2012 case.[152] To summarise the Court's reasoning. First, the Court brushed away the suggestion that the use of the expression 'cannot uphold', which it had used in several prior judgments when rejecting a claim[153] (and which it had used in *Territorial and Maritime Dispute* in relation to Nicaragua's claim to an extended continental shelf) meant that it had effectively decided the issue.[154] Second, it considered that the interpretation of the operative part of the judgment depended on the reasoning deployed in the related parts of the judgment.[155] Third, on that basis, the Court held that the reason it could not uphold Nicaragua's prior claim was because the State had not discharged its obligations under UNCLOS to provide certain technical information to the Commission on the Limits of the Continental Shelf.[156]

Accordingly, the Court characterised the prior decision (i.e., the conclusion that it 'cannot uphold' Nicaragua's claim) as establishing a *precondition* for the decision of that claim, rather than as a decision on the *merits* of that claim. It held that: 'the condition imposed by it in its 2012 Judgment in order for it to be able to examine the claim of Nicaragua contained [in the prior judgment] has been fulfilled' and then concluded that it was 'not precluded by the res judicata principle from ruling' on the dispute.[157]

As one would expect, a decision from a split bench generated some strongly worded dissents. Seven of the eight judges in the (technical) minority issued a joint dissent. They castigated the majority as having misread the 2012 judgment but also of detracting 'from the values of legal stability and finality of judgments that the principle of *res judicata* operates to protect'.[158] The dissenters criticised

[152] *Question of the Delimitation of the Continental Shelf between Nicaragua and Colombia beyond 200 nautical miles from the Nicaraguan Coast (Nicaragua v Colombia),* ICJ, Judgment (Preliminary Objections) of 17 March 2016, Joint Dissenting Opinion of Judges Yusuf, Cançado Trindade, Xue, Gaja, Bhandari, Robinson and Brower, para 2. Ultimately, the Court rejected Nicaragua's claims, see Judgment of 13 July 2023. Judge Tomka, in the minority, considered that the judgment was 'disquieting' and that it was based on a 'rule that the Court simply "invented"', Dissenting Opinion of Judge Tomka, paras 1 and 3. Several judges raised concerns about the odd procedural approach taken to address the merits, see eg Separate Opinion of Judge Xue, paras 2–9; Dissenting Opinion of Judge Charlesworth paras 37–39.

[153] See eg *Continental Shelf (Tunisia/Libyan Arab Jamahiriya),* ICJ, Judgment of 24 February 1982 paras 14–15.

[154] *Question of the Delimitation* (n 152) para 74. The Court held that: 'The Court will not, therefore, linger over the meaning of the phrase "cannot uphold", taken in isolation, in the way the Parties have done. It will examine this phrase in its context, in order to determine the meaning of the decision not to uphold Nicaragua's request for the Court to delimit the continental shelf between the Parties.'

[155] ibid paras 75–83.

[156] ibid para 84.

[157] *Question of Delimitation* (n 152) para 87.

[158] ibid, *Question of the Delimitation*, Joint Dissenting Opinion of Judges Yusuf, Cançado Trindade, Xue, Gaja, Bhandari, Robinson and Brower.

the majority for failing to properly engage with the meaning of the expression 'cannot uphold'.[159] More importantly, they argued that the majority had misread the 2012 judgment, as the basis of that decision had been Nicaragua's failure 'to prove the existence of an extended continental shelf',[160] focusing on the use of the expression 'not established' in relation to the 2012 claim because it had failed to provide the necessary evidence for doing so.[161]

The *coup de grâce*, however, is the dissenters' argument on what they called the majority's procedural incoherence.[162] In short, the dissenters contend (rightly, in my view) that if in 2012 the Court considered that the procedural requirements were not met,[163] then the correct decision would have been to find Nicaragua's claim inadmissible. But the Court did not do that then; in fact, it expressly found the claim to be admissible.[164] Perhaps unsurprisingly, the ICJ's judgment in *Delimitation of the Continental Shelf* has been considered 'concerning'[165] and one that leaves us with 'more uncertainty and less assurances'.[166] Again, this shows how a relevant category of international procedural law – *res judicata* – operates as a standard rather than as a rule.

[159] ibid para 20.
[160] ibid.
[161] ibid para 26.
[162] ibid paras 40 and ff.
[163] *Question of the Delimitation* (n 120), Separate Opinion of Judge Greenwood. This separate opinion may perhaps provide some indication as to what policy considerations may have been behind the majority's reasoning. Greenwood explains that in international law *res judicata* has substantive – rather than merely procedural – effects. He explains that: 'If the legal entitlement claimed by a party is dependent upon the existence of facts the burden of proving which rests on that party, then a finding that that party has not discharged its burden of proof amounts to a determination of whether or not it has that entitlement,' para 5. Under that principle, Colombia's jurisdictional objection should have been upheld. Nevertheless, he observed that: 'If that is correct, then the question of such entitlement is settled, between Nicaragua and Colombia, in perpetuity. Not only can Nicaragua not contest this issue with Colombia in these, or any subsequent, proceedings in the Court or any other competent tribunal . . . Such a judgment would not prevent Nicaragua from taking forward its submission to the Commission on the Limits of the Continental Shelf . . . However, no outer limits to a continental shelf beyond the 200 nautical miles from the Nicaraguan mainland . . . could be opposable to Colombia. Since a judgment creates *res judicata* only as between the parties . . . the 2012 Judgment could not prevent Nicaragua from asserting an entitlement to a continental shelf beyond 200 nautical miles against other neighbouring States. As between Nicaragua and Colombia, however, Nicaragua would have no scope for any such assertion.' Essentially, because the CLCS can establish an entitlement to an extended continental shelf, and that would be opposable vis-à-vis all UNCLOS parties (of which Colombia is not one).
[164] *Question of the Delimitation* (n 120), Joint Dissenting Opinion, para 47, the joint dissenters stated that: 'The Court had the opportunity to state in the 2012 Judgment that it considered submission of information to the CLCS . . . to be a prerequisite for delimitation and thus to declare Nicaragua's final submission inadmissible. The majority attempts to avoid confronting this fact by arguing that the Court adjudged Nicaragua's final submission . . . to be admissible but did not continue to address the submission on the merits . . . However, the majority does not explain what possible purpose would be served by declaring a claim to be admissible but not continuing to address it on the merits. Moreover, it does not explain how the Court, once it had declared a claim to be admissible, can refuse to address the claim on the merits.'
[165] Riddi 'Precarious Finality? (n 149) 401.
[166] Salas Kantor and Zavala Achurra 'The Principle of *res judicata* before the International Court of Justice' (n 149) 305.

These examples illustrate the indeterminacy that is inherent in (again, *some*) rules of international procedural law. These cases involved learned courts or tribunals carefully considering similarly (or identically) worded treaty provisions or the same legal principles and arriving at opposite results. Further, due to the decentralised nature of international adjudication, there is no hierarchically superior court that would be able to clarify the proper approach to take. In fact, as the *Kiliç* annulment committee's decisions shows, even when there are second-level review proceedings, there is reluctance to clarify the correct approach to interpretation. This takes us to the third characteristic of international procedural law mentioned above.

VI. CONCLUSION

To conclude, this chapter has explained some of the fundamental characteristics of international procedural law and how they may influence how international courts determine the scope of – and whether they exercise – their jurisdiction. First, it explains how some provisions of international procedural law are relatively indeterminate (as opposed to being *entirely* indeterminate), as they are mainly standards rather than rules, thus allowing some (but not unfettered) discretion. Second, it analysed the competence–competence principle and how this allows international courts to determine their own jurisdiction, usually with few constraints. Third, it considered the generalised lack of appellate or second level review mechanisms, which leads to the absence of authoritative interpretations of many relevant provisions (even in sub-systems where second level review mechanisms are available).

My aim in this chapter was to show that the relative indeterminacy of some provisions of international procedural law, combined with the generally high degree of autonomy that international courts have to determine their own jurisdiction and the lack of second-level review, means that, in many instances, international adjudicators will have a degree of flexibility in determining how (and whether) to exercise their jurisdiction. Basically, that those characteristics permit the use of implied avoidance techniques. The instinctive reaction many have is that this is a detrimental state of affairs that must be solved, as it jeopardises certainty[167] or, arguably, even the normativity of international procedural law. But perhaps this is a feature rather than a bug. As I argued in chapter 3, there are some instances (but not all), where the use of avoidance techniques will be normatively justified.

[167] See LL Fuller, *The Morality of Law* 2nd edn (Yale University Press, 1969) 63: '[T]he desideratum of clarity represents one of the most essential ingredients of legality.'

5

Implied Avoidance Techniques in Practice

'Predictions are hard, particularly about the future'

Nils Bohr (or Yogi Berra)

THIS CHAPTER ANALYSES SOME cases that show how some international courts have used implied avoidance techniques in practice. It is divided into two parts. The first deals with three 'older' cases, from the time international adjudication was more comfortable with non-justiciability doctrines. Those case studies show that, even when express avoidance doctrines were more widely accepted, international courts nevertheless tended to refrain from applying them, opting instead to rely on implied avoidance techniques. The second focuses on more contemporaneous cases and considers the application of the following three jurisdictional principles or doctrines, which, I argue, are sometimes deployed as implied avoidance techniques. Two out of the three doctrines identified below were developed by the ICJ: the existence of a dispute and the indispensable third-party (or *Monetary Gold*) principle. The third is from the European Court of Human Rights: the extraterritorial application of the European Convention.

Some could argue that this choice is flawed. As some scholars argue, the ICJ is the oldest of the old-style international court.[1] It lacks compulsory jurisdiction and lacks coercive enforcement mechanisms.[2] This choice could uncharitably be characterised as an attempt to 'load the dice'. A cynic could observe that if there is *one* international court that would be inclined to impliedly deploy avoidance techniques, that would be the ICJ. Despite that potential criticism, a series of case studies that leans towards the ICJ is defensible. There are several reasons for this. First, the ICJ is the only international court of general subject-matter jurisdiction. Moreover, in terms of politically sensitive disputes, these tend to find their way to the ICJ much more often than to other international courts

[1] K Alter, *The New Terrain of International Law* (Princeton University Press 2014).

[2] These points have been addressed thoroughly in chapter 2. Regarding the case study method, see generally J Gerring, *Case Study Research Principles and Practice* (CUP, 2016) 86–150. See also: WM Reisman and AR Willard, *International Incidents: The Law That Counts in World Politics* (Princeton University Press, 1988).

and tribunals. Issues of self-determination, boundaries (i.e., a State's territory), and the use of force are more likely to demand the application of implied avoidance techniques than somewhat technical disputes about, say, import duties on re-treaded tires.[3]

Second, the Court, as the principal legal organ of the United Nations, casts 'a tremendous shadow on the development of international law'.[4] The Court's clout in developing rules of international law is not seriously disputed. As Antonio Cassese stated: 'Once the ICJ has stated that a legal standard is part of customary international law, few would seriously challenge such a finding.'[5] Or, as Hernandez put it, understanding the ICJ's judgment 'is considered by the epistemic community of international lawyers as the benchmark of one's grasp of the international legal discipline'.[6]

Having said that, as set out in chapter 1, I acknowledge that an international court's institutional design – including its jurisdictional mandate and the enforcement mechanisms at its disposal (and their robustness) – may influence that international court's approach to the exercise of its jurisdiction. The legitimacy and the effectiveness of the enforcement mechanisms available vary between international courts. The proposition that an international court that has a stronger jurisdictional mandate and more effective enforcement mechanisms will be more assertive when dealing with politically sensitive disputes is intuitively plausible – and seems to have some empirical basis.[7] Put simply, the Court of Justice of the European Union (insofar as we consider it an international court) probably has less of a need to deploy implied avoidance techniques than an international court that depends on State consent to jurisdiction. To reiterate, the examples below are meant to be illustrative only. I am not attempting to map *all* the techniques or tools in the international judicial toolkit that may be used to avoid a decision. Rather, I mainly focus on selecting some examples that, in my view, are useful to show how avoidance techniques may be operating in practice.

As I mentioned at the start, any claim about the application of implied avoidance techniques is, inherently, somewhat speculative. The whole point of the application of these avoidance techniques being implied – in contrast with express avoidance techniques, such as declaring that an issue is non-justiciable – is

[3] This example is somewhat facetious, but nevertheless it strikes me as illustrative: WTO Panel Report, *Brazil – Measures Affecting Imports of Retreaded Tyres*, WT/DS332/R (adopted 17 December 2007).

[4] G Hernández, *The International Court of Justice and the Judicial Function* (OUP, 2014) 4.

[5] A Cassese, *Realizing Utopia: The Future of International Law* (OUP, 2012) 240.

[6] Hernández *The International Court of Justice and the Judicial Function* (n 4) 5.

[7] G Dimitropoulos, 'Investor–State Dispute Settlement Reform and Theory of Institutional Design' (2018) 9 *Journal of International Dispute Settlement* 535; SW Schill and G Vidigal, 'Designing Investment Dispute Settlement à la Carte: Insights from Comparative Institutional Design Analysis' (2020) 18 *Law & Practice of International Courts & Tribunals* 314; K Alter, L Helfer and MR Madsen, 'How Context Shapes the Authority of International Courts' (2016) 79 *Law & Contemporary Problems* 1.

that the court in question is not *declaring* that it is avoiding the case. The avoidance takes place discreetly, *sotto voce*. My argument is that, on a close reading of these cases, and when taking a probabilistic and inferential approach, it is possible to credibly argue that it is more likely than not that we are before the implied deployment of an avoidance technique.

I. AVOIDANCE TECHNIQUES IN PRACTICE: THREE EARLY CASES

This initial section focuses on three early examples of this trend. Given the timing of these cases, and the (even more) underdeveloped nature of international procedural law then, these international courts had less doctrinal cover than their contemporaries, which is reflected in their sometimes-blunter approach to avoidance: more express than implied. The point is that the use of avoidance techniques is as old as international adjudication itself (and arguably, as old as adjudication more generally). There are, after all, few new things under the sun – particularly in the law.

The three cases are: the *Alabama* Arbitration, the PCIJ's decision in *Free Zones of Upper Savoy and the District of Gex*, and the *Wal Wal Incident* arbitration. These cases illustrate how international courts have relied on avoidance techniques to duck particularly contentious issues, which they refrained from adjudicating (with, I argue, positive results). When read closely, and when taking context into account, it becomes apparent that those international adjudicators were relying on avoidance techniques to decline to exercise jurisdiction and thus abstain from deciding certain aspects of those disputes.

A. The Alabama Arbitration

The Alabama Arbitration is considered one of the most important cases in the history of international dispute settlement.[8] Thomas Bingham captured the historical importance of the Alabama arbitration when he compared it to *Hamlet*: a story that everyone knows – and knows how it ends.[9] The Alabama arbitration has been considered the first international dispute settled by a proper international tribunal (as opposed to a commission) and to be the 'basic model for international arbitration today'.[10]

[8] See eg JB Moore, *History and Digest of the International Arbitrations to which the United States has Been a Party* (Government Printing Office, 1898); A Cook, *The Alabama Claims* (Cornell University Press, 1975); T Bingham, 'The Alabama Claims Arbitration' (2005) 54 *International and Comparative Law Quarterly* 1.

[9] Bingham ibid 1.

[10] VV Veeder, 'The Historical Keystone to International Arbitration: The Party-Appointed Arbitrator—From Miami to Geneva' (2013) 107 *Proceedings of the ASIL Annual Meeting* 387, 390.

The political situation between the US and the UK was tense. The dispute concerned the United States' claim that the United Kingdom had breached its obligation of neutrality during the American civil war. The US alleged that the UK had allowed a series of warships, including the CCS Alabama, to be built (or repurposed) in the UK and delivered to the Confederacy.[11] The Union's naval capabilities were significantly stronger than the Confederates',[12] hence why the purported assistance to the Confederates on this front caused such offence to the Union. Ultimately, the tribunal's award was significant. It ordered the UK to pay the US US$15.5 million in gold, a sum that, according to one estimate, would today be equivalent to approximately US$225 billion.[13]

One often overlooked (albeit well-documented) aspect of this arbitration is that there was a challenge to the Tribunal's subject-matter jurisdiction in the middle of the proceedings that almost derailed the arbitration – and thus risked war between the two countries.[14] That jurisdictional challenge involved one of the most contentious issues in the arbitration: whether the tribunal had jurisdiction over the United States' *indirect* claims i.e., claims other than those directly relating to the loss of the ships and property. In this case, the indirect claims included the increase in the cost of marine insurance; the decrease in American carrying trade, including the decrease in imports and exports; and, more critically, the cost of a two-year extension of the civil war.[15] For context, the value of the indirect claims was almost ten times as high as that of the direct claims (at the time approximately $15 million and $110 million, respectively).[16]

British diplomats had been under the impression that no indirect claims would be raised in the arbitration. United States diplomats considered that the indirect claims fell within the scope of the Treaty of Washington. As VV Veeder put it, a 'diplomatic storm' arose when the United States raised the indirect claims.[17] The two States tried to solve the issue diplomatically before the hearing started, to no avail. Britain was considering walking away from the proceedings if the tribunal upheld jurisdiction over the indirect claims.[18] Indeed, one of its arguments was that the tribunal lacked jurisdiction to determine its own jurisdiction over the indirect claims (competence-competence was not widely accepted then).[19]

Roy Jenkins, in his biography of Gladstone – the British prime minister at the time the arbitration took place – considered the arbitration the 'greatest nineteenth-century triumph of rational internationalism over short-sighted jingoism' R Jenkins, *Gladstone* (Macmillan, 1995) 359.

[11] Veeder (n 10) 390.

[12] In general, see D Porter, *The Naval History of the Civil War* (Sherman Publishing Company, 1886); FJ Merli, *Great Britain and the Confederate Navy, 1861–1865* (Indiana University Press, 2004); P Silverstone, *Civil War Navies, 1855–1883* (Routledge, 2006).

[13] ibid.

[14] Veeder 'The Historical Keystone' (n 10).

[15] Bingham 'The Alabama Claims Arbitration' (n 8) 12; Veeder (n 10) 397.

[16] Bingham ibid) 12.

[17] Veeder (n 10) 397.

[18] ibid.

[19] The competence-competence principle is addressed in detail in chapter 4.

During the hearing, Britain's agent, Lord Tenterden, refused to present his final written argument. Instead, he requested the tribunal for an eight-month extension for the parties to negotiate a supplementary treaty. The general impression was that, if there was such a suspension of the proceedings, the arbitration would not resume and there would be a substantial risk of war. As John Bassett Moore put it, the tensions surrounding the Alabama dispute had not 'worn so menacing an aspect as that which they assumed after the close of the civil war in the United States'.[20] The United States' agent, Bancroft Davis, requested a five-day adjournment to obtain instructions. After the short adjournment, the tribunal made a 'spontaneous' declaration to the Parties. It noted in relation to the indirect claims that:

> The Arbitrators think it right to state that [in relation to the indirect claims] they have arrived, individually and collectively, at the conclusion that these claims do not constitute, upon the principles of international law applicable to such cases, good foundation for an award of compensation or computation of damages between nations and should upon such principles, be wholly excluded from the consideration of the tribunal . . . even if there were no disagreement between the two Governments as to the competency of the tribunal to decide thereon.[21]

Of course, the declaration was not exactly spontaneous – it was the result of intense diplomatic negotiations between the parties. It was seen as a compromise position, which simultaneously preserved the arbitration whilst allowing the United States to maintain its position that the indirect claims were covered by the Treaty of Washington. The British attorney general, Sir Roundell Palmer, who played a key role in those negotiations, noted in his memoirs that he drew up the compromise which he thought would be acceptable to both parties: 'unless the United States preferred the failure of the Treaty to the abandonment of those claims'.[22]

In retrospect, we know that the parties had surely influenced the tribunal to make its curious statement essentially declining jurisdiction over the indirect claims. However, for all practical purposes, the effect of the tribunal's note was the avoidance of the most contentious issue in the case: the United States' indirect claims. The tribunal's note thus signalled to the parties that the tribunal would abstain from deciding that issue.

Seen with modern eyes, that type of party intervention would be considered unacceptable. Yet, when viewed in its proper context (including the historical), the tribunal's approach should be positively appraised. Given what was at stake and the potential consequences, including a credible risk of the outbreak of war, the *Alabama* arbitration is rightly considered a great success. To a material extent, that success was possible given the parties' agreement – in the middle of

[20] Moore *International Arbitrations to which the United States has Been a Party* (n 8) 495.
[21] Veeder (n 10) 397.
[22] R Palmer, *Memorials: Part II, Personal and Political* (Macmillan, 1898) 237. Veeder (n 10) 400.

the proceedings – to restrict the tribunal's subject-matter jurisdiction. By removing the tribunal's jurisdiction over the indirect claims, which the UK considered either non-justiciable or outside the scope of the tribunal's subject-matter jurisdiction, the tribunal was able to ultimately decide the case. The proceedings survived. Despite considering the award to be unduly harsh, the UK complied.

To reiterate, contemporary observers considered that war between the US and the UK was a serious possibility if the proceedings failed. That grim alternative was averted. From the point of promoting minimum order, that is the best possible outcome. In short, by declining jurisdiction – and thus avoiding a decision on – the indirect claims, the most contentious issue in dispute, the *Alabama* tribunal managed to navigate away from potential catastrophe and issue an award that was both legitimate and effective and that is now correctly regarded as one of the most important awards in the history of international adjudication.[23] Importantly, it is a powerful illustration of the point that in international adjudication (as in life more generally), half a loaf tends to be better than no bread.

B. Free Zones of Upper Savoy and the District of Gex

Article 13 of the Covenant of the League of Nations restricted the category of justiciable disputes.[24] It provided that only disputes that States 'recognize to be suitable for submission to arbitration or judicial settlement' could be resolved through those means. Those restrictions seldom arose in practice (in those instances, it was much more likely that a case would not have made its way to the Permanent Court or an arbitral tribunal). But one instance where the Permanent Court had to grapple with the issue of whether a particular dispute was suitable for international adjudication was in *Free Zones of Upper Savoy and the District of Gex*.

The facts of the case are slightly complicated.[25] Some geographic context is useful:[26] Geneva is connected to the rest of Switzerland by a narrow strip of territory, a few kilometres wide.[27] It is wedged between two French regions: Upper Savoy and Gex. Being able to trade freely with those regions was critical for Geneva. There had been treaties declaring those areas free zones (i.e., territories where customs duties were not imposed) since the early 1600s. This provided stability and allowed Geneva to prosper. But by the end of the First World War, the French government wanted to abolish the free zones. Article 435

[23] Bingham (n 8) 1.

[24] The point is dealt with in more detail in chapter 2.

[25] A Gattini, 'Free Zones of Upper Savoy and the District of Gex', in A Peters (ed) *Max Planck Encyclopaedia of Public International Law*.

[26] For a useful explanation, see L Schulthess, 'The Franco-Swiss Free Zones' *Foreign Affairs* (December 1924).

[27] C Biermann, 'The Franco-Swiss Free Zones' (1923) 13 *Geographical Review* 368.

of the Treaty of Versailles (to which Switzerland was not a party, but which it accepted subject to reservations) provided that the free zones of Upper Savoy and the District of Gex were 'no longer consistent with present conditions' and further stated that both States would 'come to an agreement together with a view of settling . . . the status of these territories'.[28]

France and Switzerland were unable to agree to a new regime. France wanted to move the customs up to the border, thus effectively eliminating the free zones. Switzerland opposed this, but eventually yielded. Nevertheless, Swiss law requires that some treaties be approved by referendum. One was called – and the treaty was resoundingly rejected.[29] France was undeterred. In late 1923 – and without Switzerland's agreement – it moved its customs to the border.

Both States ultimately agreed to submit the case to the Permanent Court. Article 2 of the special agreement provided that, absent agreement between the parties, the Permanent Court would be capable of determining the applicable customs regime. The Permanent Court's initial reaction was to punt. It issued an order granting the parties further time to reach an agreement regarding the customs regime in the hope that the parties would reach an agreement in that additional time.[30] But the time expired and they did not. The Permanent Court had thus to address the merits of the dispute. That required determining the applicable customs regime, which was the most politically sensitive aspect of the dispute. Although the Court ultimately decided the dispute,[31] it refused to address that issue. To avoid doing so, the Court held that the dispute over the customs regime was not, in reality, a legal dispute, holding that:

> [T]he settlement of such matters is not a question of law, but is a matter depending on the interplay of economic interest on which no Government can afford to be controlled by an outside organ. Such questions are outside the sphere in which a Court of Justice . . . can help in the solution of disputes between two States.[32]

The PCIJ's analysis of the issue was pithy. In characterising the issue as 'not a question of law', the PCIJ was effectively declaring it non-justiciable (and thus applying what I have called 'an express avoidance' technique). Another relevant point is that, whilst refusing to draw up a new customs regime, the Permanent Court held that the regime of the free zones would 'continue in force so long as it has not been modified by agreement',[33] while at the same

[28] Schultess 'The Franco-Swiss Free Zones' (n 26).

[29] ibid.

[30] *Free Zones of Upper Savoy and the District of Gex, (France v Switzerland)*, PCIJ, Order of 6 December 1930.

[31] ibid PCIJ, Judgment of 7 June 1932. See eg Dissenting Opinion of Judge Dreyfus 208: 'The Court has, however, retained its cognizance of the other questions which were submitted to it.'

[32] *Free Zones of Upper Savoy* (n 30), Judgment, 162. The Court then decided to leave the prior customs regime in force until 1934 with the expectation that the parties would agree to a new regime by then, 171.

[33] ibid 170.

time observing that, if that were the case, Switzerland 'ought in return to grant compensatory economic advantages'.[34] In other words, the PCIJ left the status quo in place, while at the same time nudging the parties in a certain direction.[35] One issue that may have influenced the Court was that during oral argument the Swiss agent noted that 'if the zones were maintained, the [Swiss] Government would, if France so desired, agree to the terms of exchange . . . being settled by experts, failing agreement'. If the free zones were left in place, the Swiss government was open to agreeing a more stable and flexible regime going forward.

Four judges dissented.[36] In their joint dissent, Judges Altamira and Hurst considered that the PCIJ should have adjudicated the dispute.[37] They considered the Court's judgment 'should contain a settlement of the whole matter, that is to say, of all the questions raised by the execution of [Article 435 of the Treaty of Versailles], which would have been settled by the Parties themselves had they reached an agreement'.[38] The Judges considered that by failing to decide the dispute, the Court was 'omitting to carry out the express mandate of the Parties in regard to the new regulation of the zones' regime', as required by the Special Agreement.[39] In fact, the express terms of the Special Agreement did not give the Permanent Court much leeway to decline jurisdiction over all or parts of the dispute – yet nevertheless that was what ultimately happened.

Conversely, Judge Neguslesco considered that the PCIJ should have declined jurisdiction over the *entire* dispute.[40] He considered that any legal questions that would come up under the Special Agreement would be 'incidental or preliminary character' as what the parties were really asking the Court to do was to 'draw up a customs regime in their place', a task that he considered was not for the Court.[41] Judge *ad hoc* Dreyfus (of France) considered that the Permanent Court had 'not fulfilled the task entrusted to it by the Special Agreement' and that it had 'refused to fulfil the most important part of its task'.[42] He admitted that the Special Agreement required the PCIJ to 'frame a customs and economic regime', which the 'Parties themselves had failed to frame',[43] The Judge *ad hoc* considered that such requirement had effectively been the 'stumbling block' that led the Court to decline jurisdiction. Then, referring to the risk of non-compliance, Judge Dreyfus stated that:

[34] ibid 169.

[35] A Kuhn, 'The Case of the Free Zones of Upper Savoy and the District of Gex' (1932) 26 *American Journal of International Law* 801, 803.

[36] Judges Altamira, Hurst, Negulesco, and Judge *ad hoc* Dreyfus.

[37] *Free Zones of Upper Savoy* (n 30), Dissenting Opinion of Judges Altamira & Hurst, 179.

[38] ibid 181.

[39] ibid.

[40] *Free Zones of Upper Savoy* (n 30), Dissenting Opinion of Judge Neguslesco, 186.

[41] ibid 196.

[42] *Free Zones of Upper Savoy* (n 30), Dissenting Opinion of Judge Dreyfus, 200 and 207.

[43] ibid 206.

> [T]he Court saw in this provision a means whereby the Party which might possibly be dissatisfied with the future judgment could render its execution nugatory, and it considered that such a result would be both damaging to its prestige and incompatible with the binding force attached to its judgment.[44]

In other words, according to Judge *ad hoc* Dreyfus, the Permanent Court was concerned with the lack of effectiveness of an eventual judgment, and that was a factor that motivated it to decline jurisdiction over the customs regime.

Neither the majority nor the dissents address in detail the issue of the limits of the Court's judicial function and the suitability of a customs regime as something capable of being solved through international adjudication. The point was, however, addressed more extensively by Judge Kellogg's observations to the 6 December Order. Kellogg was a skilled diplomat. He had previously served as the United States' Secretary of State.[45] Kellogg was concerned with exposing the PCIJ to deciding highly politicised disputes. '[I]t is scarcely possible that it was intended', Kellogg said, 'that, even with the consent of the Parties, the Court should take jurisdiction of political questions, should exercise the functions of drafting treaties between nations or decide questions upon grounds of political and economic expediency'.[46] Kellogg proposed a definition of political questions that should *not* be addressed by international courts:

> What is a political question? It is a question which is exclusively within the competence of a sovereign State. The making of tariff regulations, the regulation of immigration, the imposition of taxes and, in short, the exercise of all governmental power necessarily inherent in a sovereign State, involve questions of this nature. In passing upon a political question there is no rule or principle of law, no norm of equity, justice or even good conscience, which the Court can apply; for, unless limited by treaties, the power of a State in this domain is unlimited.[47]

Judge Kellogg's views on sovereignty are perhaps outdated. But, given the state of international law at the time he wrote, including the number of issues that were considered to fall exclusively within a State's domestic jurisdiction, it seemed a sensible position. More importantly, Judge Kellogg noted that adjudication was only one of *many* methods to solve international disputes, emphasising that in some cases – such as those involving political disputes – it was not the most effective one. On that point he contended that:

> That these political questions often lead to conflict and that the nations are pledged by the Pact of Paris to settle all differences by pacific means is undoubtedly true; but there is ample machinery for the adjustment of these questions; diplomacy, conciliation commissions and general arbitration are available for this purpose . . . But these

[44] ibid 207.
[45] His greatest achievement was the Kellogg-Briand Pact.
[46] *Free Zones of Upper Savoy,* Order (n 30), Observations of Judge Kellogg 34.
[47] ibid 41.

> questions . . . political or economic policy are within the sovereign jurisdiction of every independent State and should not and cannot be submitted to the International Court of Justice . . . There is no need to impose upon the Court any such political questions destructive of its influence as a Court of Justice.[48]

The Permanent Court's decision in *Free Zones* is a particularly helpful illustration of the role that a more flexible notion of justiciability may play in international adjudication. In principle, the parties had agreed that the Permanent Court would be able to decide the issue. But was that a question that the Court should have been asked to solve in the first place? As Kuhn notes, that was a 'task which is essentially administrative in character'.[49] Moreover, is it really sensible to expect that an international judicial forum, with its inherent limitations, would be capable of solving disputes that years of detailed negotiations have failed to resolve? Here, there were no subjective concerns regarding the suitability of the international adjudication to solve the dispute, as both States considered that delegating the issue to an international court was a sensible solution (and probably one that would be more palatable to their domestic constituencies than a negotiated agreement).

The Court's refusal to address a key issue on the merits, and its decision to maintain the *status quo ante,* did catalyse a solution (perhaps illustrating the pro-dialogic virtues of abstention).[50] Further negotiations allowed France and Switzerland to agree on several important issues, including the delimitation of the free zones and the controls applicable within them.[51] Because the two States were not able to reach a complete agreement, they submitted the dispute to a three-member commission tasked with mediating – and, if needed, arbitrating – the dispute, which they ultimately did.[52] The arbitrators did solve the remaining (narrower) points of contention and set up a customs regime. Interestingly, the regime they set out included an 'agency of conciliation and control' a political body that would 'smooth out difficulties' in the implementation of the agreement.[53]

Overall, I consider that the Permanent Court's refusal to *positively* set up a customs regime was positive. The Court's decision to avoid deciding that issue was probably the right choice; and probably the path that contributed the most to achieving minimum order. By leaving the *status quo ante* in place, the Permanent Court provided the parties with further incentive to negotiate. And they did, substantially narrowing the issues in dispute. The alternatives the PCIJ *avoided* must also be considered. For instance, it avoided threats to its legitimacy (and

[48] ibid 42.

[49] Kuhn 'Free Zones of Upper Savoy and the District of Gex' (n 35) 803.

[50] Fostering dialogue between States is, I argue, one of the main virtues of the application of avoidance doctrines, as explained in chapter 3.

[51] MO Hudson, 'The Aftermath of the Permanent Court's Judgment in the Free Zones Case' (1934) 28 *American Journal of International Law* 322, 324.

[52] ibid 324-25.

[53] ibid 324.

to that of international adjudication more generally) by issuing a decision that would effectively require setting up substantial political and economic arrangements. This implied a non-negligible risk that the dissatisfied party would refuse to comply with the judgment, thus potentially affecting the legitimacy of the Permanent Court. It also potentially helped prevent the Permanent Court from being saddled with a series of highly politicised, somewhat intractable disputes. As Manley Hudson observed, the role of the PCIJ in this dispute was one of 'building bridges from one public attitude to the other'. He concludes that 'later events' had 'vindicated' the Court's cautious approach.[54]

C. The Wal Wal Arbitration

In contrast with the *Alabama* and *Free Zones* cases, both of which are well known and often cited, the *Wal Wal* arbitration (also known as the Italian-Ethiopian dispute) is relatively obscure.[55] That is a pity. It is an important decision in the development of international adjudication. In particular, it shows how a political organ – the Council of the League of Nations – could intervene during an arbitral proceeding to curtail the tribunal's subject-matter jurisdiction.

The *Wal Wal* arbitration's context is relevant. It took place at the start of the Abyssinia Crisis, which some consider a failure that highlighted the League of Nations' shortcomings.[56] The dispute arose from the Wal Wal incident, at the start of Fascist Italy's armed action against Ethiopia in the 1930s.[57] Arbitration was seen as a way of avoiding an escalation of the conflict. The award was issued in September 1935.[58] By then, military operations were ongoing; just a few months after the award had been issued Italy had taken Ethiopia.

The incident itself took place in December 1934, in the Wal Wal, an oasis located in the border between Ethiopia and Somalia, then Italian Somaliland (which in the 1920s was not a clearly defined territory). Italy built a fort in the Wal Wal. Between 5–7 September 1934 fighting broke out between Ethiopian and Italian and Somali troops. Ethiopia invoked the treaty of friendship and commerce between the two States. That treaty included an arbitration provision. Ethiopia also raised the issue at the League of Nations' Council. After months

[54] ibid 325.

[55] The case is examined in detail in: P Potter, The Wal Wal Arbitration (Carnegie Endowment, 1938); JH Spencer, 'The Italian-Ethiopian Dispute and the League of Nations' (1937) 31 *American Journal of International Law* 614.

[56] CG Fenwick, 'The "Failure" of the League of Nations' (1936) 30 *American Journal of International Law* 506.

[57] For a general overview of the conflict, see G Baer, *Test Case: Italy, Ethiopia, and the League of Nations* (Hoover Institution Press, 1976); D Nicolle, *The Italian Invasion of Abyssinia 1935–1936* (Bloomsbury, 2012); G Strang (ed), *Collision of Empires: Italy's Invasion of Ethiopia and its International Impact* (Routledge, 2013).

[58] L'incident de Walwal (Italy v Ethiopia) RIAA (1935) vol III, XLVI, Award (3 September 1935) 1657 (Wal Wal Award).

of diplomatic negotiations Italy ultimately agreed to arbitration. The dispute was thus removed from consideration by the League's Council.

The parties had disagreed on the scope of the arbitral tribunal's jurisdiction, particularly whether it would have jurisdiction to determine the boundary between Ethiopia and Italian Somaliland (the Ogaden-Somaliland boundary). During oral argument in the arbitration the Ethiopian agent mentioned that Ethiopia exercised sovereignty over the Wal Wal. The Italian agent argued that boundary issues had been excluded from the tribunal's jurisdiction. He further contended that Italy would walk away from the proceedings if Ethiopia even *dared* to argue that the matter was within the tribunal's jurisdiction.[59]

The Ethiopian-appointed arbitrators considered that the tribunal had jurisdiction to determine its own jurisdiction. The Italian-appointed arbitrators rejected that. At that time the panel had only four members. Because there was a disagreement, the Ethiopian-appointed arbitrators requested the appointment of a fifth arbitrator. The Italian-appointed arbitrators rejected this too.[60] The issue was submitted to the League's Secretary General and, through him, to the League's Council. The President of the Council convened a meeting. Mussolini insinuated that Italy would not attend.[61] Ethiopia rejected the claim that it had accepted the exclusion of boundary delimitations from the arbitration. The Council decided the issue in Italy's favour and thus ordered the tribunal to avoid overreaching its jurisdiction, considering that it would effectively do that if it 'bases its decision on the opinion that the place on which the incident took place was under Italy's or Ethiopia's sovereignty'.[62]

Superficially, the Council's decision could be viewed as nothing more than an interpretation of the tribunal's subject matter jurisdiction, with the caveat that, given the applicable procedure, such a decision had to be taken by an organ other than the tribunal. But that ignores context. There is more: Italy's initial reluctance to accept the submission of the dispute to arbitration, its express threat to withdraw from the proceedings, and (thinly veiled) threat not to participate in the Council's meeting show (or at least support the possibility) that the Council was trying to avoid Italy withdrawing from the proceeding by restricting the tribunal's subject matter jurisdiction midway through the arbitration with the objective of avoiding an eventual decision on the boundary delimitation issue.

More broadly, too robust action against Italy could have led to the consolidation of the Hitler-Mussolini alliance at a moment 'when the most important task of European diplomacy was to prevent just that'.[63] In other words, in terms of the potential consequences, avoiding a categorical Italian withdrawal from the League (and thus the cementing of the Hitler-Mussolini alliance) was a

[59] Potter The Wal Wal Arbitration (n 55) 33.
[60] ibid. See also *Wal Wal Award* (n 58) 1661, para 5.
[61] Potter (n 55); Spencer 'The Italian-Ethiopian Dispute' (n 55).
[62] Wal Wal Award (n 58) 1661, para 6.
[63] M Koskenniemi, *From Apology to Utopia: The Structure of International Legal Argument* (CUP, 2006) 592.

fundamental priority. An expansive view of the tribunal's jurisdiction would perhaps have accelerated that process. In a situation where the scope of the tribunal's jurisdiction was not completely clear – and where both potential outcomes were at least arguable – perhaps the Council's decision is defensible, bearing in mind that the Council is a political rather than a judicial body and thus one that may more openly weigh policy factors when reaching a determination.

As a result, the Council's approach, which basically implied *avoiding* the boundary issue, was narrowly aimed at preserving Italy's consent to have the dispute adjudicated (and impliedly aimed at preventing the consolidation of the Hitler-Mussolini alliance). Given what ultimately happened, this outcome is somewhat bittersweet. But if perhaps not outright commendable, it is at least understandable.

These old examples seek to highlight a simple point: avoidance is not new. International courts have long relied on avoidance techniques to abstain from deciding cases or particularly sensitive issues within cases. These three examples also illustrate an additional point, one that is articulated more openly than it is now: concerns about enforcement and effectiveness. These cases show that international courts did take these two factors into account when considering the extent of their jurisdiction. That was salutary. As the section below shows, I argue that, despite protestations to the contrary, concerns about enforcement and effectiveness still play a role in international adjudication – even if this is no longer so openly acknowledged.

II. CONTEMPORANEOUS CASE STUDIES

This section analyses three jurisdictional rules or doctrines that, I argue, international courts have relied on to avoid deciding certain cases or issues. These cases show how implied avoidance doctrines operate in practice. The argument that they are being used as implied avoidance techniques becomes stronger when the evolution of those doctrines is analysed in detail, as this highlights their inherent ductility and, in turn, how that ductility provides international courts with the flexibility to use them to abstain from deciding certain cases or issues. International courts can rely on those avoidance doctrines for multiple reasons, which I do not attempt to define, but they include preventing backlash, safeguarding the international court's legitimacy or authority, tempering judicialisation, achieving minimum order, promoting human rights and the eventual effectiveness and enforceability of any eventual decision.

A. The Existence of a Dispute

There are few less obvious examples of the use of a jurisdictional doctrine as an implied avoidance technique than the ICJ's use of the existence of a dispute doctrine in the *Obligation to Negotiate* judgments (the Marshall Islands cases).[64] From a doctrinal perspective, the Court's interpretation of the existence of a dispute doctrine is unpersuasive.[65] Given the substantial indeterminacy of the notion and the lack of a doctrinally robust demarcation of the concept, the Court's application of that doctrine may be called erratic: it is characterised by sudden variations of the requirements for its application.[66]

Before domestic courts, jurisdictional requirements regarding the existence of a dispute are usually focused on avoiding covert requests for advisory opinions.[67] Discussions about the existence of a dispute are thus rare.[68] These requirements are not particularly common at the international level either, yet they have surfaced with certain regularity before the ICJ.[69] As explained previously, the existence of a dispute doctrine is not based on the distinction between legal and political disputes, including because the Court has systematically rejected that distinction. Nor is the existence of a dispute doctrine supported by either the Court's Statute or, when properly understood, its case law. As to the Statute, the reference to a 'dispute' in Articles 36(2) and 38 is mainly aimed

[64] *Obligations concerning Negotiations relating to Cessation of the Nuclear Arms Race and to Nuclear Disarmament (Marshall Islands v United Kingdom),* ICJ, Judgment (Preliminary Objections) of 5 October 2016; *Obligations concerning Negotiations relating to Cessation of the Nuclear Arms Race and to Nuclear Disarmament (Marshall Islands v India),* ICJ, Judgment (Preliminary Objections) of 5 October 2016; *Obligations concerning Negotiations relating to Cessation of the Nuclear Arms Race and to Nuclear Disarmament (Marshall Islands v Pakistan),* ICJ, Judgment (Preliminary Objections) of 5 October 2016; collectively I will refer to these as the *Marshall Islands* cases or as *Marshall Islands (UK), Marshall Islands (India),* and *Marshall Islands (Pakistan).*

[65] See eg, VJ Proulx, 'The World Court's Jurisdictional Formalism and its Lost Market Share: The Marshall Islands Decisions and the Quest for a Suitable Dispute Settlement Forum for Multilateral Disputes' (2017) 30 *Leiden Journal of International Law* 925, criticising what it deemed a formalist shift in the Court's approach to jurisdictional objections. See also: A Miron, 'Establishing the Existence of a Dispute before the International Court of Justice: Between Formalism and Verbalism' (2017) *Questions of International Law* (31 December 2017); A Bianchi 'Choice and (the Awareness of) its Consequences: The ICJ's "Structural Bias" Strikes Again in the *Marshall Islands* Case' (2017) 11; L Palestini, 'Forget About Mavrommatis and Judicial Economy: The Alleged Absence of a Dispute in Cases Concerning Obligations to Negotiate' (2017) *Journal of International Dispute Settlement* 557; S Ranganathan, 'Nuclear Weapons and the Court' (2017) 111 *AJIL Unbound* 88.

[66] For a discussion of the evolution of the Court's treatment of the existence of a dispute objection, see *Obligations concerning Negotiations (Marshall Islands v India)* (n 64), Separate Opinion of Judge Donoghue; Separate Opinion of Judge Abraham; see also: MA Becker, 'The Dispute that Wasn't There: Judgments in the Nuclear Disarmament Cases at the International Court of Justice' (2017) 6(1) *Cambridge Journal of International Law* 4. I have written about this issue at length in: M Casas, 'Functional Justiciability and the Existence of a Dispute: A Means of Jurisdictional Avoidance?' (2019) 10 *Journal of International Dispute Settlement* 599. As this section shows, I am in a minority that considers the Court's decision in the *Marshall Islands* cases normatively justified.

[67] FA Hessick, 'Cases, Controversies, and Diversity' (2015) 109 *Northwestern University Law Review*; see eg *Hollingsworth v Perry* 570 US (2013).

[68] JR Siegel, 'A Theory of Justiciability' (2007) 86 *Texas Law Review* 73, 76–77.

[69] See *Application of the International Convention on the Elimination of All Forms of Racial Discrimination (Georgia v Russian Federation)*, ICJ, Judgment (Preliminary Objections) of 1 April 2011; *Marshall Islands Cases.*

at distinguishing contentious disputes from advisory proceedings.[70] Similarly, at least originally, the existence of a dispute doctrine was not created by the Court's case law. What seems to have happened is that the Court relied on the vagueness of some of its precedents to convert some dicta regarding the existence of a dispute into a jurisdictional bar – and thus as an implied avoidance technique.

The Court has repeatedly made reference to the existence of a dispute in several of its rulings, starting with the PCIJ's decisions in *Mavrommatis Palestine Concessions* and *Electricity Company of Sofia and Bulgaria*. In effect, it is oft repeated that the PCIJ laid out the foundations for the existence of a dispute jurisdictional objection in *Mavrommatis* and further elaborated those foundations in *Electricity Company*.[71] This is the general consensus.[72] Yet, when those decisions are analysed closely, it is evident that neither of them relates to the existence of a dispute as it is understood today.

(i) The Early Cases: Mavrommatis and Electricity Company

In *Mavrommatis* the Permanent Court defined a dispute as 'a disagreement on a point of law or fact, a conflict of legal views or of interests between two persons'.[73] The passage is ritually repeated in every case where the purported absence of a dispute is used to challenge jurisdiction. But the existence of a dispute was never an issue in that case. The dispute concerned the claims that Mavrommatis, a Greek national (and a concession hunter!), had against the United Kingdom arising from overlapping concessions in Palestine. Mavrommatis tried negotiating with the UK's Colonial Office but failed. Greece, exercising diplomatic protection, then filed a claim against the UK before the PCIJ.

The UK challenged the court's jurisdiction. That challenge was never based on the *absence* of a dispute; but rather on the fact that the dispute was between an *individual* and a State – not between two States. So, it was, in reality, about standing or personal jurisdiction. The Permanent Court rejected that jurisdictional challenge and authoritatively established the nationality of claims rule – also known as the Mavrommatis formula.[74] Thus, the existence of a dispute itself was never a relevant issue in that case.

[70] C Tomuschat, 'Article 36' in A Zimmermann, C Tams, K Oellers-Frahm and C Tomuschat (eds), *The Statute of the International Court of Justice: A Commentary* (OUP, 2019) 721.

[71] R Kolb, *The International Court of Justice* (Hart Publishing, 2013) 302.

[72] C Schreuer, 'What is a Legal Dispute?' in I Buffard, J Crawford, A Pellet and S Wittich (eds), *International Law between Universalism and Fragmentation* (Martinus Nijhoff, 2008) 959.

[73] *Mavrommatis Palestine Concessions (Greece v United Kingdom)*, PCIJ, Judgment of 30 August 1924, 11.

[74] ibid 12. The principle is also established in *Panevezys-Saldutiskis Railway (Estonia v Lithuania)*, PCIJ, Judgment of 28 February 1939, p 16 where the Permanent Court stated that: 'it is the bond of nationality between the State and the individual which alone confers upon the State the right of diplomatic protection'.

The next case in which the PCIJ dealt with the existence of a dispute issue was in *Electricity Company*.[75] Again, the existence of a dispute was not itself the main point of contention. There, the Permanent Court held that: 'the Belgian Government has not established the existence of such a dispute and accordingly declares that the Belgian Application cannot be entertained'.[76] Here, however, the actual issue was whether Belgium had complied with a jurisdictional precondition to attempt to solve disputes through diplomatic negotiations before submitting a claim to the PCIJ not whether the dispute itself existed.[77]

In sum, a closer reading of *Mavrommatis* and *Electricity Company* reveals that the existence of a dispute was never an issue in either case. Although those rulings include some ambiguous language, neither actually concerned the *existence* of a dispute. As I explained in chapter 4, the sources of international procedural law are often opaque. International courts are often involved in the creation of those rules – and they often do so with a remarkable degree of laxity. This is an example. While neither *Mavrommatis* nor *Electricity Company* constitute precedential basis for the existence of a dispute doctrine, the inherent indeterminacy of some rules of international procedural law have allowed subsequent international courts to rely on those precedents as an implied avoidance technique.

(ii) The Evolution of the Existence of a Dispute Doctrine

Despite the lack of textual or precedential basis for the existence of a dispute principle, the Court has applied it throughout. As Judge Abraham pointed out in his declaration in *Obligation to Negotiate*: 'the existence of a dispute . . . is not only a condition for the exercise of the Court's jurisdiction but, more fundamentally, a condition for the very existence of that jurisdiction'.[78] Despite Schreuer's warning that '[a]rguments attempting to deny the existence of a dispute have hardly ever succeeded',[79] the Court has indeed applied the existence of a dispute principle to either decline jurisdiction over cases – including politically sensitive disputes such as the *Marshall Islands* cases – but also to carve-out certain parts of disputes in others. The Court's doctrinal treatment of the existence of a dispute has sometimes been unpredictable: the variations in the case law makes it hard to draw a linear pattern in its jurisprudence.

[75] *Electricity Company of Sofia and Bulgaria (Belgium v Bulgaria)*, PCIJ, Judgment of 4 April 1939.

[76] ibid 83.

[77] The Treaty limits the jurisdiction of the Permanent Court to those disputes 'which it has not been possible to settle by diplomatic means'. Belgium had even admitted that one of the claims it was submitting to the court was new. See *Electricity Company* (n 75), Written submission of Belgium, 33 'Un nouveau grief avait du rest . . . surgi pour la compagnie' (A new claim. . . has arisen for the company; my translation).

[78] *Marshall Islands (India)* (n 64) Declaration of Judge Abraham 1.

[79] Although Schreuer asserts that it is very difficult for this jurisdiction objection to succeed, in recent years the ICJ has been more open to rely on it, as the *Marshall Islands Cases* show, see Schreuer 'What is a Legal Dispute?' (n 72) 978.

After *Mavrommatis,* the Court developed the concept of a dispute in *Interpretation of Peace Treaties*, where it held that a dispute implies that 'the two sides hold clearly opposite views concerning the question of the performance or non-performance of'[80] international obligations. The usefulness of this standard is debatable. What does 'clearly opposite views' mean? For a state to litigate a claim against another state they must have differing opinions regarding an obligation. When States *don't* have opposing views, they don't tend to engage in international litigation.

Later, the Court applied the *positive opposition* standard. In the *South West Africa* cases the Court asserted that 'it must be shown that the claim of one party is positively opposed by the other'.[81] Positive opposition requires State A to make a claim – and State B to refute that claim. Judge Morelli, with characteristic acumen, expounded on this standard in his dissenting opinion in *South West Africa,* claiming that: 'a dispute consists, not of a conflict of interests as such, but rather in a contrast between the respective attitudes of the parties in relation to a certain conflict of interests'.[82]

But this requirement quickly ran into an obstacle: silence. A State wishing to avoid litigation could simply remain silent – and thus avoid *positively opposing* the other State's claim. The Court, however, pragmatically sorted this by opting for another standard: *objective determination.* In the *Nuclear Tests* cases, the positive opposition standard was left aside. The Court held that: '[w]hether there exists an international dispute is a matter for objective determination'.[83] This change allowed the Court to circumvent strategic silence.

The objective determination standard is easy to apply when the claim is based on a specific incident (e.g., the bombing of an oil platform, or failure to respect a boundary). But since the Court has also stated that there is no obligation to formally notify the respondent State about the existence of a claim (i.e., there is no procedural requirement to give another State notice, usually through diplomatic correspondence or a *note verbale*), it is harder to objectively determine the existence of *purely legal* disputes. Two States may have conflicting positions as to the interpretation of a treaty, but unless an incident arises that requires the express articulation of those diverging views, they may simply ignore that conflict. The adoption of the objective determination standard – a functional standard that rejects formalism – grants the Court freedom to determine that a dispute exists, regardless of the conduct of the parties.[84] This flexibility has

[80] *Interpretation of Peace Treaties with Bulgaria, Hungary and Romania*, ICJ, Advisory Opinion of 30 March 1950, 74.

[81] *South West Africa (Ethiopia v South Africa; Liberia v South Africa)*, ICJ, Judgment (Second Phase) of 18 July 1966, 328.

[82] ibid, Separate Opinion of Judge Morelli, 567.

[83] *Nuclear Tests (Australia v France)*, ICJ, Judgment of 20 December 1974 para 55.

[84] *Alleged Violations of Sovereign Rights and Maritime Spaces in the Caribbean Sea (Nicaragua v Colombia)*, ICJ, Judgment (Preliminary Objections) of 17 March 2016 para 27. See also *Georgia v Russia* (n 69) para 85; *Questions of Interpretation and Application of the 1971 Montreal Convention*

been bolstered by the Court's assertion that, regardless of what the parties *actually claim*, it is the Court itself who 'determine[s] on an objective basis the subject-matter of the dispute'.[85] Again, neither the Court's Statute nor its Rules expressly grant it this power; yet, by asserting that it can do so, perhaps on the basis of its inherent powers,[86] the Court preserves some flexibility.

Nevertheless, in recent decisions the Court has heightened the threshold it applies to determine whether a dispute exists. In the words of Judge Donoghue, 'the Court's inquiry into the existence of a dispute has been more exacting'.[87] In *Application of the International Convention on the Elimination of All Forms of Racial Discrimination*, for example, the Court established that, for a dispute to exist, diplomatic communication between the States had to explicitly mention the claims 'with sufficient clarity to enable the State against which [a] claim is made to identify that there is, or may be, a dispute with regard to that subject matter'.[88] Likewise, in *Obligation to Prosecute or Extradite* the Court, relying on diplomatic correspondence regarding the potential breach of a treaty, considered that there was a dispute on that point. At the same time, however, it considered that there was *no* dispute regarding potential violations of customary international law (a controversial issue) because those alleged breaches had never been mentioned in the diplomatic exchanges.[89]

(iii) The Marshall Islands Cases

In the *Obligation to negotiate* cases the Court, yet again, modified the criteria for determining the existence of a dispute.[90] The Marshall Islands are a very small archipelagic State in the Pacific. After World War I, the Islands were a mandate territory under the League of Nations. In 1944, during World War II, the United States took control of the Islands. Two years later, the United States started atmospheric nuclear tests in Bikini Atoll. The tests lasted 12 years – and caused considerable human and environmental harm.[91]

The Marshall Islands filed claims against nine States. The five nuclear-weapon States under the NPT: China, France, Russia, the United Kingdom, and the United States,[92] and four other States that are known (or suspected)

---

arising from the Aerial Incident at Lockerbie (Libyan Arab Jamahiriya v United Kingdom), ICJ, Judgment (Preliminary Objections) of 27 February 1998, 25-26.

[85] *Nuclear Tests* (n 83) para 29. *Obligation to Negotiate Access to the Pacific Ocean (Bolivia v Chile)*, ICJ, Judgment (Preliminary Objections) of 24 September 2015 para 26.

[86] C Brown, *A Common Law of International Adjudication* (OUP, 2007); C Brown, 'The Inherent Powers of International Courts and Tribunals' (2006) 76 *British Yearbook of International Law* 195.

[87] *Marshall Islands (India)* (n 64), Separate Opinion of Judge Donoghue 1.

[88] *Georgia v Russia* (n 69) para 85.

[89] *Questions relating to the Obligation to Prosecute or Extradite (Belgium v Senegal)*, ICJ, Judgment of 20 July 2012 para 54.

[90] See also Becker 'The Dispute that Wasn't There' (n 66).

[91] *Marshall Islands (UK)* (n 64) para 44.

[92] ibid para 19.

to have nuclear weapons: North Korea, India, Israel, and Pakistan.[93] In short, the Marshall Islands argued that those States had breached their obligations to negotiate in good faith towards nuclear disarmament, either under the NPT[94] or customary international law.[95] Of those nine States, only three had accepted the Court's jurisdiction: the UK, India and Pakistan. The Marshall Islands invited the other States to accept the Court's jurisdiction for the proceedings. Unsurprisingly, they did not take up the invitation.[96]

The Court declined jurisdiction in all three cases. It held, by the thinnest of majorities, that a dispute did not exist between the parties. This was the first time the Court relied on that doctrine to decline jurisdiction over an entire dispute.[97] To start, the Court reiterated the basic concepts of the existence of a dispute doctrine, mentioned above.[98] Further, the Court held that 'a dispute exists when it is demonstrated, on the basis of the evidence, that the respondent was aware, or could not be unaware, that its views were "positively opposed" by the applicant'.[99] In fact, the Court noted that, while it could take into account conduct subsequent to the filing of the application, subsequent conduct (including statements made during the proceedings) did not 'enable the Court to find that the condition of the existence of a dispute has been fulfilled in the same proceedings' as the Court considered that would mean the respondent State 'would be deprived of the opportunity before the institution of proceedings to the claim made against its own conduct'.[100]

Having set out those principles, the Court considered that, because the Marshall Islands, despite having consistently criticised States who possessed nuclear weapons in international fora,[101] had not engaged in any bilateral diplomatic exchanges with the UK, the requirements for the existence of a dispute had not been satisfied. The ICJ held that none of those 'more general statements . . . supports the existence of a dispute, since none articulates an alleged breach'.[102]

Essentially, the Court adopted a new requirement: that of *objective awareness*,[103] which requires that the respondent State cannot be unaware of the content of the claims being brought against it. This test is vague and hard to apply. Although the Court does not specifically refer to the issue of *notice*, its reasoning relies on the fact that the respondent States were not aware of the subject matter of the Marshall Islands' claims before the start of the proceedings.[104]

[93] ibid para 22.
[94] ibid para 1.
[95] *Marshall Islands (India)* (n 64) paras 1 and ff; *Marshall Islands (Pakistan)* paras 1 and ff.
[96] Five of those States outright ignored that invitation; China expressly rejected it.
[97] *Marshall Islands (UK)* (n 64), Dissenting Opinion of Judge Crawford para 1.
[98] ibid paras 37-40.
[99] ibid para 41.
[100] ibid para 42; *Marshall Islands (India)* and *Marshall Islands (Pakistan)* (n 64), both at para 40.
[101] *Marshall Islands (UK)* at paras 46–50.
[102] ibid para 51.
[103] *Marshall Islands (India)* (n 64), Dissenting Opinion of Judge Crawford at para 1.
[104] *Marshall Islands (UK)* (n 64) para 40.

Doctrinally, the Court's decision is hard to defend. Requiring that a defendant be made aware of the claims against it is reasonable. Most domestic procedural systems have similar notice requirements. This requirement may even be more relevant at the international level, where several dispute resolution mechanisms establish obligations for the parties to attempt negotiations before initiating judicial proceedings.[105] Yet no such preconditions applied here. As Becker explains, the Court does not point to any 'legal requirement in the Statute or elsewhere' that indicates why a respondent State 'is entitled to . . . an opportunity [to react before the institution of proceedings] as a matter of course'.[106] The reason is simple: because there was no legal requirement, either in the Court's Statute, the NPT or its case law (or even under general principles of law), which required the Marshall Islands to notify the respondent States.[107] Basically, the Court pulled a new jurisdictional requirement out of a hat to decline jurisdiction.

Despite the Court essentially declining jurisdiction because of the Marshall Islands' refusal to give the respondent States proper notice of its claims against them, the Court nevertheless reiterated that there is no duty of notice under international law: '"such a formal protest is not a necessary condition" for the existence of a dispute'.[108] This is not a discrepancy between the law-in-the-books and the law-in-action; it is an internal (and frankly, quite obvious) discrepancy between what the Court is *saying* it is doing, and what it is *actually* doing in the very same judgment. So, although the Court is saying there is no notice requirement, lack of notice was *precisely* the reason the Court declined jurisdiction. The Court's approach to the existence of a dispute doctrine shows the relative indeterminacy of this procedural concept. The precedents have varied, sometimes considerably. The standard is just not clear. And this doctrinal looseness grants the Court a degree of flexibility when applying the existence of a dispute principle, including when, as here, it is deployed as an implied avoidance technique.

Several of the dissenting Judges in the *Marshall Islands* cases criticised the Court from a doctrinal perspective. They focus mainly on what they considered the majority's departure from the Court's relatively settled case law regarding the existence of a dispute and its replacement with the objective awareness standard. For example, the dissenting judges have called this change in the applicable standard 'an exercise in pure formalism'[109] (Judge Bennouna), a 'formal approach'[110] (Judge Robinson), the implementation of a 'formalistic and inflexible

[105] See eg Article XXXII of the Pact of Bogota, which only makes judicial means of settlement available when 'the conciliation procedure . . . does not lead to a solution'.

[106] Becker (n 66) 9.

[107] Note, however, that Article 43(1) of the Articles on State Responsibility for Internationally Wrongful Acts provides that: 'An injured State which invokes the responsibility of another State shall give notice of its claim to that State.'

[108] *Marshall Islands (UK)* (n 64) para 38; *Marshall Islands (India)* and *Marshall Islands (Pakistan)* (n 64) both at para 35.

[109] *Marshall Islands (UK)* (n 64), Dissenting Opinion of Judge Bennouna 1.

[110] ibid Dissenting Opinion of Judge Robinson 15.

approach'[111] (Judge Sebutinde) or as discarding a 'tradition of flexibility'[112] (Judge Crawford).[113] These points are, of course, valid. If this case is analysed without regard to its subject matter and evaluated on strictly procedural terms, the adoption of the objective awareness requirement is indeed inflexible, rigid, and formalistic.

Here, however, a merely doctrinal analysis is insufficient. Restricting the appraisal of the judgments to a purely doctrinal analysis requires assuming that half the Court is staunchly committed to strict procedural formalism while at the same time taking a lax approach to the application of its own precedents. This is an unlikely combination of contradicting legal attitudes. In fact, the deviation from the previous treatment of the existence of a dispute requirement is so stark that it would require assuming a high degree of doctrinal ineptitude from the majority (which is fanciful).

This changes when contextual factors are considered. Here, they were likely determinative.

The first, and most obvious, factor is the subject matter of the dispute: nuclear weapons. It is disingenuous to assume that any of the Court's judges were unaware of the relevance and potential impact of this case. As one of the dissenters declared, the subject matter that was before the Court was of 'a major concern of the vulnerable international community, and indeed of humankind as a whole'.[114]

Any realistic analysis of these cases must take their subject matter into account. States *care* about nuclear weapons – particularly those that have them. A brief overview of the nuclear doctrines or policies of nuclear weapon States confirms this. For example, the United States latest Nuclear Posture Review states that the US will only consider deploying nuclear weapons 'in extreme circumstances to defend the vital interests of the United States or its allies'.[115] Similarly, the UK's nuclear doctrine clarifies that it would only resort to nuclear weapons 'only in extreme circumstances of self-defence'.[116] For its part, China's nuclear doctrine states that the 'goal' of its nuclear arsenal is 'deterring other countries from using or threatening to use nuclear weapons against China'.[117] In short,

[111] ibid Dissenting Opinion of Judge Sebutinde 6.

[112] ibid Dissenting Opinion of Judge Crawford, para 10.

[113] Interestingly, Judge Crawford hints in his dissenting opinion that the Court may have perhaps managed to decline jurisdiction over the dispute on the basis of the *Monetary Gold* principle, paras 32–33.

[114] ibid, Dissenting Opinion of Judge Cançado Trindade 88.

[115] For a good explanation, see Congressional Research Service, *U.S. Nuclear Weapons Policy: Considering 'No First Use'* (CRS Insight IN10553, 29 March 2022). Available at: https://crsreports.congress.gov/product/pdf/IN/IN10553.

[116] UK Ministry of Defence, Defence Nuclear Organisation, 'The UK's nuclear deterrent: what you need to know' (GOV.UK, 6 October 2025). Available at: www.gov.uk/government/publications/the-uks-nuclear-deterrent-what-you-need-to-know/the-uks-nuclear-deterrent-what-you-need-to-know.

[117] State Council Information Office of the People's Republic of China, *China's National Defence in the New Era* (July 2019). Available at: https://english.www.gov.cn/archive/whitepaper/201907/24/content/WS5d3941ddc6d08408f502283d.html.

nuclear-weapon States consider their nuclear deterrents a 'vital interest', the likes of which were historically considered unfit for adjudication.[118] Accordingly, all or most of those States have deliberately – and expressly – excluded issues regarding their nuclear deterrent from international adjudication.[119]

Despite their shortcomings (and there are many), nuclear weapons or, more specifically, nuclear deterrence, has played a key role in achieving and maintaining minimum order. Nuclear disarmament is an issue that has received considerable diplomatic efforts, with some bilateral efforts between the US and the USSR and then the Russian Federation having some success. But believing that a decision by an international court is a silver bullet for a problem that has dodged humanity for decades is wishful thinking – at best. Thomas Schelling, one of the leading scholars on nuclear deterrence, claims that the lack of use of nuclear weapons in combat in the past sixty years is the 'most significant event' in that time – and whether that remains so in the next sixty will also be one 'of the most important questions' of our time.[120] Perhaps it is a question that is not for the judicial process to answer.

This point was cogently articulated by Judge Oda in his dissenting opinion in the *Threat or Use of Nuclear Weapons* Advisory Opinion. There, Judge Oda stated that any decision on nuclear disarmament: 'is a function of political negotiations among States in Geneva or New York and is not one which concerns Our judicial institution here at The Hague'.[121] Under this view, the Court's application of international law to this dispute *may* be influenced by the subject matter of the dispute and, more importantly, the underlying value it represents: power. The appraisal of the decision must thus consider the role of the judicial process within this broader context and take into account whether judicial intervention would have been legitimate.[122]

[118] H Lauterpacht, *The Function of Law in the International Community* (OUP, 2011) 24. See also the discussion on the Russian Memorandum of 1899 to the Third Hague Conference, discussed in detail in chapter 2, section I(D), see also: JB Scott, *Reports to the Hague Conferences of 1899 and 1907* (Clarendon Press, 1917), 98.

[119] The only one of the P-5 States to accept the ICJ's compulsory jurisdiction is the United Kingdom. Shortly after the Court's judgment in the *Marshall Islands* cases, the UK modified its declaration recognising the jurisdiction of the Court as compulsory to specifically exclude 'any claim or dispute that arises from or is connected with or related to nuclear disarmament and/or nuclear weapons, unless all of the other nuclear-weapon States Party to the Treaty on the Non-Proliferation of Nuclear Weapons have also consented to the jurisdiction of the Court and are party to the proceedings in question', see United Kingdom, Declaration recognising as compulsory the jurisdiction of the International Court of Justice (22 February 2017) para (f). In practice, the language of this reservation will, absent a sea-change in the approach that the United States, China, and Russia take to international adjudication, mean that the UK has effectively excluded any dispute regarding its nuclear deterrent from international adjudication.

[120] T Schelling, 'Nuclear Deterrence for the Future' (2006) 23 *Issues in Science and Technology* 50; T Schelling, *Arms and Influence* (Yale University Press, 2008).

[121] *Legality of the Threat or Use of Nuclear Weapons,* ICJ, Advisory Opinion dated 8 July 1996, Dissenting Opinion of Judge Oda, para 54.

[122] WM Reisman and A Schreiber, *Jurisprudence* (New Haven Press, 1986) 15.

In effect, after the Court's decision, international negotiations on a treaty banning nuclear weapons gained strength. In December 2016, a few months after the judgments were issued, the UN General Assembly called for negotiations on a new nuclear ban treaty,[123] which resulted in the Treaty on the Prohibition of Nuclear Weapons, adopted in July 2017.[124] Although nuclear-weapon States have not become parties to the Treaty, it did enter into force in January 2021, after more than 50 States ratified it.[125]

The second factor is the nature of the legal obligation or legal rule being invoked by the Marshall Islands: the purported obligation to negotiate in good faith towards nuclear disarmament. The Marshall Islands argue that this obligation arises under Article 6 of the Treaty on Nuclear Non-Proliferation, of which the UK is a party; and customary international law, as India and Pakistan are not parties to the NPT.

A cursory review of the legal obligation established in Article 6 of the NPT[126] (and in less concrete terms, under customary international law) shows that it is a *weak* obligation – if it is an obligation at all. Article 6 of the NPT sets out the parties' obligation to 'pursue negotiations in good faith . . . relating to the cessation of the nuclear arms rate at an early date and to nuclear disarmament'. There is no end date for those negotiations to take place. There is no sanction for a violation of that obligation. Nor are there any compulsory dispute resolution mechanisms contemplated. Moreover, what *is* the exact content of an open-ended obligation to negotiate in good faith? A party may well claim that it has met that obligation because it has attempted to negotiate but has been unable to reach an agreement with the other parties. Indeed, the legal obligations invoked by the Marshall Islands are thus reminiscent of the Roman law notion of *lex imperfecta,* in the international context sometimes referred to as

[123] UNGA Res 71/258 (2017).

[124] UNGA A/CONF.229/2017/8. The Treaty has been ratified by 23 States so far. It will enter into force once it has been ratified by 50 States. Unsurprisingly, no State possessing nuclear weapons have become signatories of the treaty.

[125] See 'UN treaty banning nuclear weapons set to enter into force in January' *UN News* (25 October 2020). Available at: https://news.un.org/en/story/2020/10/1076082; D Rietiker, 'The Treaty on the Prohibition of Nuclear Weapons: A Further Confirmation of the Human- and Victim-Centred Trend in Arms Control Law' in JL Black-Branch and D Fleck (eds), *Nuclear Non-Proliferation in International Law – Volume IV: Human Perspectives on the Development and Use of Nuclear Energy* (TMC Asser Press, 2019) 325, 326; H Miyazaki and A Riles, 'Theorizing Intergenerational Justice in International Law: The Case of the Treaty on the Prohibition of Nuclear Weapons' (2022) 7 *UC Irvine Journal of International, Transnational, and Comparative Law* 122; C Evans, *Assessing the Theoretical and Practical Impact of the Treaty on the Prohibition of Nuclear Weapons as a Disarmament Law Instrument* (PhD thesis, University of Reading, 2022). Available at: https://centaur.reading.ac.uk/107506/.

[126] The complete text of Article 6 of the NPT reads: 'Each of the Parties to the Treaty undertakes to pursue negotiations in good faith on effective measures relating to cessation of the nuclear arms race at an early date and to nuclear disarmament, and on a treaty on general and complete disarmament under strict and effective international control.'

lex simulata, both terms used to describe legal obligations whose breach did not entail a sanction.[127]

Although the Court's decision was purely jurisdictional, it is reasonable to ask whether the inherent weakness of the legal rule purportedly violated had any – perhaps at most a minor – influence in the Court's approach. The obligation to negotiate was a *very weak* legal prescription. Indeed, it may be argued that the NPT itself is not justiciable – or at least is only relatively justiciable, as not all of its provisions contain applicable rules.[128] When, as here, the rule itself does not provide for its application by international courts, it is worth asking whether the rule was actually meant to be applied in international dispute settlement.

The third factor is the potential effectiveness and enforceability of the Court's decision (or lack thereof). That is, the Court's appraisal of the available enforcement mechanisms and the likelihood that an eventual judgment against the nuclear weapon States would have been effective.[129] It is impossible to ignore that any potential outcome that would have challenged the respondent States' nuclear policy would almost certainly have faced extreme opposition.[130] Backlash would have surely ensued. Although predictions about future compliance are difficult, in these circumstances it is reasonable to assume that few cases in the Court's history faced so high a probability of non-compliance.[131] Therefore, the lack of any credible base for enforcing this judgment is a factor that must also be taken into account. It is hard to claim that the thought of the potential implications of an unfavourable decision on the merits never crossed the minds of a group of judges who are well-versed in the conduct of international affairs.[132] Indeed, memories of the 'specter of non-compliance' probably arose.[133]

[127] M Rheinstein, 'The Nuremberg Trial and Aggressive War' (review of Sheldon Glueck, *The Nuremberg Trial and Aggressive War* (1946)) (1947) 14 *University of Chicago Law Review* 319, 319–21. See also the distinction between myth system and operational code set out in chapters 1 and 4.

[128] T Schultz, *Transnational Legality: Stateless Law and International Arbitration* (OUP, 2014) 10.

[129] KJ Alter, LR Helfer and MR Madsen, 'How Context Shapes the Authority of International Courts' (2016) 79 *Law and Contemporary Problems* 1, particularly section III, at 5 and ff.

[130] WM Reisman, 'International Lawmaking: A Process of Communication' (1981) 75 *Proceedings of the Annual Meeting (American Society of International Law)* 101, 105; R Howse and R Teitel, 'Beyond Compliance: Rethinking Why International Law Really Matters' (2010) 1 *Global Policy* 127; K Raustiala and AM Slaughter, 'International Law, International Relations and Compliance' in W Carlsnaes, T Risse and BA Simmons (eds), *Handbook of International Relations* (SAGE, 2002) 538.

[131] KJ Alter, JT Gathii and LR Helfer, 'Backlash Against International Courts in West, East and Southern Africa: Causes and Consequences' (2016) 27 *European Journal of International Law* 293, 318; WM Reisman, 'Has the International Court Exceeded Its Jurisdiction?' (1986) 80 *American Journal of International Law* 128, 132, stating that: 'In a fragile international political system that seeks to protect itself by insulating certain matters from review through their declarations accepting the Court's jurisdiction matters of vital interest to the major powers from review even by the Security Council.'

[132] Some would argue that the fact that so many of the Court's judges come from a government background leads the Court to be systematically biased in favour of the *status quo*, see Bianchi 'Choice and (the Awareness of) its Consequences' (n 65) 85.

[133] J Dugard, 'The Nuclear Tests Cases and the South West Africa Cases: Some Realism About the International Judicial Decision' (1976) 16 *Virginia Journal of International Law* 463, 488.

Interestingly, several events that took place in the midst of oral argument signalled potential non-compliance. In fact, the three respondents, by either statement or conduct, *hinted* what their eventual attitude to an unfavourable judgment would be. Pakistan, while initially participating in the procedures and even submitting written pleadings, later refused to participate in oral argument.[134] Non-appearance has been a strong indicator of potential future compliance issues.[135] The United Kingdom also made comments during oral argument that would cast doubts over the potential effectiveness of an eventual judgment.[136]

But it was India that sent the strongest message. Oral arguments began on 7 March. On 8 March 'a reliable defense source' leaked that India had secretly carried out a test launch of a nuclear-capable missile.[137] The issue was mentioned by counsel for the Marshall Islands, calling it a case of 'contempt of court'.[138] India accepted it had test-fired a nuclear-capable, submarine-launched missile stating that 'there is no legal régime prohibiting the possession and testing of missile'.[139] The two issues may be completely unrelated; perhaps the test was already scheduled before the date for oral arguments was set. Yet the message was too obvious to be ignored. One does not need to embark on a Straussian or diplomatic-speak analysis of the issue to get the point.

These statements were made just a few months after another divisive jurisdictional ruling in *Alleged Violations*.[140] The Court's decision in that case led

[134] *Marshall Islands (Pakistan)* (n 64) para 8: 'By a letter dated 2 March 2016, Pakistan informed the Court that it would not be participating in the oral proceedings on jurisdiction and admissibility.'

[135] J Ku and C Mirasola, 'Tracking Compliance with the South China Sea Arbitral Award: China's 2017 Summer Fishing Moratorium May Rekindle Conflict with the Philippines' *Lawfare* (7 March 2017). Available at: www.lawfareblog.com/tracking-compliance-south-china-sea-arbitral-award-chinas-2017-summer-fishing-moratorium-may; JI Charney, 'Disputes Implicating the Institutional Credibility of the Court: Problems of Non-Appearance, Non-Participation, and Non-Performance' in LF Damrosch (ed), *The International Court of Justice at a Crossroads* (Transnational Publishers, 1987) 288, 292; C Paulson, 'Compliance with Final Judgments of the International Court of Justice since 1987' (2004) 98 *American Journal of International Law* 434; EA Posner and JC Yoo, 'Judicial Independence in International Tribunals' (2005) 93 *California Law Review* 1 (table stating that, in cases of compulsory jurisdiction, the Court's rulings have only encountered a 40% compliance rate). Nevertheless, those statistics should be treated with caution; there may be some factual errors, for example regarding the number of cases submitted to the Inter-American Court of Human Rights. See also the discussion about compliance and effectiveness in chapter 2.

[136] *Marshall Islands (UK)* (n 64), Public sitting held on Monday 14 March 2016, at 3 pm: *Marshall Islands (UK)*, Verbatim Record CR 2016/7, 21–22 (Sir Daniel Bethlehem QC) stating: 'This case ... would without doubt raise searching questions about the judicial function, about the equality of law in proceedings before the Court ... and about the wisdom of optional clause declarations ... The United Kingdom has had an optional clause declaration in place since 1930 ... The Court's decision on jurisdiction and admissibility will not rest behind a veil of privacy. A finding of jurisdiction would raise serious questions about the judicial function'.

[137] 'India test fires nuke capable SLBM K-4 secretly' *The New Indian Express* (9 March 2016).

[138] *Marshall Islands (India)* (n 64), Public sitting held on Monday 14 March 2016, at 10 am: Verbatim Record CR 2016/6, 8 (Mr van den Biesen).

[139] ibid, Public sitting held on Wednesday 16 March 2016, at 10 am: *Marshall Islands (India)*, Verbatim Record CR 2016/8, 9 (Mr Gill).

[140] *Alleged Violations* (n 84), decided by the casting vote of the President.

the respondent state, Colombia, to declare (quite loudly) that it would not appear before the Court in the merits phase.[141] Given that Colombia had already denounced the treaty that established the Court's jurisdiction over that case, the Pact of Bogotá, before the case was filed, this is not surprising (jurisdiction was only established by virtue of a sunset clause).[142] It is thus safe to say that there were serious doubts as to the potential effectiveness or enforceability of a judgment adverse to the nuclear weapon States; that this case came up when there were already rumblings of defiance in the other of the Court's active cases probably did not help either.

Factoring in predictions of potential compliance difficulties in judicial analysis is, of course, an extremely delicate task. It risks creating perverse incentives. Reluctant respondents would be rewarded by upping the ante and signalling adamant resistance to comply with a potential adverse judgment if they thought this may tilt the court in their favour. We may even reach a point where this is routinely seen as another tool in the recalcitrant litigator's toolkit. But, to be clear, possibilities of non-compliance do not – and should not – automatically result in avoidance. Far from it. What it does mean, however, is that compliance difficulties can be one of several factors included in the overall, prudential appraisal of how an international court should exercise its jurisdiction. This is particularly so where the legal obligations at hand are particularly vaporous and there are significant doubts about the potential effectiveness of any adverse decision.

In sum, as the arguments above show, it is possible that the Court relied on the existence of a dispute doctrine as an implied avoidance technique to abstain from deciding a politically sensitive issue that touches vital national security interests of the world's most powerful States. Despite its doctrinal shortcomings, ultimately this is a decision that may be cast in a more favourable light. It likely saved the Court from either having to muddle the law on the merits to avoid ruling against the nuclear-weapon States or from what would surely have been very overt defiance. It thus preserved the Court's legitimacy. Moreover, at a systemic level, it is a decision that illustrates maturity and realism about the limitations of the international judicial function; one that is cognizant of its intrinsic limitations. Perhaps disappointingly for some, it also confirms the often-limited role that international adjudication plays in the broader international legal process.

[141] See President Juan Manuel Santos, 'Declaración del Presidente de Colombia Juan Manuel Santos sobre decisiones de la Corte Internacional de Justicia de La Haya' (7 March 2016). Available at: http://es.presidencia.gov.co/discursos/Declaracion-del-Presidente-de-Colombia-Juan-Manuel-Santos-sobre-decisiones-de-la-Corte-Internacional-de-Justicia-de-La-Haya ('faced with such contradictions, I have decided that Colombia will NOT continue to appear, in this matter, before the International Court of Justice. . . The bilateral issues between Colombia and Nicaragua will NOT continue to be subject to the decision of a third party' (my translation)).

[142] In fairness, Colombia reconsidered and then participated fully in the proceedings.

(iv) The Existence of a Dispute Doctrine as an Issue-Selection Mechanism

As explained previously, jurisdictional avoidance techniques may be used not only to decline jurisdiction over a case, but also to abstain from deciding a specific *issue* within a case. The Court, albeit more discreetly, has also relied on the existence of a dispute principle as an implied avoidance technique to carve-out *certain aspects* of a dispute, to refrain from having to adjudicate those particular issues.[143] Two examples illustrate this.

The first is *Obligation to Prosecute or Extradite*. The case involved allegations of torture raised against Hissène Habré, Chad's former dictator.[144] This was the first ICJ case to deal with the obligation to prosecute or extradite (*aut dedere aut judicare*).[145] The Court carved out the issue of potential obligations to prosecute or extradite arising under customary international law because they were not *explicitly* mentioned in diplomatic correspondence.[146] As one commentator observes, that was a 'controversial point'.[147]

The second one is *Alleged Violations*.[148] This was one of the cases in the long-running dispute between Nicaragua and Colombia regarding their maritime boundary. One important (perhaps *the* most important) aspect of this dispute was Nicaragua's allegations that the Colombian military had used, or threatened to use, force against Nicaraguan vessels in the disputed maritime area.[149] The Court relied on statements made by Nicaraguan military officials and on the timing of the application to consider that there was no dispute regarding Colombia's purported threats to use force against Nicaragua.[150] This was by far the most controversial issue in that case. There is an indication that the Court was relying on the inherent flexibility of the existence of a dispute principle in the dissenting opinion of Judge *ad hoc* Caron, who noted that the Court 'also departs from its own jurisprudence on this requirement'.[151]

[143] For a positive appraisal of the Court's decision to avoid some cases, see E Gordon, 'The World Court and the Interpretation of Constitutive Treaties: Some Observations on the Development of an International Constitutional Law' (1965) 59 *American Journal of International Law* 794, 802 stating that: 'The Court's self-restraint, therefore, seems to be the result of a highly pragmatic assessment of the greatest marginal utility which the judicial process can bring to the resolution of international disputes.'

[144] For more general views on the case, see S Shah, 'Questions relating to the Obligation to Prosecute or Extradite (Belgium v Senegal)' (2013) 13 *Human Rights Law Review* 351; A Nollkaemper, 'Wither Aut Dedere? The Obligation to Extradite or Prosecute after the International Court of Justice's Judgment in Belgium v Senegal' (2013) 4 *Journal of International Dispute Settlement* 501.

[145] M Andenas and T Weatherall, 'International Court of Justice: Questions relating to the Obligation to Extradite or Prosecute (Belgium v Senegal), Judgment of 20 July 2012' (2013) 62 *International and Comparative Law Quarterly* 753.

[146] *Obligation to Prosecute or Extradite* (n 89) 445; Nollkaemper , 'Wither Aut Dedere? (n 144) 517.

[147] C Nielsen, 'Prosecution or Bust: The Obligation to Prosecute under the United Nations Convention against Torture' (2013) 72 *Cambridge Law Journal* 242.

[148] *Alleged Violations* (n 84).

[149] This issue takes prominence in Nicaragua's submissions. See eg *Alleged Violations* (n 84), Memorial of the Republic of Nicaragua, 3 October 2014.

[150] ibid 32–33.

[151] *Alleged Violations* (n 84), Dissenting Opinion of Judge Caron para 5.

B. Indispensable Third Parties (The Monetary Gold Principle)

The second avoidance technique I will analyse is the indispensable third-party principle, also known as the *Monetary Gold* principle.[152] International courts are, in general, not courts of general personal jurisdiction.[153] This leads to potential difficulties when attempting to adjudicate disputes involving several States, only some of which may accept an international court's jurisdiction.[154]

As with the existence of a dispute, there is no express reference to the indispensable third-party principle in the relevant sources of international procedural law. There is no express provision in the Court's Statute that sets out this principle;[155] it was entirely judge-created. As with the existence of a dispute, this is a principle that has shown a remarkable degree of plasticity in its application. It is fuzzy; its borders are hard to draw and its application is subject to a certain degree of unpredictability.

There has been substantial academic commentary criticising the Court's application of the *Monetary Gold* principle. One author goes as far as to accuse the Court of 'fundamentally misunderst[anding] what the indispensable parties' doctrine is really about' and of 'misinterpret[ing] most of the relevant concepts'.[156] Others consider that the principle's 'inconsistency with the Statute's jurisdictional architecture appears plain',[157] further noting that the Court's application of the *Monetary Gold* principle has been 'at times imprecise'[158] and riddled with 'ambiguities and inconsistencies'.[159]

Perhaps more soberly, one of the leading textbooks on the ICJ notes that '[i]t is not easy to determine when [the conditions for the operation of the *Monetary Gold* principle] are fulfilled'.[160] Or, as Dugard said, the *Monetary Gold* case was 'dangerously uncertain'.[161] Conversely, Pierre d'Argent considers that the *Monetary Gold* principle is not exactly related to the subject matter

[152] See A Orakhelashvili, 'The Competence of the International Court of Justice and the Doctrine of the Indispensable Party: From Monetary Gold to East Timor and Beyond' (2011) 2 *Journal of International Dispute Settlement* 373. This is a rather bold claim.

[153] Even some international courts that have personal jurisdiction over a series of regional States (e.g., the ECtHR), do not have *general* personal jurisdiction. Indeed, arts 32–34 of the ECHR reflects the general principle that an international court may only exercise jurisdiction over a State with its consent. See also M Den Heijer, 'Procedural Aspects of Shared Responsibility in the European Court of Human Rights' (2013) 4 *Journal of International Dispute Settlement* 361.

[154] Although *Monetary Gold* is the main authority on this issue, the Central American Court of Justice addressed the issue in the *El Salvador v. Nicaragua* dispute, regarding the Bryan-Chamorro treaty, see 'El Salvador v Nicaragua' (1917) 11 *American Journal of International Law* 674, 683.

[155] Z Mollengarden and N Zamir, 'The Monetary Gold Principle: Back to Basics' (2021) 115 *American Journal of International Law* 41, 57 and ff.

[156] Orakhelashvili 'The Competence of the International Court of Justice ' (n 152) 373.

[157] Mollengarden and Zamir 'The Monetary Gold Principle' (n 155) 71.

[158] ibid 42.

[159] ibid 45.

[160] Tomuschat 'Article 36' (n 70) 730.

[161] J Dugard, '1966 and All That, the South West Africa Judgment Revisited in the East Timor Case' (1996) 8 *African Journal of International and Comparative Law* 549, 558.

of the dispute, but rather to the Court's exercise of its jurisdiction over specific claims.[162] He argues that the application of the principle is circumscribed by how parties frame their claims.[163]

None of those scholars, however, has considered whether the Court has relied on the inherent indeterminacy of the *Monetary Gold* principle as an implied avoidance technique. This, rather than doctrinal or technical incompetence, is probably the better explanation.

(i) Corfu Channel

Perhaps ironically, the Court's jurisprudence on indispensable third parties does not start with *Monetary Gold* – but rather with another landmark judgment: *Corfu Channel*.[164] Both cases involve Albania, though, and are linked. *Corfu Channel* involved the damage suffered by British naval vessels when they struck mines in the Corfu channel, which separates Greece from Albania.[165] A key issue in the claim was who was responsible for having laid the mines in the channel.

The UK argued that either Albania had laid the mines – or that Yugoslavia had done so with Albania's consent.[166] Indeed, during the hearing, the UK's Attorney General, Sir Hartley Shawcross (of Nuremberg trial fame), while admitting that the UK was not directly raising claims against Yugoslavia, mentioned that Yugoslavia had the type of mines that had exploded and that its involvement in the matter had been 'converted into certainty by the evidence . . . before the Court'.[167]

But Yugoslavia's absence did not dissuade the Court from deciding the case. Although the Court recognised that 'the authors of the minelaying remain unknown',[168] it considered that its task was to decide the *specific issue* of whether Albania was internationally responsible for the explosions.[169] Ultimately, it considered that – regardless of who *laid* the mines – the Albanian government must have *known* about their placement in its territorial waters and, therefore, was responsible.[170] At no point, however, did the Court indicate that Yugoslavia's

[162] P d'Argent, 'The Monetary Gold Principle: A Matter of Submissions' (2021) 115 *AJIL Unbound* 149, 150.

[163] ibid. d'Argent considers that 'its application very much depends on the way grievances are articulated', noting that in *Armed Activities on the Territory of the Congo* the principle would have easily been applicable were it not for the 'DRC's carefully worded submissions'. Although how the Court re-characterised Portugal's claim in *East Timor* would call this view into question.

[164] *Corfu Channel (United Kingdom v Albania)*, ICJ, Judgment of 9 April 1949.

[165] For a general overview, see M Waibel, 'Corfu Channel Case', in A Peters (ed) *Max Planck Encyclopedia of Public International Law* (2013), vol II 792.

[166] Among other things, the UK submitted evidence from former Yugoslavian naval officers, one of whom indicated that he had seen a Yugoslavian minelayer in the area shortly before the accident.

[167] *Corfu Channel* (n 164), Minutes from the Sittings Held from 9 November 1948 to 9 April 1949, 1950 ICJ Rep. 240 (25 March 1949).

[168] *Corfu Channel* (n 164) 17.

[169] ibid.

[170] ibid 22.

potential involvement in the case – or any determination of its rights – could preclude it from adjudicating the dispute.

(ii) Monetary Gold

Just a few years later the Court took a different position in *Monetary Gold.* Procedurally, this is a (very) strange case, including because it was the *claimant* who ultimately decided to challenge the Court's jurisdiction. Some context is necessary to understand what was happening. To summarise: the Central Bank of Albania's gold reserves were deposited in Italian banks. The Nazis looted c.2.5 tons of those reserves in 1943. After the end of the war, the reparations agreement[171] determined that the monetary gold that the Nazis had looted would be proportionally distributed between the States that proved that a 'definite amount of [their] monetary gold . . . was "looted by Germany"'.[172] The broader context of reparations was delicate,[173] among other things because of Keynes' notion that the reparations regime imposed on Germany at the end of the First World War was a catalyst for the Second World War.[174]

France, the UK and the US (here, the 'Executors') were charged with implementing the reparations agreement (the Washington Agreement).[175] Both Italy and Albania were claiming the Albanian central bank's gold that the Nazi's had stolen from Rome. The Executors, rather than deciding themselves the question of ownership, submitted the dispute to arbitration. The arbitrator held that the gold belonged to Albania.[176] So far so good. But then the plot (procedurally) thickened. Italy and the UK had made separate claims over that gold (i.e., claims not under the reparations agreement) in case the arbitrator ruled in favour of Albania. Italy was claiming compensation for the expropriation of Italian interests in the Central Bank of Albania; the UK was claiming for unpaid reparations ordered under the *Corfu Channel* judgment, which Albania had not yet satisfied.[177]

Before submitting the issue to the arbitrator, the Executors decided that, if the arbitrator ruled that the gold belonged to Albania, they would 'deliver the gold to the United Kingdom in partial satisfaction of the judgment in the Corfu Channel case' unless one of two things happened: (1) Albania applied to the ICJ to determine whether the gold could be transferred to the UK; or (2) Italy

[171] Agreement on Reparation from Germany, on the Establishment of an Inter-Allied Reparation Agency and on Restitution of Monetary Gold (adopted 14 January 1946).

[172] *Monetary Gold Removed from Rome in 1943 (Italy v France)*, ICJ, Judgment (Preliminary Question) of 15 June 1954.

[173] For a general view on the subject, see RM Buxbaum, 'A Legal History of International Reparations' (2005) 23 *Berkeley Journal of International Law* 314.

[174] Generally: JM Keynes, *The Economic Consequences of the Peace* (Macmillan, 1919).

[175] *Monetary Gold* (n 172) 25.

[176] ibid 26.

[177] ibid.

applied to the Court to determine whether the gold should have been delivered to Italy or whether the Italian claims had priority.[178]

Albania had not accepted the Court's compulsory jurisdiction. It did not make any application.[179] Albania's refusal to submit to the Court's jurisdiction was questionable, particularly because Albania was one of the signatories of Recommendation 8 of the Final Act and Annex of the Paris Agreement on Reparation from Germany,[180] which provides that States should 'agree to have recourse to the International Court of Justice for the solution of every conflict of law or of competence' arising from the Reparations Agreement.[181] This was exactly the type of situation that arose in *Monetary Gold*.

Italy, however, *did* file an application. It argued that it was entitled to the gold as compensation for the Albanian communist government's unlawful expropriation (without compensation) of Italian shareholders' stake in the Central Bank of Albania. Italy also raised a second point: that its claim over the gold should have priority over that of the UK.[182] A few months later, however, Italy appeared to have changed its mind. It took the procedurally unusual step of challenging the Court's jurisdiction.[183] The crux of that argument was that the statement made by the Executors was not a 'sufficient basis upon which to found the jurisdiction of the Court'.[184] To add further complexity, despite its subsequent jurisdictional challenge, Italy – belatedly – argued that the Court *had* jurisdiction to decide the priority issue.[185] This was (yet another) change of tack.

The Court upheld Italy's preliminary objection. It considered that Italy's claim to the gold required determining whether Albania had committed an internationally wrongful act. The Court thus held that:

> [T]o determine whether Italy is entitled to receive the gold, it is necessary to determine whether Albania has committed any international wrong against Italy, and whether she is under an obligation to pay compensation to her . . . In order to decide such questions, it is necessary to determine whether the Albanian [expropriation law] was contrary to international law . . . To go into the merits of such questions would be to decide a dispute between Italy and Albania.

[178] ibid.
[179] ibid.
[180] Originally published in: Department of State Bulletin, vol XIV, No 343 (27 January 1946).
[181] 'Reparation from Germany: Final Act and Annex of the Paris Conference on Reparation, November 9–December 21, 1945' (1946) 21 *International Conciliation* 215, 238.
[182] *Monetary Gold* (n 172) 22.
[183] ibid 27.
[184] ibid.
[185] *Monetary Gold* (n 172), Pleadings, Hearing, 10 May, the Italian counsel stated that: 'the priority issue should be considered quite separately from the issue relating to the international responsibility of Albania'. Hearing, 13 May: 'The second claim is distinct from the first . . . if the Court considers that the question of priority between the respective rights of the United Kingdom and Italy can be examined in a hypothetical form, independently of the examination of the first Italian claim, the Italian Government . . . would have no objection', 164.

> The Court cannot decide such a dispute without the consent of Albania . . . Albania's legal interests would not only be affected by a decision, but would form the very subject-matter of the decision.[186]

Ultimately, even though the Court considered that the three Executors *and* Italy had conferred it jurisdiction, it could not exercise its jurisdiction over Italy's first claim (i.e., whether it was entitled to the gold).[187] The logic was straightforward: determining whether Italy was entitled to the gold depended on whether Albania had committed an internationally wrongful act – a determination that required Albania's participation in the proceedings. The Court's decision on this issue was unanimous.[188] In his declaration, President McNair questioned Italy's procedural approach, criticising their failure to (try) to make Albania a respondent to the proceedings.[189]

Further – and more problematically – the Court also declined jurisdiction over Italy's second claim (i.e., the priority claim in respect of the UK). Unlike Albania, the UK *was* a party to the proceedings. Although the Court recognised that, because of the UK's participation in the proceedings, it 'might seem' as it could adjudicate the second claim, it nevertheless refused to do so. The Court relied on the terms of the Washington Agreement, narrowly construing their jurisdictional scope. The Agreement provided that the Court could determine the issue of priority 'if this issue should arise'.[190] On that basis, the Court considered that Italy's entitlement to the monetary gold was an antecedent issue that had to be resolved first, holding that the wording of the Washington Agreement meant that the issue of priority would only arise 'if the Court had already decided that Italy had a valid claim to the gold in question against Albania'.[191]

There was only one dissent, by Judge Levi Carneiro.[192] In his view, the Court had jurisdiction over the second claim – and should have decided it. He considered that the second claim 'has been submitted – and remains submitted – to the Court, and the only States interested in its decision on this question are before the Court'.[193] Moreover, Judge Levi Carneiro considered that the Court did not need to engage in hypothetical questions of fact to decide the second claim, as it could opt to 'deal[] with it as a question of abstract law . . . It could have decided it quite simply by recognizing the character of the two claims, without

[186] *Monetary Gold* (n 172) 32.
[187] ibid 33.
[188] ibid 34. The President of the Court, Sir Arnold McNair, as well as Judges Read and Levi Carneiro issued separate opinions (the latter dissenting on another issue).
[189] ibid. Declaration of Judge McNair 35.
[190] *Monetary Gold* (n 172) 33.
[191] ibid.
[192] *Monetary Gold* (n 172), Dissenting Opinion of Judge Levi Carneiro.
[193] ibid 43.

prejudging the question of the validity of the claim which has not as yet been established'.[194]

To add to the procedural peculiarities of the case, none of the three Respondents challenged the Court's jurisdiction. The US questioned Italy's decision to challenge the Court's jurisdiction. It argued that Albania was not an indispensable third party because, under any outcome, it would never be receiving the gold. The US further contended that there was no enforcement risk as the transfer of the gold would be the result of the Executor's decision – not a decision of the Court.[195] Further, it argued that the actual dispute between the Court was one between the UK and Italy and that the Executors were 'in a position to dispose of the gold without Albania's agreement'.[196]

France queried the adequacy of Italy's jurisdictional objection and reiterated that it submitted to the Court's jurisdiction. France argued that there should be no doubt as to the Court's jurisdiction, observing – rhetorically – that the only potential issue that may lead to some worries was the 'enforcement of the judgment',[197] only to reiterate that there would be no 'problem' with the enforcement of the judgment because the 'three Respondent Governments, responsible for enforcement, are capable of proceeding, are engaged [in the proceedings] and their engagement is absolute'.[198]

Finally, the UK (which could be considered the main respondent), raised a procedurally nuanced argument. While the UK did not challenge the Court's jurisdiction, it did contend that Italy's jurisdictional objections should be considered as 'amounting to a nullification or cancellation – or to a withdrawal – of the original Application'.[199] This, it argued, meant that the Court should determine what the result should be as if 'Italy, as well as Albania, had never applied to the Court at all'.[200] Of course, the outcome of that was that the Executors would have transferred the gold to the UK in satisfaction of the *Corfu Channel* judgment. So, although the UK advanced the argument that the Court could only decide the priority issue (if it 'should arise') this argument must be analysed in the broader context of the UK's main argument that Italy's jurisdictional objections were tantamount to a withdrawal of the application – a conclusion the Court did not reach.[201]

[194] ibid 44.

[195] *Monetary Gold* (n 172), Pleadings, Statement of the Government of the United States of America on the Preliminary Question of Jurisdiction Raised by the Government of Italy, 93.

[196] ibid 94.

[197] *Monetary Gold* (n 172), Pleadings, Observations of the French Government, 85 (my translation).

[198] ibid (my translation).

[199] *Monetary Gold* (n 172), Pleadings, Observations of the British Government, 80.

[200] ibid.

[201] *Monetary Gold* (n 172), Pleadings, Hearing, 12 May, 132, Sir Gerald Fitzmaurice: 'I shall accordingly ask the Court to hold that there is no longer any valid or subsisting Italian application before the Court . . . If the Court agrees with this view . . . it would be unnecessary for the Court to determine the issues of jurisdiction.'

At a doctrinal level, analysing the Court's judgment requires nuance. As a starting point, that the decision to decline jurisdiction over the first claim was unanimous, and over the second claim, almost unanimous, should give some pause before criticising the Court's reasoning. However, some contemporaneous commentary was critical of the *Monetary Gold* judgment. Johnson considered that the Court's decision to decline jurisdiction went against 'cogent practical reasons' to do the opposite and overall considered that the approach was unsatisfactory.[202] Hersch Lauterpacht was also unimpressed. He wrote that the Court's judgment would be restricted to the 'interpretation of the technical clauses' of the Reparations Agreement but that it did not establish a decision on 'wider issues of international law'.[203] Others simply did not anticipate that the case would set out an important precedent.[204]

The most straightforward explanation for the Court's approach is that by adopting a narrow view of its jurisdictional mandate under the Washington Agreement it avoided appearing to 'flexibilise' the requirement for State-consent to its jurisdiction.[205] This is also what some modern authors make of the case.[206] Kolb, for instance, has opined that the Court's underlying motivation was to 'avoid the introduction of a back-door form of compulsory jurisdiction'.[207]

Perhaps that is all. But there are some grounds to plausibly consider that there could have been something else behind the Court's approach. The most insightful contemporary analysis is Oliver's. He starts by noting that, on its face, the Court's judgment could be viewed as a 'nicely reasoned piece of ineffectualness'.[208] Nevertheless, he explains that, based on the context of the decision and its subject matter, there may have been other considerations at

[202] DHN Johnson, 'The Case of the Monetary Gold Removed from Rome in 1943' (1955) 4 *International and Comparative Law Quarterly* 93, 104.

[203] H Lauterpacht, *The Development of International Law by the International Court* (Stevens & Sons, 1958) 33.

[204] MO Hudson, 'The Thirty-Third Year of the World Court' (1955) 49 *American Journal of International Law* 1, 6.

[205] Johnson 'The Case of the Monetary Gold' (n 202) 106. This point, of course, was addressed in chapter 2. In addition to the authorities mentioned therein, see also Hernández (n 4) 47; H Thirlway, *The Law and Procedure of the International Court of Justice: Fifty Years of Jurisprudence* (OUP, 2013) 691; J Crawford, *Brownlie's Principles of Public International Law*, 8th edn (OUP, 2012) 672; T Sparks, 'Reassessing State Consent to Jurisdiction: The Indispensable Third Party Principle before the ICJ' (Max Planck Institute for Comparative Public Law and International Law, MPIL Research Paper Series No 2020-22, 2020).

[206] AJ Grotto, 'Monetary Gold Arbitration and Case' in A Peters (ed), *Max Planck Encyclopaedia of Public International Law* para 12.

[207] Kolb *The International Court of Justice* (n 71) 568.

[208] CT Oliver, 'The Monetary Gold Decision in Perspective' (1955) 49 *American Journal of International Law* 216. That this was one of the few articles that focuses on the broader political context of the *Monetary Gold* decision may be due to the fact that Oliver, in addition to being a legal scholar, was also a diplomat. He served at one point as US Ambassador and had experience in the 'thick of the titanic challenges posed by the war's destruction and the postwar efforts . . . to repair the wreckage through the Marshall Plan', see WD Rogers, 'Covey T Oliver (1913–2007)' (2007) 101 *American Journal of International Law* 404.

play. 'It is somewhat disturbing', Oliver wrote, that the UK, as a fiduciary of the reparations, 'disposed in the twilight of their trust to enforce their own non-trustee claims against the trust assets',[209] further noting that allowing the Executors to grant the gold to the UK as satisfaction for the unpaid *Corfu Channel* judgment would be tantamount to allowing the UK to engage in self-help.[210] Indeed, Oliver opines that the Court was 'cavalierly tossed a 'hot potato' that diplomacy and international quasi-administrative law and international arbitration did not handle', further criticising the Tripartite Gold Commission for not having completely decided the issue of who was entitled to that portion of the gold.[211]

A doctrinal appraisal of the *Monetary Gold* decision should ask whether it was possible for the Court to decide the second claim – even without deciding the first claim. In my view, the answer is yes. As all three Respondent States mentioned, the second claim involved whether the UK's or Italy's claims had priority. Both the UK and Italy were before the Court. If the Court ruled that the UK claim had priority, that was the end of the matter (as the Executors had already decided that the UK was entitled to that gold). Conversely, if the Court held that Italy's claim – if ultimately sustained – would have priority, then the enforcement of that judgment would be suspended until Italy managed to establish that primary claim against Albania. If Italy failed to do so, then the gold would also been eventually transferred to the UK.

A New Haven focused appraisal of the judgment also requires nuance. Unlike most international judgments, here there were robust – indeed, almost guaranteed – grounds for enforcement. After all, the Executors *held* the gold and had accepted that it would be transferred in accordance with the Court's judgment. Leaving that issue aside, determining whether the Court's decision contributed to minimum order is not straightforward.

On the one hand, reiterating the importance of the principle of State consent to international adjudication and, potentially, rejecting the possibility of self-help, could be considered as positive effects. As Oliver points out, here the practical outcome of the Court's refusal to adjudicate the dispute was that the UK was unable to claim the gold for itself; a result that, to some, had more than a whiff of self-dealing. Avoiding having to expressly determine that issue likely averted the eventual pushback from the UK that such a decision would have generated. Although there is nothing in the judgment itself that indicates that this was the message the Court was trying to communicate, it was not such an obscure point, as some astute contemporaneous commentators picked it up.[212]

On the other hand, one potential consequence of the Court's refusal to adjudicate the dispute was that the UK and Albania were locked in a protracted

[209] Oliver ibid 220.
[210] ibid.
[211] ibid 221.
[212] See eg Oliver (n 208).

diplomatic spat that lasted for almost 40 years.[213] The two States did not have diplomatic relations during that time. The UK claimed that Albania had still not paid the compensation it owed from *Corfu Channel*; Albania claimed that the UK was retaining its monetary gold.[214]

If anything, the Court's *Monetary Gold* judgment shows the inherent flexibility in some principles of international procedural law. It is that ductility, that plasticity – and the relatively doctrinal thinness of the field more generally – that allows the Court some leeway in determining how to apply those rules and, in consequence, whether to adjudicate a case (or not). As explained above, and as Judge Levi Carneiro set out in his dissenting opinion, the Court may have well opted to decline jurisdiction over the first claim but uphold it over the second one. Ultimately, it opted not to do so. The critical point is that it would have been equally plausible for the Court to have followed Judge Levi Carneiro's suggested approach. This decision is far from single-right-answer territory.

(iii) Military and Paramilitary Activities

After *Monetary Gold*, it took almost forty years for a respondent State to invoke the indispensable third-parties principle to challenge the Court's jurisdiction. The US (unsuccessfully) did so in *Military and Paramilitary Activities in and Against Nicaragua*.[215]

There, in short, the US raised a series of jurisdictional challenges. On the issue of indispensable third-parties, it argued that the principle precluded the Court from adjudicating the dispute because doing so would involve adjudicating on the collective self-defence efforts of El Salvador, Honduras and Costa Rica, who were also involved in the conflict.[216] Those States neighbour Nicaragua and

[213] One possibility, at least in relation to the Italy–UK dispute, is that there were hopes of the parties reaching a settlement, even up to oral argument in the hearings. Indeed, at the start of the hearing, the Italian agent, Ambassador Casto Caruso, mentioned that possibility, see *Monetary Gold* (n 172), Hearing (10 May 1954) 105.

[214] The two States finally settled their dispute in 1992, signing a Memorandum of Understanding in which the UK agreed to return the monetary gold held by the Bank of England and Albania agreed to pay compensation under *Corfu Channel*, see G Marston (ed), 'United Kingdom Materials on International Law 1992' (1993) 63 *British Yearbook of International Law* 615, 781 ff.

[215] *Military and Paramilitary Activities in and Against Nicaragua (Nicaragua v United States of America)*, ICJ, Judgment of 27 June 1986. This is, of course, a controversial judgment. Reisman considered that the Court's 'creation of a valid Nicaraguan declaration is so ill-founded in the facts, in the law and in the Court's own jurisprudence as to constitute a ground of nullity', Reisman (n 131) 128; James Crawford characterised it as 'perhaps the most complex and intractable instance of serial litigation yet brought before the International Court of Justice', in 'Military and Paramilitary Activities in and against Nicaragua (Nicaragua v United States of America)' in A Peters (ed), *Max Planck Encyclopaedia of Public International Law*. Other States had previously invoked the doctrine in the context of requests to intervene in proceedings The principle was invoked by States attempting to *intervene* in proceedings – but not by respondents. See *Continental Shelf (Tunisia/Libyan Arab Jamahiriya)*, ICJ, Judgment (Application by Malta for Permission to Intervene) of 14 April 1981, 15 and see 24–28; *Frontier Dispute (Burkina Faso/Republic of Mali)*, ICJ, Judgment of 22 December 1986.

[216] *Military and Paramilitary* (n 215) 430.

they considered that Nicaragua had engaged in military action and also assisted guerrillas in their respective territories.[217] The Court rejected that argument in a single paragraph, concluding that neither El Salvador, Honduras or Costa Rica were in a position equivalent to Albania's in *Monetary Gold* and thus could not be considered 'truly indispensable' parties.[218]

(iv) Certain Phosphate Lands in Nauru

The Court did not engage with the *Monetary Gold* principle in detail in *Military and Paramilitary Activities*. It was only in *Certain Phosphate Lands in Nauru* where, despite *refusing* to decline jurisdiction on its basis, the Court engaged with the principle in detail.[219]

First, some background. Nauru is a tiny coral island in the Pacific: it is the world's smallest island nation and the world's least populated State. In the late nineteenth century, Nauru was annexed by the German Empire.[220] During the First World War, it was occupied by Australia. After that, it was under a League of Nations' mandate.[221] The mandate was carried out by Australia, New Zealand and the UK.[222] During the Second World War, it was occupied by Japan. After that, it was a UN Trust Territory, again under the joint authority of Australia, New Zealand and the UK.[223] Despite those three States having joint authority, in practice Australia *de facto* administered the territory by itself until Nauru's independence in 1968.[224]

Because it is in the migratory flightpath of several birds, Nauru had rich phosphate deposits (the result of centuries of accumulated guano). Since 1919, phosphate mining in Nauru had been managed by the British Phosphate Commissioners.[225] The phosphate mining operations were transferred to Nauru in 1967, shortly before independence.[226] Once independent, Nauru was not satisfied with the way that the commissioners had mined the phosphates claiming (unsurprisingly), that the mining operations had not been carried out with Nauru's best interests in mind. Nauru initiated proceedings against Australia. Among other things, it claimed that Australia was responsible for rehabilitating some of the phosphate lands that had

[217] ibid 430–1.
[218] ibid 431.
[219] *Certain Phosphate Lands in Nauru (Nauru v Australia)*, ICJ, Judgment (Preliminary Objections) of 26 June 1992 240.
[220] N Schrijver, 'Certain Phosphate Lands in Nauru Case (Nauru v Australia)' in A Peters (ed), *Max Planck Encyclopaedia of Public International Law* (OUP, online) para 1 (last updated September 2008).
[221] ibid.
[222] Nauru Island Agreement (2 July 1919) 113 *British and Foreign State Papers* 151.
[223] Proposed Trusteeship Agreement for the Territory of Nauru, UNGA Res 140 (II) (1 November 1947).
[224] Schrijver Certain Phosphate Lands' (n 220).
[225] *Certain Phosphate Lands* (n 219) para 59.
[226] ibid para 60.

been mined.[227] Although New Zealand and the UK had joint authority over Nauru, and although both had accepted the Court's compulsory jurisdiction, Nauru did not initiate proceedings against either; it only made claims against Australia.

Australia raised several jurisdictional objections, one of which was based on *Monetary Gold*. Australia argued that, in reality, Nauru's claim was 'not a claim against Australia itself but a claim against the Administering Authority in relation to Nauru'.[228] In consequence, Australia said, the Court could not adjudicate on Australia's responsibility without also 'adjudicating on the responsibility of New Zealand and the United Kingdom'.[229]

Indeed, because the Trusteeship Agreement established joint liability between the three administering States, Australia argued that the *Monetary Gold* principle was engaged. Australia contended that it could demand that the UK and New Zealand make a contribution to any monetary award the Court issued in favour of Nauru.[230] The Court rejected that argument, holding instead that:

> [A] finding by the Court regarding the existence or the content of the responsibility attributed to Australia by Nauru might well have implications for the legal situation of the other two States concerned, but no finding in respect of that legal situation will be needed as a basis for the Court's decision on Nauru's claim against Australia.[231]

An important aspect of the Court's judgment was its interpretation of the indispensable third-parties principle. The Court clarified that its approach in *Monetary Gold* was based on the 'link between, on the one hand, the necessary findings regarding Albania's alleged responsibility and, on the other, the decision requested of the Court regarding the allocation of gold, was not purely temporal but also logical'.[232] The Court contrasted that with what it considered was the situation here, where it held that determining the UK's or New Zealand's responsibility was 'not a prerequisite for the determination of the responsibility of Australia'.[233] In relation to joint liability, the Court observed that was:

[227] See *Certain Phosphate Lands*, Application Instituting Proceedings (19 May 1989) at 30.

[228] *Certain Phosphate Lands* (n 219) para 39.

[229] ibid.

[230] Australia raised this point in its written and oral submissions to the Court. See *Certain Phosphate Lands*, Verbatim Record CR 91/17 (Public sitting held on Wednesday 13 November 1991) 22–23 (Alain Pellet).

[231] *Certain Phosphate Lands* (n 219) 55.

[232] ibid. For a distinction between the characterisation approach and the logical approach, see P Tzeng, 'The Implicated Issue Problem: Indispensable Issues and Incidental Jurisdiction' (2018) 50 *NYU Journal of International Law & Politics* 447, 460. See also C Harris, 'Claims with an Ulterior Purpose: Characterising Disputes Concerning the "Interpretation or Application" of a Treaty' (2019) 18(3) *The Law and Practice of International Courts and Tribunals* 279.

[233] *Certain Phosphate Lands* (n 219) para 55. In his separate opinion Judge Shahabuddeen considered that 'there is nothing in the legal elements of a possible judgment in favour of Nauru which would require the judgment to be construed as *per se* constituting or amounting to a judicial determination of the responsibility of New Zealand and the United Kingdom . . . It is difficult to see what protection will be needed beyond that provided by Article 59 of the Statute of the Court' Separate Opinion of Judge Shahabuddeen, 297.

> [A] question which the Court must reserve for the merits: but it is independent of the question whether Australia can be sued alone. The Court does not consider that any reason has been shown why a claim brought against only one of the three States should be declared inadmissible in limine litis merely because that claim raises questions of the administration of the territory, which was shared with two other States.

The Court's decision to punt this issue to the merits is hard to understand. Of course, if the Court ultimately concluded that it could not adjudicate on Australia's liability without affecting the UK's and New Zealand's rights, it could have declined jurisdiction at that phase. Yet the more logical approach would be to have decided that issue at the preliminary objections stage. As Judge Schwebel observed in his dissenting opinion, the Court should refrain from adjudicating a dispute if the judgment against a State that is party to the proceedings would 'effectively determine the legal obligations of one or more States which are not before the Court'.[234]

Overall, the Court adopted a narrow interpretation of the *Monetary Gold* principle to uphold jurisdiction over Nauru's claim.[235] Doctrinally, this decision may be defensible. Nevertheless, the Court's attempt to add what it considered a *logical* – as opposed to only a *temporal* – element in the application of the doctrine could be considered a slightly artificial attempt to rationalise a preferred outcome.

The judgment has been criticised. The four dissenting opinions (by President Jennings, Vice-President Oda, and judges Ago and Schwebel) are a good place to start.[236] President Jennings considered that the interests of both the UK and New Zealand were 'inextricabl[y] involve[d]'.[237] More caustically, Judge Schwebel criticised the majority's reliance on analogies from domestic procedural law, raising a point that has been made in this book: 'jurisdiction is not consensual in national law'.[238] Judge Ago noted that, having failed to bring claims against the UK and New Zealand, Nauru must have faced the consequences of that procedural choice.[239] Finally, Vice-President Oda concluded that the Court should decline jurisdiction, among other things, because the entire dispute could only be resolved 'under the United Nations mechanism' on Trusteeship.[240] He also

[234] *Certain Phosphate Lands* (n 219), Dissenting Opinion of Judge Schwebel, 331. The Judge further observed that 'a Judgment by this Court upon the responsibility of Australia would appear to be tantamount to a judgment upon the responsibility of New Zealand and the United Kingdom . . . The answer . . . is that the protection afforded the absent States by Article 59 in the quite exceptional situation of this case would be notional rather than real'.

[235] See Orakhelashvili (n 152) 382.

[236] The identity of the dissenters is, in itself, indicative. Nevertheless, the majority included Judges Lachs, Guillaume and Shahabuddeen.

[237] *Certain Phosphate Lands* (n 219), Dissenting Opinion of Judge Jennings, 301.

[238] ibid Dissenting Opinion of Judge Schwebel, 329–30.

[239] ibid para 6.

[240] ibid Dissenting Opinion of Judge Oda, para 25.

considered that the claim was inadmissible given Nauru's delay in raising any claims regarding the phosphate mining since it became independent in 1967.[241]

Some scholars were unpersuaded. Scobbie considered it a 'disturbing development'.[242] Schrijver opined that the Court's application of the *Monetary Gold* principle has received 'serious criticism'.[243] Others seemed only to focus on the underlying subject matter of the dispute rather than on the procedural aspects.[244] In fact, in his separate opinion in *East Timor*, Judge Ranjeva insinuated that the decision in *Nauru* was a 'a departure from previous doctrine'.[245]

Again, a merely doctrinal analysis foregoes considering the (conspicuous) policy context. This was, after all, 'the first case involving a former dependent territory bringing action against a metropolitan authority for abusing its power when administering the dependent territory'.[246] The last time that particular issue arose before was in the *Northern Cameroons* case, where, as explained above, the Court declined jurisdiction (relying on an express justiciability doctrine) and faced considerable criticism, particularly from States that had recently become independent.[247] Did the subject matter and identity of the parties potentially influence the Court's decision to uphold jurisdiction? Is this the underlying reason why the Court was somewhat flexible in its approach to the *Monetary Gold* doctrine? After all, this was a doctrine that was relatively indeterminate and had only been developed in a few judgments.

The strongest I can put this is: perhaps. There are no certainties. But, approaching the issue probabilistically and inferentially, there are certainly some indicia that suggest that the Court may have considered that upholding jurisdiction would contribute to its institutional robustness and to its legitimacy as a forum for adjudicating colonial-related disputes. James Crawford, whose pragmatic instincts are often underrated, observed that the Court's judgment 'exposed a certain sympathy towards Nauru's argument'.[248]

More importantly, there are some statements in the separate opinions which, perhaps if read Straussianly, provide further support for this view.[249] For

[241] ibid paras 28–29.

[242] I Scobbie, 'Case Concerning Certain Phosphate Lands in Nauru (Nauru v Australia), Preliminary Objections Judgment' (1993) 42 *International and Comparative Law Quarterly* 710.

[243] Schrijver (n 220) 14.

[244] RF Reyes Jr, 'Nauru v Australia: The International Fiduciary Duty and the Settlement of Nauru's Claims for Rehabilitation of Its Phosphate Lands' (1996) 16 *New York Law School Journal of International and Comparative Law* 2; A Anghie, 'The Heart of My Home: Colonialism, Environmental Damage, and the Nauru Case' (1993) 34 *Harvard International Law Journal* 445.

[245] *East Timor (Portugal v Australia)*, ICJ, Judgment of 30 June 1995. See Separate Opinion of Judge Ranjeva, 130.

[246] Schrijver (n 220) 13.

[247] See eg Anghie 'The Heart of My Home' (n 244) 446. Similarly, in relation to the *South West Africa cases*, Dugard (n 161) '1966 and All That' 549 noting that in the aftermath the Court had to deploy a 'conscious and concerted effort' to 'convince the international community that it was not a bastion of colonial, Eurocentric jurisprudence'.

[248] J Crawford, '"Dreamers of the Day": Australia and the International Court of Justice' (2013) 14 *Melbourne Journal of International Law* 520, 522.

[249] President Jennings and Judge Schwebel did not consider this issue.

example, in his dissenting opinion Judge Ago clarified that he was 'no less sensitive than [his] colleagues to the frustration felt by the Nauruans'[250] to then caveat that those 'perfectly justified emotional reactions should not blind [the Court] to the fact that the questions we have to consider . . . are very specific questions of law and that it is by reference to the law, and only to the law, that they have to be answered'.[251] Vice President Oda similarly mentioned that he was aware of the 'natural and social situation in which Nauru as a relatively new independent State [was] placed' and of the 'particular relations between Australia and Nauru since the time of the League of Nations'.[252] Therefore, the Judge explained that he was 'personally . . . second to none in hoping that some measures may well be considered by Australia for promoting the rehabilitation' of the phosphate lands.[253] Finally, Judge Shahabuddeen, who was part of the majority, starts his separate opinion by reiterating the importance of the principle of equality of States.[254] He did this after clarifying that 'Nauru is one of the smallest States in the world; Australia one of the larger'.[255] Given that the principle of sovereign equality of States was not at issue, it is interesting that the Judge considered it relevant to reiterate this principle.

In any event, even if there was no underlying, unarticulated motivation to the Court's approach, the application of the *Monetary Gold* principle in *Nauru* at the very least supports the proposition that rules of international procedural law often are inherently indeterminate and thus relatively flexible.

(v) East Timor

It was not until the *East Timor* judgment,[256] decided over forty years after *Monetary Gold*, that the Court relied on the indispensable third-party principle to decline jurisdiction over a dispute. Only two years after the Court's decision in *Nauru*, the contours of the *Monetary Gold* principle shifted again.

Before going into the details of the judgment, some context is necessary.[257] Timor is an island in Southeast Asia. It is above Australia, at the end of the archipelago that constitutes Indonesia. The Netherlands and Portugal had colonised the island (the Portuguese since the sixteenth century). In 1859 the two colonial powers divided Timor: the Netherlands controlled the west of the island, whereas

[250] *Certain Phosphate Lands* (n 219), Dissenting Opinion of Judge Ago, para 1
[251] ibid.
[252] ibid Dissenting Opinion of Judge Oda, para 30.
[253] ibid.
[254] ibid Dissenting Opinion of Judge Shahabuddeen, 270.
[255] ibid.
[256] *East Timor* (n 245) 90.
[257] For a thorough overview, see M Benzing, 'Midwifing a New State: The United Nations in East Timor' (2005) 9 *Max Planck Yearbook of United Nations Law* 295, particularly section II. See also RS Clark, 'The "Decolonization" of East Timor and the United Nations Norms on Self-Determination and Aggression' (1980) 7 *Yale Journal of International Law* 2. The Court's judgment addresses this briefly (all of 3 lines, in para 11).

the Portuguese controlled the east.[258] During the Second World War Japan invaded East Timor and occupied it for three years. Following the war, Indonesia became independent from the Netherlands. By 1949, West Timor had become part of Indonesia.[259] East Timor, in contrast, remained under Portuguese rule.

On joining the UN, Portugal refused to comply with its obligations under international law in relation to administration of non-self-governing territories, including refusing to comply with any reporting requirements on the situation in East Timor.[260] This led the UN General Assembly to declare East Timor a Non-Self Governing Territory, under Chapter XI of the UN Charter.[261] East Timor was thus considered an overseas province of Portugal.[262] Portugal, then under the *Estado Novo* regime, the dictatorship led by António Salazar, adamantly rejected any possibility of self-determination or independence for its overseas territories.[263] In 1974 the *Estado Novo* regime was overthrown. The new regime accepted its obligations under Chapter XI and recognised the right of Portuguese overseas territories to become independent.[264] Although the end-goal of independence was now accepted, there remained serious questions as to *when* and *how* Portuguese colonies, including East Timor, would become independent.

In East Timor 1974-1975 was a time of political chaos. There was fighting between different factions. The Portuguese authorities packed up and left the Island. In late 1975, one faction had declared independence; another had declared independence *and* integration with Indonesia.[265] By December 1975 Indonesia had invaded and set up a 'provisional' government. Of course, it was no such thing. The next year, a 'Regional Popular Assembly' had voted for East Timor to formally become part of Indonesia.[266] The UN General Assembly and the Security Council condemned Indonesia's occupation and requested it to withdraw from East Timor. Indonesia ignored those requests.[267] It effectively controlled the territory until 1999. East Timor became an independent State in 2002.[268]

[258] Benzing ibid 300.

[259] ibid.

[260] Clark , 'The "Decolonization" of East Timor' (n 257) 3.

[261] UNGA Res 1542 (XV) (15 December 1960). This was reiterated in UNGA Res 3485 (XXX) (12 December 1975).

[262] *East Timor* (n 245) para 12.

[263] Clark (n 257) 3.

[264] See Report of the Special Committee on the Situation with Regard to the Implementation of the Declaration on the Granting of Independence to Colonial Countries and Peoples, 30 UN GAOR, 2 Supp (No 23) 34, UN Doc A/10023/Rev 1 (1975). Similarly, in the GA's Fourth Committee, Portugal reiterated its recognition of its obligations under Chapter XI. 29 UN GAOR, C4 (2080th mtg) 3, 7, UN Doc A/C 4/SR 2080 (1975).

[265] Clark (n 257) 7–8.

[266] ibid 10–11.

[267] *East Timor* (n 245) paras 13–16.

[268] JG Taylor, *The Indonesian Occupation of East Timor 1974–1989: A Chronology* (Catholic Institute for International Relations, 1990); P Hainsworth and S McCloskey (eds), *The East Timor Question: The Struggle for Independence from Indonesia* (IB Tauris, 2012). See also T Voon, 'Closing the Gap Between Legitimacy and Legality of Humanitarian Intervention: Lessons from East Timor and Kosovo' (2002) 7 *UCLA Journal of International Law and Foreign Affairs* 31.

Australia had *de facto* recognised East Timor's incorporation into Indonesia in 1978, noting that, despite objecting to the manner in which Indonesia had occupied East Timor, Indonesia's control of the territory was 'effective and covers all major administrative centres of the territory'.[269] A few years before, Australia and Indonesia had delimitated the continental shelf between their coasts. There was an undelimitated part, called the 'Timor Gap'.[270] Having failed to agree on delimitation, in 1989 Australia and Indonesia entered into a treaty setting up a zone of cooperation to jointly explore and exploit the Timor Gap's resources.[271]

In *East Timor*, Portugal claimed that by negotiating and entering into the treaty with Indonesia, Australia had violated East Timor's right to self-determination and to permanent sovereignty over their natural resources, as well as Portugal's rights as administering power.[272] Australia challenged the Court's jurisdiction including by, among other things, invoking the *Monetary Gold* principle. Australia's objection was that adjudicating the dispute would require the Court to 'rule on the lawfulness of the conduct of a third State, namely Indonesia', who was not before the Court.[273] Portugal, in turn, argued that it was only requesting the Court to adjudicate on Australia's conduct.[274] The Court upheld Australia's jurisdictional objection. It held that:

> Australia's behaviour cannot be assessed without first entering into the question why it is that Indonesia could not lawfully have concluded the 1989 Treaty, while Portugal allegedly could have done so; the very subject-matter of the Court's decision would necessarily be a determination whether, having regard to the circumstances in which Indonesia entered and remained in East Timor, it could or could not have acquired the power to enter into treaties on behalf of East Timor . . . The Court could not make such a determination in the absence of the consent of Indonesia.[275]

Additionally, while accepting that the principle of self-determination was *erga omnes*, the Court distinguished between the character of that obligation and consent to jurisdiction. The Court concluded that it could not adjudicate on the conduct of a State without its consent – even if the obligation in question was *erga omnes*.[276]

There are two important aspects of the Court's judgment. First, doctrinally, the Court arguably departed from its previous articulation of the *Monetary Gold* principle (including as recently as in *Nauru*). Several judges, both in the majority and in the minority, disagreed (to different degrees) with the Court's application of the *Monetary Gold* principle. They considered that

[269] *East Timor* (n 245) para 17.
[270] ibid para 18.
[271] ibid.
[272] ibid para 19.
[273] ibid para 24.
[274] ibid para 25.
[275] ibid para 28.
[276] ibid para 29.

this case should be distinguished. These are express doctrinal doubts as to the Court's application of an unsettled and relatively indeterminate doctrine. For example, in the majority, Judge Oda[277] considered that the *Monetary Gold* principle could be distinguished, as this dispute was 'quite different in nature'.[278] Likewise, Judge Ranjeva considered that a 'scrupulous examination' of Portugal's claims did not 'oblige the Court, as a prerequisite, to adjudicate on the lawfulness of the entry into and continued presence of Indonesia in the Territory of East Timor'.[279]

In the minority, Judge Weeramantry's dissenting opinion addressed what he considered both the procedural and substantive shortcomings of the majority's approach. On the specific issue of the application of the *Monetary Gold* principle, Judge Weeramantry considered that the Court's approach would 'lead to manifestly unreasonable results'.[280] In his view, the Court's approach meant that a 'third party's wrongdoing must be established as a prerequisite to the claim or defense', thus leading to 'manifest injustice and an unreasonable result'. Further, the judge considered that the interpretation of the *Monetary Gold* principle 'clearly extends the decision far beyond its permissible limits' and was contrary to the principle of 'individual responsibility of each State for its own acts'.[281] Judge Weeramantry also noted the change of approach from *Nauru*, a case he considered to be the 'closest to the principle involved in the present case', which was nevertheless swiftly set aside to expand the application of the *Monetary Gold* principle. Similarly, Judge *ad hoc* Skubiszewski considered that the Court had historically adopted a *narrow* interpretation of the *Monetary Gold* principle.[282] He observed that, whilst some of Indonesia's interest may be affected by a decision on Portugal's claims, those interests were not the 'very subject-matter of the decision' and Indonesia would have sufficient protection under the Court's Statute (particularly Article 59).[283]

Academic commentary was also critical. Chinkin considers that the Court's reliance on *Monetary Gold* 'can be questioned both on the authority of that case and on its different facts'.[284] Among other strongly worded criticism, Orakhelashvili considers that the judgment 'improperly extended the reach of the doctrine of indispensable third parties, applying it to circumstances to which

[277] *East Timor* (n 245), Separate Opinion of Judge Oda paras 1, 19–20. Judge Oda agreed with the result – but not with the reasoning – would have dismissed the case on the ground of Portugal's lack of standing.

[278] ibid para 8.

[279] *East Timor* (n 245), Separate Opinion of Judge Ranjeva, 132.

[280] ibid Dissenting Opinion of Judge Weeramantry, 161.

[281] ibid 162.

[282] ibid para 62. See also Dugard (n 161) 558.

[283] ibid para 67.

[284] C Chinkin, 'The East Timor Case (Portugal v Australia)' (1996) 45 *International and Comparative Law Quarterly* 712, 718, noting also that: 'The authority of Monetary Gold is also lessened by the fact that it had not been applied or extended in any subsequent case until' *East Timor*, 719.

this doctrine had not been designed to apply'.[285] Scobbie and Drew, for their part, considered that the judgment was 'threadbare' and that it proceeded on the basis of 'bare assertion rather than reasoned conclusion'.[286] The 'absence of reasoning which characterizes the judgment', these authors say, 'indicates that while the collegium could agree on the outcome, it could not agree on the details of its underlying justification'.[287] On a similar note, John Dugard observed that: 'a closer analysis of judicial precedent and general principle shows that the *Monetary Gold case* was possibly distinguishable and that the Court might have engaged in a process of balancing of conflicting interests . . . to achieve a result which allowed it to address the merits of Portugal's claims'.[288] In fact, Dugard observes that, unlike in *Monetary Gold*, where Albania was not before the Court, the 'two states between whose rights the Court was required to adjudicate – Portugal and Australia – *were* both before the Court'.[289]

Second, the underlying (and generally unarticulated) concern was that any judgment that negatively affected Indonesia's rights over East Timor would have no practical effect – that it would be ignored. This goes back to the international community's reaction to Indonesia's occupation of East Timor in 1975. Initially, both the General Assembly and the Security Council criticised the invasion.[290] Yet the Security Council's reaction was lukewarm from the start. While it requested Indonesia to withdraw its troops, the Council did not condemn the invasion, refusing to characterise it as an act of aggression or as a breach on the prohibition on the use of force.[291] Further, despite Indonesia's failure to comply with the Council's prior decisions, the Council did not take any further actions to ensure compliance.[292] Indonesia's clout (particularly its influence in the non-aligned movement, of which it was one of the main actors, together with India and Yugoslavia)[293] and deft foreign policy are probably responsible

[285] Orakhelashvili (n 152) 391.

[286] I Scobbie and C J Drew, 'Self-Determination Undetermined: The Case of East Timor' (1996) 9 *Leiden Journal of International Law* 185, 192.

[287] ibid 193. Perceptively, Scobbie and Drew also mention at 203 how the Court took some liberty in reformulating Portugal's (carefully constructed) claims to make sure that they would be more easily captured by the indispensable third-parties doctrine.

[288] Dugard (n 161) 557.

[289] ibid.

[290] See UNGA Res 3485, UN GAOR, 30th Sess, Supp No 34, paras 4–5, UN Doc A/10034 (1976) ('strongly deplor[ing] the military intervention of the armed forces of Indonesia in Portuguese Timor' and '[c]all[ing] upon the Government of Indonesia to desist from further violations of the territorial integrity of Portuguese Timor and to withdraw without delay its armed forces from the Territory in order to enable the people of the Territory freely to exercise their right to self-determination and independence'); UNSC Res 384, UN SCOR, 30th Sess, 1869th mtg (1976) (using language similar to that in UNGA Res 3485). See also: B Kondoch, 'The United Nations Administration of East Timor' (2001) 6 *Journal of Conflict and Security Law* 245, 247–48; T Grant, 'East Timor, the UN System, and Enforcing Non-Recognition in International Law' (2000) 33 *Vanderbilt Journal of Transnational Law* 273, 277–78.

[291] UNSC Res 384 (1975); UNSC Res 385 (1976).

[292] Kondoch 'Administration of East Timor' (n 290) 247.

[293] See eg, JA Braveboy-Wagner, 'Collective Diplomacy of the Global South' in B Hocking and others (eds), *Routledge Handbook of Diplomacy and Statecraft* (Routledge, 2012).

for this. As Clark explains, 'Indonesian diplomacy gradually eroded the support formerly shown for East Timor'.[294]

The Court's judgment does not expressly mention this issue. But some of the individual opinions do. Judge *ad hoc* Skubiszewski noted that there was an element of *realpolitik* in the Court's approach. He notes that the Court was 'told that recognition of conquest was unavoidable'.[295] He also mentioned allegations that a judgment adverse to Australia (and, by implication, to Indonesia) 'would not be capable of execution'.[296] Likewise, Judge Weeramantry, albeit somewhat obliquely, included sections in his dissenting opinion rebutting the premises that the 'Judgment would serve no useful purpose'[297] and that 'The Court should not give a judgment which it has no authority or ability to satisfy'.[298]

For a judgment that has generated a substantial amount of academic criticism, it is surprising that the potential underlying policy-considerations have not had more salience in scholarship, particularly when two of the dissents mention the issue. Indeed, Pierre-Marie Dupuy, who acted as counsel for Portugal in *East Timor,* some years later admitted that the Portuguese legal team knew the case faced difficulties that were 'not all purely legal'.[299] That is evident: this is a case where the relevant variables cannot be reduced to text (i.e., the doctrinally correct application of the *Monetary Gold* principle).

Properly understanding the *East Timor* decision requires, I say, taking those factors into account. Again, it is plausible that the Court's approach to the *Monetary Gold* principle – including its characterisation of Portugal's claims – were influenced by policy considerations, namely, the potential lack of effectiveness of any judgment issued that was averse to Indonesia. International adjudication may take into account enforcement and effectiveness considerations.[300] Here, the plausible expectations of compliance on the part of Indonesia would have been low to very low. The international community had already shown that it was not willing to outright condemn Indonesia's invasion of East Timor – and that it was not willing to take any material, concrete steps to make Indonesia comply with the prior resolutions. Some scholars have considered the international response to Indonesia's invasion of East Timor (including that of the General Assembly, the Security Council, and the Court) as hypocritical,[301] noting that 'many of the

[294] Clark (n 257) 11.

[295] *East Timor* (n 245), Dissenting Opinion of Judge Skubiszewski, para 162.

[296] ibid para 161.

[297] ibid Dissenting Opinion of Judge Weeramantry, 218–19.

[298] ibid.

[299] WM Reisman, 'The Hudson Medal Luncheon: "The Unity of International Law"' in (2015) 109 *American Society of International Law Proceedings of the Annual Meeting* 255.

[300] See in international adjudication the 'extent of a control base [i.e., of coercive enforcement mechanisms] is a ubiquitous consideration' WM Reisman, *Nullity and Revision: The Review and Enforcement of International Judgments and Awards* (Yale University Press, 1971) 249.

[301] WM Reisman, 'Hollow Victory: Humanitarian Intervention and Protection of Minorities' (1997) 91 *Proceedings of the Annual Meeting (American Society of International Law)* 431, 432.

types of sanctions that are actually used may prove ineffective or ephemeral'.[302] Indeed, as explained above, the diplomatic condemnation of Indonesia's invasion had simmered down a few years after the invasion. Twenty years later, the situation had not improved.

In that context, it is credible to suggest that the Court relied on the inherent indeterminacy of the *Monetary Gold* principle to decline jurisdiction to avoid having to issue a judgment on the merits that would be openly – and perhaps brazenly – defied by Indonesia (and perhaps even by Australia). This suggests that the Court may have been relying on the *Monetary Gold* principle as a jurisdictional avoidance technique.

International adjudication sometimes operates according to the principle of second-best solutions.[303] Although from a doctrinal perspective the Court's approach was – and should be – criticised, in practice the decision must take into account the wider context in which the Court was operating. When the main participants of the international process – including the Security Council – had already made clear that they were either unwilling or unable to confront Indonesia, it is perhaps expecting too much from the Court to assume that it would take up that mantle. Here, however, a decision declining jurisdiction was, for all practical purposes, a decision in favour of the status quo (i.e., accepting Indonesia's unlawful occupation of East Timor). Given the gross human rights violations committed during Indonesia's occupation, it is hard to justify this from a point of view of promoting human dignity (although it perhaps was the best alternative from a point of view of maintaining or promoting minimum order). Perhaps this is the most powerful example of how reliance on avoidance techniques is not always normatively justified.

Nevertheless, a New Haven-based appraisal of the *East Timor* judgment also requires considering the alternatives. Here, one potential alternative the Court had was to accept some of the narrower formulations of Portugal's claim, which had been carefully crafted to avoid the application of the *Monetary Gold* principle.[304] This would have enabled the Court to issue a judgment on the merits strictly focused on *Australia's* breaches of its international obligations. That alternative would perhaps have represented a happy medium: it would have provided a more doctrinally solid application of the *Monetary Gold* principle; it would have criticised Australia's decision to recognise Indonesia's invasion of East Timor; and it would have perhaps signalled to Indonesia that the international community had not stopped considering its invasion of East Timor as unlawful.

Fortunately, the dispute was solved in East Timor's favour (although by political rather than by judicial means). In 2002 it became independent – the first

[302] ibid 434.

[303] WM Reisman, *The Quest for World Order and Human Dignity in the Twenty-First Century* (Brill, 2013) 452.

[304] As considered by Judges Weeramantry and Skubiszewski.

State to become so in the twenty-first century.[305] The solution to the conflict was complex. It included a diplomatic settlement with Indonesia, temporary administration by the UN, and the deployment of peacekeeping operations. Indeed, the first years of East Timor (now Timor-Leste's) independent life were tumultuous. The difficulty in solving the situation in East Timor perhaps indicates that this was a dispute (broadly understood – not the narrow Portuguese claim) that was not suitable to be resolved through international adjudication, but rather by other political and diplomatic means.

(vi) The Monetary Gold Principle and Other International Courts

With one exception, other international courts have been reluctant to apply the *Monetary Gold* principle to decline jurisdiction over a dispute. This does not mean that they reject the principle's existence or relevance. Rather, while they acknowledge its importance, other courts and tribunals have considered that it was not applicable in the specific circumstances they were dealing with. There are several potential explanations for this. One is that this is exactly the result of the application of an inherently flexible principle, which in the hands of another body of adjudicators leads to diverging results. Another one is the availability of other avoidance techniques, including deferential standards of review, available in their toolkits. Those different tools may allow reaching the same result by another route. And, of course, there are differences in institutional design, legitimacy, and enforcement mechanisms between international courts. Some examples illustrate this.

First, ITLOS. Despite recognising that the *Monetary Gold* principle 'is a well-established procedural rule in international judicial proceedings',[306] the Tribunal has refused to apply the *Monetary Gold* principle to decline jurisdiction in two instances. The first was *M/V Norstar*, a case involving Italy's arrest and detention of a Panamanian-flagged vessel.[307] Italy had requested that Spain arrest the vessel.[308] Panama argued that the dispute should not be adjudicated because Spain, as the recipient of the request to seize the vessel, was not a party to the proceedings.[309] The Tribunal rejected that argument, holding that Spain was not an indispensable third party.[310] This was because the core of the legal interests in dispute were those of Italy – the State that had *made* the

[305] See generally Kondoch (n 290); S Chawla, 'Shaping East Timor: A Dimension of United Nations Peacekeeping' (2001) 24 *Strategic Analysis* 2291; N MacQueen, 'United Nations Transitional Administration in East Timor (UNTAET)' in JA Koops and others (eds), *The Oxford Handbook of United Nations Peacekeeping Operations* (OUP, 2015).

[306] *The M/V 'Norstar' Case (Panama v Italy)*, ITLOS, Judgment (Preliminary Objections) of 4 November 2016, para 172.

[307] ibid.

[308] ibid para 43.

[309] ibid para 173.

[310] ibid paras 172–3.

request – not those of the State that had *executed* the request.[311] The second was *Dispute concerning delimitation of the maritime boundary between Mauritius and Maldives in the Indian Ocean.*[312] The dispute concerned the delimitation of a maritime boundary involving the Chagos Archipelago.[313] The Maldives contended that the Tribunal should decline jurisdiction over the dispute because the UK, which exercised sovereignty over the Chagos Archipelago, was not a party to the dispute.[314] The Tribunal rejected that jurisdictional objection, on the basis that, among other things, according to the ICJ's *Chagos* advisory opinion it was entitled to treat Mauritius as the coastal State for maritime delimitation purposes.[315] Of course, this must be analysed in the context that – perhaps because it has such a small case-load – ITLOS has historically been extremely reluctant to decline jurisdiction over a dispute.

Second, the ECtHR. The European Court has also rejected the application of the *Monetary Gold* principle despite the principle being invoked in several high-profile disputes, including *Banković, Behrami, Saramati,* and *Hanan.*[316] All these cases involve airstrikes. The first, NATO airstrikes in Serbia;[317] the second and third, armed actions in Kosovo; and the fourth, a German airstrike in Afghanistan.[318] In all of those disputes, the European Court refused to apply the *Monetary Gold* principle.[319] Yet it nonetheless managed to either find the case inadmissible (in the first three cases) or, after finding only part of the dispute admissible, found no breach on the merits.[320] Often, the basis for doing so was the extraterritoriality doctrine, addressed below.

In *Banković,* the ECtHR held that the applicants were outside the 'jurisdiction' of the respondent States for the purposes of Article 1 of the ECHR.[321] In *Behrami* and *Saramati,* the European Court held the claims to be inadmissible on the basis that the international force that had carried out the relevant facts were part of – and under the command – of the UN's Mission in Kosovo and

[311] ibid.

[312] *Dispute concerning Delimitation of the Maritime Boundary between Mauritius and Maldives in the Indian Ocean (Mauritius/Maldives),* ITLOS, Judgment (Preliminary Objections) of 28 January 2021.

[313] ibid.

[314] ibid paras 82–83.

[315] ibid para 249. The Tribunal's reliance on the ICJ's advisory opinion is, in my view, questionable. On this, see the Separate and Dissenting Opinion of Judge Oxman, paras 28–33.

[316] The most notable being *Banković and Others v Belgium and Others* App no 52207/99 (ECtHR (GC), Decision, 12 December 2001); *Behrami and Behrami v France* App no 71412/01 and *Saramati v France, Germany and Norway* App no 78166/01 (ECtHR (GC), Decision, 2 May 2007), all concerning NATO airstrikes in Serbia; and *Hanan v Germany* App no 4871/16 (ECtHR (GC), 16 February 2021).

[317] *Banković* (n 316) paras 9–11.

[318] *Hanan* (n 316) paras 3, 21–25.

[319] To be clear, this is not a situation where the ECtHR expressly refused to apply the *Monetary Gold* principle, but rather one where, having found the applications inadmissible on *other* grounds, the Court did not consider it necessary to address the *Monetary Gold* point, see *Behrami* and *Saramati* (n 316) para 153.

[320] See eg *Hanan* (n 316).

[321] *Banković* (n 316) paras 34 and ff.

thus its actions were 'attributable to the UN' which was a 'legal entity distinct from its member states and . . . not a contracting party to the Convention'.[322] Finally, in *Hanan,* although the ECtHR found the claims admissible, it applied a substantially deferential standard of review on the merits, which took into the account the particular context of an extraterritorial armed conflict.[323]

Third, investment tribunals. Some tribunals have also refused to apply the *Monetary Gold* principle. Two examples are representative. The first one is *Chevron v. Ecuador.*[324] Ecuador argued that the *Monetary Gold* principle was applicable as deciding the investor's claim would have potentially impacted the rights of third parties – individuals involved in domestic litigation and settlement agreements related to some of the issues subject to the arbitration.[325] The Tribunal rejected Ecuador's argument. Its reasoning was based on the nature of the legal obligations at hand. Whereas the absent third-parties' rights were under Ecuadorian law, the issues in dispute arose under the Ecuador-US BIT.[326] Likewise, in *Raiffeisen Bank International AG v Croatia,*[327] a case involving foreign-currency denominated loans, Croatia argued that the *Monetary Gold* principle was applicable because any finding of liability against Croatia would render Austria liable under EU law.[328] The Tribunal rejected that argument. It considered that any finding, either on jurisdiction or liability, would at most 'indirectly' affect Austria's legal interest,[329] as 'no issue of Austrian state responsibility under the EU *acquis* or the BIT is involved' as 'Croatia is the state whose legal responsibility is being invoked'.[330]

The examples from ITLOS and the investment tribunals illustrate the inherent flexibility that some procedural doctrines have in international law. That flexibility means that they *may* be interpreted, narrowly or broadly, and be

[322] *Saramati* (n 316) paras 144-52.

[323] *Hanan* (n 316) para 198 and ff. See also M Milanovic, 'Extraterritorial Investigations in *Hanan v Germany*; Extraterritorial Assassinations in New Interstate Claim Filed by Ukraine against Russia' (*EJIL:Talk!*, 26 February 2021). Available at: www.ejiltalk.org/extraterritorial-investigations-in-hanan-v-germany-extraterritorial-assassinations-in-new-interstate-claim-filed-by-ukraine-against-russia/ stating that: 'To make a long story short, [the Court] employed a very deferential standard of review, and despite the many problems with how the investigation was conducted its conclusion was that in extraordinary circumstances states had to have a certain degree of latitude.'

[324] *Chevron Corporation and Texaco Petroleum Company v The Republic of Ecuador* (Third Interim Award on Jurisdiction and Admissibility) PCA Case No 2009-23 (27 February 2012).

[325] ibid para 3.178.

[326] ibid para 4.67, holding that: 'this Tribunal has only to decide upon questions of the Respondent's liability to the Claimants under the BIT . . . But that answer would not decide the question of the effect of the 1995 Settlement Agreement . . . If there were an inconsistency between the Respondent's obligations under the BIT and the [absent third parties'] rights as determined by the Courts in Ecuador, it would be for the Respondent to decide how to resolve that inconsistency'.

[327] *Raiffeisen Bank International AG and Raiffeisenbank Austria d.d. v Republic of Croatia* (Decision on the Respondent's Jurisdictional Objections) ICSID Case No ARB/17/34 (30 September 2020).

[328] ibid para 295.

[329] ibid.

[330] ibid. See eg *Addiko Bank AG and Addiko Bank d.d. v Republic of Croatia* (Decision on an Objection to Jurisdiction) ICSID Case No ARB/17/37 (12 June 2020) para 307; *SolEs Badajoz GmbH v Kingdom of Spain* (Award) ICSID Case No ARB/15/38 (31 July 2019) para 522.

utilised as case- or issue-selection mechanisms and thus as an implied avoidance technique. Conversely, the ECtHR's reluctance to apply the *Monetary Gold* principle to decline jurisdiction is perhaps due to the ECtHR having better tools at its disposal, including the extraterritoriality doctrine (at the jurisdictional stage) the margin of appreciation doctrine (on the merits).

Fourth, the award in *Larsen v. Hawaiian Kingdom*.[331] This is a strange case – a very strange case – decided by a strong tribunal.[332] The claim was in theory brought by an individual, Lance Paul Larsen, who alleged that the Hawaiian Kingdom (which was overthrown by the US in the late nineteenth century)[333] had breached an 1849 Treaty of Friendship, Commerce and Navigation with the United States of America by 'allowing the unlawful imposition of American municipal laws over claimant's person within the territorial jurisdiction of the Hawaiian Kingdom'.[334] Indeed, Mr Larsen was not claiming monetary damages; rather he admitted that he was trying to 'force the hand of his government to intervene . . . to successfully end the unlawful occupation of the Hawaiian Islands . . . and to end the imposition of American laws'.[335] Among other things, he claimed that, because there was no treaty of cession between the US and the Hawaiian Kingdom, the latter was sovereign.[336] In reality, however, the entire claim was concocted as a way of trying to reestablish the Hawaiian Kingdom.[337] A few years before the case was submitted to arbitration, certain Hawaiians purported to create an Acting Council of Regency and an acting government.[338] The Hawaiian Kingdom seems to have been motivated by the (misguided) thought that being listed as a 'non-Contracting State' by the Permanent Court of Arbitration implied international recognition of the Hawaiian Kingdom – and even that this was a 'reflection of . . . *opinion juris*'.[339]

The Tribunal declined jurisdiction. To do so, it invoked the *Monetary Gold* principle, holding that it could not decide the key issue before it (whether the Hawaiian Kingdom had breached its treaty obligations to Mr Larsen, 'without ruling on the legality of the acts of the United States of America. Yet that is precisely what the *Monetary Gold* principle precludes the Tribunal from

[331] *Larsen v Hawaiian Kingdom* (Award) PCA Case No 1999-01 (5 February 2001) paras 12.13–12.17.

[332] The Tribunal was composed of Professor James Crawford SC (President), Professor Christopher Greenwood QC and Gavan Griffiths QC.

[333] A good summary is at P Dumberry, 'The Hawaiian Kingdom Arbitration Case and the Unsettled Question of the Hawaiian Kingdom's Claim to Continuity as an Independent State under International Law' (2002) 1 *Chinese Journal of International Law* 655, 656 and ff.

[334] *Larsen* (n 331) para 1.

[335] ibid para 5.5.

[336] DK Sai, 'Backstory—Larsen v Hawaiian Kingdom at the Permanent Court of Arbitration (1999–2001)' (2022) 4 *Hawaii Journal of Law and Politics* 133, 155.

[337] The Hawaiian Kingdom's agent in the proceedings, Prof David Keanu Sai, is completely open about this, see Sai (n 336).

[338] ibid 154.

[339] ibid 160.

doing'.[340] A few months after the Tribunal's award, the Hawaiian Kingdom filed a 'complaint' against the US before the UN Security Council. It was ignored.[341] And a few months later the Hawaiian Kingdom purported to accept the ICJ's jurisdiction. That was also ignored.[342]

The subject matter of the dispute suggests that the Tribunal may have been keen to avoid deciding the merits of the dispute. Test the point this way: would any decision that, expressly or impliedly, determined that the US' actions in Hawaii in the late nineteenth century were internationally unlawful have any effectiveness? Taken to its logical conclusion, a decision finding illegality would support the claim that Hawaii was not a part of the US, but rather an independent State. Secession is always a fraught topic. It is questionable whether an arbitral award – particularly one issued in *this* context – would have contributed anything at all.

The decision faced some criticism. Some commentators noted (positively) that the tribunal's award 'sidestepped th[at] sensitive question',[343] yet they criticised the tribunal's approach as it could cause 'mischief in the future' and could 'establish a dangerous trend'. Those commentators considered that the tribunal should have 'douse[d] the fires of this litigation at the outset, instead of allowing it almost to burn out of control'.[344] That criticism is basically that the tribunal should have been more aggressive in applying other avoidance techniques rather than risk manipulating the *Monetary Gold* principle too strongly.

III. EXTRATERRITORIALITY

Moving away from the ICJ, the third example of a doctrine that has potentially been used as an implied avoidance technique has been the ECtHR's approach to extraterritoriality.[345] Unlike the existence of a dispute or the *Monetary Gold* principle, there *is* a basis in the European Convention for this principle – Article 1 – which provides that: 'The High Contracting Parties shall secure to everyone within their jurisdiction the rights and freedoms defined in Section I of this Convention.' The textual provision, however, is vague.[346]

[340] *Larsen* (n 331) para 12.15.

[341] Dumberry 'The Hawaiian Kingdom Arbitration Case' (n 333) 671.

[342] ibid 673.

[343] DJ Bederman and KR Hilbert, 'Lance Paul Larsen v The Hawaiian Kingdom' (2001) 95 *American Journal of International Law* 927, 928.

[344] ibid 933.

[345] As explained in chapter 3, given the procedural turn and doctrines such as the margin of appreciation, the European Court can either avoid certain issues or to be deferential on the merits, thus decreasing the need to rely on express or implied jurisdictional avoidance techniques to avoid adjudicating issues. At the European Court of Human Rights, avoidance now mainly occurs at the merits phase.

[346] E Voeten, 'Politics, Judicial Behaviour, and Institutional Design' in J Christoffersen and MR Madsen (eds), *The European Court of Human Rights between Law and Politics* (OUP, 2011) 320, noting that: 'When politicians delegate to judges the authority to interpret such abstract rights as

As with the two previous examples, the ECtHR's approach to extraterritoriality has fluctuated, constantly shifting from expansive to narrow readings of the provision. This, of course, means that the doctrine has been subject to criticism. One of the leading critics has been Milanović. He observes that although the ECtHR system is 'by far the strongest of all human rights regimes'[347] as it has strong compliance mechanisms,[348] nevertheless the ECtHR's approach to extraterritoriality is 'the most problematic' as it suffers from 'rampant casuistry and conceptual chaos'.[349] Indeed, Milanović concedes that the European Court may be using its approach to extraterritoriality as an implied avoidance technique, observing that the Court's jurisprudence was one of '(at times quite unprincipled) compromise, caused mostly by the Court's understandable desire to avoid the merits of legally and politically extremely difficult cases by relying on the preliminary issue of extraterritorial application'.[350] Similarly, Connall Mallory observes that European Court's approach to extraterritorial jurisdiction under Article 1 of the ECHR has 'at points . . . appeared settled, stable and almost intelligible', but at other times 'it has been hugely confusing, infuriatingly contradictory and lacking in any sense of direction'.[351] One potential explanation is that questions of extraterritoriality often arise in the context of the use of force. For most Convention States, the extraterritorial use of force mostly took place as part of the 'war on terror'; this, Sarah Miller argues, meant that extraterritoriality went from a 'doctrinal abstraction into an issue with profound and very real political and legal ramifications'.[352]

Three preliminary points. First, to clarify, in this context *extraterritorial jurisdiction* should be understood as referring to the jurisdiction of a *State*[353] – not the jurisdiction of a court.[354] Second, a brief overview of the different relevant

freedom of expression and respect for private and family life, they allow judges to create compounds brewed from a motley crew of ingredients including legal text, statutes, precedents, judges' policy preferences, judges' perceptions of what society values, and collegial norms . . . rights review inevitably introduces elements of subjectivity and judicial discretion.'

[347] M Milanovic, *Extraterritorial Application of Human Rights Treaties: Law, Principles, and Policy* (OUP, 2011) 4.

[348] Nevertheless, the European Court is not isolated from the community processes and contestation from key actors, mainly States. See Ø Stiansen and E Voeten, 'Backlash and Judicial Restraint: Evidence from the European Court of Human Rights' (2020) 64 *International Studies Quarterly* 770; J Petrov, 'The Populist Challenge to the European Court of Human Rights' (2020) 18 *International Journal of Constitutional Law* 476. See also the discussion on the procedural turn in chapter 3.

[349] Milanovic *Extraterritorial Application of Human Rights Treaties* (n 347) 4.

[350] ibid. See also: Milanovic 'Extraterritorial Investigations in *Hanan v Germany*' (n 323).

[351] C Mallory, 'A Second Coming of Extraterritorial Jurisdiction at the European Court of Human Rights?' (2021) 82 *Questions of International Law* 31.

[352] S Miller, 'Revisiting Extraterritorial Jurisdiction: A Territorial Justification for Extraterritorial Jurisdiction under the European Convention' (2009) 20 *European Journal of International Law* 1223.

[353] S Besson, 'The Extraterritoriality of the European Convention on Human Rights: Why Human Rights Depend on Jurisdiction and What Jurisdiction Amounts To' (2012) 25 *Leiden Journal of International Law* 857, 862.

[354] L Raible, *Human Rights Unbound: A Theory of Extraterritoriality* (OUP, 2020); Y Shany, 'Taking Universality Seriously: A Functional Approach to Extraterritoriality in International Human Rights Law' (2013) 7 *Law and Ethics of Human Rights* 47; G Ress, 'Problems of Extraterritorial

models of State jurisdiction.[355] The first model is *spatial*.[356] This basically means that a State exercises *effective control* over an area (i.e., control over that territory or space).[357] This is the model that is most widely followed in general international law.[358] The second model is *personal*.[359] In contrast to the spatial model, this model focuses on the State's control over *individuals* (e.g., a State's jurisdiction includes the activities of the members of that State's armed forces – even when they are acting outside the State's territory).[360] Third, the ECtHR's case law on extraterritoriality is vast.[361] It is beyond the scope of this book to engage with all of it. Rather, below I analyse a selection of cases that illustrate the European Court's approach – and how it has fluctuated.

A. Loizidou

One of the first cases where the European Court developed the concept of extraterritoriality was *Loizidou v Turkey*.[362] Before that, the Court's cases regarding

---

Human Rights Violations: The Jurisdiction of the European Court of Human Rights: the *Banković* case' (2002) 12 *Italian Yearbook of International Law* 51; J Ross, 'Jurisdictional Aspects of International Human Rights Law and Humanitarian Law in the War on Terror' in F Coomans and MT Kamminga (eds), *Extraterritorial Application of Human Rights Treaties* (Intersentia, 2004) 9, 23–24; EC Gillard, 'International Humanitarian Law and Extraterritorial State Conduct' in Coomans and Kamminga (eds), *Extraterritorial Application of Human Rights Treaties* (Intersentia, 2004) 25; M Happold, '*Banković* v Belgium and the Territorial Scope of the European Convention on Human Rights' (2003) 3 *Human Rights Law Review* 77, 82–84.

[355] A Demetriades, 'Reconceptualising Extraterritoriality under the ECHR as Concurrent Responsibility' (2020) 12 *European Journal of Legal Studies* 157, 166–68.

[356] Milanovic (n 347) 127 and ff.

[357] R Wilde, 'Triggering State Obligations Extraterritorially: The Spatial Test in Certain Human Rights Treaties' (2007) 40 *Israel Law Review* 503; M Giuffré, 'A Functional-Impact Model of Jurisdiction: Extraterritoriality before the European Court of Human Rights' (2021) 82 *Questions of International Law* 53.

[358] *Legal Consequences of the Construction of a Wall in the Occupied Palestinian Territory*, ICJ, Advisory Opinion dated 9 July 2004, paras 109–13; *Armed Activities on the Territory of the Congo (Congo v Uganda)*, ICJ, Judgment of 19 December 2005, paras 179, 216–17.

[359] R Lawson, 'Life After *Banković*: On the Extraterritorial Application of the European Convention on Human Rights' in Coomans and Kamminga (eds), *Extraterritorial Application of Human Rights Treaties* 83.

[360] Milanovic (n 347) 173 and ff.

[361] In addition to the cases discussed below see eg *Güzelyurtlu and Others v Cyprus and Turkey* (n 2); *Al-Skeini and Others v United Kingdom* (n 9); *Ilaşcu and Others v Moldova and Russia* App no 48787/99 (ECtHR (GC), 8 July 2004); *Marković and Others v Italy* App no 1398/03 (ECtHR (GC), 14 December 2006); *Djokaba Lambi Longa v The Netherlands* App no 33917/12 (ECtHR, 9 October 2012); *Catan and Others v Moldova and Russia* App nos 43370/04, 8252/05 and 18454/06 (ECtHR (GC), 19 October 2012); *Hirsi Jamaa and Others v Italy* App no 27765/09 (ECtHR (GC), 23 February 2012); *Al Nashiri v Poland* App no 28761/11 (ECtHR, 24 July 2014); *Husayn (Abu Zubaydah) v Poland* App no 7511/13 (ECtHR, 24 July 2014); *Jaloud v The Netherlands* App no 47708/08 (ECtHR, 20 November 2014); *Chiragov and Others v Armenia* App no 13216/05 (ECtHR (GC), 16 June 2015); *N D and N T v Spain* App nos 8675/15 and 8697/15 (ECtHR (GC), 13 February 2020).

[362] *Loizidou v Turkey* (Preliminary Objections) App no 15318/89 (ECtHR, 23 March 1995) para 62; *Loizidou v Turkey* (Merits) App no 15318/89 (ECtHR, 18 December 1996) 129.

extraterritoriality were focused on discrete issues, such as extradition or expulsion.[363] The dispute concerned the Turkish Republic of Northern Cyprus (the TRNC). Loizidou was a Greek Cypriot. She owned plots of land in the territory that subsequently became the purported TRNC.[364] After that, she could no longer access her property. Turkey challenged the Court's jurisdiction, arguing, among other things, that the claims did not concern Turkey, but rather the TRNC.[365]

For context: Cyprus has a complex history.[366] The island's population is comprised of two ethnic groups, essentially Greek Cypriots and Turkish Cypriots. There were tensions. To limit this to the most recent part of the dispute, suffice to say that following protracted diplomatic negotiations, the Greek Cypriot and the Turkish Cypriot communities reached an agreement in 1960 and the independent Republic of Cyprus was proclaimed.[367] Yet, by 1963, there was civil disorder, which only calmed down after British troops were stationed between the two sides.[368] In 1967, there was more violence and disorder. In 1974, abetted by the Greek military dictatorship, Greek Cypriot forces overthrew the government (supposedly with the intention of having Cyprus join Greece). Five days later, Turkish troops landed on the Island. They controlled one-third of the territory.[369] In late 1983, the Turkish Cypriots declared an independent State: the TRNC.[370]

The international community quickly condemned this attempt at secession. The Security Council deplored the 'purported secession of part of the Republic of Cyprus'.[371] It also called on States to refrain from recognising 'any Cypriot State other than the Republic of Cyprus'.[372] Overall, the international response has been categorical, to the point that no 'state other than Turkey has so far recognized the TRNC'.[373]

At the preliminary objections stage, the ECtHR considered that at that point it did not need to determine whether Turkey was, in fact, responsible for the conduct

[363] *Soering v United Kingdom* App no 14038/88 (ECtHR, 7 July 1989) para 91; see also *Loizidou* (Preliminary Objections) (n 362) para 52.

[364] *Loizidou* (Preliminary Objections) (n 362) para 12.

[365] ibid paras 47, 55.

[366] For a good overview, see A Jacovides, 'Cyprus: International Law and the Prospects for Settlement' (1984) 78 *Proceedings of the Annual Meeting (American Society of International Law)* 107, 108 ff; MM Hakki, 'Property Wars in Cyprus: the Turkish Position According to International Law' (2011) 15(6) *The International Journal of Human Rights* 847.

[367] Jacovides 'Cyprus' (n 366) 108.

[368] ibid 109.

[369] ibid.

[370] S Talmon, 'The Cyprus Question Before the European Court of Justice' (2001) 12 *European Journal of International Law* 727.

[371] UNSC Res 541 (18 November 1983) UN Doc S/RES/541; UNSC Res 550 (11 May 1984) UN Doc S/RES/550.

[372] UNSC Res 550 (n 371).

[373] Talmon (n 370) 728; S Talmon, 'The Constitutive Versus the Declaratory Theory of Recognition: Tertium Non Datur?' (2005) 75 *British Yearbook of International Law* 101; A Dolunay and F Kasap, 'Still Unrecognized State: Self-Determination and the "Status of the TRNC" Court Decisions' (2020) 13 *Journal of Politics and Law* 1.

subject to the claim.[374] Rather, it only had to determine whether the acts potentially fell within Turkey's jurisdiction (despite having occurred outside Turkey's territory).[375] The Court considered that they could. It held that under Article 1:

> [T]he concept of 'jurisdiction' . . . is not restricted to the national territory of the High Contracting Parties . . . In addition, the responsibility of Contracting Parties can be involved because of acts of their authorities, whether performed within or outside national boundaries, which produce effects outside their own territory . . .

Bearing in mind the object and purpose of the Convention, the responsibility of a Contracting Party may also arise when, as a consequence of military action – whether lawful or unlawful – it exercises effective control of an area outside its national territory. The obligation to secure, in such an area, the rights and freedoms set out in the Convention derives from the fact that such control is required, whether it be exercised directly, through its armed forces, or through a subordinate local administration.

Because the TRNC had been occupied by Turkish troops, the Court considered that the relevant acts *did* fall within Turkey's jurisdiction.[376] This is one example of the ECtHR's relying on the spatial model of jurisdiction to apply the European Convention extraterritorially.[377] Scholars have characterised the ECtHR's approach to the extraterritorial application of the Convention in different ways, with the main emphasis being on Turkey's '*effective control*' over the territory of the TRNC.[378]

From a doctrinal perspective, some scholars have criticised the European Court's decision in *Loizidou*. As Milanović explains, the judgment's grounding on prior case law was 'flimsy'.[379] In fact, that author challenges the Court's reliance on certain precedents, particularly *Drozd*,[380] relating to acts of State that have effects outside the State's territory, where he says the Court 'somewhat surreptitiously added the words "whether performed within or outside national boundaries"'.[381] Others, however, consider that the Court's approach was sound, as it could be justified on the basis of the Court's doctrine of interpreting the European Convention as a 'living instrument'.[382]

374 *Loizidou* (Preliminary Objections) (n 362) para 61.

375 Interestingly, when it came to decide the merits, while the European Court ruled that Turkey was internationally responsible, it avoided deciding the issue of the legality of the presence of Turkish troops in the TRNC, see B Rudolf, 'Loizidou v Turkey' (1996) 90 *American Journal of International Law* 98.

376 *Loizidou* (Preliminary Objections) (n 362) para 63.

377 Besson 'The Extraterritoriality of the European Convention on Human Rights' (n 353) 860; Demetriades 'Reconceptualising Extraterritoriality' (n 355); Milanovic (n 347) 127.

378 Besson (n 353) 872.

379 Milanovic (n 347) 127.

380 *Drozd and Janousek v France and Spain* App no 12747/87 (ECtHR, 26 June 1992).

381 Milanovic (n 347) 127.

382 For an overview of this doctrine more generally, see G Letsas, 'The ECHR as a Living Instrument: Its Meaning and Legitimacy' in A Føllesdal, B Peters and G Ulfstein (eds), *Constituting Europe: The European Court of Human Rights in a National, European and Global Context* (CUP, 2013) 106.

Moreover, the wording of Article 1 of the Convention allows for some flexibility. That provision does not necessarily equate jurisdiction to territory; hence a reading of the term 'jurisdiction' that takes into account effective control is at least plausible. Further, the notion that 'jurisdiction' is sometimes understood as the State's authority, including the authority to regulate the conduct of persons, is broadly accepted in general international law.[383] In fact, this was how the European Commission had previously interpreted that provision in its prior decisions.[384]

Evaluating the ECtHR's judgment must also take into account the broader context of the situation in the TRNC. The decision has much that is commendable. By indicating the possibility that Turkey could be held internationally responsible for human rights violations taking place in the TRNC, the Court was attempting to incentivise Turkey to avoid subsequent violations. Moreover, but for the establishment of the TRNC, the claimants would have enjoyed protection under the Convention, as Cyprus is a party to the ECHR.[385] That approach enjoyed international support, as there was widespread condemnation of the TRNC. As mentioned above, the Security Council had condemned the TRNC's attempt at secession – and no State other than Turkey had recognised it. Considering potential enforcement mechanisms, the ECtHR is in a relatively robust place (at least relative to other international courts). These factors suggest that the Court was well placed to adopt an expansive view of its own jurisdiction in this specific case. Therefore, it is possible that, as the ICJ did in *Nauru*, the European Court was relying on the plasticity of the notion of jurisdiction under Article 1 of the Convention to *uphold* jurisdiction and adjudicate the claim.

B. Banković

This case concerns a claim regarding NATO airstrikes in the Federal Republic of Yugoslavia during the Kosovo War in April 1999.[386] In short, under the leadership of Slobodan Milosević, Serbia had embarked on an ethnic cleansing campaign

[383] V Lowe, 'Jurisdiction' in Malcolm D Evans (ed), *International Law* 2nd edn (OUP, 2006) 335; M Shaw, *International Law* 6th edn (CUP, 2008) 645; C Ryngaert, *Jurisdiction in International Law,* 2nd edn (OUP, 2015); see also: M Akehurst, 'Jurisdiction in International Law' (1972–73) 46 *British Yearbook of International Law* 14 and see also the discussion on this issue in chapter 2.

[384] *X v Federal Republic of Germany* App no 1065/61 (European Commission of Human Rights, 25 September 1965); *Ilse Hess v United Kingdom* App no 6231/73 (European Commission of Human Rights, 28 May 1975).

[385] Regarding the 'espace juridique' doctrine, see Milanovic (n 347) 173 ff; Raible, *Human Rights Unbound* (n 354).

[386] *Banković* (n 316) paras 6–11; H Charlesworth, 'International Law: A Discipline of Crisis' (2002) 65 *Modern Law Review* 377, 378; C Greenwood, 'International Law and the NATO Intervention in Kosovo' (2000) 49 *International and Comparative Law Quarterly* 926; J Sperling and M Webber, 'NATO: from Kosovo to Kabul' (2009) 85 *International Affairs* 491; WM Reisman, 'Kosovo's Antinomies' (1999) 93 *American Journal of International Law* 860.

aimed at removing ethnic Albanians from Kosovo. This led to internal strife and gross human rights violations. Continued diplomatic efforts failed. Sanctions were tried but failed. Although it had condemned Serbia's conduct and characterised the situation in Kosovo as a threat to international peace and security,[387] the Security Council did not go beyond that. It was gridlocked due to Russia's veto.[388] In March 1999, without obtaining Security Council authorisation, NATO decided to carry out a campaign of airstrikes against Serbia.[389] Although the Security Council had not authorised the use of force against Serbia, early on the bombing campaign the Council refused to condemn NATO's military campaign.[390]

A NATO airstrike struck a Serbian television station, killing 16.[391] The relatives of the victims brought proceedings against all NATO member States that were party to the ECHR. The Court characterised the 'essential question' in the dispute as follows: 'whether the applicants and their deceased relatives were, as a result of that extra-territorial act, capable of falling within the jurisdiction of the respondent States'.[392] Relying on the Convention's *travaux*, as well as in the notions of jurisdiction under general international law, the Grand Chamber considered that 'Article 1 of the Convention must be considered to reflect this ordinary and essentially territorial notion of jurisdiction',[393] further recognising that 'other basis of jurisdiction being exceptional and requiring special justification in the particular circumstances of each case'.[394] Overall, the Grand Chamber rejected the applicant's argument. Essentially, it held that the notion of 'effective control' requires States to ensure Convention rights 'in a manner proportionate to the level of control exercised in any given extra-territorial situation'.[395] The Grand Chamber held that:

> [T]he applicants' submission is tantamount to arguing that anyone adversely affected by an act imputable to a Contracting State, wherever in the world that act may have been committed or its consequences felt, is thereby brought within the jurisdiction of that State for the purpose of Article 1 of the Convention.
>
> The Court is inclined to agree that . . . the text of Article 1 does not accommodate such an approach to 'jurisdiction' . . . the Court is of the view that the wording of

[387] UNSC Res 1199 (23 September 1998) UN Doc S/RES/1199; UNSC Res 1203 (24 October 1998) UN Doc S/RES/1203; UNSC Res 1160 (31 March 1998) UN Doc S/RES/1160.

[388] MJ Glennon, 'The New Interventionism: The Search for a Just International Law' (1999) 78(3) *Foreign Affairs* 2.

[389] North Atlantic Council, 'Statement on Kosovo' (23 April 1999). Available at: www.nato.int/cps/en/natohq/official_texts_27451.htm.

[390] R Wedgwood, 'NATO's Campaign in Yugoslavia' (1999) 93 *American Journal of International Law* 828, 830–1. Noting that a draft resolution tabled by Russia, Belarus, and India 'was defeated by a vote of 12-3. The permanent members of the Council did not have occasion to exercise a veto, since the numerical tally fell far short of passage'.

[391] *Banković* (n 316) para 11.

[392] ibid para 54.

[393] ibid para 61.

[394] ibid.

[395] ibid para 75.

> Article 1 does not provide any support for the applicants' suggestion that the positive obligation in Article 1 to secure 'the rights and freedoms defined in Section I of this Convention' can be divided and tailored in accordance with the particular circumstances of the extra-territorial act in question.[396]

Finally, the Grand Chamber held that the 'Convention was not designed to be applied throughout the world, even in respect of the conduct of Contracting States', clarifying that, in its desire to avoid a 'gap or vacuum in human rights' protection', it had nevertheless 'establish[ed] jurisdiction only when the territory in question was one that, but for the specific circumstances, would normally be covered by the Convention'.[397] In consequence, the Grand Chamber ruled that the extraterritorial conduct of the respondent States did not fall within the Court's jurisdiction for the purposes of Article 1 of the European Convention, declining jurisdiction over the NATO airstrikes in Yugoslavia. The judgment was unanimous.[398]

The *Bankovic* decision has been heavily criticised. Raible considers that the decision was 'infamous'.[399] Similarly, one of its strongest critics, Milanović, considers that the ECtHR's judgment in *Bankovic* was 'the result of the Court's less than transparent weighing of different policy considerations', which sought to arrive at a 'superficial, legalistic rationale that would justify making the extraterritorial application of the ECHR *exceptional*'.[400] Other scholars observe that, in *Bankovic*, the ECtHR was acting 'in a way that is inconsistent with its own previous case law on similar interpretative issues'.[401] Mallory opines that the Court had 'called an abrupt halt to its stable line of jurisprudence' and accuses it of almost 'totally disregarding its previous decisions which had steadily expanded the reach of the Convention's obligations'.[402] And the list goes on.[403]

The crux of the criticism of *Bankovic* seems to rest on the fact that the European Court did not continue its trend of expanding its jurisdiction in the context of extraterritoriality. The question is whether that expansion was doctrinally justified. Perhaps it was not. There is one important distinction between the situation in *Loizidou* and the situation in *Bankovic*: in the former, both Cyprus (the entire island) and Turkey were party to the European Convention; in the

[396] ibid.
[397] ibid para 80.
[398] Because this was a Grand Chamber decision there were 16 judges on the bench.
[399] L Raible, 'Extraterritoriality Between a Rock and Hard Place' (2021) 82 *Questions of International Law* 7.
[400] Milanovic (n 347) 54.
[401] LE Popa, 'Treaty Interpretation at the European Court of Human Rights' in E Popa (ed), *Patterns of Treaty Interpretation as Anti-Fragmentation Tools: A Comparative Analysis with a Special Focus on the ECtHR, WTO and ICJ* (Springer, 2018) 217.
[402] Mallory 'A Second Coming of Extraterritorial Jurisdiction' (n 351).
[403] See eg Lawson 'Life After *Banković*' (n 359) 83 and ff; Popa (n 401); Wilde 'Triggering State Obligations' (n 357) 503; A Orakhelashvili, 'Restrictive Interpretation of Human Rights Treaties in the Recent Jurisprudence of the European Court of Human Rights' (2003) 14 *European Journal of International Law* 529.

latter, Serbia was not. Moreover, although the NATO States were carrying out a series of air strikes, their degree of control over the territory that was being struck was not at all comparable with the control that Turkey exercised over the TRNC.

Although the ECtHR has been flexible in its approach to the interpretation of Article 1, it does not appear to me that the text of the Convention strongly militated in favour of either outcome. And it does not appear to me that the Court's case law, as represented by *Loizidou*, required the extraterritorial application of the Convention in *Bankovic*. One potential explanation for the criticism is that the Court refused to view its jurisdiction as a one-way ratchet (i.e., as ever-expanding), but rather opted to restrain that expansion. Some do not consider that an acceptable outcome.

In any event, this is a hard judgment to appraise. Not only is the main issue legally complex, but the underlying issue (and its political context) was fraught.[404] Starting with the latter, Richard Falk observed that few international incidents have 'provoked [such] extremely divergent interpretations'.[405]

On the one hand, some consider NATO's intervention lawful. In this camp we find Christopher Greenwood, who observed that the underlying *values* of the international system and the UN Charter, did not 'rest exclusively on the principles of non-intervention and respect for sovereignty', but also on 'respect for human rights and the 'dignity and worth of the human person'.[406] On that basis, he considered that NATO's actions were justified when there existed a 'most serious humanitarian emergency involving large scale loss of life'.[407] Similarly, Reisman considered that NATO's action in Kosovo 'did not accord with the design of the United Nations Charter'.[408] Nevertheless, he viewed the airstrikes as justified because the 'Security Council was paralyzed', thus leaving only two options, to: 'forgo formally lawful action under the Charter or to forgo the lives and human rights of the Kosovars'.[409] Further noting that: 'when military force was brought into play, the ensemble of strategies that until then had failed, finally worked'.[410] In that same line, Glennon considered that the 'old rules on peacekeeping and peacemaking . . . should not be mourned', concluding that the 'horror of ethnic cleansing' in Kosovo meant that 'pressure built to use force against him, whether the U.N. Charter allowed it or not'.[411] And, as Wedgwood queried, 'How can an effort so broadly supported in its objectives – to stem

[404] The editorial comments section of (1999) 93(4) *American Journal of International Law* has interesting commentary from: Louis Henkin, Ruth Wedgwood, Jonathan Charney, Christine Chinkin, Richard Falk, Tomas Franck, and Michael Reisman.

[405] RA Falk, 'Kosovo, World Order, and the Future of International Law' (1999) 93 *American Journal of International Law* 847.

[406] Greenwood , 'International Law' (n 386) 929.

[407] ibid 931.

[408] Reisman, *Kosovo's Antinomies* (n 386) 860.

[409] ibid.

[410] ibid.

[411] Glennon 'The New Interventionism' (n 388).

Belgrade's expulsion of ethnic Albanians from Kosovo and block a gross violation of international law – be so uncertain in its legal basis?'[412].

That there is a degree of support for the bombing campaign is unsurprising. NATO's aerial campaign in the FRY is considered as having ended the Kosovo War. And, after all, the NATO air strikes were only carried out after 'all efforts to achieve a negotiated, political solution to the Kosovo crisis had failed'.[413] The situation in Kosovo was a humanitarian catastrophe. Genocide was being carried out.[414] Perhaps it was then UN Secretary General Kofi Annan who put it best. He considered the bombing 'tragic' but then caveated that: 'there are times when the use of force may be legitimate in the pursuit of peace'.[415] Moreover, there is also an important element of *temporal* context. NATO's intervention in Kosovo happened only a few years after the genocide and ethnic cleansing in Rwanda, which was broadly seen as a failure of the international community. 'If, in those dark days and hours leading up to the genocide', Annan again posited, 'a coalition of States had been prepared to act in defense of the Tutsi population, but did not receive prompt Council authorization, should such a coalition have stood aside and allowed the horror to unfold?'[416]

Others, however, disagreed – and strongly. 'When the primary responsibility of the Security Council for international ordering is displaced', Christine Chinkin argues, 'those that seek to act in its place must be especially mindful of their responsibilities'.[417] She further considered that the bombing campaign had been 'disproportionate, as it had an 'excessive . . . impact on the human rights of one civilian population'.[418] Jonathan Charney took a similar line. He considered that the bombing campaign '[i]ndisputably . . . violated the United Nations Charter and international law', which meant that the intervention 'risked destabilizing the international rule of law' and weakened the prohibition on the use of force.[419] And in a balanced criticism, Bruno Simma feared that the intervention indicated that NATO would start to carry out 'enforcement action in place of the UN without . . . authorization'.[420] Simma considered that the NATO

[412] Wedgwood 'NATO's Campaign in Yugoslavia' (n 390).

[413] *Banković* (n 316) para 8. Although note that Falk (n 405) considers at 855 that 'flexible diplomacy was not pursued' and that 'there are some grounds for supposing that a more flexible approach might have achieved acceptable results without recourse to war'.

[414] See eg, *Application of the Convention on the Prevention and Punishment of the Crime of Genocide (Bosnia and Herzegovina v Serbia and Montenegro)*, ICJ, Judgment of 26 February 2007, 43.

[415] Secretary-General's Statement on NATO Military Action Against Yugoslavia, UN Press Release SG/SM/6938 (24 March 1999).

[416] Secretary-General Presents his Annual Report to General Assembly, UN Press Release SG/SM/7136, GA/9596 (20 September 1999).

[417] CM Chinkin, 'Kosovo: A "Good" or "Bad" War?' (1999) 93 *American Journal of International Law* 841.

[418] ibid 845.

[419] JI Charney, 'Anticipatory Humanitarian Intervention in Kosovo' (1999) 93 *American Journal of International Law* 834, 834.

[420] B Simma, 'NATO, the UN and the Use of Force: Legal Aspects' (1999) 10 *European Journal of International Law* 1, 21.

campaign was 'illegal due to the lack of Security Council authorization', but he acknowledges that NATO members 'made every effort to get as close to legality as possible'.[421]

These views above show that the policy considerations of the NATO bombing campaign are nuanced. Reisman captured the complexity of the issue when he observed that no lawyer 'can look back at the incident without disquiet'.[422] Yet the underlying motivations of the *Bankovic* judgment are, in my view, more straightforward. There are two main issues to consider, in addition to the point already mentioned about the relatively open-nature and vagueness of the provision at play (Art. 1 of the European Convention). This degree of indeterminacy afforded the ECtHR some flexibility to determine whether to adjudicate the dispute.

First, the discussion above shows that States were divided regarding the legality of NATO's intervention in Yugoslavia. Assuming jurisdiction over the case would have required the European Court to directly adjudicate on the legality of the bombing campaign – a topic that understandably the Court may have preferred to avoid given its political sensitivity. Albeit there is a question mark over the legality of NATO's intervention, the campaign seems to have contributed to minimum order and the respect of human rights; it stopped the ethnic cleansing and gross human rights violations that were taking place in Kosovo. Therefore, a judgment from the European Court finding the NATO States internationally responsible for human rights violations would have potentially worked to undermine minimum order and the respect of human rights, including by disincentivising future instances of humanitarian intervention.

Second, although it is reasonable to assume that the European Court was institutionally robust enough to overcome any backlash from a decision against the NATO States, the fact remains that such a decision would have likely generated (possibly quite substantial) backlash. The effectiveness and enforceability of an adverse judgment would have been scarce. The case was brought against *all* NATO members that were also party to the European Convention: 17 States in total.[423] The collection of respondent States constitutes a substantial number of the members of the Council of Europe – and includes those that have the most clout.[424]

On this basis, the European Court's approach of avoiding the issue may be justified. This was achieved by using extraterritoriality as an implied avoidance technique. Neither the Convention's text, nor the Court's jurisprudence *required*

[421] ibid 22.

[422] Reisman, *Kosovo's Antinomies* (n 386) 860.

[423] Belgium, the Czech Republic, Denmark, France, Germany, Greece, Hungary, Iceland, Italy, Luxembourg, the Netherlands, Norway, Poland, Portugal, Spain, Turkey and the United Kingdom.

[424] In an interesting, concurrent dispute, the ICJ (unanimously) declined jurisdiction over Serbia's claim against a series of NATO States regarding the bombing campaign, see eg *Legality of Use of Force (Serbia and Montenegro v United Kingdom)*, ICJ, Judgment (Preliminary Objections) of 15 December 2004, 1307.

a different outcome. Although some consider that international jurisdiction should continually and irrevocably expand (particularly in the human rights context), the reality of the international legal process is dynamic. Whereas the Court had previously considered that it was correct to expand the extraterritorial scope of the Convention, in this case it unanimously considered that that was not the correct approach. In my view, that was a fair call.

C. Al-Skeini

The Grand Chamber's decision in *Al-Skeini* represents yet another shift in the European Court's approach to extraterritoriality, now moving away from *Bankovic*.[425] The case relates to the conduct of UK troops during the 2003 invasion of Iraq. Between May 2003 until June 2004 UK troops were responsible for controlling the South-East of Iraq, which includes Basra, the second-largest city in the country.[426] During that time, those troops were in charge of public order.[427] In short, the claim concerned six Iraqi citizens that were killed by British troops in Basra (one of them while held in a detention facility in a UK military base).[428] The claimants alleged that all six were under the UK's jurisdiction when they were killed and that the UK had breached Article 2 of the Convention by failing to carry out an effective investigation of their deaths.[429] The UK admitted that the European Convention applied in its military bases in Iraq (and their detention facilities),[430] but denied that the Convention applied extraterritorially in Iraq more generally.[431]

The ECtHR rejected the UK's arguments and upheld jurisdiction. The Grand Chamber considered that the Convention applied extraterritorially in these circumstances. The Chamber, while acknowledging that jurisdiction was '*primarily*' territorial,[432] also recognised that there were exceptions to this principle.[433] Those exceptions include: (i) actions of diplomatic or consular agents operating abroad;[434] (ii) cases where, because of another State's invitation or acquiescence, a State 'exercises all or some of the public powers';[435] (iii) situations where 'a State's agents operating outside its territory may bring the

[425] Indeed, both judgments were issued on the same day: *Al-Skeini v United Kingdom* (n 361). A related, also relevant case, was decided the same day: *Al-Jedda v United Kingdom* App no 27021/08 (ECtHR, 7 July 2011). *Al-Jedda* is an important authority on, among other things, attribution of conduct to States and international organisations.
[426] *Al-Skeini* (n 361) para 20.
[427] ibid para 21.
[428] ibid para 63.
[429] ibid para 3.
[430] ibid.
[431] ibid paras 110 and ff.
[432] ibid paras 131 and ff.
[433] ibid, para 133.
[434] ibid, para 134.
[435] ibid, para 135.

individual thereby brought under the control of the State's authorities into the State's Article 1 jurisdiction',[436] and (iv) cases where a State, following military action (whether lawful or unlawful) 'exercises effective control of an area outside the national territory'.[437]

Ultimately, the ECtHR *refrained* from deciding whether the UK had effective 'overall control' over Basra. Instead, the Grand Chamber focused on another of the exceptions: the UK's exercise of public powers and governmental authority in that region.[438] The Grand Chamber found that, because the UK *did* exercise those powers, an exception to the territorial principle of jurisdiction applied and thus the Convention applied extraterritorially (over the entire area controlled by the UK – not only military bases). The European Court held that:

> [F]ollowing the removal from power of the Ba'ath regime and until the accession of the Interim Government, the United Kingdom (together with the United States) assumed in Iraq the exercise of some of the public powers normally to be exercised by a foreign government. In particular, the United Kingdom assumed authority and responsibility for the maintenance of security in South East Iraq. In these exceptional circumstances, the Court considers that the United Kingdom, through its soldiers engaged in security operations in Basra . . . exercised authority and control over individuals killed in the course of such security operations, so as to establish a jurisdiction link between the deceased and the United Kingdom for purposes of Article 1 of the Convention.[439]

The Court's decision on admissibility and jurisdiction was unanimous.[440] It also generally ruled against the UK on the merits, finding it had breached its obligations under Article 2 of the Convention.[441]

Although the Grand Chamber's decision was unanimous, two judges filed concurrent opinions: Judges Rozakis and Bonello. Only the latter opinion is relevant.[442] It is one of the most trenchant criticisms of the European Court's approach to extraterritoriality. (Judge Bonello retired shortly after filing this concurrence.) The judge's views are candid (perhaps *too* candid) and, given his privileged vantage point, they are worth considering:

[436] ibid, para 136.
[437] ibid, para 138.
[438] Arguably, a functional approach, see M Loughlin, 'The Functionalist Style in Public Law' (2005) 55(3) *University of Toronto Law Journal* 361.
[439] *Al-Skeini* (n 361) para 149. The case had previously gone through UK domestic courts, culminating in a judgment from the House of Lords, which concluded, based on *Bankovic*, that the Convention did not apply extraterritorially in Iraq: *R (Al-Skeini) v Secretary of State for Defence* [2007] UKHL 26. In subsequent judgments, the European Court has found that the Convention applies extraterritorially in militarily occupied territory, see *Hassan v United Kingdom* App no 29750/09 (ECtHR, 16 September 2014).
[440] *Al-Skeini* (n 361) paras 75–76.
[441] ibid, with a caveat in dispositive point 5 in relation to one of the applicants.
[442] ibid.

> The Court's case-law on Article 1 of the Convention . . . has, so far, been bedeviled by an inability or an unwillingness to establish a coherent and axiomatic regime, grounded in essential basics and even-handedly applicable across the widest spectrum of jurisdictional controversies . . .
>
> Up until now, the Court has . . . spawned a number of 'leading' judgments based on a need-to-decide basis, patchwork case-law at best . . . As the Court has . . . always tailored its tenets to sets of specific facts, it is hardly surprising that those tenets then seem to limp when applied to sets of different facts . . . they then betray an awkward fit and the cohabitation of [different strands of case-law] is, overall, quite problematic. . .
>
> The truth seems to be that Article 1 case-law has . . . enshrined everything and the opposite of everything.[443]

There is extensive commentary on *Al-Skeini*. Overall, the academic reaction was positive. Besson opined that the Court 'reorganized and clarified' the different categories of jurisdiction and that the judgment 'promis[ed] a fresh start in the Court's case law on extraterritoriality'.[444] Similarly, Milanović considers that these two judgments are 'as close as we've ever come to the European Court overruling *Bankovic*. And good riddance'.[445] Some, however, criticised the judgment, considering that even though the ECtHR expanded the extraterritorial application of the Convention, the European Court still was 'more restrictive' than UN human rights bodies.[446]

Doctrinally, and contrary to several commentators, I do not find that the Court in *Al-Skeini* overruled *Bankovic*. While there was some refinement as to the exceptions that triggered the extraterritorial application of the Convention, the differences in the underlying situations in *Bankovic* and *Al-Skeini* are sufficient to distinguish the case. In my view, there is an important categorical and conceptual difference between targeted strikes and a full military occupation. It is true, however, that the European Court framed the exceptions in relatively wide language. Judge Bonello is right when he says that the Court has refused to set out a bright-line rule, 'a coherent and axiomatic regime'. In my view, however, that is both intentional and even commendable. By keeping the language somewhat vague, the ECtHR was keeping some flexibility to determine the extraterritorial application of the Convention. This flexibility may allow the Court – in some cases, mainly those at the margin – to take contextual elements into consideration when determining whether the Convention applies extraterritorially, an issue that will, more often than not, come up when assessing the lawfulness of military conduct abroad, one of the most politically sensitive issues that will come before the European Court. It thus makes sense for the Court to have at least *some* discretion.

[443] *Al-Skeini* (n 361), Concurring Opinion of Judge Bonello, paras 4–7.
[444] Besson (n 353) 872.
[445] M Milanovic, 'European Court Decides Al-Skeini and Al-Jedda' *EJIL: Talk!* (7 July 2011).
[446] Raible (n 354) 1435.

By focusing on the exercise of public authority, the ECtHR essentially left open the possibility of deciding that other scenarios of the use of force abroad remain outside the scope of the Convention (i.e., situations like those in *Bankovic,* or drone strikes), as in those cases the State would not be exercising public authority in the location of the strike.[447] Put simply, the European Court's decision to leave parts of the extraterritoriality doctrine in the realm of relatively vague standards – rather than narrow, bright-line rules – is doctrinally defensible. And, from the perspective of the New Haven school, it is positive. The Court's decision to uphold jurisdiction here contributed to minimum order and to the respect of human rights. The UK's extrajudicial execution of Iraqi citizens – carried out in a territory the UK had military control over and was occupying by force – was a gross human rights violation. Holding the UK to account for the conduct of its troops in a territory *it was occupying* is positive.

Further, when viewed in tandem with *Bankovic* the Court's distinction of the situation there, which only concerned airstrikes, and the situation in *Al-Skeini,* which concerned an occupation, is sensible. Although some criticised NATO's decision to not deploy ground forces in Yugoslavia, within the range of possible military interventions, the deployment of targeted airstrikes – as opposed of the deployment of an occupying ground force – seems to be the alternative that would most likely lead to the avoidance of surplus violence.

In terms of prospective effectiveness, the situation is again different than that in *Bankovic.* Unlike the military action there, which had the support of the entire NATO alliance, the military action in Iraq, whilst nominally multilateral, had considerably narrower support. Further, rather than having to potentially face 17 States contesting the judgment, the UK was the sole respondent State. Similarly, Mallory recognises that the ECtHR needs to balance the expansion of its jurisdiction with potential compliance concerns, particularly those that could threaten the 'important strategic, economic and political interests in [States'] overseas endeavours', further observing that as a 'strategic actor', the European Court is thus 'mindful of its own legitimacy and authority in respect of both rights' protection and state compliance'.[448]

Al-Skeini is an interesting judgment because it highlights the ductility of many of the rules of international procedural law on matters of jurisdiction and admissibility. In this case, the European Court decided to uphold jurisdiction, but the relatively vagueness of the Court's treatment of extraterritoriality meant that the issue was both rationally and causally indeterminate. The opposite result would have been equally plausible.

[447] Milanovic (n 445) considers that the way the Court framed its judgment meant that *Bankovic* could still apply, and that, for instance 'the current bombing of Libya by a number of European States could *not* fall under Art. 1 ECHR'.

[448] Mallory (n 351).

D. Georgia

The final case analysed in this section shows how the European Court relied *again* on the flexibility of the rules on extraterritoriality. *Georgia v. Russia (II)*[449] is an inter-State case related to the five-day hostilities between Georgia and Russia over South Ossetia and Abkhazia.[450] Very briefly, following attacks by secessionists in South Ossetia (an ethnic enclave that had fought a separatist war against Georgia in the 1990s), the Georgian military attacked the regional capital, Tskhinvali. Then, Russian troops intervened on the secessionists' side, briskly taking over South Ossetia and pushing back the Georgian troops. After five days of conflict, a ceasefire was reached. For some months afterwards, Russia kept a heavy military presence in South Ossetia.

One of the main aspects of the judgment is its distinction between the five days of active hostilities and the period of Russian occupation that took place after the ceasefire. First, the Court found that the Convention did not apply extraterritorially during the *active* phase of the hostilities. The ECtHR held that, under the *spatial* model of jurisdiction, Russia did not exercise effective control over South Ossetia during the active phase of the hostilities, as military operations 'carried out during an international armed conflict' do not imply '"effective control" over an area', as fighting for control by definition means no control.[451]

Second, the Court considered whether the *personal* model of jurisdiction was applicable, under the 'State agent authority and control' principle. Again, it concluded that it did not. It held that, after *Bankovic*, it had ruled that the 'decisive factor' to establish 'State agent authority and control' was the 'exercise of physical power and control over the persons in question'.[452] Yet the Court distinguished the application of that principle, considering that those cases involved 'isolated and specific acts involving an element of proximity'.[453] Here, unlike in *Bankovic,* Russia had not just engaged in air or artillery strikes – it had also deployed ground forces. The Court nevertheless held that:

> By contrast, the active phase of hostilities which the Court is required to examine in the present case in the context of an international armed conflict is very different, as it concerns bombing and artillery shelling by Russian armed forces seeking to put the

[449] *Georgia v Russia (II)* App no 38263/08 (ECtHR (Grand Chamber), 21 January 2021).

[450] See generally C King, 'The Five-Day War: Managing Moscow After the Georgia Crisis' (November/December 2008) 87(6) *Foreign Affairs* 2; CV Pallin and F Westerlund, 'Russia's War in Georgia: Lessons and Consequences' (2009) 20(2) *Small Wars & Insurgencies* 400; RE Hamilton, 'August 2008 and Everything After: A Ten-Year Retrospective on the Russia–Georgia War' (Foreign Policy Research Institute, 22 October 2018). Available at: www.fpri.org/article/2018/10/august-2008-and-everything-after-a-ten-year-retrospective-on-the-russia-georgia-war/..

[451] *Georgia v Russia* (n 449) para 127.

[452] ibid para 131.

[453] ibid para 132.

> Georgian army *hors de combat* and to establish control over areas forming part of Georgia . . .
>
> [T]he Court attaches decisive weight to the fact that the very reality of armed confrontation and fighting between enemy military forces seeking to establish control over an area in a context of chaos not only means that there is no 'effective control' over an area . . . but also excludes any form of 'State agent authority and control' over individuals.[454]

Importantly, the Court considered that it was not suited to adjudicate claims arising from the *active* part of hostilities, observing that those situations were 'predominantly regulated by legal norms other than those of the Convention (specifically, international humanitarian law or the law of armed conflict)'.[455] Further, the Court noted that if the State-parties wished the Court to carry out those tasks they would need to 'provide the necessary legal basis for such a task'.[456] Note the difference in the ECtHR's approach in *Ukraine v Russia,* where it distinguished *Georgia v Russia (II)* on somewhat weak grounds, claiming that there had been no context of chaos there and also that IHL applied in tandem with the protections of the European Convention.[457] Given the subject matter of that case, the European Court can perhaps be forgiven for this abrupt doctrinal shift.[458]

Turning back to *Georgia,* the Court did rule that the Convention applied extraterritorially *after* the active phase of hostilities, once Russian troops (or their proxies) were occupying South Ossetia, Abkhazia and the buffer zone.[459] Basically, the Court considered that both the presence of Russian troops (between August and October 2008) and, subsequently, the Ossetian and Abkhazian authorities' dependency on Russia, meant that Russia had 'effective control' over those territories.[460] On this point, the European Court was almost unanimous, with only a single dissent.

The Court's decision in *Georgia* was controversial, both internally and externally. Some of the dissenting opinions severely criticised the majority's approach. In general, the dissents disapproved of the Court's approach to extraterritoriality and, in many instances, criticised what they perceived was a revival of the Court's *Bankovic* judgment. Somewhat unusually, several of the dissents

[454] ibid paras 133, 137.

[455] ibid para 141.

[456] ibid para 142.

[457] *Ukraine and the Netherlands v Russia* Apps nos 8019/16, 43800/14, 28525/20 and 11055/22 (ECtHR (Grand Chamber), 9 July 2025) para 361.

[458] Arguably this shift happened previously, in *Ukraine and the Netherlands v Russia* (dec) App nos 43800/14, 8019/16 and 28525/20 (ECtHR (Grand Chamber), 25 January 2023) (MH17). This judgment also demonstrates the importance of effectiveness considerations in international law. Whilst the decision is unquestionably legitimate and, at least on paper, ensures respect for human rights in the middle of atrocities, the elephant in the court room remains its absolute lack of any type of effectiveness. Perhaps, after all, *silent enim leges inter arma*.

[459] *Georgia v Russia* (n 449) paras 161–75.

[460] ibid para 174.

were framed in relatively emotional language. For example, Judge Lemmens noted that he 'regret[s] that the majority have taken a step back and restricted the scope of the Convention where human rights are at great risk'.[461] In a joint dissent, Judges Yudkivska, Wojtyczek and Chanturia (the Georgian judge on the Court) accused the majority of confirming the roman maxim *silent enim leges inter arma* ('in times of war law falls silent').[462] The joint dissenters also argued that the majority opted to 'evade the core debate' regarding extraterritoriality'[463] and that this led to a 'continuing state of confusion' regarding the doctrine'.[464] Also writing individually, Judge Chanturia considered that the Court had not only 'resuscitate[d] the otherwise lifeless *Bankovic* precedent', but also that it had taken a 'step backwards'[465] in the protection of human rights.[466]

Judge Grozev, in turn, while admitting that the doctrine of 'effective control' did not 'provid[e] a workable criterion in the context of armed conflict',[467] considered that the interpretation that would favour the objectives of the Convention (and that would avoid any vacuums or black holes) would be for the Court to consider that acts of war are covered by extraterritoriality.[468] But the most strident dissent came from Judge Pinto De Albuquerque. He considered that the European Court's position was 'morally and legally untenable',[469] characterised the majority's reasoning as relying exclusively on a 'classical *ad terrorem fallacy*' and a 'ruminat[ion] about catastrophic worst-case scenarios'.[470] He concludes – rather grandiloquently – claiming that the 'Court will face a gargantuan task to restore the damage to its credibility caused by this judgment'.[471]

The majority, perhaps understandably, does not expressly rebut those criticisms. There is a soft rebuttal in the concurring opinion of Judge Keller. She notes that the minority's view, which would have had the ECtHR adjudicate on the active period of hostilities, was 'founded on an overly expansive vision of the Court as an adjudicator of the totality of armed conflict', contrasting that with the 'principled yet realistic' approach of the majority.[472]

[461] *Georgia v Russia* (n 449), Partly Dissenting Opinion of Judge Lemmens, para 3.

[462] *Georgia v Russia* (n 449), Joint Partly Dissenting Opinion of Judges Yudkivska, Wojtyczek and Chanturia, para 1. Perhaps it is worth mentioning that Judge Yudkivska is Ukrainian and Judge Chanturia, Georgian.

[463] ibid para 14.

[464] ibid.

[465] *Georgia v Russia* (n 449), Partly Dissenting Opinion of Judge Chanturia, para 14.

[466] Interestingly, the judge expressly mentioned policy considerations in his dissent, noting that: 'Collective public order, however, cannot exist without peace reigning in the territories of the member States. How can this Court act as the guarantor of peace and public order in Europe if it turns its back on an armed conflict occurring within the member States' legal space?' ibid para 53.

[467] *Georgia v Russia* (n 449), Partly Dissenting Opinion of Judge Grozev, para 170.

[468] ibid paras 171–72.

[469] *Georgia v Russia* (n 449), Partly Dissenting Opinion of Judge Pinto De Albuquerque, para 22.

[470] ibid para 24.

[471] ibid para 30.

[472] *Georgia v Russia* (n 449), Concurring Opinion of Judge Keller, paras 4–5.

Unsurprisingly, there has been broad academic criticism of the judgment. The main focus of the criticism has been twofold: first, the zigzagging nature of the Court's approach to extraterritoriality; second, the Court's refusal to adjudicate on potential human rights violations carried out during the active phase of the hostilities. Dzehtsiarou considers that a consequence of the Court's decision in *Georgia* is that it is 'ready to give up on massive human rights violations because they are too difficult to deal with'[473] and he considers that the ECtHR 'allowed the rupture of European Public Order'.[474] In a similar vein, Raible says that, in *Georgia*, the Court 'contracted [its] interpretation of the extraterritorial scope of the ECHR'.[475] She also observes that by narrowing the extraterritorial scope of the Convention the Court was going 'against the grain of wider trends'.[476]

One interesting aspect of academic criticism is that (unusually), a few commentators quickly perceived that the European Court had relied on the flexibility (or doctrinal muddle) surrounding the extraterritoriality doctrine to avoid deciding the dispute. Mallory considered that the majority represented 'the wing of the Court that is conscious of the risks of an overly expansive approach to . . . jurisdiction'. He observes that 'state interventions increasing dramatically' in recent cases involving extraterritoriality, observing that States had 'become far more active in attempting to shape the meaning of extraterritorial jurisdiction within effective proceedings'.[477]

Similarly, Milanović opined that, although the judgment was 'very important', it was also 'very disappointing'.[478] He further observed that the 'Court's policy-driven motivations . . . are entirely transparent'. The Court is 'fearful of political backlash',[479] Milanović says, and sees inter-State disputes, particularly those that are 'dealing with armed conflict', as a source of 'existential danger, which it wants to avoid dealing with as much as it is possible to do so'.[480] Milanović admits that he understands the ECtHR's position, considering that it is explained:

[473] K Dzehtsiarou, 'The Judgement of Solomon that Went Wrong: Georgia v Russia (II) by the European Court of Human Rights' (Völkerrechtsblog, 26 January 2021). Available at: https// voelkerrechtsblog.org/the-judgement-of-solomon-that-went-wrong-georgia-v-russia-ii-by-the -european-court-of-human-rights/.. Further criticising that 'The Court, which was designed to be a bulwark against totalitarianism and ultimately prevent war, decided not to deal with massive human rights violations as they are too complex and demanding'.

[474] ibid.

[475] Raible 'Extraterritoriality Between a Rock and Hard Place' (n 399) 20.

[476] Miller 'Revisiting Extraterritorial Jurisdiction' (n 352) 22. Again, viewing jurisdiction as a unilateral ratchet.

[477] Mallory (n 351) 43. In addition, consider all the factors related to the 'procedural turn', discussed in chapter 3.

[478] Milanovic (n 323).

[479] Raible (n 399) 26, also considers that the Court did 'not want to get involved for fear of backlash', criticising also what she considers the Court's lack of principled reasoning in reaching that conclusion.

[480] ibid.

> [B]y a fundamental apology v. utopia tension between considerations of universality ('doing the right thing') and effectiveness ('we're not best placed to do this, and if we try the whole thing may blow up in our face') . . . The Court . . . does not really want to deal with these cases, where it feels there is little good it can actually do, while the danger of political blow-back detrimental to the whole Convention system is too high to ignore.[481]

Despite that, Milanović questions the Court's reliance on the doctrinal flexibility (the 'supposed intricacies') of the extraterritoriality principle. Instead, he would prefer the Court to have avoided the issue at the merits stage, 'rather than by distorting the notion of Art. 1 jurisdiction and turning it into a disguised, opaque and arbitrary non-justiciability doctrine'.[482] Essentially, Milanović is saying that the Court relied on extraterritoriality as an implied avoidance technique. And of course it did. Yet it is worth questioning whether, despite the doctrinal imprecision that results from the use of extraterritoriality as an implied avoidance technique, some sort of merits-avoidance would have been best, including because that could have resulted in a decision that did not find that Russia's conduct was unlawful – arguably a worst result.

Appraising the ECtHR's *Georgia* decision is hard. Perhaps it is more difficult than all the other cases discussed in this Chapter. Doctrinally, the majority's approach to the effective control principle, albeit criticised by the minority and by commentators, is defensible. It is logical to conclude that a State does not exercise effective control over a territory it is fighting over with another State (the 'context of chaos'). While the pull of universalism, which is very strong in human rights scholarship, would logically oppose the recognition of areas (e.g., live hostilities) where international human rights law does not apply, that conclusion is potentially misguided. The fact that there may be scenarios where the European Convention does not apply does not mean that those scenarios are completely lawless. International humanitarian law still applies – and nothing in the judgment puts that in doubt. On the issue of the relative indeterminacy of the extraterritoriality principle, it is questionable that the European Court allowed the doctrine to fluctuate (yet again). *Al-Skeini* had provided some conceptual clarity. Although it is obvious that some doctrinal uncertainty provides the Court with flexibility and the possibility of relying on extraterritoriality as an implied avoidance technique. Ultimately, the Court was concerned with restricting the application of the Convention to hostilities, possibly *the* issue that the Court was keenest to avoid, as explained below.

The judgment is also hard to evaluate from a policy-oriented perspective. From the point of view of maximising the possibility of enforcement, the Court could be forgiven for having considered (in those naïve times) that a judgment that was not *completely* against Russia was more likely to be effective and

[481] ibid.
[482] Milanovic (n 323).

complied with. Although some have considered that this was the Court's underlying motivation,[483] I am not persuaded, for two reasons. First, by then Russia had a long history of not complying with the European Court's judgments. Indeed, one year later, Russia had withdrawn from the European Convention, after it had been excluded from the Council of Europe – the strongest sanction the Convention mechanism had at its disposal.[484] By the time it left the Convention, Russia had 2,129 judgments against it pending compliance.[485] In this context, a finding that Russia had committed human rights violations during the active phase of the hostilities was unlikely to be the straw that broke the camel's back. At that time (i.e., after the South Ossetia war and after annexing Crimea) Russia was well into 'what's-another-stripe-on-a-tiger' territory.

Second, it is plausible that the Court's concern actually related to *other* States (e.g., those States with political clout and with a more robust tradition of taking the Court's judgment seriously). Those same States, as Mallory explains, had taken an increased interest in disputes concerning the extraterritorial scope of the Convention. Indeed, the very topic, given that it normally comes up when States use force abroad, is quite politically sensitive. So, whilst the Court could reasonably expect that Russia would not comply with an adverse judgment (and thus that factor should not have weighed too much in its assessment), it could have reasonably been concerned with backlash from *other* States, reluctant to find themselves subject to Convention obligations in the course of hostilities (and this is a point on which it is possible to draw a distinction with military occupation).

From the point of view of contributing to minimum order, it is unlikely that any decision from the Court could have significantly moved the needle. For that matter, neither could a decision from the ICJ (which also declined jurisdiction in a related dispute).[486] The main contribution to minimum order in this dispute was the negotiation of an effective ceasefire. This was achieved through political/diplomatic means.[487] It is hard to see how this could have been achieved through international adjudication, for instance, through the order of interim measures. It is through the political processes that minimum order was re-established. Again, this shows the limits of international adjudication. Particularly,

[483] Dzehtsiarou 'The Judgement of Solomon that Went Wrong' (n 473).

[484] Council of Europe, 'Russia ceases to be a Party to the European Convention on Human Rights on 16 September 2022' (Newsroom, 23 March 2022). Available at: www.coe.int/en/web/portal/-/russia-ceases-to-be-a-party-to-the-european-convention-of-human-rights-on-16-september-2022; Council of Europe, Newsroom, *Russia ceases to be a party to the European Convention on Human Rights* (16 Sept. 2022).

[485] ibid, stating that '2,129 judgments and decisions have yet to be fully implemented by Russia and remain pending before the Committee of Ministers'.

[486] *Application of the International Convention on the Elimination of All Forms of Racial Discrimination* (n 69) 70.

[487] RD Asmus, *A Little War That Shook the World: Georgia, Russia, and the Future of the West* (Palgrave Macmillan, 2010) 5: 'Western diplomatic intervention became obsessed with finding a formula that . . . ended the fighting and essentially papered over the larger political issues at stake.'

it highlights how critical decisions, those dealing with acute incidents, are often taken, not through court judgments, but rather through other more authoritative processes. And that's OK. This type of conflict calls for some humility – or at least realism – regarding the capacity of the adjudicative function to address these international crises. As I have explained before, international adjudicators often play a relatively limited role in the broader international legal process.[488]

Therefore, my view is that the Court's decision in *Georgia*, while far from perfect, has at least some positive aspects. By refusing to expand the Convention's extraterritorial scope to active hostilities, the Court possibly preserved its legitimacy and avoided strong backlash from States (other than Russia) that take their Convention obligations seriously, but also occasionally use force abroad. Similarly to how the ICJ proceeded in *Obligation to Prosecute* or in *Alleged Violations,* the ECtHR relied on extraterritoriality as an implied avoidance technique to *carve out* (i.e., to withdraw from adjudication) some aspects of the dispute, i.e., it operated as an issue-selection mechanism. The European Court has effectively promoted human dignity by holding those States accountable for a substantial number of human rights violations committed abroad. Perhaps prudence and pragmatism advised against extending that accountability to the context of *active* hostilities (again, an area where those States are still bound by international humanitarian law). And the ECtHR relied on an implied avoidance doctrine to reach that result.

IV. CONCLUSION

To conclude, this chapter has sought to identify several examples where implied avoidance techniques were applied in practice. These examples have illustrated how international courts use the relative indeterminacy of rules of international procedural law to deploy implied avoidance techniques to abstain either from deciding a case or an issue. As the examples analysed above suggest, the relative doctrinal indeterminacy of parts of international procedural law does not always result in avoidance. In some instances, such as *Certain Phosphates in Nauru* or *Al-Skeini*, it may operate to allow the Court to *adjudicate* a dispute, including in circumstances where there would have been doubts about its capacity to do so (at least under a narrow construction of the relevant jurisdictional rules).

Further, the chapter showed how often the indeterminacy of the relevant procedural rules means that, doctrinally, there often is no single right answer when dealing with complex issues of international procedural law. Perhaps international procedural law will eventually develop enough doctrinal 'thickness' for that not to be the case. And perhaps it should. But it is not at that point yet.

[488] See chapter 1.

At least for now, we are often far from a bivalent, 'rules-are-results' territory. Instead, the sparsity of doctrine leads to flexibility and a modicum of discretion in the application of those relevant principles. There may be some positive aspects of this, including because it allows those courts to rely on that doctrinal indeterminacy as implied avoidance techniques.

Finally, I have argued that the implied application of avoidance techniques may sometimes be justified, on both pragmatic and normative grounds. A policy-oriented approach, which considers that decisions should have both legitimacy and effectiveness, allows taking those factors into account. This includes, among other things, openness to considering whether a decision will be effective, whether it will likely be enforceable, whether it protects the legitimacy and authority of an international court and whether it promotes minimum order and respect for human rights. But a decision, whether it avoids a case or whether it goes on to decide it on the merits, will only be appraised positively if it satisfies both criteria of legitimacy and effectiveness. In consequence, not all applications of avoidance techniques will be justified. Some will not, as argued above. But when those criteria are satisfied, then I argue that the implied use of avoidance techniques is justified. It allows international courts to incorporate prudential and pragmatic considerations into their analysis; it allows them to have some control over the disputes and issues they adjudicate; and, critically, it is an important tool to navigate potentially very sensitive issues that may lead to backlash and, in some instances, to hard blows being dealt to international adjudication more generally. This is particularly so when international adjudication faces the potentially lethal combination of an increase in the judicialisation of mega political disputes and a growing – and aggressive – backlash from some quarters against international adjudication and international law more generally.

6

Conclusion

'It ain't over till it's over'

Yogi Berra

HERE I SET OUT my conclusions in summary. As I explained in detail in the Introduction, I have approached the issues covered in this book with what I hope is a good dose of epistemic humility – including an awareness that my analysis involves some degree of speculation. Because of that, I suggested approaching the issue inferentially and probabilistically. All of this means accepting that, on some of my core claims, it will be difficult, if not impossible, to formulate any bright-line rules or to come to any hard-and-fast conclusions. Nonetheless, with those caveats in place, I argue that it is possible to make the following points.

First, there is a high probability that some avoidance is happening in international courts. This includes jurisdictional avoidance, as well as other forms of avoidance techniques that happen at the merits or remedies stages. This should not be surprising. It is now relatively well accepted that there is avoidance in domestic courts, including apex courts. If that is the case there, why should it be different at the international level, where courts operate on a weaker institutional context and, to an important degree, depend on State consent?

A close reading of the three case studies set out in the prior chapter suggests that avoidance is the likelier explanation rather than mere discrepancies in the application of black-letter law or, even worse, significant doctrinal incompetence. In my view, there are substantial grounds to argue that international courts have at times used the existence of a dispute, the indispensable third party or *Monetary Gold* principle, and the extraterritorial application of the European Convention on Human Rights as avoidance techniques. Those are only examples.

Second, there are different types of avoidance. The type covered in this book is jurisdictional avoidance, understood as an international court's abstention from issuing a decision on the merits of a case or issue. This is achieved by declining jurisdiction over them, declaring them inadmissible or, more rarely, by holding them to be non-justiciable. Jurisdictional avoidance may not be the most relevant type of avoidance. There seems to be an ongoing shift towards other types of avoidance techniques, mainly those focused on the review of the merits.

Those include the strategic application of standards of review, adopting a more deferential approach to judging State conduct (e.g., the margin of appreciation doctrine, the State's right to regulate), or excluding some issues from international adjudication by using exception clauses or reservations.

Third, jurisdictional avoidance mainly operates as a case- or issue-selection mechanism. Essentially, this means that avoidance techniques are used to allow an international court to have, in some cases, some say as to what cases or issues it decides – even when the court's formal procedural rules do not provide that it will have the capacity to select cases or issues.

Fourth, avoidance techniques may be applied expressly or impliedly. Express avoidance techniques are those where the court openly acknowledges that it is refraining from adjudicating a case or issue, mainly because of its subject matter. The paradigmatic example of an express avoidance technique is a declaration of non-justiciability, where a court holds that it will refrain from deciding a dispute because the subject-matter is not suitable for adjudication. Although in some domestic legal systems express avoidance techniques are still used with some regularity, international courts are extremely reluctant to rely on them. Historically, attempts to objectively establish the categories of dispute which were suitable for international adjudication failed. In the few instances where international courts have come close to holding that they are applying an express avoidance technique and that they are abstaining from deciding a case or issue because of its subject matter, they have been criticised.

In contrast, with implied avoidance techniques an international court is not openly acknowledging that it is applying an avoidance technique. The avoidance technique is not expressly articulated; it happens impliedly, covertly, *sub silentio,* between the lines (Straussianly). In the context of jurisdictional avoidance, the implied use of avoidance techniques operates through the application of jurisdictional and admissibility doctrines. That is, the avoidance technique is deployed through an international court's approach to issues of jurisdiction and admissibility. Importantly, the implied deployment of avoidance techniques suggests a lack of judicial candour. International courts are not openly saying that they are applying or interpreting certain jurisdictional doctrine – say, the *Monetary Gold* principle – in a particular way to decline jurisdiction over a case because they would prefer to refrain from deciding the dispute on the merits. So, claiming that a certain decision constitutes the use of an implied avoidance technique, by definition, requires speculation.

Fifth, international courts may rely on the rules of jurisdiction and admissibility as implied avoidance techniques because of the inherent characteristics of those rules. International procedural law is mainly judge-created. Many of its rules are relatively indeterminate; they are vague or fuzzy. In fact, many of the rules of international procedural law are, in reality, standards or evaluation rules. They allow for a plurality of answers rather than a single right answer. They are not bivalent. This means that, for all practical purposes, international procedural law is not doctrinally thick enough to require specific answers in most cases. This ductility, in turn, provides international courts with some flexibility in their application, so they can occasionally rely on them as implied avoidance techniques.

International courts' potential to rely on the relative indeterminacy of international procedural law as an avoidance technique is bolstered by two additional features of international procedural law. The first is international courts' wide discretion to ascertain their own jurisdiction. This is reflected in the competence–competence principle, which establishes that, in general, an international court will be able to ascertain the extent of its own jurisdiction. The second is the general lack of appellate or second level review mechanisms. Taken together, all those characteristics enable international courts to deploy implied avoidance techniques. Look at it this way: international courts are: (1) applying relatively vague and ill-defined rules on jurisdiction and admissibility; (2) are determining themselves the breadth of their own jurisdiction; and (3) ensuring that determination will normally not be subject to any (or any effective) type of appellate or second-level review.

Sixth, not all decisions in which an international court abstains from deciding a case will be an instance of avoidance. International procedural law is *relatively* – not absolutely – indeterminate. There will be many instances where a decision declining jurisdiction over a case or declaring a claim inadmissible will be the result of the straightforward application of black-letter law and entirely unrelated to any avoidance concerns. In my view, for a jurisdictional decision to constitute an instance of avoidance requires a plausible belief that the underlying – albeit unarticulated – motivation for that decision was the international court's preference for abstaining from deciding the merits of the dispute.

It is hard, if not impossible, to systematise and create a list of the specific issues or concerns that may lead an international court to rely on an avoidance technique to abstain from deciding a dispute on the merits. Ultimately, I argue that this is a prudential issue, which will depend on each court's judgment and wisdom. Without being exhaustive, those issues may include: the subject matter of the dispute, particularly when it involves 'mega-political' issues of particular public salience and political sensitivity (e.g., issues involving essential security interests or the use of force); concerns about the potential backlash that a decision may generate, including when it could seriously jeopardise the authority and legitimacy of an international court or even threaten its very existence; or when there is a high likelihood that a decision will be ineffective or will be unenforceable. Again, these are just meant to be examples.

Seventh, sometimes the use of implied avoidance techniques may be normatively justified. This justification is contingent on the particular circumstances of the case, including what the likely consequences of a decision would be, both for the particular dispute *and* for the international court in question. There are situations where abstention may be the option that contributes the most to minimum order. This could be for multiple reasons, including because the dispute could be best addressed by other means, such as diplomatic or political ones, because an eventual judgment will contribute to further inflame tensions rather than leading to the peaceful settlement of a dispute, or because a judgment on the merits will probably involve significant backlash and may threaten the authority, legitimacy or even existence of an international court.

Having said that, in my view, the fact that avoidance techniques involve international courts relying on the relative indeterminacy of international procedural law does not, in itself, mean that it is normatively objectionable. As explained above, some rules of international procedural law are relatively indeterminate – and that provides international courts with some flexibility in their application.

Eighth, accepting that avoidance takes place, and that it may be normatively justified, is linked with accepting that there are limits to the international judicial function. Although there has been an increase in the judicialisation of international affairs, it has been neither uniform nor particularly solid. Just look at the recent, significant instances of backlash against international courts. Politically salient and sensitive issues – including 'mega political' issues – are making their way more regularly to the dockets of international courts. Yet this has not necessarily occurred in tandem with the institutional strengthening of international courts. They are dealing with ever-more complicated and sensitive issues without always having developed the necessary clout to do so properly. This means that international courts may lack both the authority and the legitimacy to decide some of those issues. Even when they do, their judgments may not always be effective; they may lack teeth or be unenforceable.

This book has discussed pathological judicial romantics, who consider that international courts have quasi-magical qualities that will allow them – via judgment – to solve momentous, sometimes intractable, international disputes. The world is facing very serious challenges. International cooperation has a key role to play in addressing them. In fact, for many of those problems, it will be indispensable. Negotiations are hard. Diplomacy is hard. Solving hard problems is, well, hard. International adjudication is an important mechanism for the peaceful settlement of disputes and may have a role to play in arriving at those solutions, particularly when viewed transnationally and considering the effects that international judgments may have domestically and on different compliance constituencies. In all likelihood, international courts will not be the protagonists of those solutions. Critically, given the difficulties in finding political solutions, international adjudication runs the risk of being seen as a hack or cheat code to go around those difficulties. There is, after all, the temptation of trying to get through litigation what one failed to win through negotiation. In any event, it is potentially hubristic to consider that a judgment by an international court – notwithstanding how learned its judges and how benign their intentions – will be capable of solving intractable problems like climate change or nuclear disarmament. To be clear: that is not meant in any way to denigrate the international judiciary. A hammer is a great tool – but it's not very useful for painting your walls.

In sum, avoidance techniques have arguably been, and may continue to be, a useful instrument in the international judicial repertoire. They may allow international courts to occasionally exercise their prudential judgment to select the cases and issues they decide, potentially to curb the excesses of judicialisation. This may allow them to preserve their authority and legitimacy and direct disputes to the best channel for their solution. Courts are not the be-all-and-end-all of international law. Life is not, after all, the Jessup moot. And, although it is not the most aesthetically attractive proposition, sometimes the best decision will be *not* to decide.

Sometimes, international courts need to take Alexander Bickel's advice and exercise their passive virtues. But only sometimes.

Bibliography

—— 'In Memoriam: Mr Auguste Beernaert' (1913) 7 *American Journal of International Law* 371, 373–74.

—— 'The Northern Cameroons Case' (1964) *Duke Law Journal* 550.

Abbott KW and others, 'The Concept of Legalization' (2000) 54 *International Organization* 401.

Abebe D and Ginsburg T 'The Dejudicialization of International Politics?' (2019) 63 *International Studies Quarterly* 521.

Abi-Saab G, *Les exceptions préliminaires dans la procédure de la Cour internationale* (1967).

Acemoglu D, Johnson S and Robinson J, 'Institutions as the Fundamental Cause of Long-Run Growth' in P Aghion and SN Durlauf (eds), *Handbook of Economic Growth* (Amsterdam, Elsevier, 2005).

Akehurst M, 'Jurisdiction in International Law' (1972–1973) 46 *British Yearbook of International Law* 145.

Akhtar A, 'Act of State, State Immunity and Judicial Review in Public International Law' (2016) 7(3) *Transnational Legal Theory* 354.

Alderton M, 'The Act of State Doctrine: Questions of Validity and Abstention from Underhill to Habib' (2011) 12 *Melbourne Journal of International Law* 1.

Alexander L, 'What Are Principles, And Do They Exist?' (2013) 33 *Institute for Law and Philosophy.*

Alexy R, 'Constitutional Rights and Proportionality' (2014) 22 *Revus: Journal for Constitutional Theory and Philosophy of Law* 51.

Alford RP, 'The Proliferation of International Courts and Tribunals: International Adjudication in Ascendance' (2000) 94 *Proceedings of the ASIL Annual Meeting* 160.

Allan TRS, *Law Liberty and Justice* (Oxford, Clarendon Press, 1994).

Allee TL and Huth PK, 'Legitimizing Dispute Settlement: International Legal Rulings as Domestic Political Cover' (2006) 100 *American Political Science Review* 219.

—— 'The Pursuit of Legal Settlements to Territorial Disputes' (2006) 23 *Conflict Management and Peace Science* 285.

Allen A, Costelloe D, Fitzmaurice M, Gragl P, Guntrip E, 'Introduction' in S Allen, D Costelloe, M Fitzmaurice, P Gragl and E Guntrip (eds), *The Oxford Handbook of Jurisdiction in International Law* (Oxford, Oxford University Press 2019).

Allen RJ and Pardo MS, 'Relative Plausibility and Its Critics' (2019) 23 *International Journal of Evidence & Proof* 5.

Alter K, *Establishing the Supremacy of European Law: The Making of an International Rule of Law in Europe,* (Oxford, Oxford University Press, 2003).

——*The European Court's Political Power: Selected Essays* (Oxford, Oxford University Press, 2009).

——*The New Terrain of International Law* (New Jersey, Princeton University Press, 2014).

——'Critical Junctures and the Future International Courts in a Post-Liberal World Order' (2018) 140 *iCourts Working Paper Series* 30.

——and Madsen MR, 'Beyond Backlash: The Consequences of Adjudicating Mega-Politics' (2022) 84 *Law and Contemporary Problems* 219.

—— and Zürn M, 'Conceptualising Backlash Politics: Introduction to a Special Issue on Backlash Politics in Comparison' (2020) 22 *British Journal of Politics and International Relations* 563, 576–77.

—— Gathii JT and Helfer LR, 'Backlash against International Courts in West, East and Southern Africa: Causes and Consequences' (2016) 27 *European Journal of International Law* 293.

——Hafner-Burton E and Helfer L, 'Theorizing the Judicialization of International Relations' (2019) 63 *International Studies Quarterly* 449.
——Helfer L and Madsen MR, 'How Context Shapes the Authority of International Courts' (2016) 79 *Law & Contemporary Problems* 1.
——Helfer L and Madsen MR, 'International Court Authority in a Complex World' in K Alter, L Helfer and MR Madsen, *International Court Authority* (Oxford, Oxford University Press, 2018).
—— Romano CPR and Shany Y, 'Mapping International Courts and Tribunals, the Issues and Players' in K Alter, C Romano and Y Shany (eds), *The Oxford Handbook of International Adjudication* (Oxford, Oxford University Press, 2014).
Altman A, 'Legal Realism, Critical Legal Studies, and Dworkin' (1986) 15 *Philosophy & Public Affairs* 205.
Alvarez JE, 'Global Judicialization Revisited' (2015) 109 *American Journal of International Law* 677.
Alvarez-Jiménez A, 'The WTO AB Report on Mexico – Soft Drinks, and the Limits of the WTO Dispute Settlement System' (2006) 33 *Legal Issues of Economic Integration.*
Alvarez Zarate JM, 'Legitimacy Concerns of the Proposed Multilateral Investment Court: Is Democracy Possible?' (2018) 59 *Boston College Law Review* 2765.
Alves das Chagas C, *Judicial Avoidance: Balancing Competences in Constitutional Adjudication* (Oxford, Hart, 2023).
Ama O (ed), *International Investment Law Reform: Contemporary Issues and Solutions* (Abingdon, Routledge, 2025).
Amirfar C and Lawry White M, 'The Paris Agreement's Conciliation Annex: If Not Now, Then When?' (2021), *ASIL Insights*, 25(17).
Andenas M and Weatherall T, 'International Court of Justice: Questions relating to the Obligation to Extradite or Prosecute (Belgium v Senegal), Judgment of 20 July 2012' (2013) 62 *International and Comparative Law Quarterly* 753.
Anghie A, 'The Heart of My Home: Colonialism, Environmental Damage, and the Nauru Case' (1993) 34 *Harvard International Law Journal* 445.
Arai-Takahashi Y, *The Margin of Appreciation Doctrine and the Principle of Proportionality in the Jurisprudence of the European Court of Human Rights* (Antwerp, Intersentia, 2002).
Arnardóttir OM, 'Organised Retreat? The Move from "Substantive" to "Procedural" Review in the ECtHR's Case Law on the Margin of Appreciation' (2015) 4 *European Society of International Law Conference Paper Series.*
Arsanjani MH and Reisman WM, 'Babel and BITs: Divergence Analysis and Authentication in the Unusual Decision of *Kiliç v Turkmenistan*' in D Caron, S Schill, A Cohen Smuty and E Triantafilou (eds), *Practising Virtue: Inside International Arbitration* (Oxford, Oxford University Press, 2015) 407.
Asmus RD, *A Little War That Shook the World: Georgia, Russia, and the Future of the West* (New York, Palgrave Macmillan, 2010).
Atiyah PS and Summers RS, *Form and Substance in Anglo-American Law: A Comparative Study in Legal Reasoning, Legal Theory and Legal Institutions* (Oxford, Clarendon Press, 1987).
Austin J, *The Province of Jurisprudence Determined* (Cambridge, Cambridge University Press, 1995).
Baaij CJW, 'EU Translation and the Burden of Legal Knowledge' in S Šarčević (ed), *Language and Culture in EU Law* (Abingdon, Routledge, 2015).
Baer G, *Test Case: Italy, Ethiopia, and the League of Nations* (Stanford, Hoover Institution Press, 1976).
Bagley PJ, 'On the Practice of Esotericism' (1992) 53 *Journal of the History of Ideas* 231.
Balch TW, *Legal and Political Questions between Nations* (Philadelphia, Allen, Lane and Scott, 1924).
Barak A, *The Judge in a Democracy* (Princeton, Princeton University Press, 2008).

——'Proportionality (2)' in M Rosenfeld and A Sajó (eds), *The Oxford Handbook of Comparative Constitutional Law* (Oxford, Oxford University Press, 2012).
Barber N, Ekins R and Yowell P (eds), *Lord Sumption and the Limits of the Law* (Oxford, Hart, 2018).
Barkow RE, 'More Supreme than Court? The Fall of the Political Question Doctrine and the Rise of Judicial Supremacy' (2002) 102 *Columbia Law Review* 237.
Bartels L and Paddeu F (eds), *Exceptions in International Law* (Oxford, Oxford University Press, 2020).
Barro R, 'Democracy and the Rule of Law' in B Bueno de Mesquita and H Root (eds), *Governing for Prosperity* (New Haven CT, Yale University Press, 2000).
Basdevant J, Jeze G and Politis N, 'Les principes juridiques sur la competence des jurisdictions internationales et, en particulier, des Tribunaux Arbitraux Mixtes organises par les Traites de paix de Versailles, de Saint-Germain, de Trianon (1927) 44 *Revue du Droit Public et de las science politique en France et a l'etranger* 45.
Beales ACF, *The History of Peace: A Short Account of the Organized Movements for International Peace* (New York, L. MacVeagh, Dial Press, 1931).
Beaumont B, Brodlija F, Ashdown R and Terrien A, *The Future of Investor-State Dispute Settlement: Reforming Law, Practice and Perspectives for a Fast-Changing World* (Alphen aan den Rijn, Wolters Kluwer, 2024).
Becker MA, 'The Dispute that Wasn't There: Judgments in the Nuclear Disarmament Cases at the International Court of Justice' (2017) 6(1) *Cambridge Journal of International Law* 4.
Bederman DJ and Hilbert KR, 'Lance Paul Larsen v The Hawaiian Kingdom' (2001) 95 *American Journal of International Law* 927.
Beneš E, 'The League of Nations: Successes and Failures' (1932–1933) 11 *Foreign Affairs* 66.
Benvenisti E, 'Margin of Appreciation, Consensus and Universal Standards' (1998–1999) 31 *New York University Journal of International Law and Politics* 843.
Benzing M, 'Midwifing a New State: The United Nations in East Timor' (2005) 9 *Max Planck Yearbook of United Nations Law* 295.
Berge TL, 'Dispute by Design? Legalization, Backlash, and the Drafting of Investment Agreements' (2020) 64 *International Studies Quarterly* 919.
Berlia G, *Jurisprudence des tribunaux internationaux en ce qui concerne leur compétence* (Paris, Recueil Sirey, 1955).
Berridge GR and James A, 'Demarche' in GR Berridge and A James, *A Dictionary of Diplomacy* 2nd edn (Basingstoke, Palgrave Macmillan, 2003).
Bertelsen S, 'A Margin for the Margin of Appreciation: Deference in the Inter-American Court of Human Rights' (2021) 19 *International Journal of Constitutional Law* 887.
Besson S, 'The Erga Omnes Effect of Judgments of the European Court of Human Rights – What's in a Name?' in S Besson (ed), *The European Court of Human Rights After Protocol 14* (Schulthess 2011).
—— 'The Extraterritoriality of the European Convention on Human Rights: Why Human Rights Depend on Jurisdiction and What Jurisdiction Amounts to' (2012) 25 *Leiden Journal of International Law* 857.
Bethlehem D, 'The Secret Life of International Law' (2012) 1 *Cambridge Journal of International and Comparative Law* 23.
Bianchi A, 'Textual Interpretation and (international) law reading: the myth of (in)determinacy and the genealogy of meaning' in P Bekker, R Dolzer and M Waibel (eds) *Making Transnational Law Work in the Global Economy* (Cambridge, Cambridge University Press, 2010) 54.
—— 'Choice and (the Awareness of) its Consequences: The ICJ's "Structural Bias" Strikes Again in the *Marshall Islands* Case' (2017) 111 *AJIL Unbound* 81.
Bickel AM, 'Foreword: The Passive Virtues' (1961) 75 *Harvard Law Review* 40.
—— *The Least Dangerous Branch: The Supreme Court at the Bar of Politics* 2nd edn (New Haven CT, Yale University Press, 1986).

Biermann C, 'The Franco-Swiss Free Zones' (1923) 13 *Geographical Review* 368.
Binder C, 'The Prohibition of Amnesties by the Inter-American Court of Human Rights' (2011) 12 *German Law Journal* 1203.
—— 'Necessity Exceptions, the Argentine Crisis and Legitimacy Concerns: Or the Benefits of a Public International Law Approach to Investment Arbitration' in T Treves, F Seatzu and S Trevisanut, *Foreign Investment, International Law and Common Concerns* (Abingdon, Taylor & Francis, 2013).
Bingham T, 'The Alabama Claims Arbitration' (2005) 54 *International and Comparative Law Quarterly* 1.
Bishop RD and Marchili SM, *Annulment Under the ICSID Convention* (Oxford, Oxford University Press, 2012).
Blasi V, 'The Role of Strategic Reasoning in Constitutional Interpretation: In Defense of the Pathological Perspective' (1986) *Duke Law Journal* 696.
Bobbitt P, 'Constitutional Fate', (1980) 58(4) *Texas Law Review,* 719.
—— *Constitutional Fate: Theory of the Constitution* (New York, Oxford University Press, 1984).
Bogdandy Av and Venzke I, *In Whose Name? A Public Law Theory of International Adjudication* (Oxford, Oxford University Press, 2014).
Boisson de Chazournes L, 'The Principle of Compétence de la Compétence in International Adjudication and its Role in an Era of Multiplication of Courts and Tribunals' in RD Sloane, Arsanjani, MH, Cogan, D and Sloane, R (eds), *Looking to the Future: Essays in Honor of W Michael Reisman* (Leiden, Brill, 2010).
Bork RH, 'The Limits of "International Law"' (1989) 3 *The National Interest.*
Bowett D, 'Jurisdiction: Changing Patterns of Authority over Activities and Resources' (1983) 53 *British Yearbook of International Law* 1.
Boyle J, 'The Politics of Reason: Critical Legal Theory and Local Social Thought,' (1985) 133 *University of Pennsylvania Law Review* 685.
Bradley C and Posner E, 'The Real Political Question Doctrine' (2023) 75 *Stanford Law Review* 1031.
Braveboy-Wagner JA, 'Collective Diplomacy of the Global South' in BJC McKercher (ed), *Routledge Handbook of Diplomacy and Statecraft* (Abingdon, Routledge, 2012).
Brierly JL, 'The General Act of Geneva, 1928' (1930) 11 *British Yearbook of International Law* 119.
Brown C, 'Review Essay: The Proliferation of International Courts and Tribunals: Finding Your Way Through the Maze' (2002) 3(2) *Melbourne Journal of International Law.*
—— 'The Inherent Powers of International Courts and Tribunals' (2006) 76 *British Yearbook of International Law* 195.
—— *A Common Law of International Adjudication* (Oxford, Oxford University Press, 2007).
Brown Scott J, *Reports to the Hague Conferences of 1899 and 1907* (Oxford, Clarendon Press, 1917).
——*The Project Relative to a Court of Arbitral justice* (Washington, The Endowment,1920).
Brownlie I, 'The Justiciability of Disputes and Issues in International Relations' (1967) 42 *British Yearbook of International Law* 123.
—— *'The Reality and Efficacy of International Law'* (1982) 52 *British Yearbook of International Law* 1.
—— 'The Peaceful Settlement of International Disputes' (2009) 8 *Chinese Journal of International Law* 267.
Broz JL, Frieden J and Weymouth S, 'Populism in Place: The Economic Geography of the Globalization Backlash' (2021) 75 *International Organization* 464.
Buergenthal T, 'Proliferation of International Courts and Tribunals: Is It Good or Bad?' (2001) 14 *Leiden Journal of International Law* 267.
Bungenberg M and Reinisch A, *From Bilateral Arbitral Tribunals and Investment Courts to a Multilateral Investment Court: Options Regarding the Institutionalization of Investor-State Dispute Settlement* (Springer, 2020).

Burke-White W, 'Proactive Complementarity: The International Criminal Court and National Courts in the Rome System of International Justice' (2008) 49 *Harvard International Law Journal* 53.
Buxbaum RM, 'A Legal History of International Reparations' (2005) 23 *Berkeley Journal of International Law* 314.
Byers M, *Custom, Power and the Power of Rules: International Relations and Customary International Law* (Cambridge, Cambridge University Press, 1999).
——*The Role of Law in International Politics* (Oxford, Oxford University Press, 2000).
Calvo C, *Le Droit international théorique et pratique: précédé d'un exposé historique des progrès de La science du droit des gens,* Vol. *3* (Paris, HardPress 2010).
Cançado Trindade AA, *International Law for Humankind: Towards a New Jus Gentium* (Leiden, Martinus Nijhoff, 2010).
Caron DD, 'War and International Adjudication: Reflections on the 1899 Peace Conference' (2000) 94 *American Journal of International Law* 4.
——and Shirlow E, 'Dissecting Backlash: The Unarticulated Causes of Backlash and its Unintended Consequences' in G Ulfstein and A Føllesdal (eds), *The Judicialization of International Law: A Mixed Blessing?* (Oxford, Oxford University Press, 2018).
Casas M, 'Nationalities of Convenience, Personal Jurisdiction, and Access to Investor-State Dispute Settlement' (2016) 49 *NYU Journal of International Law and Politics.*
——'Functional Justiciability and the Existence of a Dispute: A Means of Jurisdictional Avoidance?' (2019) 10 *Journal of International Dispute Settlement* 599.
——'Dejudicialization and Non-Judicialization in International Law' (2025) *Yale Journal of International Law* 107.
—— 'The Enforcement of Intra-EU Arbitral Awards: Some Additional Policy Considerations' (2025) 42 *Journal of International Arbitration* 77.
Cassel D, 'Does International Human Rights Law Make a Difference?' (2001) 2 *Chicago Journal of International Law* 121.
Cassese A, *Realizing Utopia: The Future of International Law* (Oxford, Oxford University Press, 2012).
Cavallaro J and Brewer SE, 'Reevaluating Regional Human Rights Litigation in the Twenty-First Century: The Case of the Inter-American Court' (2008) 102 *American Journal of International Law* 768.
Cetra R and Nascimento J, 'Counting Coins: Funding the Inter-American Human Rights System', in Due Process of Law Foundation (ed), *The Inter-American Human Rights System: Changing Times, Ongoing Challenges* (Dejusticia, Colombia, 2016) 53.
Chambers J II (ed), *The Eagle and the Dove: The American Peace Movement and United States Foreign Policy 1900–1922* (New York, Syracuse University Press, 1991).
Charlesworth H, 'International Law: A Discipline of Crisis' (2002) 65 *Modern Law Review* 377.
Charney JI, 'Disputes Implicating the Institutional Credibility of the Court: Problems of Non-Appearance, Non-Participation, and Non-Performance' in LF Damrosch (ed), *The International Court of Justice at a Crossroads* (Dobbs Ferry, NY, Transnational Publishers, 1987) 288.
—— 'Anticipatory Humanitarian Intervention in Kosovo' (1999) 93 *American Journal of International Law* 834.
Charnovitz S 'WTO Appellate Body Roundtable' (2005) 99 *Proceedings of the Annual Meeting of the American Society of International Law* 175–87.
Chatfield C, *The American Peace Movement: Ideals and Activism* (New York, Twayne, 1992).
Chayes A and Chayes AH, 'On Compliance' (1993) 47 *International Organization* 175.
Chayes A, Ehrlich T and Lowenfeld AF, *International Legal Process* (Boston, Little Brown, 1968).
Chawla S, 'Shaping East Timor: A Dimension of United Nations Peacekeeping' (2001) 24 *Strategic Analysis* 2291.
Cheng B, *General Principles of Law: As Applied by International Courts and Tribunals* (Cambridge, Cambridge University Press, 2006).

Cheng TH, *When International Law Works* (New York, Oxford University Press, 2012).
Chiam M, 'Public Invocation of International Law and Legacies of the Iraq War' (2021) 9 *London Review of International Law L* 271.
Chiassoni P, 'Legal Interpretation without Truth' (2016) 29 *Revus – Journal for Constitutional Theory and Philosophy of Law* 93.
Chinkin C, 'The East Timor Case (Portugal v Australia)' (1996) 45 *International and Comparative Law Quarterly* 712.
—— 'Kosovo: A "Good" or "Bad" War?' (1999) 93 *American Journal of International Law* 841.
Clark G and Sohn LB, *World Peace Through World Law: Two Alternative Plans,* 3rd edn (Cambridge MA, Harvard University Press, 1966).
Clark RS, 'The "Decolonization" of East Timor and the United Nations Norms on Self-Determination and Aggression' (1980) 7 *Yale Journal of International Law* 2.
Cohen M, 'Sincerity and Reason-Giving: When May Legal Decisions Makers Lie' (2009) 59 *De Paul Law Review* 1091.
—— 'Form, Formula and Constitutional Ethos: The Political Question/Justiciability Doctrine in Three Common Law Systems' (2011) 59 *American Journal of Comparative Law* 675.
——'When Judges Have Reasons Not to Give Reasons: A Comparative Law Approach' (2015) 72 *Washington and Lee Law Review* 483.
Cohrs PO, 'The First "Real" Peace Settlements after the First World War: Britain, the United States and the Accords of London and Locarno, 1923–1925' (2003) 12 *Contemporary European History* 1.
Colangelo AJ, 'Spatial Legality' (2012–2013) 107 *Northwestern University Law Review* 69, 106.
Coleman JL, 'Truth and Objectivity in Law' (1995) 1 *Legal Theory* 33.
Comanducci P, 'Principios jurídicos e indeterminación del derecho' (1998) 21(II) *Doxa: Cuadernos de Filosofía del Derecho* 89.
Contesse J, 'Resisting the Inter-American Human Rights System' (2019) 44 *Yale Journal of International Law* 179.
—— 'Judicial Interactions and Human Rights Contestations in Latin America' (2021) 12 *Journal of International Dispute Settlement* 271.
——'The Rule of Advice in International Human Rights Law' (2021) 115 *American Journal of International Law* 367.
Cook A, *The Alabama Claims* (Syracuse, NY, Cornell University Press, 1975).
Cope KL and Versteeg M, 'Review Essay: The Interpretation of International Law by Domestic Courts' (2017) 111 *American Journal of International Law* 538.
Cory HM, *Compulsory Arbitration of International Disputes* (New York, Columbia University Press, 1932).
Costelloe D, *Legal Consequences of Peremptory Norms* (Cambridge, Cambridge University Press, 2017).
Curti ME, *The American Peace Crusade 1815–1860* (Durham, NC, Duke University Press, 1929).
Crawford J, *Brownlie's Principles of Public International Law,* 8th edn (Oxford, Oxford University Press, 2012).
——'"Dreamers of the Day": Australia and the International Court of Justice' (2013) 14 *Melbourne Journal of International Law* 520.
——*Chance, Order, Change: The Course of International Law* (Leiden, Brill, 2014).
——'Military and Paramilitary Activities in and against Nicaragua (Nicaragua v United States of America)' in A Peters (ed), *Max Planck Encyclopaedia of Public International Law.*
Creamer CD, 'Between the Letter of the Law and the Demands of Politics: The Judicial Balancing of Trade Authority within the WTO' (Working Paper, 2015).
Cross FB, 'Political Science and the New Legal Realism: A Case of Unfortunate Interdisciplinary Ignorance' (1997) 92 *Northwestern University Law Review* 251.
Dagan H, 'The Realist Conception of Law' (2007) 57 *University of Toronto Law Journal* 607.
Damrosch LF, *Enforcing International Law through Non-Forcible Measures* (Martinus Nijhoff 1998).

d'Amato A, 'Is International Law Really "Law"?' (1985) 79 *Northwestern University Law Review* 1293.
d'Argent P, 'The Monetary Gold Principle: A Matter of Submissions' (2021) 115 *AJIL Unbound* 149.
d'Aspremont J, *The Epistemology of the Secret: International Law as Revelation* (Cambridge, Cambridge University Press, 2025).
Davey WJ, 'Has the WTO Dispute Settlement System Exceeded Its Authority? A Consideration of Deference Shown by the System to Member Government Decisions and its Use of Issue-Avoidance Techniques' (2001) 4 *Journal of International Economic Law* 79.
——and Sapir A, 'The Soft Drinks Case: The WTO and Regional Agreements' (2009) 8 *World Trade Review* 5.
Davis C, *Why Adjudicate?* (Princeton NJ, Princeton University Press, 2012).
Davis KC, *Discretionary Justice: A Preliminary Inquiry* (Baton Rouge, Louisiana State University Press, 1969).
——and Blodgett Bermeo S, 'Who Files? Developing Country Participation in GATT/WTO Adjudication' (2009) 71 *Journal of Politics* 1033.
De Brabandere E, *Investment Treaty Arbitration as Public International Law* (Cambridge, Cambridge University Press, 2014).
Delaney E, *'Analyzing Avoidance: Judicial Strategy in Comparative Perspective'* (2016) 66 *Duke Law Journal* 1.
Demetriades A, 'Reconceptualising Extraterritoriality under the ECHR as Concurrent Responsibility' (2020) 12 *European Journal of Legal Studies* 157.
Demirkol B, 'Interpretation of the Dispute Settlement Clause in Turkish Investment Treaties with Turkic States' (2016) 32 *Arbitration International* 29-43.
Den Heijer M, 'Procedural Aspects of Shared Responsibility in the European Court of Human Rights' (2013) 4 *Journal of International Dispute Settlement* 361.
Derrig R, *The New Haven School: American International Law* (Oxford, Oxford University Press, 2025).
Deutsch JG, 'Neutrality, Legitimacy, and the Supreme Court: Some Intersections between Law and Political Science' (1967) 20 *Stanford Law Review* 169.
Dickinson A, 'Acts of State and the Frontiers of International Law' (2018) 14 *Journal of Private International Law* 1.
Dimitropoulos G, 'Investor–State Dispute Settlement Reform and Theory of Institutional Design' (2018) 9 *Journal of International Dispute Settlement* 535.
—— 'The Conditions for Reform: a Typology of "Backlash" and Lessons for Reform in International Investment Law and Arbitration' (2020) 18 *The Law and Practice of International Courts and Tribunals* 416.
Dixon R, 'Creating Dialogue About Socioeconomic Rights: Strong-Form Versus Weak-Form Judicial Review' (2007) 5 *International Journal of Constitutional Law* 391.
Djukic D, *The Right to Appeal in International Criminal Law* (Leiden, Brill, 2019).
Dolunay A and Kasap F, 'Still Unrecognized State: Self-Determination and the "Status of the TRNC" Court Decisions' (2020) 13 *Journal of Politics and Law* 1.
Donaldson V, 'The Appellate Body: Institutional and Procedural Aspects' in PFJ Macrory, AE Appleton and MG Plummer (eds), *The World Trade Organization: Legal, Economic and Political Analysis* vol 1 (New York, Springer, 2005) 1277.
Douglas Z, 'The MFN Clause in Investment Arbitration: Treaty Interpretation Off the Rails' (2011) 2 *Journal of International Dispute Settlement* 97.
Dubin MD, 'Elihu Root and the Advocacy of a League of Nations, 1914–1917' (1966) 19 *Western Political Quarterly* 439.
Dugard J, 'The Nuclear Tests Cases and the South West Africa Cases: Some Realism About the International Judicial Decision' (1976) 16 *Virginia Journal of International Law* 463.
——'1966 and All That, the South West Africa Judgment Revisited in the East Timor Case' (1996) 8 *African Journal of International and Comparative Law* 549.

Dumberry P, 'The Hawaiian Kingdom Arbitration Case and the Unsettled Question of the Hawaiian Kingdom's Claim to Continuity as an Independent State under International Law' (2002) 1 *Chinese Journal of International Law* 655.
Dunlap CJ, 'Lawfare Today: A Perspective' (2008) 3 *Yale Journal of International Affairs* 146.
——'Does Lawfare Need an Apologia?' (2010) 43 *Case Western Reserve Journal of International Law* 121.
Dupont C, Schultz T, Yackee J, 'Investment Arbitration and Political Systems Theory' in T Schultz and F Ortino (eds), *Oxford Handbook of International Arbitration* (Oxford, Oxford University Press, 2019).
Durand G, 'L'acte de gouvernement, l'exemple afghan' (2022) *Actualité juridique Collectivités territoriales* 111.
Dworkin R, 'The Model of Rules' (1967) 35 *University of Chicago Law Review* 14.
—— 'No Right Answer' (1978) 53 *NYU Law Review* 12.
——*A Matter of Principle* (Cambridge MA, Harvard University Press, 1985).
—— 'On Gaps in the Law' in P Amselek and N MacCormick (eds), *Controversies about Law's Ontology* (Edinburgh, Edinburgh University Press, 1991).
——'The Supreme Court Phalanx' *The New York Review of Books* (27 September 2007).
Dzehtsiarou K, 'The Judgement of Solomon that Went Wrong: Georgia v Russia (II) by the European Court of Human Rights' (Völkerrechtsblog, 26 January 2021).
Ehrlich I and Posner RA, 'An Economic Analysis of Legal Rulemaking' (1974) 3 *Journal of Legal Studies* 257.
Ekins R and Gee G, 'Putting Judicial Power in its Place' (2017) 36 *University of Queensland Law Journal* 375–398.
Ellis J, 'General Principles and Comparative Law' (2011) 22 *European Journal of International Law* 949.
Enabulele AO, 'Sailing against the Tide: Exhaustion of Domestic Remedies and the ECOWAS Community Court of Justice' (2012) 56 *Journal of African Law* 268.
Endicott TAO, *Vagueness in Law* (Oxford, Oxford University Press, 2000).
——'The Reason of the Law' (2003) 48 *American Journal of Jurisprudence* 83.
European Court of Human Rights, Registry, *Practical Guide on Admissibility Criteria*, Section II 'Grounds for Inadmissibility Relating to the Court's Jurisdiction', 64, last updated 28 February 2025.
C Evans (2022) *Assessing the Theoretical and Practical Impact of the Treaty on the Prohibition of Nuclear Weapons as a Disarmament Law Instrument* (PhD thesis, University of Reading).
Falk RA, 'Kosovo, World Order, and the Future of International Law' (1999) 93 *American Journal of International Law* 847.
Fallon R, 'The Linkage between Justiciability and Remedies and Their Connections to Substantive Rights' (2006) 92 *Virginia Law Review* 633.
—— 'A Theory of Judicial Candor' (2017) 117 *Columbia Law Review* 2265.
Farber DA, 'Legal Pragmatism and the Constitution' (1988) *Minnesota Law Review* 1343.
——'Toward a New Legal Realism' (2001) 68 *University of Chicago Law Review* 279.
Feller AH, 'Some Observations on the Calvo Clause' (1933) 27 *American Journal of International Law* 461.
——*The Mexican Claims Commissions: 1923–34* (New York, Macmillan, 1935).
Fenwick GG, 'The "Failure" of the League of Nations' (1936) 30 *American Journal of International Law* 506.
Fitzmaurice G, 'The Law and Procedure of the International Court of Justice, 1951–54: Questions of Jurisdiction, Competence and Procedure' (1958) 34 *British Yearbook of International Law* 1.
——'Vae Victis, or Woe to the Negotiators!: Your Treaty, or Our "Interpretation" of It?' (1971) 65 *American Journal of International Law* 358.
Flemes D, Nolte D and Wehner L, 'Una comunidad de seguridad regional en formación: la unasur y su Consejo de Defensa/A regional security community in the making: Unasur and its South American Defence Council (2011) 44 *Estudios Internacionales* 105.

Fouchard F, *The Standard of Review before the International Court of Justice: Between Principle and Pragmatism* (Oxford, Hart, 2024).
Fontana D,'Docket Control and the Success of Constitutional Courts', in T Ginsburg and R Dixon (eds), *Comparative Constitutional Law* (Cheltenham, Edward Elgar, 2011) 624.
Fontanelli F, *Jurisdiction and Admissibility in Investment Arbitration: The Practice and the Theory* (Leiden, Brill, 2018).
——'Once Burned, Twice Shy: The Use of Compromissory Clauses before the International Court of Justice and Their Declining Popularity in New Treaties' (2021) 104 *Rivista di Diritto Internazionale* 7.
—— and Tanzi A, 'Jurisdiction and Admissibility in Investment Arbitration: A View from the Bridge at the Practice' (2017) 16(1) *Law and Practice of International Courts and Tribunals* 3–20.
Franck T, *The Power of Legitimacy Among Nations* (Oxford, Oxford University Press, 1990).
Freeman AV, 'Recent Aspects of the Calvo Doctrine and the Challenge of International Law' (1946) 40 *American Journal of International Law* 121.
Friedman B, 'Dialogue and Judicial Review' (1992–1993) *Michigan Law Review* 81 577.
——'The Wages of Stealth Overruling (With Particular Attention to *Miranda v Arizona*)' (2010) 99 *Georgetown Law Journal* 1.
Friedman E, 'Evasion Strategies in International Documents: When "Constructive Ambiguity" Leads to Oppositional Interpretation' (2017) 14(4) *Critical Discourse Studies* 385.
Frishman O and Benvenisti E, 'National Courts and Interpretative Approaches to International Law: The Case against Convergence' in HP Aust and G Nolte (eds), *The Interpretation of International Law by Domestic Courts: Uniformity, Diversity, Convergence* (Oxford, Oxford University Press, 2016) 317.
Fuller L, *The Morality of Law* 2nd edn (New Haven CT, Yale University Press, 1969).
Gaillard E, 'Establishing Jurisdiction Through a Most-Favoured-Nation Clause' (2005) 233 *New York Law Journal* 105.
Gallus N, *The Temporal Jurisdiction of International Tribunals* (Oxford, Oxford University Press, 2017).
Gal-Or N, 'The Concept of Appeal in International Dispute Settlement' (2008) 19 *European Journal of International Law* 43.
Garcia de Enterria E, *Democracia, jueces y control de la administración*, 5th edn (Navarra, Civitas, 2000) 171.
Gattini A, 'Free Zones of Upper Savoy and the District of Gex' in A Peters (ed) *Max Planck Encyclopaedia of Public International Law*.
George BJ, 'Extraterritorial Application of Penal Legislation' (1966) 64 *Michigan Law Review* 609.
Gerards J and Brems E (eds), *Procedural Review in European Fundamental Rights Cases* (Cambridge, Cambridge University Press, 2017).
Gillard EC, 'International Humanitarian Law and Extraterritorial State Conduct' in F Coomans and MT Kamminga (eds), *Extraterritorial Application of Human Rights Treaties* (Antwerp, Intersentia, 2004).
Giuffré M, 'A Functional-impact Model of Jurisdiction: Extraterritoriality Before the European Court of Human Rights' (2021) 82 *Questions of International Law* 53.
Glasgow G, *From Dawes to Locarno – Being a Critical Record of an Important Achievement of European Diplomacy 1924–1925* (New York, Harper & Brothers 1926).
Glennon MJ, 'The New Interventionism: The Search for a Just International Law' (1999) 78(3) *Foreign Affairs* 2.
Goldsmith J and Levinson D, 'Law for States: International Law, Constitutional Law, Public Law' (2009) 122 *Harvard Law Review* 1791.
Gordon E, 'The World Court and the Interpretation of Constitutive Treaties: Some Observations on the Development of an International Constitutional Law' (1965) 59 *American Journal of International Law* 794.

Graebner R, 'Dialogue and Divergence: The Vienna Convention on Consular Relations in German, American, and International Courts' (2011) 42 *Georgetown Journal of International Law* 605.

Grant T, 'East Timor, the UN System, and Enforcing Non-Recognition in International Law' (2000) 33 *Vanderbilt Journal of Transnational Law* 273.

Greenwood C, 'International Law and the NATO Intervention in Kosovo' (2000) 49 *International and Comparative Law Quarterly* 926.

Grimm D, 'Types of Constitutions' in M Rosenfeld and A Sajó (eds), *The Oxford Handbook of Comparative Constitutional Law* (Oxford, Oxford University Press, 2012).

Gross L, 'Limitations on the Judicial Function' (1964) 58 *American Journal of International Law* 415.

——'On the Justiciability of International Disputes' in *Essays on International Law and Organization* (Dobbs Ferry, NY, Transnational Publishers 1984).

—— 'Underutilization of the International Court of Justice' (1986) 27 *Harvard Journal of International Law* 571.

Grotto AJ, 'Monetary Gold Arbitration and Case' in A Peters (ed), *Max Planck Encyclopaedia of Public International Law.*

Guillaume G, 'Advantages and Risks of Proliferation: A Blueprint for Action' (2004) 2 *Journal of International Criminal Justice* 300.

Gunther G, 'The Subtle Vices of the "Passive Virtues"—A Comment on Principle and Expediency in Judicial Review' (1964) 64 *Columbia Law Review* 1.

Guzman AT, 'A Compliance-Based Theory of International Law' (2002) 90 *California Law Review* 1823.

—— 'The Design of International Agreements' (2005) 16 *European Journal of International Law* 579.

Hafner-Burton EM, Victor DG and Lupu Y, 'Political Science Research on International Law: The State of the Field' (2012) 106 *American Journal of International Law* 47.

Hageman ED, 'Judicial Candor and Extralegal Reasoning: Why Extralegal Reasons Require Legal Justifications (And No More)' (2015) 91 *Notre Dame Law Review* 405.

Hainsworth P and McCloskey S (eds), *The East Timor Question: The Struggle for Independence from Indonesia* (London, IB Tauris, 2012).

Hakki MM, 'Property Wars in Cyprus: the Turkish Position According to International Law' (2011) 15(6) *The International Journal of Human Rights* 847.

Haltom W and Silverstein M, 'The Scholarly Tradition Revisited: Alexander Bickel, Herbert Wechsler, and the Legitimacy of Judicial Review' (1987) 4 *Constitutional Commentary* 127

Hamilton A, 'No. 78' in C Rossiert (ed), *The Federalist Papers,* (New American Library, 1961).

Hamilton RE, 'August 2008 and Everything After: A Ten-Year Retrospective on the Russia–Georgia War' (Foreign Policy Research Institute, 22 October 2018).

Happold M, '*Banković* v Belgium and the Territorial Scope of the European Convention on Human Rights' (2003) 3 *Human Rights Law Review* 77.

Harris BV, 'Judicial Review, Justiciability and the Prerogative of Mercy' (2003) 62 *CLJ* 631.

Harris C, 'Claims with an Ulterior Purpose: Characterising Disputes Concerning the "Interpretation or Application" of a Treaty' (2019) 18(3) *The Law and Practice of International Courts and Tribunals* 279.

Hart HLA, *The Concept of Law,* 3rd edn (Oxford, Oxford University Press, 2012).

Hart HM, Sacks AM, Eskridge Jr, Wm and Frickey, P)*The Legal Process: Basic Problems in the Making and Application of Law* (St Paul MN, Foundation Press, 1994).

Hathaway O and Shapiro SJ, 'Outcasting: Enforcement in Domestic and International Law' (2011) 121 *Yale Law Journal* 252.

Hawkins D and Jacoby W, 'Partial Compliance: A Comparison of the European and Inter-American Courts of Human Rights' (2010) 6 *Journal of International Law and International Relations* 35.

Hedges RY, 'Justiciable Disputes' (1928) 22 *American Journal of International Law* 560.

Heiskanen V, 'Ménage à trois? Jurisdiction, Admissibility and Competence in Investment Treaty Arbitration' (2013) 29(1) *ICSID Review – Foreign Investment Law Journal.*

Helfer LR, 'Overlegalizing Human Rights: International Relations Theory and the Commonwealth Caribbean Backlash Against Human Rights Regimes' (2002) 102 *Columbia Law Review* 1832.
——'The Effectiveness of International Adjudicators' in CPR Romano, KJ Alter and Y Shany (eds), *The Oxford Handbook of International Adjudication* (Oxford, Oxford University Press, 2013).
——'The Benefits and Burdens of Brighton' (2012) 1(1) *ESIL Reflections*.
——and Slaughter AM, 'Toward a Theory of Effective Supranational Adjudication' (1997) 107 *Yale Law Journal* 273.
Hellman D, 'The Importance of Appearing Principled' (1995) 37 *Arizona Law Review* 1107.
Henckels C, 'Overcoming Jurisdictional Isolationism at the WTO–FTA Nexus: A Potential Approach for the WTO' (2008) 19 *European Journal of International Law* 571.
——'Indirect Expropriation and the Right to Regulate: Revisiting Proportionality Analysis and the Standard of Review in Investor-State Arbitration' (2012) 15 *Journal of International Economic Law* 223.
Henkin L, 'Is There a "Political Question" Doctrine?' (1976) 85 *Yale Law Journal* 597.
——*How Nations Behave* (New York, Columbia University Press, 1979).
Hernández GI, *The International Court of Justice and the Judicial Function* (Oxford, Oxford University Press, 2014).
—— 'The Judicialization of International Law: Reflections on the Empirical Turn' (2014) 25 *European Journal of International Law* 919.
Hessick FA, 'Cases, Controversies, and Diversity' (2015) 109 *Northwestern University Law Review*.
Highet K, 'Litigation Implications of the US Withdrawal from the Nicaragua Case' (1985) 79 *American Journal of International Law* 992.
Higgins R, 'Policy Considerations and the International Judicial Process' (1968) 17 *International and Comparative Law Quarterly* 58, 62.
—— *Problems & Process: International Law and How We Use It* (Oxford, Oxford University Press, 1994).
Hillebrecht C, *Saving the International Justice Regime* (Cambridge, Cambridge University Press,, 2021).
Hirschl R, *Towards Juristocracy* (Cambridge MA, Harvard University Press, 2004).
Holmes OW, *The Common Law* (Cambridge MA, Belknap Press, 2009).
Horwitz MJ, *The Transformation of American Law 1870–1960: The Crisis of Legal Orthodoxy* (Oxford, Oxford University Press, 1992).
Howse R, 'Reading Between the Lines: Exotericism, Esotericism, and the Philosophical Rhetoric of Leo Strauss' (1999) 32 *Philosophy and Rhetoric* 60.
——*Leo Strauss Man of Peace* (Cambridge, Cambridge University Press, 2014).
——and Teitel R, 'Beyond Compliance: Rethinking Why International Law Really Matters' (2010) 1(12) *Global Policy* 127.
Hsieh PL, 'New Investment Rulemaking in Asia: Between Regionalism and Domestication' (2023) 22 *World Trade Review* 173.
Hudson MO, 'Legal and Political Questions' (1924) 18 *Proceedings of the American Society of International Law at Its Annual Meeting* 126.
——'Present Status of the Hague Conventions of 1899 and 1907' (1931) 25 *American Journal of International Law* 114.
——'The Aftermath of the Permanent Court's Judgment in the Free Zones Case' (1934) 28 *American Journal of International Law* 322.
——'The Inter-American Treaties of Pacific Settlement' (1936–1937) 15 *Foreign Affairs* 165.
—— *The Permanent Court of International Justice: 1920–1942* (New York, The Macmillan Company, 1943).
——'The Thirty-Third Year of the World Court' (1955) 49 *American Journal of International Law* 1.
Hull W, *The Two Hague Conferences and their Contribution to International Law* (Boston MA, Ginn & Company, 1908).

Huneeus A, 'Courts Resisting Courts: Lessons from the Inter-American Court's Struggle to Enforce Human Rights' (2011) 44 *Cornell International Law Journal* 493.

—— 'Compliance with Judgments and Decisions' in CPR Romano, KJ Alter and Y Shany (eds), *The Oxford Handbook of International Adjudication* (Oxford University Press, 2013) 439.

Hunt M, 'Sovereignty's Blight: Why Contemporary Public Law Needs the Concept of "Due Deference"' in N Bamforth and P Leyland (eds), *Public Law in a Multi-Layered Constitution* (Oxford, Hart Publishing, 2003).

Huq AZ, 'The People Against the Constitution' (2018) 116 *Michigan Law Review* 1123.

Idleman SC, 'Prudential Theory of Judicial Candor' (1994–1995) 73 *Texas Law Review* 1307.

Institut de Droit International, '*Project de réglement pour la procedure arbitrale internationale'*, Session de La Haye – 1875, *Annuaire* (1877).

——'*La Classification des conflits comportant un reglement judiciare, rapport par M.M. Ph. Marshall-Brown et N. Politis', Annuaire* (1922).

—— '*L'extension de l'arbitrage obligatoire et la competence obligatoire de la Cour Permanente de Justice Internationale*', *Annuaire* (1927).

ICSID, *Background Paper on Annulment* (2024).

Issacharoff S, 'Democracy's Deficits' (2018) 85 *University of Chicago Law Review* 485.

Jackson M, 'Judicial Avoidance at the European Court of Human Rights: Institutional Authority, the Procedural Turn, and Docket Control' (2022) 20 *International Journal of Constitutional Law* 112

Jessup P, 'A Record of the Arbitration Treaties' (1928) 138 *The Annals of the American Academy of Political and Social Science* 120.

——'The Palmas Island Arbitration' (1928) 22 *American Journal of International Law* 735.

—— *Transnational Law* (New Haven CT, Yale University Press, 1956).

Jacobson J, 'The Conduct of Locarno Diplomacy' (1972) 34 *Review of Politics* 67.

Jacovides A, 'Cyprus: International Law and the Prospects for Settlement' (1984) 78 *Proceedings of the Annual Meeting (American Society of International Law)* 107.

John A, 'Inarticulate and Unconscious: Non-Justiciability before the International Court of Justice' (2021) 20 *The Law & Practice of International Courts and Tribunals* 77.

Johnson DHN, 'The Case of the Monetary Gold Removed from Rome in 1943' (1955) 4 *International and Comparative Law Quarterly* 93.

——'The Case concerning the Northern Cameroons' (1964) 13 *International and Comparative Law Quarterly* 1143.

Johnstone I and Ratner S (eds), *Talking International Law: Legal Argumentation Outside the Courtroom* (Oxford, Oxford University Press, 2021).

Juillard P, 'Calvo Doctrine/Calvo Clause' (2007) in A Peters (ed) *Max Planck Encyclopedia of Public International Law.*

Jully A, 'Propos orthodoxes sur l'acte de gouvernement' (2019) 43 *Civitas Europa* 165.

Jütersonke O, *Morgenthau, Law and Realism* (Cambridge, Cambridge University Press, 2010).

Kairys, D, 'Law and Politics' (1984) 52 *George Washington Law Review* 243.

—— 'Legal Reasoning', in D Kairys (ed), *The Politics of Law* 3rd edn (New York, Basic Books, 1998).

Kamarowsky L, De Westman S and Lacointa J, *Le Tribunal International* (Paris, G Pedone-Lauriel, 1887).

Kanargelidis J, 'New Anti-Dumping Rules Applied by Canada: The Zeroing Debate' *Mondaq Business Briefing* (7 September 2005).

Kavanagh E, 'Judicial Restraint in Pursuit of Justice' (2010) 60 *University of Toronto Law Journal* 23.

Kebbon N, 'The World Court's Compulsory Jurisdiction under the Optional Clause – Past, Present and Future' (1989) 58 *Nordic Journal of International Law* 257.

Kelman M, *A Guide to Critical Legal Studies* (Cambridge MA, Harvard University Press, 1987).

Kelsen H, *Introduction to the Problems of Legal Theory* (Oxford, Clarendon Press, 1997).

Kennedy David, *International Legal Structures* (Baden-Baden, Nomos, 1987).

Kennedy Duncan, 'Form and Substance in Private Law Adjudication' (1976) 89 *Harvard Law Review* 1685.
Keohane RO, Moravcsik A and Slaughter AM, 'Legalized Dispute Resolution: Interstate and Transnational' (2000) 54 *International Organization* 457–88.
Keynes JM, The Economic Consequences of the Peace (London, Macmillan, 1919).
Keys B, 'Diplomat's Two Minds: Deconstructing a Foreign Policy Myth' (2020) 44 *Diplomatic History* 1.
King C, 'The Five-Day War: Managing Moscow After the Georgia Crisis' (November/December 2008) 87(6) *Foreign Affairs* 2.
King JA, 'Institutional Approaches to Judicial Restraint' (2008) 28 *Oxford Journal of Legal Studies* 421.
Kingsbury B, 'The Concept of Compliance as a Function of Competing Conceptions of International Law' (1998) 19 *Michigan Journal of International Law* 345.
——'Foreword: Is the Proliferation of International Courts and Tribunals a Systemic Problem?' (1999) 31 *NYU Journal of International Law and Politics* 679.
——'International Courts: Uneven Judicialization in Global Order', in J Crawford and M Koskenniemi (eds), *The Cambridge Companion to International Law* (Cambridge, Cambridge University Press, 2012).
Klein DB, 'Foreword to Republication of "A Beginner's Guide to Esoteric Reading"' (2015) 12 *Econ Journal Watch* 293.
Kleinlein T, 'The Procedural Approach of the European Court of Human Rights: Between Subsidiarity and Dynamic Evolution' (2019) 68 *International and Comparative Law Quarterly* 91.
Kress K, 'Legal Indeterminacy' (1989) 77 *California Law Review* 283.
Koh HH, 'Why Do Nations Obey International Law' (1996–1997) 106 *Yale Law Journal* 2599.
——'The 1994 Roscoe Pound Lecture: Transnational Legal Process' (1996) 75 *Nebraska Law Review*.
——'The 1998 Frankel Lecture: Bringing International Law Home' (1998) 35 *Houston Law Review* 624.
—— 'Is There a New New Haven School of International Law? Commentary' (2007) 32 *Yale Journal of International Law* 559.
—— *The Trump Administration and International Law* (Oxford, Oxford University Press, 2018).
—— 'Transnational Legal Process and the "New" New Haven School of International Law' in JL Dunoff and MA Pollack (eds), *International Legal Theory: Foundations and Frontiers* (2022) 101.
—— 'The Yale School of International Law' (2024) 9/22 *The Yale Journal of International Law Online* 1.
Kolb R, *The International Court of Justice* (Oxford, Hart, 2013).
Konar H, 'Termination of Treaties as a Political Question: The Role of Congress after Goldwater v Carter Comment' (1980–1981) 4 *Fordham International Law Journal* 81.
Kondoch B, 'The United Nations Administration of East Timor' (2001) 6 *Journal of Conflict and Security Law* 245.
Korzun V, 'The Right to Regulate in Investor-State Arbitration: Slicing and Dicing Regulatory Carve-outs' (2017) 50 *Vanderbilt Journal of Transnational Law* 355.
Koskenniemi M, *The Gentle Civilizer of Nations, the Rise and Fall of International Law 1870–1960* (Cambridge, Cambridge University Press, 2001).
——*From Apology to Utopia: The Structure of International Legal Argument* (Cambridge, Cambridge University Press, 2005).
Kotuby C and Sobota L, *General Principles of Law and International Due Process: Principles and Norms Applicable in Transnational Disputes* (Oxford, Oxford University Press, 2017).
Kritsiotis D, 'International Law and the Relativities of Enforcement' in J Crawford and M Koskenniemi (eds), *The Cambridge Companion to International Law* (Cambridge, Cambridge University Press, 2012).

Krisch N, 'The Backlash against International Courts' *Verfassungsblog* (16 December 2014).
Kronman A, 'Alexander Bickel's Philosophy of Prudence' (1985) 94 *Yale Law Journal* 1567, 1569.
Kruger P, 'From the Paris Peace Treaties to the End of the Second World War' in B Fassbender and A Peters (eds), *Oxford Handbook on the History of International Law* (Oxford, Oxford University Press, 2012).
Krugman Ray L, 'Justice Ginsburg and the Middle Way' (2003) 68 *Brooklyn Law Review* 629.
Ku J and Mirasola C, 'Tracking Compliance with the South China Sea Arbitral Award: China's 2017 Summer Fishing Moratorium May Rekindle Conflict with the Philippines' *Lawfare* (7 March 2017).
Kuhn A, 'The Case of the Free Zones of Upper Savoy and the District of Gex' (1932) 26 *American Journal of International Law* 801.
Kunz J, 'International Arbitration in Pan American Developments' (1948–1949) 27 *Texas Law Review* 182.
Kuran T, *Private Truths, Public Lies: The Social Consequences of Preference Falsification* (Cambridge MA, Harvard University Press 1997).
Lamm V, *Compulsory Jurisdiction in International Law* (Cheltenham, Edward Elgar, 2014).
Landau D, 'Populist Constitutions' (2018) 85 *University of Chicago Law Review* 521.
Langford M and Behn D, 'Managing Backlash: The Evolving Investment Treaty Arbitrator?' (2018) 29 *European Journal of International Law* 551.
——and Fauchald OK, 'Backlash and State Strategies in International Investment Law' in T Gammeltoft-Hansen and T Aalberts (eds), *The Changing Practices of International Law: Sovereignty, Law and Politics in a Globalising World* (Cambridge, Cambridge University Press, 2018).
Lauterpacht H, *Private Law Sources and Analogies of International Law: With Special Reference to International Arbitration* (London, Longmans, Green & Co, 1927).
——'The Doctrine of Non-Justiciable Disputes in International Law' (1928) *Economica* 277.
——'The Absence of an International Legislature and the Compulsory Jurisdiction of International Tribunals' (1930) 11 *British Yearbook of International Law* 134.
—— *The Development of International Law by the International Court* (London, Stevens & Sons, 1958).
——*The Function of Law in the International Community* (Oxford, Oxford University Press, 2011).
Lawson KL, 'The Constitutional Twilight Zone of Treaty Termination: Goldwater v Carter Note' (1979–1980) 20 *Virginia Journal of International Law* 147.
Lawson R, 'Life After *Banković*: On the Extraterritorial Application of the European Convention on Human Rights' in F Coomans and MT Kamminga (eds), *Extraterritorial Application of Human Rights Treaties* (Antwerp, Intersentia, 2004).
League of Nations, *Arbitration and Security* (1927).
Leiter B, 'American Legal Realism' in M Golding and W Edmundson (eds), *The Blackwell Guide to the Philosophy of Law and Legal Theory* (Blackwell 2005) 52.
——*Naturalizing Jurisprudence: Essays on American Legal Realism and Naturalism in Legal Philosophy* (Oxford, Oxford Univeristy Press, 2007).
—— 'Legal Realisms, Old and New' (2013) 47 *Valparaiso University Law Review* 949.
Leff AA, 'Law and' (1978) 87 *Yale Law Journal* 989.
Leflar RA, 'Some Observations concerning Judicial Opinions' (1961) 61 *Columbia Law Review* 810.
—— *One Life in the Law* (Fayettiville, University of Arkansas Press, 1985).
Letsas G, 'Two Concepts of the Margin of Appreciation' (2006) 26 *Oxford Journal of Legal Studies* 705.
—— 'The ECHR as a Living Instrument: Its Meaning and Legitimacy' in A Føllesdal, B Peters and G Ulfstein (eds), *Constituting Europe: The European Court of Human Rights in a National, European and Global Context* (Cambridge, Cambridge University Press, 2013).
Levy D, *Maxims for Thinking Analytically: The Wisdom of Legendary Harvard Professor Richard Zeckhauser* (Dan Levy, 2021).

Leys S, 'The Art of Interpreting Nonexistent Inscriptions Written in Invisible Ink on a Blank Page' *The New York Review of Books* (11 October 1990).

Linos K and Pegram T, 'The Language of Compromise in International Agreements' (2016) 70 *International Organization* 587.

Llamzon AP, 'Jurisdiction and Compliance in Recent Decisions of the International Court of Justice' (2007) 18 *European Journal of International Law* 815.

Llewellyn K, *The Bramble Bush* (Oxford, Oxford Universiy Press, 2008).

Lloyd L, '"A Springboard for the Future": A Historical Examination of Britain's Role in Shaping the Optional Clause of the Permanent Court of International Justice' (1985) 79 *American Journal of International Law* 28.

Loder BCJ, 'The Permanent Court of International Justice and Compulsory Jurisdiction' (1921–22) 2 *British Yearbook of International Law* 6.

Lonardo L, '*How the Court Tries to Deliver Justice in Common and Foreign Security Policy, Where the Need for Judicial Protection Clashes with Principles of Conferral and Institutional Balance*' (2024) 9 *European Forum* 830.

Loughlin M, 'The Functionalist Style in Public Law' (2005) 55(3) *University of Toronto Law Journal* 361.

Lowe V, 'Jurisdiction' in MD Evans (ed), *International Law* 2nd edn (Oxford, Oxford University Press, 2006).

——*International Law* (Oxford, Oxford University Press, 2009).

Lowenfeld A, 'Public Law in the International Arena: Conflict of Laws, International Law, and Some Suggestions for Their Interaction' (1979) 163 *Recueil des Cours* 311.

Lugg A and others, 'Why is There No Investor-State Dispute Settlement in RCEP? Bargaining and Contestation in the Investment Regime' (2024) *Business and Policy (First View)* 1.

Lupu Y, Verdier PH and Versteeg M 'The Strength of Weak Review: National Courts, Interpretative Canons, and Human Rights Treaties' (2019) 63 *International Studies Quarterly* 507.

Ma D, 'A BIT Unfair: An Illustration of the Backlash against International Arbitration in Latin America' (2012) *Journal of Dispute Resolution* 571.

MacCormick N, *Legal Reasoning and Legal Theory* (Oxford, Clarendon Press 1978).

——*Rhetoric and The Rule of Law* (Oxford, Oxford University Press, 2005).

MacQueen N, 'United Nations Transitional Administration in East Timor (UNTAET)' in JA Koops, T Tardy, N MacQueen and PD Williams (eds), *The Oxford Handbook of United Nations Peacekeeping Operations* (Oxford, Oxford University Press, 2015).

Madsen MR, Cebulak P and Wiebusch M, 'Backlash Against International Courts: Explaining the Forms and Patterns of Resistance to International Courts' (2018) 14 *International Journal of Law in Context* 197.

Mallory C, 'A Second Coming of Extraterritorial Jurisdiction at the European Court of Human Rights?' (2021) 82 *Questions of International Law* 31.

Mancini GF, 'The Making of a Constitution for Europe' (1989) 26 *Common Market Law Review* 595.

Mann FA, *The Doctrine of International Jurisdiction, The Hague Academy Collected Courses 111* (Leiden, Brill, 1964).

—— *The Doctrine of International Jurisdiction Revisited After Twenty Years,* The Hague Academy Collected Courses 186 (Leiden, Brill, 1984).

Marchand CR, *The American Peace Movement and Social Reform 1898–1918* (Princeton NJ Princeton University Press, 1972).

Marshall G, 'Justiciability', in AG Guest (ed), *Oxford Essays in Jurisprudence* (Oxford, Oxford University Press, 1961).

Marston G (ed), 'United Kingdom Materials on International Law 1992' (1993) 63 *British Yearbook of International Law* 615.

Martin L, 'Against Compliance' in J Dunoff and M Pollack (eds), *Interdisciplinary Perspectives on International Law and International Relations: The State of the Art* (Cambridge, Cambridge University Press, 2012).

Matsushita M, 'Some Thoughts on the Appellate Body' in PFJ Macrory, AE Appleton and MG Plummer (eds), *The World Trade Organization: Legal, Economic and Political Analysis* vol 1 (New York, Springer, 2005).
——'The Dispute Settlement Mechanism at the WTO: The Appellate Body—Assessment and Problems' in M Daunton, A Narlikar and RM Stern (eds), *The Oxford Handbook on the World Trade Organization* (Oxford, Oxford University Press, 2012) 511.
—— Schoenbaum J, Mavroidis P and Hahn M, *The World Trade Organization: Law, Practice, and Policy* 3rd edn (Oxford, Oxford University Press, 2015).
Maupin JA, 'MFN-based Jurisdiction in Investor-State Arbitration: Is There Any Hope for a Consistent Approach?' (2011) 14(1) *Journal of International Economic Law* 157.
Mavroidis P, *The Process before the Appellate Body* (Cambridge, Cambridge University Press, 2022).
McDougal M, 'International Law, Power and Policy: A Contemporary Conception' (1953) 82 *Recueil des Cours de l'Académie de Droit International* 137.
——'Remarks at the 79th Annual Meeting of the American Society of International Law' (1985) *Proceedings of the American Society of International Law, McDougal's Jurisprudence: Utility, Influence, Controversy*.
——and Feliciano F, *Law and Minimum World Public Order* (New Haven CT, Yale University Press, 1961).
——Lasswell HD and Miller JC, *The Interpretation of Agreements and World Public Order: Principles of Content and Procedure* (New Haven CT, Yale University Press, 1967).
——Lasswell HD and Reisman WM, 'Theories about International Law: Prologue to a Configurative Jurisprudence' (1967–1968) 8 *Virginia Journal of International Law* 188.
McEvoy AF, 'A New Realism for Legal Studies' (2005) *Wisconsin Law Review* 433.
McGlynn Gaffney Jr E, 'Goldwater v Carter: The Constitutional Allocation of Power in Treaty Termination Symposium: Goldwater v Carter' (1979–1980) 6 *Yale Studies in World Public Order* 81.
McGoldrick D, 'The Boundaries of Justiciability' (2010) 59 *International and Comparative Law Quarterly* 981.
McLachlan C, 'The Assault on International Adjudication and the Limits of Withdrawal' (2019) 68 *International and Comparative Law Quarterly* 499.
—— Shore L and Weiniger M, *International Investment Arbitration: Substantive Principles* 2nd edn (Oxford, Oxford University Press, 2017).
Mejia-Lemos D, 'Venezuela's Denunciation of the American Convention on Human Rights' (2013) 17(1) *ASIL Insights*.
Melzer A, *Philosophy Between the Lines: The Lost History of Esoteric Writing* (Chicago IL, University of Chicago Press, 2014).
Merli FJ, *Great Britain and the Confederate Navy, 1861–1865* (Bloomington IN, Indiana University Press, 2004).
Merry SE, 'New Legal Realism and the Ethnography of Transnational Law' (2006) 31 *Law & Social Inquiry* 975.
Methymaki E, 'Thinking Beyond International Adjudication: Inspections as Instruments of Order Production in the International System' (2022) 21 *Law and Practice of International Courts and Tribunals* 520.
Meyer RS, *Peace Organizations Past and Present: A Survey and Directory* (Jefferson NC, McFarland, 1988).
Milanovic M, *Extraterritorial Application of Human Rights Treaties: Law, Principles, and Policy* (Oxford, Oxford University Press, 2011).
—— 'European Court Decides Al-Skeini and Al-Jedda' *EJIL: Talk!* (7 July 2011).
——'Georgia v Russia No 2: The European Court's Resurrection of Bankovic in the Contexts of Chaos' (EJIL:Talk!, 25 January 2021).
—— 'Extraterritorial Investigations in *Hanan v Germany*; Extraterritorial Assassinations in New Interstate Claim Filed by Ukraine against Russia' (EJIL:Talk!, 26 February 2021).

Miles CL, 'Indeterminacy' in J d'Aspremont and S Singh, *Concepts for International Law* (Cheltenham, Edward Elgar, 2019).
——'Implied terms in Treaties' (2025) 119 *American Journal of International Law* 57.
Miles TJ and Sunstein CR, 'The New Legal Realism' (2008) 75 *University of Chicago Law Review* 831.
Miller D, *My Diary at the Conference of Paris* (New York, Appeal Printing, 1924).
——*Drafting of the Covenant* (New York, P Putnam's Sons, 1928).
Miller GM, 'Treaty Termination under the United States Constitution: Reassessing the Legacy of Goldwater v Carter Notes' (1994–1995) 27 *New York University Journal of International Law and Politics* 859.
Miller S, 'Revisiting Extraterritorial Jurisdiction: A Territorial Justification for Extraterritorial Jurisdiction under the European Convention' (2009) 20 *European Journal of International Law* 1223.
Mills A, 'Rethinking Jurisdiction in International Law' (2014) 84 *British Yearbook of International Law* 87–139.
Miranda J and Sanchez Miranda M, 'Chronicle of a Crisis Foretold: How the WTO Appellate Body Drove Itself into a Corner' (2023) 26 *Journal of International Economic Law* 435.
Miron A, 'Establishing the Existence of a Dispute before the International Court of Justice: Between Formalism and Verbalism' (2017) *Questions of International Law* (31 December 2017).
Miyazaki H and Riles A, 'Theorizing Intergenerational Justice in International Law: The Case of the Treaty on the Prohibition of Nuclear Weapons' (2022) 7 *UC Irvine Journal of International, Transnational, and Comparative Law* 122.
Mollengarden Z and Zamir N, 'The Monetary Gold Principle: Back to Basics' (2021) 115 *American Journal of International Law* 41.
Moore JB, *History and Digest of the International Arbitrations to which the United States has Been a Party* (Washington DC, Government Printing Office, 1898).
Morgenthau H, *La Notion du Politique et la Théorie des differends internationaux* (Paris, Recueil Sirey, 1933).
——Thompson K and Clinton D, *Politics Among Nations* 7th edn (New York, McGraw-Hill Education, 2005).
Mortensen J, 'The Travaux of Travaux: Is the Vienna Convention Hostile to Drafting History?' (2013) 107 *American Journal of International Law* 780.
Mosler H, 'The Area of Justiciability: Some Cases of Agreed Delimitation in the Submission of Disputes to the International Court of Justice', in J Makarczyk (ed) *Essays in International Law in Honour of Manfred Lachs* (Leiden, Brill, 1984).
Muñoz Machado S, *Tratado de derecho administrative y derecho público general* (Madrid, BOE, 2015).
Murdock JO and Gobbi HJ, 'The Inter-American Juridical Committee' (1960) 9 *American Journal of Comparative Law* 596.
Murphy S, 'The Concept of International Law' (2009) 165, *Proceedings American Society International Law Annual Meeting* 6.
Murungu CB, 'Towards a Criminal Chamber in the African Court of Justice and Human Rights' (2011) 9 *Journal of International Criminal Justice* 1067.
Nardell G and Rees-Evans L, 'The Agreement Terminating Intra-EU BITs: Are Its Provisions on "New" and "Pending" Arbitration Proceedings Compatible with Investors' Fundamental Rights?' (2021) 37 *Arbitration International* 197.
Neal TC and V Torbjorn (eds), *The Global Expansion of Judicial Power* (New York, New York University Press, 1995).
Newbury MV, 'Foreign Act of State – A Practical Guide' *Amicus Curiae* Series 2, No 1(1) 7.
Nicolle D, *The Italian Invasion of Abyssinia 1935–1936* (London, Bloomsbury, 2012).
Nielsen C, 'Prosecution or Bust: The Obligation to Prosecute under the United Nations Convention against Torture' (2013) 72 *Cambridge Law Journal* 242.

Nollkaemper A, 'Wither Aut Dedere? The Obligation to Extradite or Prosecute after the International Court of Justice's Judgment in Belgium v Senegal' (2013) 4 *Journal of International Dispute Settlement* 501.
Nourse V and Shaffer G, 'Varieties of New Legal Realism: Can a New World Order Prompt a New Legal Theory?' (2009) 25 *Cornell Law Review* 61.
Novak G, *Global Lawmaking and Social Change* (Oxford, Hart, 2024).
Odermatt J, 'Patterns of Avoidance: Political Questions Before International Courts' (2018) 14 *International Journal of Law in Context* 221.
Ogus A, 'Quantitative Rules and Judicial Decision Making' in P Burrows and CG Veljanovski (eds), *The Economic Approach to Law* (London, Butterworths, 1981).
Oliver CT, 'The Monetary Gold Decision in Perspective' (1955) 49 *American Journal of International Law* 216.
——'Goldwater v Carter: Crisis in American Constitutional Arrangements for the Conduct of International Relations Symposium: Goldwater v Carter' (1979–1980) 6 *Yale Studies in World Public Order* 11.
Ottolenghi M and Prows P, 'Res Judicata in the ICJ's Genocide Case: Implications for Other Courts and Tribunals' (2009) 21 *Pace International Law Review* 37.
Orakhelashvili A, 'Restrictive Interpretation of Human Rights Treaties in the Recent Jurisprudence of the European Court of Human Rights' (2003) 14 *European Journal of International Law* 529.
——*Peremptory Norms in International Law* (Oxford, Oxford University Press, 2008).
—— 'The Competence of the International Court of Justice and the Doctrine of the Indispensable Party: From Monetary Gold to East Timor and Beyond' (2011) 2 *Journal of International Dispute Settlement* 373.
Oxman B, 'Jurisdiction of States' in A Peters (ed), *Max Planck Encyclopedia of Public International Law* (2007).
Paddeu F and Waibel M, 'Necessity 20 Years On: The Limits of Article 25' (2022) 37 *ICSID Review – Foreign Investment Law Journal* 160.
Paiement P, 'Urgent Agenda: How Climate Litigation Builds Transnational Narratives' (2020) 11 *Transnational Legal Theory* 121.
Palchetti P, 'Making and Enforcing Procedural Law at the International Court of Justice' (2019) *Questions of International Law/Questions de Droit International*.
Palestini L, 'Forget About Mavrommatis and Judicial Economy: The Alleged Absence of a Dispute in Cases Concerning Obligations to Negotiate' (2017) *Journal of International Dispute Settlement* 557.
Pallin CV and Westerlund F, 'Russia's War in Georgia: Lessons and Consequences' (2009) 20(2) *Small Wars & Insurgencies* 400.
Palmer R, *Memorials: Part II, Personal and Political* (London, Macmillan, 1898).
Paparinskis M, 'Revisiting the Indispensable Third Party Principle' (2020) 103 *Rivista di Diritto Internazionale* 49.
——'Long Live Monetary Gold* Terms and Conditions Apply' (2021) 115 *American Journal of International Law* 154.
Patterson E, *Jurisprudence: Men and Ideas of the Law* (St Paul MN, Foundation Press, 1953).
Paulson C, 'Compliance with Final Judgments of the International Court of Justice since 1987' (2004) 98 *American Journal of International Law* 434.
Pauwelyn J, 'The Transformation of World Trade' (2005) 104 *Michigan Law Review* 1.
——and Hamilton RJ, 'Exit from International Tribunals' (2018) 9 *Journal of International Dispute Settlement* 679.
Pelc KJ, 'The Politics of Precedent in International Law: A Social Network Application' (2014) 108 *American Political Science Review* 547.
Peller G, 'The Metaphysics of American Law' (1985) 73 *California Law Review* 1151.
Pellet A and Muller D, 'Article 38' in A Zimmermann, C Tams, K Oellers-Frahm, C Tomuschat (eds), *The Statute of the International Court of Justice: A Commentary* (Oxford, Oxford University Press, 2019).

Perez AF, 'The Passive Virtues and the World Court: Pro-Dialogic Abstention by the International Court of Justice' (1997) 18 *Michigan Journal of International Law*, 399.
Peters A, 'The Refinement of International Law: From Fragmentation to Regime Interaction and Politicization' (2017) 15 *International Journal of Constitutional Law* 671.
Petrov J, 'The Populist Challenge to the European Court of Human Rights' (2020) 18 *International Journal of Constitutional Law* 476.
Phelps C, *The Anglo-American Peace Movements in the Mid-Nineteenth Century* (New York, Columbia University Press, 1930).
Plessix B, *Droit administratif général* 2nd edn (London, LexisNexis, 2018).
Politis N, *The New Aspects of International Law* (Washington DC, Carnegie Endowment for International Peace, 1928).
Pomerance M, 'Case Analysis: The ICJ and South West Africa (Namibia): A Retrospective Legal/Political Assessment' (1999) 12 *Leiden Journal of International Law* 425.
Popa LE, 'Treaty Interpretation at the European Court of Human Rights' in LE Popa (ed), *Patterns of Treaty Interpretation as Anti-Fragmentation Tools: A Comparative Analysis with a Special Focus on the ECtHR, WTO and ICJ* (Cham, Springer, 2018).
Popelier P, 'Procedural Rationality Review after Animal Defenders International: A Constructively Critical Approach' (2019) 15 *European Constitutional Law Review* 272.
Porter D, *The Naval History of the Civil War* (New York, Sherman Publishing Company, 1886).
Posner E, 'Evaluating the Effects of International Law: Next Steps' (2010) 1(3) *Global Policy* 334.
——'Liberal Internationalism and the Populist Backlash' (2017) 49 *Arizona State Law Journal* 795, 813.
——Yoo JC, 'Judicial Independence in International Tribunals' (2005) 93 *California Law Review* 1.
Posner RA, *The Problems of Jurisprudence* (Cambridge MA, Harvard University Press, 1990).
——*How Judges Think* (Cambridge MA, Harvard University Press, 2010).
Post R and Siegel R, '*Roe* Rage: Democratic Constitutionalism and Backlash' (2007) 42 *Harvard Civil Rights-Civil Liberties Law Review* 373.
Potter P, *The Wal Wal Arbitration* (Washington, Carnegie Endowment, 1938).
Pound R, 'Law in Books and Law in Action' (1910) 44 *American Law Review* 12.
—— *An Introduction to the Philosophy of Law* (New Haven CT, Yale University Press, 1922).
—— 'Hierarchy of Sources and Forms in Different Systems of Law' (1933) 7 *Tulane Law Review* 475.
Pozen D, 'The Leaky Leviathan: Why the Government Condemns and Condones Unlawful Disclosures of Information' (2013) 127 *Harvard Law Review* 512.
Proulx VJ, 'The World Court's Jurisdictional Formalism and its Lost Market Share: The Marshall Islands Decisions and the Quest for a Suitable Dispute Settlement Forum for Multilateral Disputes' (2017) 30 *Leiden Journal of International Law* 925.
Przetacznik F, 'The Compulsory Jurisdiction of the International Court of Justice as a Prerequisite for Peace' (1990) 68 *Revue de Droit International de Sciences Diplomatiques et Politiques*.
Radin M, 'In Defence of an Unsystematic Science of Law' (1942) 51 *Yale Law Journal* 1271.
Raible L, *Human Rights Unbound: A Theory of Extraterritoriality* (Oxford, Oxford University Press, 2020).
——'Extraterritoriality Between A Rock and Hard Place' (2021) 82 *Questions of International Law* 7.
Ralston JH, *International Arbitration from Athens to Locarno* (Lawbook Exchange, 2004).
——and Permanent Court of International Justice, *The Law and Procedure of International Tribunals Being a Résumé of the Views of Arbitrators upon Questions Arising under the Law of Nations and of the Procedure and Practice of International Courts* (Washington DC, Byrne & Co, 1926).
Ranganathan S, 'Nuclear Weapons and the Court' (2017) 111 *AJIL Unbound* 88.

Ratner SR, 'Land Feuds and their Solutions: Finding International Law Beyond the Tribunal Chamber' (2006) 100 *American Journal of International Law* 808.
Raustiala K, 'Compliance and Effectiveness in International Regulatory Cooperation' (2000) 32 *Case Western Reserve Journal of International Law* 387.
—— 'Form and Substance in International Agreements' (2005) 99 *American Journal of International Law* 581.
——and Slaughter AM, 'International Law, International Relations and Compliance' in W Carlsnaes, T Risse and BA Simmons (eds), *Handbook of International Relations* (London, SAGE, 2002).
Reed L and others, *Guide to ICSID Arbitration* 2nd edn (Alphen aan den Rijn, Kluwer Law International, 2011).
Reichenbach C, 'The Missing Dispute Resolution Mechanisms in International Climate Change Agreements' (2023) 3 *Global Energy Law and Sustainability* 129.
Reinisch A, 'The Proliferation of International Dispute Settlement Mechanisms: The Threat of Fragmentation vs. the Promise of a More Effective System? Some Reflections From the Perspective of Investment Arbitration', in I Buffard, J Crawford, A Pellet and S Wittich (eds), *International Law Between Universalism and Fragmentation, Festschrift in Honour of Gerhard Hafner* (Leiden, Brill, 2008).
—— 'Necessity in Investment Arbitration' (2010) 41 *Netherlands Yearbook of International Law* 138.
—— 'The Use and Limits of *Res Judicata* and *Lis Pendens* as Procedural Tools to Avoid Conflicting Dispute Settlement Outcomes' (2004) 3 *Law and Practice of International Courts and Tribunals* 37, 44 (2004).
Reisman WM, *Nullity and Revision: The Review and Enforcement of International Judgments and Awards* (New Haven CT, Yale University Press, 1971).
——'Myth System and Operational Code' (1976–1977) 3 *Yale Studies in World Public Order* 229.
——'International Lawmaking: A Process of Communication: The Harold D Lasswell Memorial Lecture' (1981) 75 *Proceedings of the American Society of International Law* 101.
——'Has the International Court Exceeded its Jurisdiction?' (1986) 80 *American Journal of International Law* 128.
——'Sovereignty and Human Rights in Contemporary International Law' (1990) 84 *American Journal of International Law* 866, 872.
—— 'The View from the New Haven School of International Law' (1992) 86 *Proceedings of the Annual Meeting (American Society of International Law)* 118.
——'The Constitutional Crisis in the United Nations' (1993) 87 *American Journal of International Law* 83.
——'Hollow Victory: Humanitarian Intervention and Protection of Minorities' (1997) 91 *Proceedings of the Annual Meeting (American Society of International Law)* 431.
—— 'Theory about Law: Jurisprudence for a Free Society' (1999) 108 *Yale Law Journal* 935, 939.
——'Kosovo's Antinomies' (1999) 93 *American Journal of International Law* 860.
——'The Manley O. Hudson Lecture: Why Regime Change is (Almost Always) A Bad Idea' (2004) 98 *American Journal of International Law,* 515.
—— *The Quest for World Order and Human Dignity in the Twenty First Century* (Leiiden, Brill, 2013).
——'Canute Confronts the Tide: States versus Tribunals and the Evolution of the Minimum Standard in Customary International Law' (2015) 30 *ICSID Review* 616.
——'The Hudson Medal Luncheon: "The Unity of International Law"' in (2015) 109 *American Society of International Law Proceedings of the Annual Meeting* 255.
——'Negotiating and Maintaining Investment Treaties: Mechanisms for Anticipating and Controlling Textual Drift' (2019) 9 *Journal of International and Comparative Law* 75.
—— and others, 'The Enforcement of International Judgments' (1968) 62 *Proceedings of the American Society of International Law* 13–25.

——and Schreiber A, *Jurisprudence* (New Haven CT, New Haven Press, 1986).
—— and Willard AR, *International Incidents The Law That Counts in World Politics* (Princeton NJ, Princeton University Press, 1988).
—— and Wiessner S and Willard AR, 'The New Haven School: A Brief Introduction' (2007) 32 *Yale Journal of International Law* 575.
Remmer KL, 'Investment Treaty Arbitration in Latin America' (2019) 54 *Latin American Research Review* 795.
Ress G, 'Problems of Extraterritorial Human Rights Violations: The Jurisdiction of the European Court of Human Rights: The *Banković* case' (2002) 12 *Italian Yearbook of International Law* 51.
Reyes RF, 'Nauru v Australia: The International Fiduciary Duty and the Settlement of Nauru's Claims for Rehabilitation of Its Phosphate Lands' (1996) 16 *New York Law School Journal of International and Comparative Law* 2.
Rheinstein M, 'The Nuremberg Trial and Aggressive War' (review of Sheldon Glueck, *The Nuremberg Trial and Aggressive War* (1946)) (1947) 14 *University of Chicago Law Review* 319.
Riddi N, 'Precarious Finality? Reflections on *res judicata* and the Question of the Delimitation of the Continental Shelf Case' (2018) 31 *Leiden Journal of International Law* 383.
Rietiker D, 'The Treaty on the Prohibition of Nuclear Weapons: A Further Confirmation of the Human- and Victim-Centred Trend in Arms Control Law' in JL Black-Branch and D Fleck (eds), *Nuclear Non-Proliferation in International Law – Volume IV: Human Perspectives on the Development and Use of Nuclear Energy* (The Hague, TMC Asser Press, 2019) 325.
Riley J, 'A Multilateral Approach to Investor-State Dispute Settlement Issues in the Asia-Pacific Region' (2021) 14 *Journal of East Asia and International Law* 147.
Roach K, 'Dialogic Judicial Review and its Critics' (2004) 23 *Supreme Court Law Review* 249.
Roberts A, 'Traditional and Modern Approaches to Customary International Law: A Reconciliation' (2001) 95 *American Journal of International Law* 757.
Rogers WD, 'Covey T Oliver (1913–2007)' (2007) 101 *American Journal of International Law* 404.
Romano CPR, 'The Proliferation of International Judicial Bodies: The Pieces of the Puzzle' (1999) 31 *NYU Journal of International Law and Politics* 709.
——'The Shift from the Consensual to the Compulsory Paradigm in International Adjudication: Elements for a Theory of Consent' (2006–2007) 39 *NYU Journal of International Law and Politics* 791
Rosenne S, *The Law and Practice of the International Court, 1920–2005* (Leiden, Brill, 2006).
Ross J, 'Jurisdictional Aspects of International Human Rights Law and Humanitarian Law in the War on Terror' in F Coomans and MT Kamminga (eds), *Extraterritorial Application of Human Rights Treaties* (Antwerp, Intersentia, 2004).
Roussel S and Nicolas C, 'De l'injusticiabilité des actes de gouvernement' (2018) *Actualité Juridique Droit Administratif* 491.
Roux T, *The Politics of Principle: The First South African Constitutional Court, 1995–2005* (Cambridge, Cambridge University Press, 2013).
Rudolf B, 'Loizidou v Turkey' (1996) 90 *American Journal of International Law* 98.
Rupp HG, 'Some Remarks on Judicial Self-Restraint'(1960) 21 *Ohio State Law Journal* 507.
Ryngaert C, *Jurisdiction in International Law,* 2nd edn (Oxford, Oxford University Press, 2015).
Sabine G, 'Review of Persecution and the Art of Writing' (1953) 63 *Ethics* 220.
Sai DK, 'Backstory—Larsen v Hawaiian Kingdom at the Permanent Court of Arbitration (1999–2001)' (2022) 4 *Hawaii Journal of Law and Politics* 133.
Sainz Borgo JC, 'La salida de Venezuela de la Comunidad Andina' (2007) 38 *Politeia* 136.
Sagan SD, *The Limits of Safety: Organizations, Accidents, and Nuclear Strategy* 4th edn (London, Palgrave Macmillan, 2019).
Salas Kantor B and Zavala Achurra ME, 'The Principle of *res judicata* before the International Court of Justice: in the Midst of Comradeship and Divorce between International Tribunals' (2019) 10 *Journal of International Dispute Settlement* 288.

Sands P, 'Reflections on International Judicialization' (2016) 27 *European Journal of International Law* 885.
Sarzo M, 'Res judicata, Jurisdiction ratione materiae and Legal Reasoning in the Dispute Between Nicaragua and Colombia before the International Court of Justice' (2017) *The Law & Practice of International Courts and Tribunals* 16(2) 224–44.
Sauvant KP, Ong M, Lama K and Petersen T, 'The Rise of Self-Judging Essential Security Interest Clauses in International Investment Agreements', (2016) *Columbia FDI Perspectives* 188.
Schabas WA, 'International Criminal Courts' in CPR Romano, K J Alter and Y Shany (eds), *The Oxford Handbook of International Adjudication* (Oxford, Oxford University Press, 2013).
Schacter O, 'Remarks at the 79th Annual Meeting of the American Society of International Law' (1985) 79 *Proceedings of the American Society of International Law, McDougal's Jurisprudence: Utility, Influence, Controversy* 272.
Schäfer A, 'Cultural Backlash? How (Not) to Explain the Rise of Authoritarian Populism' (2022) 52 *British Journal of Political Science* 1977.
Schauer F, *Playing by the Rules: A Philosophical Examination of Rule-Based Decisionmaking in Law and in Life* (Oxford, Clarendon Press, 1991).
——'The Tyranny of Choice and the Rulification of Standards' (2005) 14 *Journal of Contemporary Legal Issues* 803.
Schlag P, 'Rules and Standards' (1985) 33 *UCLA Law Review* 379.
Schreuer C, 'What is a Legal Dispute?' in in I Buffard, J Crawford, A Pellet and S Wittich (eds), *International Law between Universalism and Fragmentation* (The Hague, Martinus Nijhoff, 2008) 959.
——'Jurisdiction and Applicable Law in Investment Treaty Arbitration' (2014) 1 *McGill Journal of Dispute Resolution* 2.
Schrijver N, 'Certain Phosphate Lands in Nauru Case (Nauru v Australia)' in A Peters (ed), *Max Planck Encyclopaedia of Public International Law* (2008).
Schulthess L, 'The Franco-Swiss Free Zones' *Foreign Affairs* (December 1924).
Schultz T, *Transnational Legality: Stateless Law and International Arbitration* (Oxford, Oxford University Press, 2014).
Schwarzenberger G, 'Present-Day Relevance of the Jay Treaty Arbitrations' (1978) 53 *Notre Dame Law Review* 715.
Schwartzman M, 'Judicial Sincerity' (2008) 94 *Virginia Law Review* 987.
Schelling T, *The Strategy of Conflict* (New Haven CT, Yale University Press, 1966; reissued 2008).
——'Nuclear Deterrence for the Future' (2006) 23 *Issues in Science and Technology* 50.
——*Arms and Influence* (New Haven CT, Yale University Press, 2008).
Schill S, 'Allocating Adjudicatory Authority: Most-Favoured-Nation Clauses as a Basis of Jurisdiction—A Reply to Zachary Douglas' (2011) 2 *Journal of International Dispute Settlement* 353.
——and Briese R, '"If the State Considers": Self-Judging Clauses in International Dispute Settlement' (2009) 13 *Max Planck Yearbook of United Nations Law* 61.
—— and Vidigal G, 'Designing Investment Dispute Settlement à la Carte: Insights from Comparative Institutional Design Analysis' (2020) 18 *Law & Practice of International Courts & Tribunals* 314.
Schlink B, 'Proportionality (1)' in M Rosenfeld and A Sajó (eds), *The Oxford Handbook of Comparative Constitutional Law* (Oxford, Oxford University Press, 2012).
Scobbie I, 'Towards the Elimination of International Law: Some Radical Scepticism about Sceptical Radicalism' (1990) 61 *British Yearbook of International Law* 339.
—— 'Case Concerning Certain Phosphate Lands in Nauru (Nauru v Australia), Preliminary Objections Judgment' (1993) 42 *International and Comparative Law Quarterly* 710.
—— 'Res judicata, Precedent and the International Court: A Preliminary Sketch' (1999) 20 *Australian Yearbook of International Law* 299.

——and C J Drew, 'Self-Determination Undetermined: The Case of East Timor' (1996) 9 *Leiden Journal of International Law* 185

Shaffer G and Pollack MA, 'Hard vs Soft Law: Alternatives, Complements, and Antagonists in International Governance' (2010) 94 *Minnesota Law Review* 706.

Shaffer G and Ginsburg T, 'The Empirical Turn in International Legal Scholarship' (2012) 106 *American Journal of International Law* 1.

Shah S, 'Questions relating to the Obligation to Prosecute or Extradite (Belgium v Senegal)' (2013) 13 *Human Rights Law Review* 351.

Shany Y, *The Competing Jurisdiction of International Courts and Tribunals* (Oxford, Oxford University Press, 2003).

——'Jurisdiction and Admissibility' in CP Romano, KJ Alter and C Avgerou (eds), *The Oxford Handbook of International Adjudication* (Oxford, Oxford University Press, 2013).

—— 'Taking Universality Seriously: A Functional Approach to Extraterritoriality in International Human Rights Law' (2013) 7 *Law and Ethics of Human Rights* 47.

——*Assessing the Effectiveness of International Courts* (Oxford, Oxford University Press, 2014).

——*Questions of Jurisdiction and Admissibility before International Courts* (Cambridge, Cambridge University Press, 2015).

Shapiro DL, 'Jurisdiction and Discretion' (1985) 60 *New York University Law Review* 543.

——'In Defense of Judicial Candor' (1987) 100 *Harvard Law Review* 731.

Shapiro M and Stone Sweet A, *On Law, Politics, and Judicialization* (Oxford, Oxford University Press, 2002).

Sharma R, 'Is There Any Role for Linguists Among Lawyers in Arbitration' (2016) 9 *Contemporary Asia Arbitration Journal* 249.

Shaw M, *Rosenne's Law and Practice of the International Court* 5th edn (Leiden/The Hague Brill/ Nijhoff, 2016) vol II.

——*International Law,* 8th edn (Cambridge, Cambridge University Press, 2017).

Sherry S, 'Putting the Law Back in Constitutional Law: Symposium – Is American Constitutional Law in Crisis: Association of American Law Schools Section on Constitutional Law (January 2009)' (2008) 25 *Constitutional Commentary* 461.

Shirlow E, *Judging at the Interface: Deference to State Decision-Making Authority in International Adjudication* 116 (Cambridge, Cambridge University Press, 2021).

Shihata IFI, *The Power of the International Court to Determine its Own Jurisdiction: Compétence de la Compétence* (The Hague, Martinus Nijhoff, 1965).

Shoyer AW, Solovy EM and Koff AW, 'Implementation and Enforcement of Dispute Settlement Decisions' in PFJ Macrory, AE Appleton and MG Plummer (eds), *The World Trade Organization: Legal, Economic and Political Analysis* vol 1 (New York, Springer, 2005) 1341.

Siegel JR, 'A Theory of Justiciability' (2007) 86 *Texas Law Review* 73.

Silverstone P, *Civil War Navies, 1855–1883* (London, Routledge, 2006).

Simma B, 'NATO, the UN and the Use of Force: Legal Aspects' (1999) 10 *European Journal of International Law* 1.

——and Müller AT, 'Exercise and Limits of Jurisdiction', in J Crawford and M Koskenniemi (eds) *The Cambridge Companion to International Law* (Cambridge, Cambridge University Press, 2012) 134.

Simmons B, 'See you in "Court"? The Appeal to Quasi-Judicial Legal Processes in the Settlement of Territorial Disputes', in PF Diehl (ed), *A Road Map to War: Territorial Dimensions of International Conflict* (Nashville TN, Vanderbilt University Press, 1999) 205.

Singer JW, 'The Player and the Cards: Nihilism and Legal Theory' (1984) 94 *Yale Law Journal* 1.

——'Legal Realism Now' (1988) 76 *California Law Review* 467.

Singh N, *The Role and Record of the International Court of Justice* (The Hague/Martinus Nijhoff, 1989).

Sobenes Obregon E, 'Res Judicata and the Test of Finality' (2018) 5 *Journal of Territorial and Maritime Studies*' 75.

Soley X and Steininger S, 'Parting Ways or Lashing Back? Withdrawals, Backlash and the Inter-American Court of Human Rights' (2018) 14 *International Journal of Law in Context* 237.

Solum LB, 'Legal Theory Lexicon: Rules, Standards, Principles, Catalogs, and Discretion' (*Legal Theory Blog*, 8 August 2021).

Sornarajah M, 'Right to Regulate and Safeguards' in UNCTAD (ed), *The Development Dimension of Foreign Direct Investment: Policy and Rule-Making Perspectives* (United Nations, 2003).

Sossin L, *Boundaries of Judicial Review: The Law of Justiciability in Canada* (Ontario, Carswell, 1999).

Spano R, 'Universality or Diversity of Human Rights – Strasbourg in the Age of Subsidiarity' (2014) 14 *Human Rights Law Review* 487.

—— 'The Future of the European Court of Human Rights: Subsidiarity, Process-Based Review and the Rule of Law' (2018) 18 *Human Rights Law Review* 473.

Spencer JH, 'The Italian–Ethiopian Dispute and the League of Nations' (1937) 31 *American Journal of International Law* 614.

Spracher WC, 'Mired in Gray: Juggling Legality, Lawfulness, and Ethics as an Intelligence Professional' (2016) 33 *American Intelligence Journal* 101.

Sparks T, 'Reassessing State Consent to Jurisdiction: The Indispensable Third-party Principle before the ICJ' (Heidelberg, Max Planck Institute for Comparative Public Law and International Law, MPIL Research Paper Series No 2020-22, 2020).

Spedding J, Ellis RL and Heath D (eds) *The Works of Francis Bacon* (Cambridge, Cambridge University Press, 2013).

Sperling J and Webber M, 'NATO: from Kosovo to Kabul' (2009) 85 *International Affairs* 491.

Staton JK and Moore WH, 'Judicial Power in Domestic and International Politics' (2011) 65 *International Organization* 553.

Steiger H, 'Plaidoyer pour une juridiction internationale obligatoire' in J Makarczyk (ed), *Theory of International Law at the Threshold of the 21st Century: Essays in Honour of Krzysztof Skubiszewski* (Alphen aan den Rijn, Kluwer Law International, 1996).

Stephenson M, '"When the Devil Turns . . .": The Political Foundations of Independent Judicial Review' (2003) 32 *Journal of Legal Studies* 59.

Stevens W, 'The Poems of our Climate' in *Wallace Stevens, Collected Poems* (London, Faber and Faber, 2006).

Stevenson JR, 'Case Concerning the Northern Cameroons (Cameroon v United Kingdom), Preliminary Objections' (1964) 58 *American Journal of International Law* 488.

Stiansen Ø and Voeten E, 'Backlash and Judicial Restraint: Evidence from the European Court of Human Rights' (2020) 64 *International Studies Quarterly* 770.

Stone-Sweet A, *The Judicial Construction of Europe* (Oxford, Oxford University Press, 2004).

——and Brunell TL, 'The European Court of Justice, State Noncompliance, and the Politics of Override' (2012) 106 *American Political Science Review* 204.

——and Mathews J, *Proportionality Balancing and Constitutional Governance: A Comparative and Global Approach* (Oxford, Oxford University Press, 2019).

Strang G (ed), *Collision of Empires: Italy's Invasion of Ethiopia and its International Impact* (Abingdon, Routledge, 2013).

Strauss L, *Persecution and the Art of Writing* (Chicago IL, University of Chicago Press, 1988).

Summers LM, 'The Calvo Clause' (1932) 19 *Virginia Law Review* 459.

Sumption J, *Trials of the State* (London, Profile Books, 2020).

Sunstein C, 'Problems with Rules' (1995) 83 *California Law Review* 953.

——'The Supreme Court 1995 Term Foreword: Leaving Things Undecided' (1996) 110 *Harvard Law Review* 7.

—— *One Case at a Time: Judicial Minimalism on the Supreme Court* (Cambridge MA, Harvard University Press, 2001).

——'If People Would be Outraged by Their Rulings, Should Judges Care?' (2010) 60 *Stanford Law Review* 155.

——'On the Expressive Function of Law' (2021) 144 *University of Pennsylvania Law Review* 2022.
Suzuki E, 'The New Haven School of International Law: An Invitation to Policy-oriented Jurisprudence' (1970) 1 *Yale Journal of World Public Order* 1–48.
Taft WH, 'A World League to Enforce Peace' (1915) 2 *The New York Times Current History of the European War* 667.
Talmon S, 'The Cyprus Question Before the European Court of Justice' (2001) 12 *European Journal of International Law* 727.
—— 'The Constitutive Versus the Declaratory Theory of Recognition: Tertium Non Datur?' (2005) 75 *British Yearbook of International Law* 101.
Taylor BD III and others (eds), *International Criminal Law Practitioner Library: International Criminal Procedure* (Cambridge, Cambridge University Press, 2011).
Taylor JG, *The Indonesian Occupation of East Timor 1974–1989: A Chronology* (London, Catholic Institute for International Relations, 1990).
Thiebaut R, 'The Role of Transnational Legal Process in Advancing a Sustainable Agenda within the Brics' (2024) 12 *Journal of Law and Sustainable Developments.*
Thirlway H, *The Law and Procedure of the International Court of Justice: Fifty Years of Jurisprudence* (Oxford, Oxford University Press, 2013).
Titi C, *The Right to Regulate in International Investment Law* (Baden-Baden/Oxford Nomos/Hart, 2014).
——'The European Union's Proposal for an International Investment Court: Significance, Innovations and Challenges Ahead' (2017) 1 *Transnational Dispute Management.*
Tomuschat C, 'Article 36' in A Zimmermann, C Tams, K Oellers-Frahm, C Tomuschat (eds), *The Statute of the International Court of Justice: A Commentary* (Oxford, Oxford University Press, 2019) 724.
Tropper J and Reinisch A, 'The 2020 Termination Agreement of Intra-EU BITs and Its Effect on Investment Arbitration in the EU – A Public International Law Analysis of the Termination Agreement' (2022) 16 *Austrian Yearbook on International Arbitration* 301.
Tushnet M, 'Law and Prudence in the Law of Justiciability: The Transformation and Disappearance of the Political Question Doctrine' (2002) 80 *North Carolina Law Review* 1203
Tzeng P, 'Jurisdiction and Applicable Law Under UNCLOS' (2016) 126 *Yale Law Journal* 242.
—— 'The Implicated Issue Problem: Indispensable Issues and Incidental Jurisdiction' (2018) 50 *NYU Journal of International Law & Politics* 447.
UNCTAD, *Most-Favoured-Nation Treatment: A Sequel* (New York/Geneva, United Nations, 2010).
Unger RM, *Knowledge and Politics* (Tampa FL, Free Press, 1975).
Van den Bossche P, 'The Demise of the WTO Appellate Body: Lessons for Governance of International Adjudication?' (2021), *World Trade Institute Working Paper No 02/2021.*
Vattel ED, Lapradelle AD and Ghequiere Fenwick C, *Le Droit Des Gens Ou Principes de La Loi Naturelle Appliqués à La Conduite et Aux Affaires Des Nations et Des Souverains* (Washington DC, Carnegie Institution, 1916).
Veeder VV, 'The Historical Keystone to International Arbitration: The Party-Appointed Arbitrator – From Miami to Geneva' (2013) 107 *Proceedings of the ASIL Annual Meeting* 387.
Vesnic MR, *Deux Précurseurs Français du Pacifisme* (Paris, A Pedone, 1911).
Vila MI, 'Subsidiarity, Margin of Appreciation and International Adjudication Within a Cooperative Conception of Human Rights' (2017) 15 *International Journal of Constitutional Law* 393.
Voeten E, 'Politics, Judicial Behaviour, and Institutional Design' in J Christoffersen and MR Madsen (eds), *The European Court of Human Rights between Law and Politics* (Oxford, Oxford University Press, 2011).
—— 'Public Opinion and the Legitimacy of International Courts' (2013) 14 *Theoretical Inquiries in Law* 411.

——'Populism and Backlashes Against International Courts' (2020) 18 *Perspectives on Politics* 407.
Voigt C, 'Institutional Arrangements and Final Clauses (Articles 16–29)', in D Klein, MP Carazo, M Doelle, J Bulmer and A Higham (eds), *The Paris Agreement on Climate Change: Analysis and Commentary* (Oxford, Oxford University Press, 2017).
von Mehren AT, 'Adjudicatory Jurisdiction: General Theories Compared and Evaluated' (1983–1984) 6 *Tel Aviv University Studies in Law* 50.
Voon T, 'Closing the Gap Between Legitimacy and Legality of Humanitarian Intervention: Lessons from East Timor and Kosovo' (2002) 7 *UCLA Journal of International Law and Foreign Affairs* 31.
Waibel M, 'Corfu Channel Case', in A Peters (ed) *Max Planck Encyclopedia of Public International Law* (2013).
——Kaushal, A, Chung, K-H and Balchin, C (eds), *The Backlash Against Investment Arbitration: Perceptions and Reality* (Alphen aan den Rijn, Kluwer, 2010).
Waldron J, 'The Core of the Case Against Judicial Review' (2006) 115 *Yale Law Journal* 1346.
——'The Concept and the Rule of Law' (2008) 43 *Georgia Law Review* 55.
——'Are Sovereigns Entitled to the Benefit of the International Rule of Law?' (2011) 22 *European Journal of International Law* 315–43.
Waltz KN and Sagan SD, *The Spread of Nuclear Weapons: An Enduring Debate* 3rd edn (WW Norton & Company, 2012).
Webb P and Bergsmo M, 'International Criminal Courts and Tribunals, Complementarity and Jurisdiction', in A Peters (ed) *Max Planck Encyclopedia of Public International Law* (2010).
Wedgwood R, 'NATO's Campaign in Yugoslavia' (1999) 93 *American Journal of International Law* 828.
Weiler JHH, 'The Transformation of Europe' (1991) 100 *Yale Law Journal* 2403.
Weill S, *The Role of National Courts in Applying International Humanitarian Law*, (Oxford, Oxford University Press, 2014).
Westlake J, *International Law* (Cambridge, Cambridge University Press, 1910).
Whipple J, 'Leibniz's Exoteric Philosophy', in *Stanford Encyclopedia of Philosophy* (Fall 2022 edn).
White AD, *Autobiography of Andrew Dickson White* (Washington DC, Library of Congress, 2016).
White G, 'International Court of Justice: Judgment in Case concerning the Northern Cameroons. The Judicial Function' (1965) 23 *Cambridge Law Journal* 9.
White GE, 'The Inevitability of Critical Legal Studies' (1984) 36 *Stanford Law Review* 649.
White TR, 'Limitations Upon the Initiation of War' (1925) 19 *Proceedings of the American Society of International Law at Its Annual Meeting* 102.
Wiessner S, 'The New Haven School of Jurisprudence: A Universal Toolkit for Understanding and Shaping the Law' (2010) 18 *Asia Pacific Law Review* 45.
——and Willard AR, 'Policy-Oriented Jurisprudence Focus Section: International Theory' (2001) 44 *German Yearbook of International Law* 96.
Wilde R, 'Triggering State Obligations Extraterritorially: The Spatial Test in Certain Human Rights Treaties' (2007) 40 *Israel Law Review* 503.
Williams JF, 'The Place of Law in International Affairs: Paper Read on February 28th, 1928' (1928) 7 *Journal of the Royal Institute of International Affairs* 94.
——'Model Treaties for the Pacific Settlement of Disputes – Mutual Assistance and Non-Aggression' (1929) 7 *International Affairs* 407.
—— 'Treaty Revision and the Future of the League of Nations' (1931) 10 *International Affairs* 326.
—— 'Justiciable and Other Disputes' (1932) 26 *American Journal of International Law* 31.
Wright JS, 'Professor Bickel, the Scholarly Tradition, and the Supreme Court (1971) 84 *Harvard Law Review* 797.
Xue H, *Jurisdiction of the International Court of Justice* (Leiden, Brill, 2017).
Yourow HC, *The Margin of Appreciation Doctrine in the Dynamics of Human Rights Jurisprudence* (Alphen aan den Rijn, Kluwer Press, 1996).

Yusuf A, 'Remarks' (2021) 115 *Proceedings of the ASIL Annual Meeting* 215.
Zarbiyev F, 'On the Judge Centredness of the International Legal Self' (2021) 32 *European Journal of International Law* 1139.
Zarra G, 'Right to Regulate, Margin of Appreciation and Proportionality: Current Status in Investment Arbitration in Light of *Philip Morris v Uruguay*' (2017) 14 *Brazilian Journal of International Law* 95.
Zeppos S, 'Judicial Candor and Statutory Interpretation' (1989) 78 *Georgetown Law Journal* 353.
Zimmermann L, Deitelhoff N, Lesch M, Arcudi A and Peez A, *International Norm Disputes: The Link Between Contestation and Norm Robustness* (Oxford, Oxford University Press, 2023).

Index

www.ingramcontent.com/pod-product-compliance
Ingram Content Group UK Ltd.
Pitfield, Milton Keynes, MK11 3LW, UK
UKHW020248290926
15470UKWH00002B/805

9 781509 993550